# The Politics of School Decentralization

*Lexington Books Politics of Education Series*
Frederick M. Wirt, Editor

Michael W. Kirst, Ed., *State, School, and Politics: Research Directions*

Joel S. Berke and Michael W. Kirst, *Federal Aid to Education: Who Benefits? Who Governs?*

Al J. Smith, Anthony Downs, M. Lewis Lachman, *Achieving Effective Desegregation*

Kern Alexander, K. Forbis Jordan, *Constitutional Reform of School Finance*

George R. LaNoue and Bruce L.R. Smith, *The Politics of School Decentralization*

# The Politics of School Decentralization

George R. La Noue
and
Bruce L. R. Smith

**Lexington Books**
D.C. Heath and Company
Lexington, Massachusetts
Toronto          London

Clothbound edition published by Lexington Books.

**Library of Congress Cataloging in Publication Data**

La Noue, George R
 The politics of school decentralization.

 1. Schools—Centralization—United States.
2. School management and organization—United States.
3. Education, Urban—United States. I. Smith, Bruce
L.R., joint author. II. Title.
LB2819.L27        379'.1535        73-178918
ISBN 0-669-74609-6
ISBN 0-669-74617-7 (pbk)

Published simultaneously in Canada.

Printed in the United States of America.

**International Standard Book Number:** { clothbound  0-669-74609-6
                                          { paperback   0-669-74617-7

**Library of Congress Catalog Card Number:** 73-178918

# Contents

# List of Tables

# Preface

The idea of writing this book first occurred to us in the fall of 1968. The emerging movement toward decentralization and broader participation in urban politics seemed to be a trend of considerable importance for social scientists, for public administrators, indeed for all those concerned with public affairs. The movement promised to restructure government to satisfy new citizen needs and interests, but its theoretical assumptions were untested and its practical effects unknown. Throughout the winter of 1968 and spring of 1969, long faculty club luncheons turned increasingly to seeking an operational way to research these issues.

In this pursuit, we were greatly aided by our late colleague, Wallace S. Sayre, Eaton Professor in the Department of Political Science at Columbia, whose wisdom and steadiness were an unfailing source of encouragement. One of our chief regrets in this project is that he did not live to see the end product and to give us the benefit of his critical assessment of our ideas. We wish to dedicate the book to his memory.

By the summer of 1969, it was apparent that the first battles in the struggle to decentralize cities were being fought in urban school systems. The conflict in Ocean Hill-Brownsville had given national prominence to the community control concept and the idea seemed to be spreading. Consequently, we undertook a preliminary survey of school decentralization in ten cities with a grant from the Center for Urban Education of New York City. Another grant from the Horace Mann-Lincoln Institute at Teachers College to George La Noue permitted additional research. The cutbacks in federal financial support for the regional educational laboratories and educational research in general, however, prevented our use of some desirable data gathering techniques and in commissioning research in the various cities. Most of the research costs for the project we have borne ourselves.

Necessity sometimes assists virtue. Rather than attempting a comprehensive history of school decentralization controversies, we have looked at the movement in broader perspective and have sought to define its most important political and theoretical implications.

During our research period (1969-72), we made at least five visits to each city. In each we sought out all relevant local reports and research, and interviewed dozens of school officials, politicians, community activists and others who influenced school decentralization politics. Smith was responsible for Los Angeles and Washington, D.C. and wrote Chapters 5 and 6; La Noue for St. Louis, Detroit and New York City and wrote Chapters 4, 7 and 8. The writing was done largely in 1972 and the case study chapters were completed roughly in their order of presentation in the book. Although there was a division of labor in writing and field work, the book is genuinely a joint effort. We worked closely together throughout the project to improve the comparative nature of the research.

In an undertaking of this size it is impossible to thank everyone who has been helpful. We received valuable assistance from so many people in various stages of the project that a full listing would take pages. In addition, a number of people whom we interviewed in different cities offered assistance only on the condition of anonymity. It would be remiss, however, not to mention a few who made major contributions. Frederick Wirt, the general editor in this series, was both encouraging and a penetrating critic of our early drafts. We also owe a special thanks to David Colton, Larry Doss, Norman Drachler, Lawrence Feinberg, the late Sam Hamerman, Wilson K. Jordan, Patricia Miner, Irna Moore, William Rivera, Daniel Schlafly, David Seeley, and Albert Shanker. Marvin Pilo, Ken King, Robert Simmelkjaer and Arnold Howitt were helpful as research assistants on specific topics. Our wives, Patricia and Elise, grew so tired of the project and its pre-emption of leisure that it is only with some trepidation that we mention them here and express our appreciation for their understanding and support. Finally, we must add the conventional acknowledgement that any remaining errors of fact or interpretation are solely our responsibility—a claim that we do not imagine will be seriously disputed.

Washington, D.C.                                        **George R. La Noue**
New York City
                                                       **Bruce L. R. Smith**
January, 1973

# The Politics of School
# Decentralization

# 1 The Political Setting of Decentralization

Few ideas in American political history have had such resilience and varied appeal as has decentralization. The idea of government "close to the people" has been an article of faith since colonial days and has reappeared in different guises in each new epoch in the nation's history. The subtleties of any historical period, of course, defy easy summary, but it is possible to discern a dominant *motif* as each succeeding age has taken up anew the continuing decentralist-centralist debate. Considered a progressive doctrine by the advocates of Jeffersonian democracy, decentralization later became the rationale for Southern secessionism. John C. Calhoun's doctrine of concurrent majorities held that economic and other interests were so distinctive in different parts of the country that each section should have a veto over national policies. The logical result of this doctrine was to leave most public policy decisions to the separate states—a position which the leaders of the Confederate States of America themselves found frustrating and ultimately destructive to their cause. After the Civil War, the idea of decentralization was linked to the cause of limited government in the period of industrial growth. The "national idea" in the first half of the twentieth century was reflected in the progressive expansion of the federal government's role in solving state and local problems.[1] The doctrine of states rights and the constitutional argument for "dual federalism" gave way to the forces that saw in centralization a fuller realization of the ideals of American democracy. There seems little doubt that, for most of this century, the centralist tradition has been the carrier of innovation, while the decentralizers have sought consolidation and slow change in order to maintain continuity with the American past.

By the middle 1960s, the ideological and political spectrum had shifted considerably. While centralization was still proposed by some progressive voices as a solution to certain problems like pollution control, selective service, and welfare reform, decentralization became fashionable among liberals. Somewhat in the style of a modern Jeffersonianism, new forces emerged that saw in decentralization the basis for efficiency, progress, and a restored sense of legitimacy in the institutions of government.[2] In part, the quest for urban decentralization and greater community participation in decision-making reflected the awakening political consciousness of big city black and Spanish-speaking citizens. The appeal of the idea also stemmed in part from cultural trends stressing the importance of individual autonomy and self-expression.[3] Some of the recent converts would surely have amazed those who defended the states-rights or neighborhood-schools version of decentralization in the race and oil controversies in the 1950s. Consider, for example, spokesmen for Black Power who insist that their groups must control all public services in their communities, or New Left leaders who embrace decentralization as an alternative to large scale organization. Perhaps the most flamboyant advocates of decentralization, authors Norman Mailer and Jimmy Breslin, in their rollicking put-on campaign in the New York mayoralty election of 1969, suggested not only that the city become the fifty-first state, but that any racial, religious, ideological, or sexual community within the city be permitted self-government. In spite of their belief that dirty air and snarled transport were the city's worst problems, their slogan was "all power to the neighborhoods." It was a sign of the times that their ideas were not regarded as wholly implausible by many New Yorkers.

Conservatives, too, could embrace the new thrust toward decentralization because it seemed to offer the prospects of less government spending, smaller units of authority, and ethnic and class homogeneity in one's own enclave. The 1968 Republican National Convention declared in its platform that decentralization of power was needed to "preserve personal liberty, improve efficiency, and provide a swifter response to human problems." The appeal of the decentralization ideology reflected a deep feeling of discontent with contemporary society shared by many disparate groups. The decentralization idea, indeed, seemed to be a classic case of political opposites gathering under a common banner. The ideas had filtered so deeply into the nation's political consciousness that President Nixon, in his 1971 State of the Union Address, spoke the rhetoric if not the substance of community control in his call for a "new American revolution."

There were ironies within ironies in the concept, and the loose coalition that held aloft the banner of decentralization was extremely fragile. Bureaucrats seeking to cultivate supportive clientele groups could endorse the idea of a larger role for the "community" in policy formation, provided the community did not really seek such a role. Community activists, having once achieved status and recognition, might resist the further involvement of other community representatives. The cities have wanted power and resources decentralized to their level, but they have been wary when neighborhoods seek a further devolution of powers. Similarly, the states have sought a larger role in the federal system, and generally have been less enthusiastic about decentralization when their municipalities petition for home rule.

In much of the recent debate, the arguments have been cast in terms of the merits of one government structure or another, but there has been a volatile political process underlying the structural arguments. Republicans, who started out by strongly opposing the idea, have sometimes dramatically shifted position as the possibilities of breaking up Democratic strongholds in the cities gradually became apparent. Democrats, once champions of more decentralization, have backed off from it when strains in the party's traditional ethnic alliances have surfaced over the issue. The structural arguments have only thinly disguised the underlying quests for dominance in state and local politics and the struggles over policy priorities.

To see the matter in its full complexity, one must look beyond the rhetoric and surface squabbles surrounding the politics of decentralization. For the battles over decentralization intersect with a number of broader trends affecting the cities—such as erosion of party loyalties, the fiscal crisis affecting state and local governments, the drive for regionalism and metropolitanism, and the cultural urge toward self-expression that has had an impact on the political arena. The relation between the forces seeking decentralization and the older metropolitan consolidation reform movement is particularly intricate. The metropolitan government idea continues to show vitality, and by one 1971 estimate there were twenty important experiments in metropolitanism underway in the United States.[4] On the surface, the metropolitan idea seems to conflict sharply with the impulse toward greater decentralization and wider citizen involvement in administration. An underlying assumption is that the present balkanized network of overlapping and sometimes conflicting jurisdictions is a chief barrier to effective government in the metropolitan areas. The usual solution, in the metropolitan reformer's view, is to strengthen general political authority—the structure of state, county, and local government—*vis-à-vis* the special districts, authorities, functional bureaucracies, and special purpose units of government. This would seem to imply that it is undesirable to fragment still further the structure of local government. Yet some commentators have urged that decentralization is a prerequisite to metropolitanism on the theory that the only way to overcome suburban fears of being completely dominated by the central city would be to break up the city into governmental units more nearly comparable in size to the suburbs.[5]

There is a substantial body of reform thought that seeks both the consolidation of functions at the metropolitan level and greater local participation and decentralization.[6] Usually, the desire has been to tap the financial resources of the wider community, while at the same time involving smaller constituencies in the delivery of services. Again, while much of the public discussion has concerned government structure, the political realities underlying the debate remain critical. Blacks fear that merging with outlying suburbs would mean a dilution of their newly-won political power in the central cities. Suburbanites are concerned over sharing the burdens of rising welfare and educational costs in the central cities. For many public officials, there are the stakes of status and office—the fear of losing power and influence by relinquishing the autonomy of their governmental units.

The net result of the intersection of these forces is an extraordinarily complex and tangled set of issues. It is difficult to tell whether the drive for decentralization will bring deep-rooted changes in the American political system or will pass away as swiftly as it emerged, or whether some middle trajectory will be followed. The task of scholarly analysis is not made easier by the high degree of emotionalism and ideological fervor that has usually surrounded the subject.

This book seeks to clarify some of the large questions arising in the wake of the decentralization movement by taking a close look at one policy arena—urban education. We have chosen to focus on education for several reasons. First, education has been the field in which most developments in urban decentralization have taken place. Although the decentralization of numerous functions—including police, health, sanitation, and other services—has been discussed (and in some cases limited experiments have been attempted), it is in the field of education where the most significant implementation has occurred. The education field is apt to be a serious test of whether the goals sought by reforms—greater responsiveness, efficiency, increased citizen participation—can in fact be achieved. Second, we have chosen to concentrate on education because it constitutes one of the central functions of state and local government. Educational expenditures account for 40.5 percent of all state and local government expenditures. In recent years, the costs have risen sharply for all public education, from $18 billion in 1960 to $45.7 billion in 1970. In the process, education has been increasingly drawn into political controversy and subjected to public scrutiny. Developments within the field of education are likely to have an increasing effect on wider political trends, and in turn, to be influenced by political decisions.

It has also seemed to us that close attention to the decentralization movement in urban education would enable the scholarly observer to gain a better perspective on some of the interesting new trends in American politics. The erosion of party loyalties, the emergence of the public-sector unions as a strong metropolitan political force, the reformist impulses that have helped make volatile political processes no longer dominated by established interest groups, the "equality revolution" and the involvement of lay citizens in the administrative process—all have played a part in the school decentralization drama. There has been much talk in recent years of a "crisis of authority" in America and of drastic and impending changes that are either taking place or should take place in the conduct of the nation's affairs. As a general postulate, we believe that scholars should not dodge such concerns or shrink from addressing large questions with high normative content. To add to enlightened public debate, as well as to enrich the theoretical bases of their own disciplines, it is important that social scientists should address themselves to issues that matter to people.

Accordingly, we seek in this book to clarify such broad questions as: How "responsive" are governmental institutions? Is public policy insensitive (or overly sensitive) to the wishes of minorities? What mixture of professional and lay judgment leads to what kinds of policy outcomes, and whose interests are mainly served? Our aim is to address ourselves to such questions in a disciplined fashion so that we can report our findings as the result of research and not as mere polemic. We find appealing the proposition, advanced by James Q. Wilson, that the concern with substantive issues:

" . . . has traditionally been part of political science since Aristotle . . . The best empirical political science has . . . usually (but not always) been that which has tried to explain why one goal rather than another is served by government . . . Such a concern draws together the empirical and philosophical aspects of political inquiry so that those that try to explain why something is as it is and those who speculate on whether it should be as it is might reasonably be regarded as members of the same discipline . . . "[7]

This book belongs to the new tradition—or rather, the re-emergence of an older tradition—that makes attention to public policy matters a central concern of research. With this approach, certain assumptions of past research on urban government are at least altered in emphasis and, in some respects, are recast into a rather different perspective. It is roughly true to say that the early students of municipal government in the United States concentrated mainly on formal and legal governing arrangements and on the administrative minutiae of service delivery (often with a view to improving "efficiency" defined in fairly narrow terms). After the World War II, in reaction to the view that local government was mainly an "administrative" matter, there was a shift in scholarly attention from formal government structure toward informal and extra-legal distribution of influence. The kinds of questions asked were: Who governs? Who has influence in which kinds of community politics? The policy approach takes some of the aspects of the earlier research—the search for more efficient municipal services and the awareness that political realities underlie formal structure—and combines them into a perspective emphasizing the performance of the urban governing system. There is less interest in who governs than in what difference it makes who governs, whose interests are served, and how well policies meet the "needs" of the governed.

In more formal language, political scientists have often been concerned with the inputs to the governing system—political parties, interest groups, elite and mass behavior—i.e., the factors shaping the pattern of demands to which governments in some sense must respond. There has typically been less concern with the conversion process—that is, how the variety of stimuli flowing in upon the government are screened and translated into policy.

There is a need to go beyond the focus on the agenda of government action to the public policies that actually emerge from the contests of politics and, in turn, to the effect these policies have in either sustaining or eroding the basis of support for the political system. This book is a modest effort to contribute to an understanding of the conversion process—the process by which demands for governmental action become or fail to become translated into public policy. We are interested in explaining the trajectory of a movement like school decentralization once it has become a salient political issue. How do urban governments respond to a demand for significant change in structure and policy objectives? How do professional interests, institutional obstacles, leadership styles, and other factors modify, adapt, intensify, or dilute political demands in the course of translating them into public policy? This is not primarily a book concerned with output, e.g., the effect of decentralization on educational performance—test scores, reading improvement, and the like. Unavoidably, however, from time to time we do make cautious inferences about the educational consequences of various decentralization experiments. And it is our hope that this study will stimulate more systematic research on ways to measure the effectiveness of governmental outputs and thus to judge the performance of urban government.

Care and precision are required in defining the boundaries of the subject. What is new in the current cries for decentralization and greater community participation that arouses our interest? Decentralization, as noted above, is shop-worn as a slogan; the small community has long occupied a legitimate place in American political thought; and "participatory," when used as a modifier of democracy, clearly reinforces the values already implicit in that concept.

As a point of departure, it is appropriate to recognize which elements are truly novel in the current drive for urban decentralization, and which are modern manifestations of older political problems and ideas. Clearly, much of what the decentralization movement has sought amounts to a change in the emphasis given certain traditional values. As Herbert Kaufman has shown, the administrative tradition in the U.S. has involved an equilibrium between three values that partly reinforce and partly conflict with each other—representativeness, bureaucratic competence, and strong executive leadership.[8] One value may predominate in administrative practice until its disadvantages lead to opposing reform suggestions. The contemporary concern with representativeness is just one part of a cycle. As disadvantages grew with the system resulting from earlier reformist impulses towards increased professionalism and bureaucratic efficiency, the move to make administrative structures more representative and "closer" to their clienteles gathered momentum. In turn, criticism is likely to arise over favoritism, lack of uniformity, inefficiency, and other problems associated with decentralization and lay involvement in administration, and a swing back towards other values may be anticipated. Although a cyclical process is the result, change does occur, for different interests are mobilized in each succeeding period.

In considerable part, what is at issue in the current decentralization debate, then, is not something wholly novel, but rather a reappearance in modern form of traditional problems—the weighing of conflicting objectives, each with some legitimacy. The debate still has a certain Jeffersonian and Hamiltonian flavor, as the virtues of grass roots democracy are vigorously assailed and defended. One man's "participatory democracy" is another man's "mob rule." Yet the elements of continuity should not obscure the complex and salient differences with the past. The contemporary battles over decentralization seem to be distinctive in several respects: (1) Decentralization is now being called the answer to special urban problems; in the past, it was said to be tailored to the needs of yeoman rural America (the suburb is more nearly the model that decentralists have in mind for the central city, not the rural township or village). (2) The emphasis on direct democracy, on the involvement of the "people" rather than interest groups or other intermediary associations, is in marked contrast to older notions of the community that stressed the organic character of society and its associational life. (3) The range and magnitude of lay participation sought in the affairs of government are unusual (not since Jacksonian days has there been such thoroughgoing distrust of the professional and exaltation of the layman).[9]

The first expressions of the modern decentralization movement can be found in the field of physical planning in the 1950s.[10] "Advocacy planning" began to call attention to the special needs of ghetto populations in the central city and provided the rationale for a new kind of relationship between the professional and lay client. In the mid 1950s, the Federal Urban Renewal program required the formation of neighborhood level groups that would participate in the planning process. Earlier, citizen participation had been called for in the 1949 Urban Renewal Act, but this had been interpreted in most cities to mean the creation of blue-ribbon city-wide panels interested mainly in downtown slum clearance. The Ford Foundation's "gray-areas" program and Mobilization for Youth gave further impetus to the idea of citizen involvement.

Then, in the middle 1960s, came the major expansion in programs embodying the concepts of decentralization and greater citizen involvement. The advisory council, representing residents of the target area or the clientele group served, was often the means by which citizens were involved in programs. The landmark legislation includes the Community Mental Health Act of 1963, Title II of the Economic Opportunity Act of 1964, Titles I and III of the Elementary and Secondary Education Act of 1965, the Demonstration Cities Act of 1966, and many implementing programs and guidelines followed from the legislation. By one count in 1971, some 180 new federal programs in the social services area had been initiated since 1965, many of which reflected the influence of the concepts of community participation. And, of course, the federal programs have triggered a wide array of local initiatives. Cities have sought to decentralize municipal services through greater field office operations, multi-service centers unifying the delivery of services, neighborhood city halls, the extension of the Mayor's office in various communities through rumor complaint centers or information units, and other devices designed to bridge the gap between the citizen and governmental institutions. The new initiatives have reflected all the complexities of traditional federalism, with the added dimension of special ethnic and race problems, interest group activity, and volatile political processes in the cities.

The cluster of phenomena loosely referred to as "decentralization," "neighborhood government," the "community revolution," "participation," "citizen involvement," etc., is our primary focus. The book attempts to sort out and bring conceptual order to the tangled lines of development of the decentralization movement.

In discussing a reform movement like decentralization, it is appropriate to note the role that periodic waves of reform have played in American politics. Reform is a venerable part of the American political tradition, awakening broad appeal in a culture noted for its preoccupation with change and progress. Yet there is also a deep ambivalence toward the reformist crusades. Reform movements have frequently led to results far different from the ideals sought. Past experiments with administrative decentralization have often resulted in serious disadvantages, as in the selective service system,[11] the wartime administration of price controls, agricultural grazing districts,[12] local health centers,[13] river basin administration,[14] and various other programs. The local field offices, instead of providing flexible administration of broad program objectives, have frequently tended toward arbitrariness, idiosyncratic decisions, and an inability to resist powerful special interests.

Nor is the weight of evidence regarding small units of government in the rural setting—village councils, town meetings, special districts—especially favorable from the perspective of the contemporary reformer. Closed oligarchies have not been uncommon in the rural setting, participation has been low, and most important, small constituencies have almost invariably tended to strengthen the dominant interests in the district at the expense of minority rights. And participation, if carried to excess, is not without its perils. The drive for open government can become inverted into the traditional anti-power bias of the American political culture, whereby little can happen because so many groups have veto power. The progressive era legacy of direct democracy—and in particular the device of the referendum—is generally believed to have been turned to the advantage of special interests.

Nonetheless, the scholar should proceed on something like the assumption that where there's smoke, there's (at least some) fire. There is something of great interest in a movement that appeals to a wide variety of people and that becomes a *Leitmotif*, if not the major theme, of a decade's political history. In this book, we will seek to identify what precisely has happened in the course of the decentralization movement. What forces have helped give rise to the school decentralization movement? What are its prospects for further growth in other policy areas, or for its decay? Do the programs embodying the decentralist assumptions in some sense "work," given the realities of the American constitutional scene? Can authority be "relegitimated" by such experiments in devolution, or will the effect be the opposite? How far can the values of openness, representativeness, and the drawing in of a wide range of society's creative energies be incorporated into the administrative process without incurring unacceptable costs in the loss of discipline, orderliness, and professionalism?

The questions that arise go to the roots of the crisis of authority affecting many social and political institutions in the country today. Can modern urban America be one nation with a common political tradition? Or are there differing principles of legitimacy underlying political demands in the modernization process, and thus the prospect of a "looser" political system with different areas of geography or of policy controlled by those with sharply conflicting values?[15] How is a more genuine community, in politics and social life, to be achieved—by dissolving uniform standards in order to accommodate group differences, or by further strengthening such standards? The subject deserves a thorough, careful, and fair-minded appraisal in its broad outline and in its details. No pretense is made that this study exhausts or even recognizes all the crucial dimensions of so complex a subject, but we hope that it begins to frame the right questions and points the way to further systematic research.

Ultimately, what is at stake in this debate is the nature and stability of the American political system and its ability to adapt to change. There is a deep and insistent belief in the country that the institutions of society have grown aloof from human needs; and there is a strong desire to recover a sense of community that seems missing in modern life. This sense of estrangement has had powerful political appeal in many sectors of society, especially among those who have traditionally lacked power and status. It will continue to be felt in many ways throughout the nation's social and political life. Yet is seems unlikely to us that significant policy issues, such as public education in the inner cities, will be detached from the wider political context and become the exclusive province of a narrowly-based clientele or geographical unit. The issues raised by the decentralization movement are too deep-rooted and controversial to engage the attention of a limited constituency. The resolution of such issues inevitably will involve a broad spectrum of interests, and the clash of values will reflect and reshape the basic working of the political system.

# 2

## The Development of the School Decentralization Movement

It is not surprising that the issue of urban decentralization should be contested first in educational politics. The performance of public schools is a matter of concern to most city dwellers, whether they are students or parents, employers or real estate salesmen. Consequently, citizens have always expected a more direct access to school politics than any other kind. In most American communities school taxes are the only levies subject to direct referendum. The elected school board is one of the few remaining links to an earlier grass-roots citizen-operated democracy. It is a very special kind of politics.

### The Characteristics of School District Politics

Although districts for sanitation, recreation, public health, mosquito control, etc., exist in many places, public schools have about the only type of functional district Americans know or care much about.

The origin of the school district extends far back into the colonial period. The first public school legislation, the Massachusetts General Court Act of 1647, required each town to set up a school; but as settlers gradually moved into more remote areas, some additional arrangements for education had to be made. To meet this need, school districts were formed on an *ad hoc* basis by the residents of the new territory. It was not until the end of the eighteenth century, however, that these districts were given the legal right to operate schools and levy school taxes. Since the districts were often too small to provide an adequate fiscal base and had very parochial constituencies, Horace Mann thought that the legislation granting them authority was a disaster, but the pattern spread.[1] Apart from the South, where county governance evolved from the parish system of the Church of England, and in Hawaii, which has a unified state system, the independent school district became the national pattern.

Many of the districts were composed of one "little red schoolhouse," and as late as 1940, there were 110,000 separate districts. Many of them did not actually operate schools, but paid tuition for students to attend other schools, thereby providing a tax haven for local residents. Some had the purpose of segregating whites from blacks, or rural pupils from city pupils. Still others survived because in the pre-federal thruway era the distances in the vast prairie and plains lands made any other arrangement impractical. But mostly because of their titles and salaries, customs and identifications, governmental units of any kind are hard to kill.

11

Yet school districts have been eliminated—indeed slaughtered—by the thousands. By 1972, there were less than 17,300, a drop of 85 percent in thirty years. The reasons are many.[2] As the family farm declined and the great migration to the cities began, the number of rural schools and school districts fell precipitously. There were 8,100 fewer public schools in 1970 than in 1960, most of the loss occurring in rural areas. Even in places with stable populations, school district mergers have proceeded rapidly. Sometimes the motivation came from parents who realized that their children needed larger schools with more equipment and teachers if they were to be competitive in college admissions. James Conant's book, *The American High School Today*, established that a high school graduating class of a hundred was the minimum size to support a modern curriculum, and to obtain that number often required mergers.[3] As the states began to expand their financial support of local schools, they became aware of the inefficiencies of small districts and often required consolidation as a condition of state aid. The contemporary school district, then, usually operates several schools and employs a specialized faculty and a differentiated administrative staff. The form of district governance, however, has changed very little.

The names vary. School board is the most common, but school committee, school trustees, school commissioners, and school inspectors are also used. The function of the school board originated in the Massachusetts school ordinance of 1647, which commanded every town to choose men to manage "the prudential affairs" of education. In short, the school board was intended to implement state rules, to make local policies, and to provide administrative oversight.

All those functions could, of course, be carried out by some municipal or county department of education, but they are not. The school district-school board arrangement is preserved because Americans believe education ought to be separate from partisan politics. Some districts (about 18%) have partisan elections, and in others non-partisanship is *pro forma*, but generally the partisan aspects of some school politics are publicly de-emphasized or even outlawed.[4] The myth that educational policy-making is non-political serves several important functions.[5] Educational professionals foster it in order to reduce their vulnerability and accountability. By discouraging broad participation, the ability of upper classes and established ethnic groups to dominate policy is enhanced. Finally, the myth of non-partisanship represents a not unreasonable reaction to some egregious abuses of public school funds and personnel by political machines. So, in order to keep the schools out of the hands of politicians, they are turned over to friends and neighbors who are willing to donate their time on the school board.

Under the scrutiny of researchers, however, the small-town school board turns out to be less than the ideal form of representative government that its folklore suggests. Its members, like the members of most other legislative bodies, are drawn from a fairly narrow stratum of the population. Blue collar workers and ethnic minorities are not often represented. Some of the classic sociological studies have found that dominance of elite families often extends to the public schools through representation on the boards.[6] School board elections are nonissue-oriented and the campaigns not very competitive. Candidates are often selected by closed caucuses or drafted to run. Once in office, board members in small districts sometimes lack the skills to make modern educational policy or are so intent on pushing a particular interest that they plunge the board into controversy.[7] Criticism by academics, however, has done very little to undermine the popularity or the independence of the school board-school district arrangement in America.[8] Though consolidation has made the districts larger and more heterogeneous, they still are the symbol of local control of education, and that is a very popular symbol. Though the size and shape of many districts may be irrational from a managerial perspective, people are attached to them. Though turning over a multi-million dollar school corporation to the deliberations of the local druggist or clergyman may not seem fiscally prudent, schools are generally honestly, if unimaginatively run. Though expecting an unpaid staffless board of laymen to keep up with educational innovations and to promote educational accountability may seem unrealistic, many still prefer the values of friends and neighbors to the skills of educational technicians. Indeed, how good is the record of the PPBS specialists and the performance contractors in education?

The school board-school district arrangement, then, is partly a pragmatic defense of local values and interests and partly an emotional attachment to indigenous institutions.[9] For many suburban, small-city, and rural inhabitants it is something significant to identify with. Not only because it defines athletic loyalties by creating cohorts of Wildcats or Pirate fans, but because it represents one of the last remaining sources of community in contemporary America, the school district will survive as long as local values are important.

## The Crisis in Urban School Governance

Criticism of school governance has been the common theme in volume after volume of recent writings on urban education.[10] During the 1960s, it became evident to many that the school policy-making arrangements that originated in rural and small-town America and that were adopted comfortably by the suburbs were breaking down in the cities. For one thing, in a quarter of our largest cities, school reformers of another era aiming to take schools out of politics created appointive boards with elaborate screening systems. They succeeded so well in insulating school officials from popular demands that contemporary reformers found it almost impossible to change school policies. But even in many cities with regular board elections, there were widespread feelings that school officials were not sensitive or accountable.

What are the origins of the crisis in urban school government? Cunningham and Nystrand have suggested that traditional patterns of representation in small towns and suburbs are not workable in the cities for several reasons.[11] Education is a personal or a family matter, but the sheer numbers in a city make it difficult for individuals to have direct contact with policy-makers. This problem is compounded for the poor and members of the minority groups who are often unrepresented on city-wide boards. From the schools' point of view, it is difficult to know who should be consulted. Communities within the city that are meaningful to people are often hard to define, and the demands and tactics of organized interest groups continue to escalate, leaving little time for speculation on local preferences. Finally, internal factors such as transient students, collective bargaining for school personnel, and external inputs in the form of new state and federal regulations have led to ever more bureaucratic standardization, which further reduces the influence of local citizens.[12]

These developments come at a time when it seems that almost all parents have discovered the importance of education for their children. Surveys show that the desire to send children to college is almost universal in every class and ethnic group. Consequently, educational competition begins earlier, lasts longer, and is more intense than ever before.

In this competitive context, parts of our urban school system have failed miserably. Whether this is largely a matter of rising expectations (by most quantitative standards urban schools are better now than twenty or fifty years ago), or whether there has been an actual decline in productivity, is politically irrelevant. Parents want improvements now, and many believe active participation in school politics is the remedy.

The new demand for participation in school governments is not strictly an educational phenomenon, however. Like other American institutions, schools have been affected by a general shift in cultural norms regarding decision-making styles. Churches, political parties, professional groups, and other organizations are finding that previously passive members are now insisting on new forms of involvement for laymen and accountability for leaders.

The current participatory ethic is particularly important to members of minority groups. Excluded by discrimination, ignorance, and apathy from most types of political participation in the past, many blacks, Puerto Ricans, and Mexican-Americans now see schools as the focal point for working out new principles of representation. In some cities, these groups seek traditional integrationist goals of access to—and jobs in—the larger system. In other places, leaders demand total control over the segment of the system in minority-group neighborhoods.

In the struggles over these demands, school systems have often found that the minority groups' principal ally was the federal government. The community action phase of the Anti-Poverty Program, Model Cities, and Title III of the Elementary and Secondary Education Act, among others, were set up to encourage local participation in policy-making as a concommitant or even a prerequisite to achieving substantive goals. Federal money was used to finance local elections and to establish special governments for these programs in inner-city neighborhoods. If the regular city and school governments did not cooperate, funds for the whole program could be held up. These programs, then, not only increased the expectations of participation for many former political drop-outs, but they also created new sets of local leaders with neighborhood rather than city-wide support and perspectives. Schools quickly became the institutional battlegrounds for the testing of these new forces.

Thus the challenge to traditional forms of urban school government has been caused both by inadequacies of structure and performance in the schools and by broader social and political trends over which the schools had no control. For many who were concerned about the desperate condition of urban public education, decentralization of the schools has seemed to be a necessary step toward reform.

## The Case for School Decentralization

The argument for urban school decentralization essentially comes from two different sources: (1) specialists in public school administration who have long recognized the dysfunctional consequences of large educational systems; and (2) a political alliance of minority groups and white liberals.

In 1938, the influential Educational Policies Commission of the National Educational Association declared:

Centralized administration of education is likely to result in mediocrity and in the lack of local adaptability. Centralization in the control, administration, and financing of education is very apt to lead to a mediocre school system and a lack of progressive development of the program of public education. With well-developed local units for the administration of schools, it is certain that some communities will develop leadership which will be effective in improving education. . . . Most of the great reforms in education have originated in the schools of some local community. They were not decreed by a central authority.[13]

That statement was mostly a defense of the traditional arrangement in small-town and rural districts. But scholars like Paul Mort, then the most prominent student of educational administration in the country, began to explore the idea of decentralized city schools. The problem that concerned him was adapting school programs to local conditions. He began to formulate hypotheses about adaptability in large and small systems,[14] and in 1940, one of his students, Francois S. Cillie, began the first empirical research on this subject.[15] Sixteen schools in New York City were matched with schools in six suburban communities in the New York metropolitan area. There are some methodological problems in this study, but Cillie's general findings that schools in the decentralized communities had flexible curriculums and more teacher participation in educational policy seem plausible. Other studies of city systems by Eby, Hicks, and Westby echoed that conclusion and urged that more autonomy be given building principals and that parent groups be more active.[16]

Though the research on which these conclusions were based was at best suggestive rather than definitive, the concept that city school systems would benefit from delegating more administrative authority became generally accepted among students of school administration. Thus, when Conant and others were successfully recommending the consolidation of rural and small-town districts, other writers were calling for administrative decentralization in the cities. A series of reports during the 1960s (Chicago-Havighurst; Booz-Allen-Hamilton; District of Columbia-Passow; Louisville-Cunningham; Milwaukee-Stiles; New York-Gittell; and Philadelphia-Odell) all concluded that some kind of decentralization would be beneficial.

Most of these research studies or reports, however, were based on concepts of efficiency, innovation, or accountability, and they were not specifically directed to the needs of the minority communities. The kind of decentralization attractive to minority groups was a reinterpretation of these values or an emphasis on different ones. It called not for administrative delegation but community control.

An analysis of all the origins of the community control thrust among minority groups, particularly black leaders, goes beyond the scope of this book. Much of the philosophy and history of the movement can be found in Stokely Carmichael and Charles Hamilton's *Black Power: The Politics of Liberation in America* (1967). In their chapter called "The Search for New Forms," the authors focus on control of the schools as a key element in the new black politics:

We must begin to think of the black community as a base of organization to control institutions in that community. Control of the ghetto schools must be taken out of the hands of "professionals," most of whom have long since demonstrated their insensitivity to the needs and problems of the black child. These "experts" bring with them middle-class biases, unsuitable techniques and materials; these are, at best, dysfunctional and at worst destructive. . . .

Black parents should seek as their goal the actual control of the public schools in their community: hiring and firing of teachers, selection of teaching materials, determination of standards, etc. This can be done with a committee of teachers. The traditional, irrelevant "See Dick, See Jane, Run Dick, Run Jane, White House, Nice Farm" nonsense must be ended. The principals and as many teachers as possible of the ghetto schools should be black. The children will be able to see their kind in positions of leadership and authority. It should never occur to anyone that a brand new school can be built in the heart of the black community and then given a white person to head it. The fact is that in this day and time, it is crucial that race be taken into account in determining policy of this sort. Some people will, again, view this as "reverse segregation" or as "racism." It is not. It is emphasizing race in a positive way: not to subordinate or rule over others but to overcome the effects of centuries in which race has been used to the detriment of the black man.[17]

About the same time *Black Power* was written, a clash between minority-group parents and the school establishment in New York began to receive nationwide publicity. At first, the conflict was over integration, curriculum, and school architecture, but (in many eyes) the main issue at Harlem's I.S. 201 soon became the racial control of the school (see Chapter 8). To articulate the goals of the parents, a black professor at the Columbia School of Social Work, Preston Wilcox, drafted one of the first specific adaptations of the community control philosophy to a specific school situation.[18] He urged the creation of a school-community committee in order to "activate parents in the ghetto to assume a kind of responsibility which the dominant society has failed to exercise." The committee selected by the parents was to be a kind of school board with the power to hire a principal, review administrative performance, and operate remedial and enrichment programs for children and adults in the community.

When it was first proposed, Wilcox's suggestion that black parents should have some special power in ghetto schools was considered extreme, even by some sympathetic respondents.[19] Shortly, however, several other theoretical defenses of a much more all-encompassing community control were advanced, this time by white liberal intellectuals.

In his book *Neighborhood Government* (1969), Milton Kotler argues that within cities neighborhood corporations with as few as 6,500 residents should set local import-export policies, control prices, rents, licensing, banking, and health, education, and welfare programs. This proposal was not aimed so much at the particular problems facing blacks in the cities, but at the general proposition that:

... the neighborhood originates as a political unit and declines as its local liberties are destroyed; the object of local power can be nothing less than re-creating neighborhood government which has political autonomy and representation in larger units.[20]

Alan Altschuler's book *Community Control* (1970), however, is subtitled "The Black Demand for Participation in Large American Cities" and focused on racial tensions. Both because of its advantages in creating opportunities for political experience and economic mobility for blacks, and because it might reduce conflict between blacks and whites by giving each a turf, Altschuler believed community control was necessary for many municipal services, including schools. He conceded that not enough research existed to support these conclusions, but he insisted nevertheless that:

... like sailors in a hurricane, we can ill afford to drift. We must estimate our bearings, on the meager information we have, and act. We may have a little time for experimentation. If so, we would do well to exploit it vigorously. But we probably will not. Societies are transformed by revolution and inadvertence, but they rarely conduct experiments to improve political forecasting. In the end, if community control becomes reality, it will probably do so little more because of experimental findings than white altruism. It will be a product of protest and pragmatic compromise.[21]

In a companion volume, *The Ecology of Public Schools: An Inquiry into Community Control*, (1971) Leonard Fein examines the political philosophy of the movement.[22] Fein is concerned less with community control as a device for improving educational achievement than as a means of restructuring the polity. From the author's perspective, not only have the integration efforts of the 1960s been a practical failure, but they are based on a misguided value system. The individualistic, secular, liberal ethic they represented is not compatible with black needs. The balance of power in the schools should be shifted from the state back toward organic communities. No plan is detailed, but Fein uses the parochial school concept as a way in which community control might be worked out for blacks.

Much of the explicit thinking about the application of the community control concept to particular urban educational problems has come from Mario Fantini, the Ford Foundation's educational expert during the late 1960s, and Marilyn Gittell, Professor of Political Science and director of the Ford-funded Institute for Community Studies. Most of the supporting theory for the community-control variant of school decentralization has been developed at the Institute. In their book, *Community Control and the Urban School*, (1971) Fantini and Gittell (with Richard Magat of Ford) affirm that, "We believe that the community-control movement, born of human deprivation, can direct the public school to a more humanistic purpose and performance."[23] Their analysis is that the lack of achievement in minority-group schools stems principally from irrelevant curriculum, alien school culture, and apathetic or unprepared professionals.[24] The remedy is to increase parental participation and influence in order to redirect the school and to forge new links between school and community.

Although most of the argument for decentralization as an educational reform is necessarily based on anecdote and inference, its logical structure can be represented in four hypotheses.

1. Decentralization will permit more people to participate in educational decision-making than will other forms of school system governance.

2. This participation will increase the influence of minority groups in the system as a whole; and in neighborhoods where minority groups are a majority, they will control the schools.

3. This realignment of political power through decentralization will lead to more (a) relevant curricula, (b) professional accountability, (c) minority group role models and (d) assurance among students that they can control their own

fate—all of which will result in better education than comes from centralized systems with their characteristics of economy of scale, merit standards, and specialized schools.

4. By improving the education of minority groups, decentralization will in the long run outdo centralization in providing such groups better access to jobs and social benefits and in hastening their integration into a wider society.

Decentralization also has implications for the school's political socialization role. While the public schools have historically inculcated Americanism and allegiance to certain generalized political norms, the pluralism of their constituencies, the ethos of professional educators, and the watchfulness of the federal courts have checked most tendencies toward overt partisan or sectarian indoctrination. Some of the advocates of community control, however, reject the white middle-class character of the socialization process and clearly hope to use the schools to encourage ethnic solidarity and challenge traditional American myths.

Moreover, decentralization inevitably becomes involved in the current urban ethnic competition.[25] At stake is not only the symbolic prize of who "controls" the school, but also thousands of very tangible jobs and contracts. Furthermore, since for many the control and character of the schools seem to be an important factor in choice of residence, the outcome of the school decentralization controversy may be critical in deciding which ethnic groups will stay in the cities.

Finally, some see school decentralization as the test of the viability of decentralizing other municipal functions or of creating neighborhood government in the cities. Every success or failure in school decentralization can be used by those whose real interest is in the future of city hall.

*A Strategy for Research*

The techniques for evaluating the claims and theoretical assumptions underlying the community control movement have themselves been subject to controversy. In the early days of the movement, those who wondered whether enough evidence existed to warrant restructuring schools or whether decentralization was the right direction were met with a reply that shifted the burden of proof. Mario Fantini argued:

The first question (of the skeptic) usually is: What evidence is there that neighborhood control of urban schools improves student achievement? The answer is that if there is no evidence, it is because there really are no community-controlled urban public schools . . . However, what we do have ample evidence of is the massive failure that the standard, centrally controlled, urban school has produced. It is ironic, therefore, that those in control of a failing system should ask others offering constructive, democratically oriented alternatives to show results before there has been any chance for full implementation.[26]

When the Institute for Community Studies published an analysis of the three New York demonstration districts, considerable attention was given to the problem of finding an appropriate methodology. In their introduction, the authors state:

. . . The evaluative documentary history of these experiments in public education suffers from the same syndrome that plagued the demonstration districts: the traditional academic criteria to measure and interpret social data are unfortunately, generally, inappropriate. When one attempts to measure, through quantitative analyses alone, the record of a social change experiment, one ends up with an unreal picture. It matters little in using the aggregate data approach how many poor school board members attend local board meetings, for example; the fact is that these percentages cannot be expected to be as high as in local suburban districts of affluent whites who have a long tradition of elected boards. The determinative factor is what impact this experience had upon the new participants as well as what impact on policy these participants had. Too many of our criteria are based on middle-class behavior patterns with emphasis on voting, registering, and belonging to organizations. In short, a wholly different orientation is needed in evaluating social change forces.[27]

The proper timing and the character of the evaluation are, of course, complicated and legitimate questions. But policy scientists cannot long put off an assessment of a movement as potentially significant as school decentralization even if the findings must be labeled tentative. Too much is at stake. Nor can evaluation be left to partisans. As Terry Clark has noted:

What a considerable portion of the literature on decentralization to date amounts to is special pleading for a particular solution. . . . Very little attempt is made to develop ideas coherent enough to warrant the term 'theory,' and the casual use of favorable examples seldom justifies the label of empirical research.[28]

Several major assumptions underlay the research strategy of this book.

1. At the time of our research, school decentralization was potentially a nationwide phenomenon and the study had to be comparative. The events at Ocean Hill-Brownsville had received so much publicity and had been so polarizing ideologically that neither sound theory nor rational public policy could be based on a study of New York alone.

2. There are no typical American cities. Consequently, this research includes an analysis of a large number of cities for which comparative demographic and political data could be found or developed as well as a manageable number of

case studies. We rejected as unrealistic the approach of using fictitious names for cities or political actors. (Everybody knows Floyd Hunter's Regional City is Atlanta.) Also, the reader deserves to know just what the author is describing in order to impose his own validity check. This decision had little effect on our access to information, but it will no doubt increase local criticism of our findings.

3. The case studies should not be snapshots but should have some chronological dimension. Too often in the past, economy and efficiency have dictated that researchers describe the educational policy process of cities or even states within a very narrow time frame. If the researcher happened on a polity at a very atypical time, all of his comparative judgments might be skewed. Consequently, our case studies cover a three-year period, which is not enough but has more than exhausted energy and resources.

4. Comparative research should strive for generalization and theory, but it must respect and state clearly the limits of its data and sample size. There is constant professional, publisher, and public pressure to overstate conclusions and to overreach data. Too often the authors' judgments are portrayed as quantifiable variables which "prove" scientific conclusions. Graphs, chi square tests, and other paraphernalia of science are used to mask the fragile, subtle nature of conclusions that should follow from this kind of work.

Choosing cities for case studies of this type requires some value judgments as well as more objective standards. Questionnaires were sent out to each of the twenty-nine cities with populations over 500,000 to discover the places in which decentralization was an issue. During the summer of 1969, field research was conducted in nine cities to narrow the field to a more manageable five. Finally, factors of diversity of decentralization patterns, geographical balance, and ease of access to key actors led us to choose St. Louis, Washington, Los Angeles, Detroit, and New York. Subsequent evaluation of developments in other cities make us to believe that these are the cities in which decentralization has been the biggest issue.

The traditional criticism of case studies is that they do not produce generalizable findings. We have tried to meet this quite valid objection in two ways. First, in Chapter 3 we have attempted to use aggregate data to test certain broad hypotheses about decentralization. Second, in researching our case studies, although most interviews were unstructured, we have used a common set of questions for every city to facilitate generalization. The key questions follow:

1. *Who are the new decentralization activists?*

Although the rhetoric of the movement assumes a mass participation of "the people" or "the community," it is more probable that decentralization politics will create additional elites to represent the newly recognized groups or neighborhoods. The task of analysis is to identify the recruitment of these new activists, their backgrounds, constituencies, financial support, ideologies, tactics, and policy goals.

2. *How has the decentralization movement affected the more traditional participants in public school politics?*

We will be concerned with defining the role and attitudes of school boards, bureaucracies, teacher organizations, parent associations, civil rights groups, political parties, mayors, and state officials. Special attention will be given to two new participants that have played critical roles in decentralization politics: foundations and anti-poverty groups.

3. *How are decentralized boundaries being drawn?*

A school district is not only an educational unit, but it defines a political relationship as well. If the "community" is to control a district, who is the community—parents, poor people, indigenous organizations, or functional interest groups? Suzanne Keller reports finding four distinct definitions of community in the literature: those based on natural geographical boundaries, those based on neighborhood services, those based on the cultural characteristics of the residents, and those based on the perceptions of the residents.[29]

4. *What is the impact of decentralization on school personnel practices?*

Growing alongside the drive for greater lay participation is the increasing militancy of teacher organizations. To what extent are these two trends reciprocal and in inevitable conflict? How have the issues been drawn in areas of certification, accountability, and tenure?

5. *How much does decentralization cost? Who should pay?*

Recently the decentralization movement has had to confront two important financial trends. The first is the wave of austerity that has paralyzed many new educational experiments and has added to the scrutiny given to the fiscal implications of any change in educational administration. The second trend is toward equalization of school finances among districts. If successful, this will centralize financial responsibility for schools. Will it then be easier or harder to decentralize educational policy-making?

6. *What is the effect of decentralization on providing services and educational achievement?*

Decentralization advocates claim that their reform will close the gap between the school and the community and create a more realistic educational experience. To the extent that this change exacerbates ethnic or class struggles, however, it might have a dysfunctional impact on the learning atmosphere and on discipline in the schools. By creating smaller districts, decentralization may increase the cultural diversity and relevance of the curriculum for some groups, but it may also decrease the availability of programs for other students with special needs (vocational training or special programs for the handicapped, for example).

7. *What is the effect of decentralization on integration and equality of opportunity?*

A decade ago it seemed clear to many liberals that the national interest required the subordination of parochial social values to the broader and overwhelmingly integrationist goals of the nation. A characteristic expression of this view was that "national survival now requires educational policies which are not subject to local veto . . . it is becoming increasingly clear that local control cannot in practice be reconciled with the ideals of a democratic society."[30] Yet by the end of the 1960s, despite (or perhaps in part because of) the passage of landmark legislation embodying many of the goals sought by the Civil Rights movement, the momentum behind further integration had largely dissipated in the Congress (although it continued in the courts through judges appointed in the Kennedy and Johnson eras). Some observers saw integration as a wholly dead issue. As Leonard Fein noted, the "historic alliance of interest and purpose between white liberals, schooled in Enlightenment doctrines, and Negro leaders seeking an integrated future, has now come undone."[31] In its place, he urged a new vision of a multi-ethnic society to replace post-integrationist doctrine. Still, strong advocates of community control have found it difficult to abandon integration, if only because of its symbolic appeal, and have frequently insisted on the eventual compatibility between community control and integration. Is this a realistic vision or is community control a new theory of separate-but-equal education?

8. *What is the effect of decentralization on the future of urban school government and on broader doctrines of federalism?*

Some see decentralization as the reform most necessary to save urban public school systems. How enduring is this movement likely to be? Can it be reconciled with the growing role of state and federal governments in educational policy? Does decentralization represent the first step in balkanizing the cities, or is it a prelude to a new metropolitanism?

These are the major questions we will be exploring in the case studies. Before turning to the cases studies, however, it seems worthwhile to ask whether there are any basic demographic or school-related factors that suggest an explanation of the trend toward decentralization of school systems in various cities.

# 3

# The Social Correlates of School Decentralization

The emphasis on writers and theoreticians of community control (Chapter 2) is warranted because the decentralization movement has never had much organizational structure. Indeed, even the term movement is something of a misnomer. There are many differences among its advocates, even though they would all restructure school systems into smaller units. Although school decentralization has been endorsed at one time or another by the NAACP, CORE, the Chamber of Commerce, the NEA and even the AFT, there has never been any coalition of major groups to achieve such a goal. Nor, as one can see from the groups listed, is there likely to be. Even so, an attempt was made to organize a national federation to support community-control schools, but the organization never could secure funding, and it has not had any influence in local disputes or state legislatures.

So while the integration and school financing reform movements have produced carefully-timed, well-planned, political and legal campaigns to achieve their goals, decentralization has no comparable organization or strategy.[1] There have been great differences in the way cities across the country have responded to the decentralization ideology. Some cities, often with considerable controversy, have substantially decentralized their school systems, while in other cities decentralization has hardly been discussed. This chapter attempts to consider whether there are any basic demographic or school-related factors that might suggest an explanation for the decision to decentralize school systems in various cities. Clearly this is a formidable task and we can hardly aspire to be definitive. As was already pointed out, dissatisfaction with urban schools stems from a complex of internal and external problems and it is unlikely that a single concern would lead a city to decentralize its schools. Nevertheless, the criticisms of decentralization advocates seem to cluster around four general complaints about urban public school systems. They are that these systems are too large, too segregated, too unproductive, and too unresponsive. By creating propositions from these criticisms and then testing them, we may be able to identify the factors that seem most strongly related to decentralization.

## Classification of School Systems

School decentralization may be defined as the transfer of legitimate decision-making authority in the areas of personnel (recruitment and discipline), curriculum, and budget from central boards and bureaucracies to local areas within the city. It may take two principal forms: administrative delegation and community control. In the first system, administrative authority in defined areas is transferred from the top of the bureaucracy to field units. Selection of local administrators and determination of basic policies remain central prerogatives. In community-control systems, local units assume not only administrative but also legislative power. The administrators are selected by and are legally responsible to the neighborhood groups or boards which legislate policy for the local units.

Two centralized types are also possible: the classic bureaucratic monopoly described in *110 Livingston Street*[2] and a system in which the central bureaucracy is responsive to lay participation.

For our purposes, therefore, cities may be classified in four basic ways:

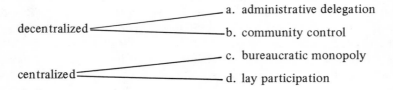

decentralized
  a. administrative delegation
  b. community control

centralized
  c. bureaucratic monopoly
  d. lay participation

There are three problems with this classification system. First, there are not many pure types, and some difficult decisions must be made in classifying the cities. Even before the rhetoric of decentralization became popular, school systems evolved responses to neighborhood pressures that produced some functional decentralization without structural recognition (the Banneker district in St. Louis in the early 1960s for example). On the other hand, there are system-initiated citizen advisory committees with much publicity and little real power in many cities. How can one make sure that they are not simply updated versions of PTA's rather than organs of meaningful community participation? Paper proposals for subsystems and demonstration schools exist in many cities, but there is little real intent to implement them.[3] Case studies can probe subtle questions of real allocation of power, but in classifying our sample of cities in this chapter we relied on formal structural tests of authority. Do the rules (state laws, board policies, administrative handbooks, etc.) of the system permit area administrators or local boards to make personnel, budgetary, or curriculum decisions?

There is also some difficulty combining administrative delegation and community control for purposes of analysis. Theoretically, the two kinds of decentralization may have different purposes, proponents, and results. But as currently implemented, they are not really opposites but points on a continuum. Strict community control exists nowhere, and administrative delegation as it has worked out in New York, Chicago, Detroit, and St. Louis has always had its participatory features. Today, both kinds of decentralization are likely to be responses to similar pressures and this book will use the broad term decentralization though occasionally referring to a specific form.

The second problem is that current federal programs (ESEA's Title I and Title III, OEO, and Model Cities, etc.) all require both target areas and some form of citizen participation. Some cities have acted to minimize these federal programs, while in others (Chicago and San Francisco for example) they have been the spearhead of the community-control movement. If the only decentralization in a system is that imposed by federal programs, and if there has been little spillover to the rest of the school system, we will still classify that city as centralized.

Finally, there is the problem that the proposed classification of the cities provides only a static snapshot that reveals little about the dynamics of the decentralization movement. To examine this aspect, a second kind of typology should—ideally—be used:

1. City schools decentralized before 1960.
2. City schools decentralized after 1960.
3. City schools still centralized, but decentralization on the public agenda. (School board or other official agency has held hearing or set up studies.)
4. City schools still centralized, but some pressure in the community for decentralization.
5. City schools still centralized and no pressure.

For the purposes of this chapter, however, we will simply compare cities with centralized or decentralized school systems.

**Data Gathering**

In order to test our hypotheses, we selected a sample of the twenty-nine cities with populations of over 500,000 in 1965. We visited about one-third of these cities in preparation for case studies, and questionnaires were sent to the other cities. The information thus obtained has been supplemented by a number of private reports prepared for the Urban Coalition, the Center for Urban Education, and other agencies interested in citizen participation.

We found that eight of the twenty-nine cities had partly decentralized school systems. In 1970 these include New York, Detroit, Los Angeles, St. Louis, Washington, D.C., Seattle, Chicago, and Philadelphia. Their school decentralization ranges from state imposed system-wide plans in New York and Detroit to the tentative steps toward administrative delegation taken in St. Louis and Philadelphia. For classification and testing purposes, these cities will all be regarded as having decentralized school systems, even though none of them is completely decentralized.

Baltimore, Boston, Atlanta, San Antonio, Houston, and New Orleans have area administrators, but according to the reports we have received, these administrators have little policy discretion. In addition, a number of other cities such as Cincinnati, Denver, Minneapolis, Pittsburgh, and San Francisco are discussing decentralization but have not yet taken formal steps. The other cities among the twenty-nine largest indicate that they have no plans and few pressures for decentralization. All school systems in cities in these three categories will be considered centralized.

Gathering aggregate data on school systems is frequently a frustrating task. In some cases we have been able to depend on previous researchers; in other instances, such as when trying to gather comparative achievement scores, we were almost totally unsuccessful. Nevertheless, we were able to accumulate enough data to provide tests, sometimes very tentative ones, of almost all of our hypotheses.[4] To illustrate the results of the tests, we have employed the Pearson product-moment coefficient of correlations. A summary of the correlations is reported in Table 3-1.

**Table 3-1**
**Summary of Correlation Coefficients of Hypothesis Relating Demographic and Political Variables to School Decentralization**

| Hypotheses | Pearson Product-Moment Correlation Coefficient |
|---|---|
| 1. The larger the city the more likely decentralization. | .57 |
| 2. The faster the relative growth of the city the less likely decentralization. | .18 |
| 3. The larger the public school enrollment the more likely decentralization. | .59 |
| 4. The faster the relative growth of the public school enrollment the less likely decentralization. | −.16 |
| 5. The larger the absolute number of non-whites in the city the more likely decentralization. | .69 |
| 6. The higher the percentage of non-whites in the city the more likely decentralization. | .23 |
| 7. The larger the relative growth of non-whites in the city the more likely decentralization. | .16 |
| 8. The larger the absolute number of non-white students in the public school system the more likely decentralization. | .65 |
| 9. The larger the relative number of non-white students in the public school system the more likely decentralization. | .32 |
| 10. The higher the number of Negro teachers, the less likely decentralization. | −.66 |
| 11. The higher the percentage of Negro teachers, the less likely decentralization. | −.20 |
| 12. The more integration of black students the less likely decentralization. | .01 |

**Table 3-1** (cont.)

| Hypotheses | Pearson Product-Moment Correlation Coefficient |
|---|---|
| 13. The more integrated the black teachers the less likely decentralization. | .08 |
| 14. The more the city schools are integrated overall the less likely decentralization. | .04 |
| 15. In school systems with 20 percent black students or more, the greater the integration the less likely decentralization. | .18 |
| 16. The greater the residential segregation in 1960 the more likely decentralization. | −.26 |
| 17. The more progress a city made in residential desegregation between 1940 and 1960, the less likely decentralization. | −.36 |
| 18. The higher the alienation toward the system (dropout rates among all students) the more likely decentralization. | −.23 |
| 19. The higher the alienation toward the system (dropout rate among non-whites) the more likely decentralization. | −.28 |
| 20. The greater the alienation toward the system (the difference in dropout rates between whites and non-whites) the more likely decentralization. | −.06 |
| 21. The higher the alienation toward the system (vandalism rates), the more likely decentralization. | −.01 |
| 22. The greater the representation of blacks on the city council, the more likely decentralization. | .15 |
| 23. Cities with elected school boards are less likely to have decentralization. | .17 |
| 24. Cities with boards elected by wards are less likely to have decentralization than cities with at-large boards. | −.13 |
| 25. School systems that are fiscally dependent are less likely to be decentralized. | −.11 |

## Size Factors

As the correlation (.57) shows, large cities school systems are more likely to be decentralized than smaller cities. Of the ten largest cities in 1960, all but Houston, Cleveland, and Baltimore have some decentralization, and Baltimore is seriously considering more change. It may be that the demand for decentralization has been strongest in the large cities because people are more likely to feel lost, alienated, and unable to participate in or to control their environment. Another possibility is that after bureaucracies reach a certain size, they may begin to decentralize in order to manage their functions. Whether the system is expanding and thus creating new jobs and other incentives seems to have very little relationship to decentralization.


## Minority Group Presence


School decentralization is considered to be a more salient issue for non-whites than for whites. Both the thrust of separatist ideology and the failure of the public schools to educate non-whites might create support for decentralization. There is a substantial correlation (.69) between the size of the non-white population and decentralization, although that is probably more a reflection of overall city size rather than the specific non-white population. The lists of the largest cities in total population and those with the largest non-white population overlap considerably. The absolute size of the non-white population is considerably more highly correlated with decentralization than either relative size (.23) or growth (.16).

Because the non-white population is younger and more likely to be enrolled in public schools, a number of cities such as Baltimore, Chicago, Detroit, Philadelphia, Cleveland, Memphis, St. Louis, and New Orleans have non-white majorities in their school systems, but not in the city at large. The correlation (.32) of non-white public school system population is slightly higher than the correlation (.23) of city non-white population with school decentralization.

One of the principal objections minority groups have to the public school system today is that racial and cultural bias and irrelevant criteria in hiring and promotion have discriminated against teachers from their groups. They claim that their children would learn better from teachers of their own background. Decentralization in its community control version might be a remedy. Consequently, where large numbers of minority group teachers are already in the school system, there might be less demand for decentralization. The (−.66) relationship, however, suggests just the opposite.

Nor is the percentage of black teachers (−.20) related to decentralization. Los Angeles and New York have a comparatively small percentage of minority group teachers, while Washington, Detroit, and St. Louis have a high percentage. The patterns of decentralization emerging in these cities do not appear to be related in any simple or clearcut fashion to the percentage of minority group teachers in the school system.

In addition to the dissatisfaction over too few minority school teachers, there is also a demand for more administrators from minority groups. Unfortunately, we have not been able to obtain aggregate data on administrators. On the basis of information we have received in our interviews, however, the lack of minority group administrators has been a significant factor in the drive to decentralize the

Boston, Los Angeles, and New York school systems. In Philadelphia, the presence of black administrators has insured some access to and therefore some support of the system. However, the large number of Detroit's black administrators did not prevent a state-mandated decentralization of the schools.

## Integration

It may be argued that it is not the number of minority group children, but the extent to which they have been integrated that will determine the pressure on the system for decentralization. It is suggested, for example, that the failure of the board of education in New York to make good on its promise of integrating I.S. 201 was the catalyst for the community control movement. A counter hypothesis is that integration endangers existing minority group elites by opening up leadership positions to outsiders and threatening eventual assimilation. For example, the period of greatest growth of Catholic and Jewish parochial schools occurred not during periods of widespread hostility, but at a time when acceptance in America seemed to portend eventual loss of traditional group identity. Thus, the prospect of integration may produce either pressures for the creation of private schools or for community control of public schools to insure group solidarity.

The degree of student integration, however, shows no relationship (.01) to decentralization. The degree of faculty integration, which might be a measure of opportunity within the school system, also has a very low correlation (.08) with decentralization.

Decentralization, it may be argued, is related to residential segregation in two ways. Ghettos may create both the reality and the appearance of community. They may also create tangible and intangible deprivations. These factors could lead to demands for community control. All American cities are highly segregated residentially, of course, but in some cities conditions are slowly improving. Correlating the Taeuber Index of residential segregation with school decentralization, however, shows a negative relationship (−.26) between segregation and decentralization.

## Alienation and Achievement in School Systems

If the public school systems in our cities were educating students according to expectations, many believe that the rather radical step of decentralization would never have been considered. Is there any relationship between educational output and decentralization?

That depends on how much achievement and how much alienation the system produces. Generally, we do not have the data to do much with our hypotheses. Obtaining comparative reading scores and college admissions rates has proved very difficult. Decentralization, however, seems not to be related to either the total dropout rate (−.23) or the non-white dropout rate (−.28). It might be argued that absolute rates of achievement and alienation are not so important as the differences between non-whites and whites, or perhaps even between city and suburb. At this time, we have only the data to test the former, but it still shows a (−.06) correlation. There is no relationship (−.01) between per capita vandalism rates and decentralization. In short, then, until further tests can be made with new data, there is no evidence that the demand for decentralization has any relationship to educational outputs.

**Political Factors**

If the demand for school decentralization is in part a demand for status, recognition, and self-determination by minority groups, it might be that a high degree of representation in regular political bodies would decrease the need to control the schools. On the other hand, the existence of such political power might make it easier to decentralize the schools once any demand was made. This is a difficult hypothesis to test, but a comparison of the degree of black representation on city councils and decentralization shows that there is a slight correlation (.15) between greater representation and decentralization.

Perhaps decentralization is more related to the character of school government. The method of selecting a school board and governing a school system presumably should affect the reality and image of the schools' responsiveness. Of course, lay participation may spring from less formal and more effective sources than elections; but generally it is argued that elections act to increase representation and responsiveness. Although there may be some slight trend toward more decentralization in cities with appointed boards, Los Angeles, Detroit, and St. Louis are examples of cities with elected boards moving toward decentralization (43 percent decentralized in cities with appointed boards versus 25 percent in cities with elected boards).

It might be argued that election by ward would insure neighborhood representation, thus decreasing the need for decentralization; or it might be that local leaders already organized around educational issues would be in a position to insist on decentralization. There are only three cities in our sample with boards elected by ward, so it is impossible to generalize. The three have both centralized and decentralized school systems. Similarly, political scientists frequently have argued that partisan elections facilitate the participation of lower-class people. However, there is only one city in our sample (Indianapolis) that has a formal partisan election for school boards, so no generalization can be made.

## Summary

The effort to test hypotheses on school decentralization with aggregate data has produced only modest results. The size of the city seems to be the most significant variable, but that is not very surprising. Of more interest is the finding that the *percentage* of non-whites in a school system or city seems not to be as important as the *number* of non-whites. Also worth consideration is the finding that neither school integration (faculty or students) nor residential segregation appears to bear much relationship to decentralization. Finally, if the data on dropout rates and school vandalism provide any sort of test at all, school decentralization seems not to be related toward educational alienation or achievement. Nor do political relationships seem to explain much about school decentralization

There are several objections to this kind of analysis and all generalizations must be treated gingerly. Clearly, while this analysis can point to potentially interesting relationships and eliminate others, it cannot show the dynamics of the decentralization movement or suggest a theory of causation. It may be that our classification scheme is too arbitrary; we may find out if other cities decentralize in the next five years. It may also be that different kinds of aggregate data or more sophisticated analytical techniques may uncover more interesting similarities among the decentralized cities than size. But for now this analysis will serve to shift the burden of proof to those who believe that integration, educational alienation, or political characteristics can provide a simple explanation for school decentralization.[5]

It seems likely that the politics of school decentralization is too complicated and elusive to be captured by tests using aggregate data. Detailed case study investigations in various cities are necessary if we are to understand the dynamics of the decentralization phenomenon.

# 4  St. Louis: The Politics of Participatory Gradualism

St. Louis needed the Arch—that 630-foot stainless steel monument that frames the city's birthplace on the banks of the Mississippi. Created by Eero Saarinen, the Arch took four years to build from planning to completion in 1965 and cost more than $15 million but it was worth it. Until its construction, about the only symbolic links for the metropolitan area were the baseball and football Cardinals. Professional sports, however, are a notoriously fickle source of community pride. Now it is the Arch, a symbol imprinted on municipal garbage cans and tourists brochures, that represents St. Louis. It is a hopeful symbol. On a clear day the Arch can even be seen in the suburbs.

Confidence is not something St. Louis has always had in itself. Founded below the confluence of the Missouri and Mississippi rivers by French fur traders in 1763, St. Louis did not begin its boom until the beginning of the California gold rush. Between 1850 and 1860, the "Gateway to the West" doubled in population to 160,773 and then doubled again over the next decade. By 1870, it was the nation's third largest city. One hundred years later, St. Louis had slipped to eighteenth largest and it was casting an anxious eye at Kansas City to see that it maintained its dominance within the state. St. Louis' 1970 population (668,000) represented a loss of almost 200,000 residents in the twenty years since 1950.

Although many of the descendants of the German and Irish immigrants who flooded the city before the Civil War still reside in its southern neighborhoods, 44 percent of the St. Louis population was black by 1970 (up from 18 percent in 1950). Furthermore, the city had a growing number of poor people. In the last decade, St. Louis had the highest ratio of increase in public assistance recipients to total population of all major cities in the United States.

Like other urban areas, St. Louis has developed a mostly white suburban ring. About 1965, St. Louis County surpassed the city in size and it is still growing rapidly. Consequently, the victory for home rule that the city won in 1876 has become a considerable liability. The city and the county of St. Louis have almost completely separate governments.[1] Since the county now has both a stronger tax base and a larger population, the city's position in the traditionally hostile state legislature is even weaker. In the county are located the metropolitan airport, two of the three area universities, and the county seat (Clayton), which is becoming the new office center of the area. It also nourishes a formidable suburban mythology about the evils of the city. A fine new expressway system exists, however, to speed suburbanites to Busch Stadium and other downtown sites whenever they find it necessary to enter the city.

35

Although St. Louis is more and more a city of the poor and uneducated and has lost some of its middle-class amenities, it still has many advantages. The city has a diverse industrial base and a reservoir of structurally sound housing along tree-lined streets. Its population may be becoming more stable, and its medium size creates the possibility of open dialogue among its leadership elites.

Since 1968, the St. Louis school system has been moving cautiously toward more community participation with a series of carefully controlled experiments. Its supporters say that this plan creates learning structures that will teach both parents and school officials how to solve educational problems, while opponents insist that the establishment is simply buying time by co-opting local movements. In 1970, black citizens made few decisions in St. Louis (of the eighteen city-wide elective posts, only one—license collector—was held by a black). Sometime before 1980, blacks will probably be in the majority in St. Louis. Given the temper of the times and the problems of the schools, an important element in the city's future is whether a gradualist policy of participation will succeed politically or educationally.

Whether St. Louis public school problems are matters of image or performance depends mainly on what one believes is possible given the nature of modern American cities. Under the leadership of William Torrey Harris and others in the latter part of the nineteenth century, St. Louis public schools enjoyed a progressive reputation for pioneering kindergartens, co-education, school libraries, and bicultural (German-American) education. More recently, the system has had a bad national press. Gittell and Hollander found its schools resistant to innovation, inadequately financed, and the school board aloof and cautious.[2] Patricia Doyle, writing a few years later in the *Saturday Review*, added: "The St. Louis schools exude a [conservative] mentality rooted partly in tradition, partly in fear."[3]

Examining the facts, about 25 percent of St. Louis public high school freshmen do not graduate. This percentage is about average for large cities, but there has been substantial criticism from St. Louis businessmen that the diploma is no longer a very good indicator of basic literacy in the recipient. Therefore, since 1970, a diploma is now contingent upon passing a Proficiency and Review test in reading, language, spelling, and arithmetic. No longer are there prestige academic high schools in the public system, but examination of the scholarship lists shows that it is at least possible to get into good colleges from any St. Louis high school. Furthermore, the system has established an extensive work-study program with local businesses. And although, on the average, eighth grade students lagged about four months behind the national norm in reading test scores, St. Louis, unlike other systems with students from similar socio-economic backgrounds, has managed to keep retardation from worsening as schooling progresses.

For many middle-class white parents, what is really wrong with the St. Louis public schools is that their basic constituency is now black and poor. About 70 percent of public school students come from poverty areas of the city and 17 percent are from welfare families. In 1970, two of every three students in the schools were black.[4]

One of the system's proudest boasts is that it "desegregated" all its schools within a year after the 1954 *Brown v. Board of Education* decision.[5] That is true, but St. Louis was one of the northernmost cities to have legally segregated schools in the first place; moreover, the dropping of *de jure* segregation has had, in the long run, very little effect on *de facto* segregation. In 1970, only fifteen of the system's 165 schools were integrated by the U.S. Civil Rights Commission's standards.[6] Yet even this much integration has been extraordinarily difficult to achieve, given the attitudes confronting the board. In 1965, fifteen school districts in Missouri still had *de jure* segregation, and a 1969 Survey Research Center analysis of racial attitudes in large cities found St. Louisans among the least liberal. While nationally 33 percent of white parents wanted their children to have only white friends, the figure rose to 50 percent in St. Louis.[7] Furthermore, in St. Louis whites can easily implement their sentiments by fleeing to the suburbs, as many have done. Or if political or business reasons require continued residence in the city, children can be transferred to St. Louis' large Catholic and Lutheran parochial school systems, which are overwhelmingly white.

Given these constraints, the school system has not tried very energetically to integrate. A freedom of choice plan exists, but there has been almost no busing for integration purposes. No attempts were made to pair schools or set up educational parks, although the feeder arrangement for a technical high school was changed to keep it from becoming all black. Neither has much effort been made to integrate the staff (over 90 percent of the black teachers are in segregated schools). For one thing, during most of the 1960s the city had a difficult time attracting teachers under any conditions.

Blacks have been more successful in obtaining employment within the system. In 1970, three of the six district superintendents were black, as were half of the principals and the teachers. The school board and the headquarters staff at 911 Locust Street have been disproportionately white, however, leading one teacher to remark: "It is impossible to move that intransigent mountain. There is a black educational subsystem controlled by whites in this city."

St. Louis, then, has a school system that seemed to many incapable of overcoming the pathologies of the inner city. Its schools appeared not very integrated, not very academically successful, and dominated by socially elite whites in a city that was increasingly lower-class black. In some cities, this would be a recipe for angry crowds at school board meetings, intimations of violence, or militant demands for community control. This has not happened in St. Louis. But in 1969, the Report of the blue-ribbon Education Task Force of the Mayor's Council on Youth warned:

There is an undercurrent of dissatisfaction with the present educational structure in St. Louis. . . . The Committee is convinced that conditions exist in the St. Louis area which will emerge as a force for decentralization. While there is time, we strongly recommend that a worthwhile plan be developed for meaningful citizen participation.

But short of the community-control model, which has never been seriously advocated by any group in the city, what are the structures and attitudes necessary for meaningful citizen participation? This is the problem St. Louis citizens and school leadership were grappling with during the three years of this study.

### The Government of the St. Louis Schools

Much of the comparative stability and gradualism in the St. Louis schools is rooted in the success of the reform movement that won control of the school board in the early 1960s.

The struggle to keep the schools out of the hands of the Democratic political machine was waged by St. Louis reformers for decades. As the public school system evolved in the nineteenth century, it was operated by a board of twenty members, some elected by wards, some at-large. A historian of the schools, H.C. Morrison, has described the results of this arrangement:

In practical operation this old board had degenerated in its last days to the point where it was often frankly engaged in playing partisan politics. Its meetings were at times spectacles of rancorous division among its members on issues not at all related to the essential interests of the school system. It was under suspicion of more or less extensive graft. Its executive officers were entirely the creation of the board, deriving their powers essentially from the board, and, for the most part, little better than figure-heads in the conduct of the school system.[8]

The reformers had some success in 1897, when they obtained from the state legislature a new school charter requiring a smaller 12-member board, elected at-large, and a division of executive authority between a Superintendent of Instruction and a Commissioner of School Buildings. As so often happens, however, the machine outlasted the fervor of the reformers and won almost all of the subsequent elections under the new structure. The new post of Commissioner became the source of patronage within the system, while the Superintendent was relatively free to pursue educational policy. The board operated on a rigid committee system that kept those matters separate, an arrangement perpetuated for decades.

As the city's population changed after World War II, the machine finally weakened and a new reform coalition of predominantly upper-class whites and middle-class blacks formed to challenge it.[9] Their first electoral success was in

1949, but it was not until 1953, when Daniel Schlafly was elected, that the reform movement began to exert major influence. From his position on the board, Schlafly publicized the corruption issue, financed lawsuits against school personnel, and finally forced a building commissioner out of office. During this period, due to illness of an opposition member, the reformers held a one-vote working majority. But in 1955, the voters—reacting in part to the reformers' support of school desegregation—returned the machine candidates to power. In Schlafly's words:

The first board meeting after the labor-ward politicans sweep of the 1955 election was sickening. The new majority arrived late for the meeting because of an extended private champagne victory dinner, paid for by the taxpayers. In rapid succession, the Board repealed anti-conflict-of-interest and other rules that the reform majority had put into effect to gain efficiency and prevent dishonesty."[10]

The reformers continued to fight, however, and in the 1961 election the Citizens Association for Public Schools elected all five candidates and took control of the board. The new board, not surprisingly, elected Schlafly as president.

From a certain perspective, St. Louis provides a rather dramatic example of lay participation. In an open contest, a citizen's association with 700 dues-paying members and a membership of 20,000 rose up to defeat a political machine and take control of school policies. But the number of citizens who can participate directly in this style of politics is rather limited. It takes 6,000 signatures to get on the ballot and, since the elections are city-wide, a candidate must not only be well-known, but able to spend up to $30,000. For the members of Schlafly's slate, the problem is somewhat simpler, since he can personally arrange for a public relations firm to handle publicity and supply campaign financing.

The slate (now called the Citizen Committeee for Quality Education) has not lost an election since the 1960s and controls every seat on the board. In 1970, three of the twelve members were black (before the slate's efforts, the board was all white), but they were very middle-class and there was a feeling that the board was hand-picked by Schlafly. Indeed, the Citizen Committee fades away between elections, and it is difficult to describe its organizational pattern, except that it is a group summoned by Schlafly at election time.

It is said of Daniel Schlafly that while some rich men like to run horses or yachts, Mr. Schlafly likes to run a school system. Owner of a lucrative family beverage business, Schlafly estimates that he has spent half of his time for the last eighteen years on education. Even after all those hundreds of committee meetings, he maintains his enthusiasm for working on education problems, and St. Louis voters have not lost their enthusiasm for him and his slate.

One of the major goals of the reformers was the creation of "unit rule," i.e., the abolition of the autonomous offices of instructional superintendent, building commissioner, auditor, and treasurer. This separation of powers, established by earlier reformers and virtually unique among American school governments, was apparently a source of both corruption and inefficiency. The practice had powerful friends, however, among the building trades unions and city politicians. Since unit rule required the approval of the Missouri legislature, the struggle lasted for nearly a decade. Finally, in 1967, embarrassed by the scandals revealed in the St. Louis schools, the legislature granted "unit rule."

To fill the position of St. Louis' first general Superintendent of Schools in this century, the board picked William Kottmeyer, the previous Superintendent of Instruction and a veteran of thirty-five years in the system. Despite this background, Bill Kottmeyer fits few bureaucratic stereotypes. He viewed the office of Superintendent as the master teacher of the school system and the city as his classroom. In weekly broadcasts from his office over the school's radio station and in his annual school report—which must be the most literate and candid in the country (the 1969 version features ten of his satirical poems on the foibles of education)[11]—the Superintendent taught his view of educational issues. The city has not always been willing to be so instructed, however; and even his associates conceded that his impressive intellectual and financial talents (royalties from the nearly two hundred reading textbooks and learning materials that he has written have made him independently wealthy) were barely enough to compensate for the all-encompassing cynicism with which he sometimes viewed his fellow men.

Kottmeyer had the benefit of the kind of classical education popular among St. Louis German families at the turn of the century. He believed in a disciplined education of logic and hard work that produced Horatio Algers like himself, but he recognized that these values are often hard to sell in the new constituency of the St. Louis public schools.

Kottmeyer and Schlafly tried to balance their desire to preserve standards (a tracking system, under attack elsewhere,[12] is an accomplishment Schlafly has said he would like to have inscribed on his tombstone) with the need for compensatory education (hence the emphasis on decreasing class size and community schools). Another part of the balancing act was a rhetorical but not a fiscal commitment to integration. A few children have been bused, but generally only to relieve crowding and new schools have been built in black neighborhoods. For Kottmeyer and Schlafly, the issue was not one of ideals, but of demographic and fiscal reality. Almost every attempt at integration in St. Louis has resulted in an all-black school within a few years at the cost of substantial neighborhood hostility. More "victories" of idealism like these, the leadership felt, would cost the system all of its remaining white constituency.

Integration might be more feasible if the system were not boxed in by an archaic fiscal provision in the Missouri Constitution requiring that school bond issues must receive a two-thirds majority. The system has not won any of these referenda since 1962, although it has received at least 50 percent of the vote in each election. Consequently, school buildings in St. Louis are, on the average, about fifty years old. The elections are often close. The yes vote in 1970 reached 63.3 percent, but the votes in the white wards were enough to defeat the bond issue.

Nor does the school system do well in the once rural and now suburban dominated state legislature.[13] Although St. Louis produces 25 percent of the state revenue (principally by sales tax—suburban legislators defeated an increase in the state income tax in 1970), it gets back only 12 percent. The St. Louis schools are unusually dependent on local property taxes, but industry is moving to the suburbs and the city has lost 7,600 retail and wholesale jobs in a six-year period.[14]

To add to the financial problem, the city government has generally viewed the fiscally independent schools as competitors for tax funds, and of course, few politicians are eager to assist the vigorous politics-is-a-dirty-business reform group that now controls the school board. After a recent bond issue, Paul Berra, Chairman of the Democratic Central Committee, said, "We all know there is a need for more cooperation (between the political parties and schoolmen). But since patronage jobs were removed from the schools, most politicians lost interest in the schools." At election time the Mayor and labor and business leaders endorse the bond issue, but do not campaign for it.

Public education in St. Louis, then, is increasingly a "black school system" dependent on white political leadership and property holders who are either apathetic about education or who send their children to private schools. The vote in the black wards is always solidly pro-school funds, but the turnouts are low.

To overcome that trend, the board proposed in 1968 that county and city school systems be merged. The metropolitan area would be divided into ten districts, each with an elected board that would have general personnel selection and curriculum powers. The Metropolitan School Board (MSB) would be appointed by the Governor from a slate nominated by three area university presidents. According to the proposal, the MSB would be authorized to recruit and examine personnel, engage in collective bargaining, maintain and construct all school buildings, provide accounting, research, and special services for the local districts and, most important, set, collect, and distribute taxes. The plan also suggested that the junior college should be operated by the MSB and even invited Catholic and Lutheran schools to join the system. What was being proposed, then, was a powerful new body (MSB) for education coordination controlled by appointed elites, together with a new form of decentralized local boards whose membership would be directly elected.

Such a system would create formidable political problems, but it might also assure substantial fiscal equity and racial balance. The merits of the plan, however, were hardly debated. It received little sympathy in the affluent suburbs and was viewed skeptically by blacks who realized that it might reduce their existing political influence. The plan was quickly killed in the state legislature, but it remains "the" solution for the board, particularly Dan Schlafly. Indeed, some think the board's interest in this "radical foreign policy" is merely an attempt to divert attention from the more conservative arrangements now governing the city system.

One conceivable solution to this dilemma would be to attempt to increase support of the system by increasing participation in decision-making. But Daniel Schlafly finds it difficult to become enthusiastic about actually sharing decision-making. Like other socially elite reformers who have struggled to overcome the evils of partisan interference in schools, he has less than complete faith in the will and wisdom of the "people." He has taken steps to see that parents and teachers have channels of communication for their problems and grievances, but he stops short of sharing power. Consequently, most school business is transacted in closed committee meetings. The agenda is not circulated. One must observe careful procedures before getting permission to address the board, and there are comparatively few public hearings. The board's minutes contain little more than a list of contracts and formal announcements.

The system's leadership is sensitive to electoral pressure. In 1969, a young white minister, Carl Dudley, ran as candidate for the board with support from a coalition of militant black poverty workers, liberal whites, and labor. The Schlafly slate refused to debate him and ran their campaign through the media. Dudley lost by about 9,000 votes, but his race still had an effect. During the campaign, the Schlafly slate increased its rhetoric about the need for citizen participation, and the board has since responded with some moves to operationalize that slogan.

As it has developed, citizen participation through school decentralization has taken three forms in St. Louis: the community schools, the districts and their parent congresses, and the Murphy-Blair District Education Board. The educational and political potential of each of these is considerably different.

## Citizen Participation in the St. Louis Schools

### Community Schools

The community school idea goes back at least to John Dewey's concept of "the school as a social center," expressed in 1902.[15] Put simply, the community school seeks to break down the barriers between formal education and community activity by encouraging neighborhood residents to use school facilities to enrich their lives. Community schools, therefore, are not restricted to a particular age group or curriculum but remain free to meet expressed neighborhood needs. Sometimes this amounts to no more than a school that is open "after hours" to adults and that offers a variety of "non-academic" courses. But occasionally it has meant that the school was directly involved in community development, and that neighborhood residents made the fundamental policies for the school. Of course, a "community school" can contain any combination of these ingredients.

The first major experiments with community schools occurred in the mid-1930s in Flint, Michigan. These schools were supported by the Mott Foundation, which to this day is a principal promoter and financial backer of this movement. The community school concept gained additional impetus when it was endorsed by the National Advisory Commission on Civil Disorders in 1967. Currently, more than 250 cities have community schools of some type.

In St. Louis, a kind of community school program existed as early as 1957. In the Banneker district in the heart of the ghetto, Sam Shepard, a black educator, began a series of programs aimed at increasing student motivation.[16] Although Shepard was able to obtain some federal and foundation money, he was never able to tap additional school system funds, and so most of his program had to depend on changing attitudes rather than on additional facilities and staff. Slogans were coined; competitions were begun; but most of all parents were involved. They were not only welcomed in the schools, but asked to sign the Parent's Pledge listing ten ways they would support their children in school. Advisory councils were formed, and parents readily turned out for meetings.

What caught the attention of the media was not the increased participation, but the fact that preliminary tests showed significantly increased student achievement. A few years later, however, according to a report of U.S. Commission on Civil Rights, the novelty had worn off and Banneker students were once again below the national average. Charisma had failed to overcome the lack of tangible support. Morale remained high, though, and Banneker parents are still among the best organized in the city.

Interest in the community school concept continued to grow in St. Louis, partly because there was a clear-cut eductional need. More than half of St. Louis's adult population has attended school for eight years or less. The board also saw the political necessity of generating more citizen interest and participation in the schools. Consequently, in 1967, the board began a version of the community school at the Ford Elementary School as a demonstration project. The school attracted 1,400 youths and adults in its first year. With the aid of grants from the Rockefeller and Danforth Foundations, eight more community schools were opened, and in 1970 Model Cities funds were used to establish five more.

The community schools are actually operated by the board in regular school buildings, using largely the regular school staff to teach after-school courses. The curriculum, the clientele, and the governance of these schools are different, however. Their courses range from karate and hatmaking to remedial work in basic subjects. These programs attracted about 1,000 persons a week, and of these some 40 percent were adults. Generally, evaluators report that the curricular side of the community schools has been quite successful, the courses popular, and attendance good.

The chain of command for the community school focuses upon a coordinator for each school's program. He reports to the city-wide director of community schools, who in turn reports to the Superintendent. But there is also a parallel structure of lay committees designed to create the sort of citizen involvement that gives community schools their purported distinction. At the top is the St. Louis Community School Council, appointed by the Health and Welfare Council of Metropolitan St. Louis. The Community School Council (leaders from industry, labor, and the professions) serves primarily to raise funds and coordinates the program with business. It does not normally interfere with educational policies.

Each school has its own community school advisory council that is supposed to advise the staff on program priorities and relationships with the neighborhood. Generally, the councils are composed of twenty to twenty-five organizational leaders who have responded to invitations from school officials. There are no elections, and the more militant groups are not represented. A formal evaluation by the Governmental Research Institute (G.R.I.) of community schools in 1970 states flatly:

... the local advisory councils should be encouraged, and must themselves be willing to function as effective voices for the community. This has not been achieved. More effort should be made to draw all elements of the community into the program including . . . those members of the community who have the least contact with and are therefore more suspicious of the community school.[17]

It is unlikely that this will occur. Militant black groups have not been allowed to use the after-school facilities. In general, the community development possibilities have been ignored or avoided. Instead, the community schools function much like suburban YMCA's—offering recreational and vocational opportunities to local residents on an individual basis. This is a worthwhile activity, but requires little in the way of community decision-making. Consequently, the councils have had difficulty discovering their role. Not surprisingly, attendance has been poor and the G.R.I. report concludes:

Very little has been done in the areas of training for advisory council members, organizing community participation and interest and referral of identified community problems to appropriate agencies.[18]

The St. Louis community schools have not become the articulators of community problems and the advocates of solutions that many had hoped for.

## The Districts and Parent Congresses

While the community schools created the possibility of a flexible response to neighborhood educational needs and a measure of local participation, St. Louis has also made more direct attempts at decentralization.

The first such efforts began in 1953, when the directors of elementary education were transferred from downtown to four field units. Nine years later, the directors were given greater authority and the title of assistant superintendents. A fifth district was created and in 1964 a sixth. It was in this period that Sam Shepard created the programs that gave the Banneker district its special visibility.

The next step in the system's gradual administrative delegation was an experiment placing both the high school and its feeder elementary schools under a single district administrator. A pilot project incorporating this concept began in the South Grand District in 1966. The Enright District followed a year later, and by 1968 the entire system had adopted this pattern. To implement administrative decentralization of the districts, each assistant superintendent was given a three- or four-man staff.

Whether these structural changes were seriously intended to facilitate meaningful community participation is difficult to establish. The public relations statements put out by the system always mentioned citizen participation as a goal, but no formal power was ever delegated. Each district enrolled about 17,000 students and was geographically compact, so that a neighborhood role in school policies was theoretically possible. Furthermore, as early as 1960 the system had created in each district local assemblies called Parent Congresses, which—given the chance—might have functioned as decision-makers.

Traditionally, public school parents in St. Louis wishing to participate in school affairs have joined either the city's affiliate of the national PTA or the indigenous Patrons Alliance. Both function largely as school-support agencies furnishing some funds and services to local schools. As in most cities, this kind of school activity is quiet, generally noncompetitive, and not very productive. Only about 11 percent of the 150,000 parents in St. Louis belong to parent organizations, and most of those members do not attend meetings.[19] Parents who are more active or angry choose instead to influence the city-wide board elections or work through pressure groups. From the PTA or the PA, however, generally come the delegates forming the Parent Congresses. Despite the legislative implications of their name, throughout most of the 1960s the Congresses functioned largely as an audience for school policies. Their meeting schedules were erratic, and the district superintendents controlled the chair and the agenda. There is no record that they ever made or even pressured for any significant change of policy.

In 1969, responding in part to Carl Dudley's campaign and realizing the inadequacies of the Congresses as either a support or participatory device, the board moved to strengthen them. First, it regularized the selection process for Congress members and officers and established a monthly meeting.[20] Secondly, it gave each Congress the right to establish the agenda "with the cooperation and assistance" of the District Superintendent and the responsibility for communicating its decisions to the district. Most important, two members of the board of education were assigned as liaisons to each of six Congresses, thereby establishing direct communication and the beginning of a feeling of neighborhood responsibility within the board.

It took some time for the Parent Congresses to adjust to their new status. Too frequently they functioned as gripe sessions, taking the opportunity to press grievances against principals in front of Board members. Leadership and attendance were erratic. The Congresses did not see themselves in a policy role and votes were seldom taken.

Then, in an effort to stimulate more local leadership and build decision-making capacities, the board gave each Congress a budget of one dollar for each child or about $17,000 for each district. To preclude the money's use for community organization or more political purposes, it was stipulated that it had to be spent for school activities. At any rate, a step had been taken toward giving the Congresses a policy role. Some Congresses were unable to establish priorities and simply divided the money on a per capita basis among the schools. In a few cases, however, they asserted their authority by rejecting the package designed by the district superintendent and substituting their own.

Since the Congresses have no formal role in selecting the district superintendent or otherwise holding him accountable, the key to the effectiveness of the district arrangement as a decentralization-participation device is the role the district administrator chooses to play. As in most school systems, questions about the autonomy or status of an official cannot be answered very definitively by examination of the system's published rules. In St. Louis there tend to be fewer published rules than in most large school systems. When asked about their role, the district superintendents reply that they are responsible for seeing that their district "keeps running." Nothing exists which states exactly the scope of their authority in that murky area between implementation and policy-making, but by custom they exercise certain powers.

In 1970, the district superintendents were veterans of the system averaging over sixty years of age. They were appointed by the Superintendent and board without formal consultation with the community. All had tenure as teachers, but their administrative status was dependent on the continued confidence of the Superintendent and Board. When a district superintendent in a white district criticized the busing of black students into his district in 1967 and made some comments which were interpreted as racist, he was summarily dismissed. There were no hearings or consultations with neighborhood leaders.

The district superintendents are not powerless, however. They not only pick their own four-man staff, but they can also veto the selection of other administrators in their district down to the level of department chairmen. Furthermore, they prepare and submit the budgets for the schools in their area and sit in on the budget-cutting sessions. In an arrangement that could develop into a cabinet form of government, the Superintendent and his staff and the six district administrators meet to consider problems every Tuesday.

The district superintendents interviewed insisted that their powers were growing, but it is difficult to measure that empirically. Because of the high rate of student mobility in St. Louis districts, they have had to accept uniform curriculums and have little influence in these matters. Despite Kottmeyer's rhetoric about the need to decentralize, he felt restrained from delegating more power, partly by his assessment of the leadership capacities of the incumbent district administrators and perhaps by his own personality. The district super-intendents seem willing to let their authority rest on custom and their knowledge of bureaucratic skills. As veterans of the system, they know that such an arrangement avoids confrontation and permits the greatest exercise of their skills. At least it is true that they have not chosen to maximize the other alternative to power—strengthening the Parent Congresses and entrenching themselves in a constituency.

## The Murphy-Blair District Education Board

While most St. Louis experiments in decentralization have been imposed from the top, there is at least one significant effort that has some grass-roots elements in it. Tucked into a curve near the Mississippi River, the Murphy-Blair neighborhood contains some 20,000 people. Eighty percent of them are Ozark whites, and the rest are blacks who moved in from the surrounding areas. During the 1930s, an active community life existed, but the post-Depression return of affluence led those who could to leave the district's decaying Baltimore-style row houses, most built before the Civil War. The area became a leaderless port of entry for Southerners migrating to St. Louis.

The neighborhood might have remained a forgotten pocket of poverty, apathy, and ignorance except for a remarkable institution, the Grace Hill Settlement House.[21] Modeled after Hull House in Chicago and founded with Episcopal money, Grace Hill has been serving the neighborhood since 1903. Following the trend of settlement houses in the 1950s, it related to the pathologies of its neighborhood mainly through social group work and recre-ational programs. In 1965, Grace Hill received a contract to operate a Headstart program. Other Headstart schools in St. Louis were run by the school board, and the board, fearing that it might eventually have to divide the program with the Catholic Archdiocese, attempted to cancel Grace Hill's contract. The settlement house then appealed to Washington. Appeals to federal authority make other locals fearful, and even the city-wide CAP agency sided with the school system, but Grace Hill won. At that time, OEO was in the mood to encourage diversity.

The contract was not only important symbolically; it made Grace Hill into an educational entrepreneur and re-focused the organization's attention on community development. Although by 1971 Grace Hill's OEO funding had dropped from its 1967 high of $225,000 to $180,000, there was money enough to permit the organization to hire personnel for its additional tasks.

In 1967, Murphy-Blair and four surrounding neighborhoods were declared Model Cities area of St. Louis. Grace Hill had lobbied intensely to have Murphy-Blair included in the Model Cities area, and later the agency received $11,000 from the federal government for planning. The result of this process was a document about the size of the St. Louis phone directory. "The Murphy-Blair Residents Plan," assembled by Grace Hill and an architectural firm engaged in advocate planning, is composed of program proposals covering areas of need. The needs ranged from a resident bus service to a series of health and service centers, and the total cost was estimated at $2 million. If all had been funded and implemented, Murphy-Blair would have had a neighborhood government almost as comprehensive as that advocated by Milton Kotler.[22]

One chapter of the plan was devoted to the subject of "How can we run our neighborhood—resident—school participation in planning."[23] It proposed four separate participatory groups: parent groups, school cabinets, District Education Board, and Community School Board. The base parent groups were essentially revitalized Mothers Clubs and PTAs, but the School Cabinet was a new device. Composed of parents, the Cabinet would "listen to specific complaints brought by parents and may decide to serve as an advocate for a parent in dealing with the school. The Cabinet may also seek to mobilize the school's base groups in regard to particular issues." The plan also suggested the creation of a Murphy-Blair District Education Board formed of representatives of the School Cabinets and other education programs in the district. Since the plan proposed a separate body, the Murphy-Blair Community School Board, to design and manage the community school program, the authority of the DEB was not clear. The implication, however, was that it would represent the concerns of the residents about the operation of all regular public school programs. The annual cost, including the salaries of a "parent participation specialist and two parent participation coordinators, was budgeted at $63,779."

As the plan was being implemented, several modifications were made. Grace Hill already operated Headstart in the neighborhood, but a new vehicle was needed if the residents and the agency were to increase their influence over the regular public schools and to control the local community school. Consequently, a Murphy-Blair District Education Board (DEB) was created, but the separate Community School Board idea was dropped.

In order to have the proper status, it was necessary to secure an agreement with the board of education granting formal recognition. The main question was whether a member of the city board and the District Superintendent would sit on the DEB. Their membership, of course, would make DEB more than just another pressure group. During a board meeting, at which several members insisted that St. Louis avoid the Ocean-Hill Brownsville example, Superintendent Kottmeyer gave an impassioned speech in favor of the DEB arrangement. The board firmly stated that DEB powers were only to be "advisory," but it agreed to recognize the Murphy-Blair group.

The selection process for the DEB is complicated, reflecting the participatory ethos and the more practical need to touch base with a number of constituencies. According to its laws, the DEB is incorporated as a non-profit corporation in the state of Missouri. Of its twenty-five directors, ten may be nonresidents, of these three are from Grace Hill, two from the school system—the District Superintendent and a School Board member—and five who can provide experience beneficial to DEB, largely university people who had previous contact with Grace Hill. The other fifteen members must be residents: four elected from geographical areas, eight chosen by the parent groups, two representing Catholic and Lutheran parochial schools, and one elected at-large. The political advantages of combining election and appointment are obvious, but to the extent that the DEB exercises real power, its representative character could be challenged legally as a violation of the one-man-one-vote principle.

The DEB began operation in December 1968, and its educational role has developed by evolution. Sometimes it has acted as a traditional school support, for example, by sponsoring school clubs and providing tutors. Its School Forum (called the School Cabinet in the plan) concept, and its struggle to control the local community schools, however, have cast it in a more overtly political role.

One finding of the neighborhood survey was that many parents felt they were unable to talk effectively to teachers and other school officials. "They won't listen to us," was heard repeatedly. The School Forum was designed to remedy this communication problem by creating small groups of parents in each school who serve with the DEB staff as intermediaries, and on occasion, as a grievance committee, when residents have problems with the school. According to a DEB memorandum, the Forum works as follows:

If a parent has a problem related to the school which he feels he cannot solve by himself, he may bring this problem before the Forum. The following procedure is used by the Forum when handling a problem or complaint:

1. The parent presents his problem and answers questions of Forum members.
2. The Forum makes a list of questions to ask the principal, with or without the parent present.
3. The Forum decides whether or not to submit questions in person or by memorandum.
4. Communicating to the principal: a.
   a. The Forum prepares a memo *or* makes an appointment for visit to the principal.

  b. The Forum presents questions (or a memo is sent) and gives the principal the option of answering them or preparing a reply by stated date.
5. The Forum puts together all the facts that have been gathered and makes a judgment.
6. The Forum makes a recommendation based on its judgment, and explains the recommendation to the parent and the school.[24]

Sometimes the problem is a frightened mother who believed her children would be beaten up coming home from school and who could not convince anyone in the school of their potential plight. A DEB staff member intervened, and the school principal ended up walking the children home that particular evening. Another time when a teacher was accused of choking a child, the School Forum used a more formal grievance proceeding. The reluctance of local school officials to participate has been overcome by the fact that their refusal would be brought to the attention of the DEB, where, of course, the district superintendent sits. There is thus an incentive to settle problems through the Forum procedure.

Originally, the Forum membership was to be drawn from established parent groups (PTA and Patron Alliance), but it soon was apparent that these were not the parents having difficulty communicating with school officials; rather, they were quite supportive of challenged authority. Grace Hill staff encouraged more alienated parents to join the Forum, thereby angering the principals and some teachers and dividing the DEB. Consequently, the Forum was controversial for a while, but had the DEB decided to abolish it, Grace Hill would have re-established it under its aegis.

The conflict over control of the community school in the district, when the DEB really exercised its political muscle, illustrates the possibilities and constraints of such activity. The St. Louis community school program was largely financed with foundation funds, which by 1970 were running out. Consequently, schoolmen looked hopefully to the Model Cities program to continue and expand such schools. The existing community schools had been almost exclusively system-initiated, but the Model Cities program called for considerable community participation. The DEB hoped to receive a federal contract directly for a school in the Murphy-Blair area, while the school system insisted that it would run these community schools as it had the others.

In October, 1969, the DEB articulated six demands regarding its role in the projected new community school.

1. The Community School Board must be more than an advisory board—it should have the power and the means to do a survey to determine what kinds of programs the neighborhood wants and should have control of all programs.
2. The hiring of all Community School staff be done in accordance with procedure set by the Neighborhood Workers Council; i.e., the qualifications and duties of each position are to be evaluated and reviewed by the

Neighborhood Workers Council; the job description is posted in the neighborhood for a certain length of time.

3. The hiring and firing of the director be done by the Community School Board.

4. The Community School Program seek to make the school the focal point, the gathering point in the neighborhood, where meetings of all kinds would be held and where other cultural and recreational activities would also be held.

5. The relation of the Model Cities' Community Schools to the other community schools run by the Board of Education be made clear, i.e., that the Model Cities' Community Schools have part in the overall policy-making done by the Board of Education's Advisory Board.

6. That the Block Captains System be paid to do a survey of the neighborhood to determine the desires of the neighborhood.[25]

The DEB did not actually want to operate the community school, but it wanted an agreement that would give it leverage to exert pressure. Some of its leaders felt that, after the decline of patronage and the ward system, St. Louis had no efficient mechanism for the delivery of neighborhood services. For that reason, the DEB demanded a role in personnel selection. Also, it must be conceded, neighborhood organizations have become increasingly dependent on federal subcontracts to provide them with money and staff to maintain their advocate role.

Consequently, DEB decided to petition the Model City agency not to release the money for the Community School Program until the St. Louis Board of Education "looked into" the DEB's proposal. The DEB also sought and won the support of some of the surrounding neighborhoods. The board's official position was that since "the Community School should obviously become an integral part of the local elementary school program, it appears that the primary administrative responsibility for the conduct of the program would logically devolve upon the school principal." Although it is true that the programs were to take place in the elementary school, it was not so obvious that an after-school program serving adults from throughout the Model Cities area should be administered by an already over-burdened elementary school principal.

The issue was less a matter of logic than of power. The central board was determined to maintain its control over the Community Schools, which were one of its most popular and publicized programs. Furthermore, the DEB was no docile Parent Congress (indeed, it would have nothing to do with its local PC), and the central board looked suspiciously at any neighborhood willing to use political methods to achieve its goals. At first the board declared that it did not have the legal authority to subcontract with Murphy-Blair. But the Model City Director pointed out that although HUD regulations did not require such contracts, they clearly permitted them. Then the board challenged the representative nature of the DEB, arguing that other Model City neighborhoods were not included. Finally, the board insisted that failure to place the community schools under the direct authority of the elementary school principal could impede the coordination of janitorial and other services.

The Murphy-Blair board thought there was a bigger issue at stake, as one of its spokesmen noted:

I happen to believe that we have reached a cross-road in the development of public education in our big cities. The problem is not simply lack of funds. The problem is also lack of confidence on the part of increasingly large segments of the public. To remedy the latter situation we badly need to invent new organizational arrangements, rather than to extend old ones. We need to distribute decision-making power more broadly, rather than to concentrate it more narrowly. We need to start with premises which focus on curriculum and learning rather than on units of command and coordination of janitorial services.[26]

The central board was not convinced, however, and both sides began to appeal to the Model Cities agency in Washington. Several not entirely consistent directives were issued, but in general they required that the board of education be the direct contractor after the neighborhood groups had approved the package. When the Murphy-Blair DEB saw the board's proposals, it not only refused to grant its approval but lined up allies from other neighborhoods. Since the law requires that the city formally approve the grant request, the DEB also sought support from the Board of Aldermen. This pressure was successful; the Aldermen refused to pass the grant request and instructed the school board to negotiate with the neighborhoods. The board, however, felt that time was on its side and so began to stall. The Nixon administration had begun its reorganization of HUD, and the new appointees and their policies were less inclined to favor neighborhood agencies in disputes with school boards. Indeed, signals were given that if St. Louis could not resolve its problems, the $500,000 would not be reserved indefinitely. Perhaps some other needy and more Republican city would be found.

In March of 1970 an agreement was reached. The Murphy-Blair DEB did not receive a subcontract or indeed any money, except $5,000 for a neighborhood survey on directions for the new community school. But the DEB was given veto power over school personnel, and the general principle was that, "None of the money granted to the board of education, by the Model City Agency, for the development of Community Schools, would be spent without the approval of the local Community School Boards."[27]

It was a compromise, but it granted more of a potential role to the DEB than had ever been given to any other neighborhood organization in St. Louis. Such compromises, however, are not always easy to interpret or enforce. There have been several disputes, particularly over personnel procedures, but the March agreement has given the DEB some leverage. When the School Board proposed that a community school coordinator should have a salary of $14,000 and academic requirements that would have eliminated Murphy-Blair residents from consideration, the DEB came in with a counterproposal. Finally, a compromise was reached that there should be a $10,000 coordinator and a $6,000 assistant coordinator as a resident-in-training for the job. Such are the victories of the movement for neighborhood participation in St. Louis.

But the future for the Murphy-Blair DEB is not completely bright. Federal agencies are less and less inclined to fund private groups in the inner city, so money is generally scarce. The DEB model has not spread to other neighborhoods. It has had some difficulties playing the role of neighborhood advocate and steam valve while actually operating programs. The first function is more attuned to the lower class residents or the "neighbors" as they are called, while the second seems to require middle-class skills. Whether the seed planted in Murphy-Blair will wither or blossom cannot be predicted.

## The Future of School Decentralization in St. Louis

One Saturday in late November 1969, St. Louis school activists gathered in the plush Chase-Park Plaza Hotel for an all-day conference. The Danforth Foundation, which for several years had been looking for ways to stimulate the school system, had put up the money to invite almost 800 delegates from community organizations in the city. The conference was unprecedented in St. Louis, and the board of education was not at all certain it wanted to participate. An open refusal, however, would not stop the conference, and it might have further undermined the board's public image and its relationship with the Foundation. Following the old political strategy of if-you-can't-beat-them-join-them, the board finally decided to become a co-sponsor.

The meeting was intended to create new discussions of St. Louis school governance and to be a rallying point for those interested in new participatory structures. No formal conference votes were taken, but a summary of the recommendations of the working groups was compiled and made public. The first three policy recommendations were:

1. The St. Louis Board of Education should be decentralized to provide a separate school board for each of the six school districts.
2. In addition to six district boards, there should be a Central Board of Education which should include two people from each district.
3. The Central Board would collect taxes, set the tax rates, and disperse funds to the district boards. District boards would have all other powers.[28]

While other conference groups supported variations of these recommendations, the consensus for a change in the governing structure was unmistakable.

For the first time, the board's policy of participatory gradualism had been challenged by a broad spectrum of responsible people. Indeed, even the call for community control was finally heard in St. Louis.

A few months after the conference there was a major change in the system's top personnel. William Kottmeyer, at age 59, resigned as Superintendent. Some have suggested that he was discouraged by the growing aggressive style of school politics in the city and the increasingly gloomy financial picture, but those who know him best believe that his passion for creating new curriculum materials was the real motivation. After proclaiming its desire to conduct a national search to fill the position, the board chose Clyde Miller, a long-time city resident and veteran of the school system. The choice was criticized by those who wanted a black man for the job (indeed, Sam Shepard left St. Louis after the decision was made), but two other blacks within the system were appointed Deputy Superintendent and acting personnel director. After his selection Miller spent his first year on a sabbatical at Yale studying school management and he has shown more interest in changing school patterns than his school establishment background might indicate.

The system's more formal response to the conference was made in a one-inch-thick volume of rebuttals and appendices which discussed conference recommendations. Some of minor conference proposals, were accepted immediately. But the major part of the volume is directed to explaining the system's attempts to increase participation and challenging the concept of further community control. The systems' rebuttal pointed naturally enough to the community schools and their advisory boards. Furthermore, it suggested that there were many other advisory boards (ten, in fact, ranging from the Federally-required Title I Advisory Committee to the Banneker District Elementary Student Advisory Committee) of which most of the conference delegates were not even aware. The response even pointed with pride to the Murphy-Blair board as a pilot project that "is allowing us, in a controlled manner, to gain experience in community control."[29]

Most of the rebuttal, however, was concerned with articulating the premises that led to the creation of the districts and their Parent Congresses. It called the Parent Congresses "one of the most promising structures involving the grass roots community in the schools" and even said that the Congresses function "in a role similar (within legal limits) to a school board." While these phrases certainly exaggerated the existing role of the Congress, the document does provide an unusually candid statement of the leadership's philosophy of decentralization.

Both the system and the community would suffer, we feel, from hasty and precipitous unloading of responsibility without preparing for it. Our intention has been to decentralize in phases, to plan the evolution. Recent experience in other large cities underscores the hazard of hasty and ill-considered changes. Our position is that the changes can still be radical, if we train ourselves for them beforehand.[30]

While on one hand this philosophy may be viewed as a tough-minded incremental approach to reform, on the other it may reflect a paternalistic, almost colonial, "We'll tell the natives when we think they are ready" attitude.

A few months later, the system moved again to increase the symbols of participation.[31] The six districts were reduced to five, but each district was divided into two administrative units based on a single high school and its feeder schools. Since each adminstrative unit has its own Parent Congress, the number of units has increased to ten. The realignment also meant that parents could expect to belong to a single Parent Congress, regardless of which grade their children were in. More importantly, the role of the district superintendent as the articulator of his district's needs rather than as central board emissary was further defined. District curriculum committees composed of teachers were created with the central office curriculum division serving only as consultants. The board's press release declares, "It is assumed that unprecedented curriculum variations among the five districts will result from this reorganization."

All these moves appear to be quite reasonable and may even turn out to increase decentralization and participation. But, as with such past decisions, there was very little community participation in the decision to create more participation. The reshuffling of the districts and the Parent Congresses was simply announced unilaterally by 911 Locust Street. Although the changes might in the long run tangibly increase the role of the Parent Congresses, symbolically the way it was done may lessen their sense of functioning in a role "similar to a school board." Consequently, it is not surprising that in the 1970-71 school year, according to headquarters staff, the Parent Congresses did not seem to develop a clear understanding of their role, and participation lagged.

Nor is it very surprising that the Parent Congresses were unable to deliver citizen support for the system when it counted most. In St. Louis increases in school taxes require a simple majority vote at a special election. The system has generally won a tax increase in the required biennial referenda, but the votes have been close. Consequently in the spring of 1971, the board decided to run a "decentralized campaign" for voter support. The board first met with the presidents of the Parent Congresses to ask if they could support the budget package. After obtaining their largely *pro forma* approval, a dinner was held for about 1,000 Parent Congress members to gain their support. From that meeting each district developed an election strategy, and some funds were distributed to the districts for local campaigns. Leadership, however, was in the hands of the district superintendent rather than the parents.

A few months later when the returns came in, it was apparent that the "decentralized campaign" had failed. Although the vote on the public school question was closer than either the junior college or convention center results, the required majority was not obtained. New school taxes have been difficult to pass in many cities in recent years. In St. Louis, the decentralist strategy was not able to reverse the pattern of opposition to public school taxes in white neighborhoods and apathy in black areas.

The loss of the tax levy was a severe blow to the system's gradualist approach to decentralization. In the new austerity budget drawn up after the election, the board decided that neither the allotments to the Parent Congresses nor those to the community schools were priorities high enough to be preserved. The cuts that ended—temporarily, at least—the two most publicized attempts at local participation caused little comment. The Parent Congresses—the "local school boards"—made no public protest, even though they would have to continue without funds. The community schools are trying to survive with private money.

In other cities it seems likely that, austerity budget or not, such unilateral reduction of funds for local groups by the central government would have been greeted by some dissent, even resistance. Realistically, of course, neither the Parent Congresses nor the community schools had effectively influenced policy, so there was little substantive loss of power. But the system had been rhetorically committed to participation through those agencies since 1969, and there was a symbolic loss. Once again the board had made it clear that participation would occur on its terms and only on its terms. Why has there been so little effective pressure for community control in St. Louis? Why does an issue dominate the politics of one city and be nonexistent in another? Compared to many other cities, community control was a non-issue, or at least an erratic, poorly articulated issue in St. Louis. Researching why something did not happen is always difficult,[32] but some speculation may be useful.

Social scientists have developed two general theoretical approaches in the study of community decision-making. To simplify an enormously complex literature,[33] the pluralist school seeks to understand community power by analyzing the participants in major decisions, while the elitists believe that power is so often exercised covertly that they focus their attention on those perceived to be influential and examine the agenda and rules in a community to see who benefits. Our research, which attempts to describe the politics of a particular policy question rather than the general distribution and relationship of power in a city, is tied to neither approach but is informed by both.

In other cities, a community control movement has required either a major center of political opposition to the school establishment or an issue that it can use to mount an attack. Neither has been present in St. Louis. Unlike Detroit, St. Louis school officials have not been pressed very hard on integration and have avoided the organization of neighborhoods around that issue. Nor, since St. Louis teachers are divided organizationally and are comparatively powerless, has there been a feeling of hostility toward them such as existed among community groups in New York and Detroit.

Most important, it has not been possible to organize any significant element against the school establishment. Since the Citizens Committee for Quality Education headed by Daniel Schlafly gained power in the 1950s, it has not been seriously challenged. St. Louis' dominant Democratic Party has not been interested in educational issues. Mayor Alphonso Cervantes has expressed sentiments that are compatible with increasing participation. For example, he told the National Advisory Commission on Civil Disorders:

We have found that ghetto neighborhoods cannot be operated on from outside alone. The people within them should have a voice, and our experience has shown that it is often a voice that speaks with good sense, since the practical aspects of the needs of the ghetto people are so much clearer to the people there than they are to anyone else.[34]

But he has not applied this perspective to education. The Mayor's office has little legal leverage on the schools in St. Louis, and so long as Schlafly has agreed not to run for mayor (at one time he might have had either party's nomination), Cervantes has been willing to keep hands off education. Indeed, the Mayor does not even have an identifiable educational aide on his staff.

In most cities it has been the black community that has created the community control movement. But in St. Louis, although there are many black school critics, there are few effective leaders. Congressman William Clay is the leading black spokesman; he has strongly criticized the schools but naturally focused most of his attention on Washington. A Council of Black People does exist, but it is not a powerful lobbying force. While the NAACP is not very active in St. Louis, CORE has a strong polemical voice but little organization.

Perhaps a part of the black reticence to press for community control is that most leaders can remember the pre-1954 legally segregated St. Louis schools. The black separatist ideology, which is so strong in some cities, has few roots in St. Louis. Community control sounds dangerously near "separate but equal" to some St. Louis blacks. Further, although it is not very often voiced, some blacks are not very eager to divide up a city in which they will probably be a majority before the end of the decade.

There is also the more subtle influence that St. Louis is no longer a very large city. Since the school system enrolls 110,000 students, it could reasonably be divided into districts; but the city itself has a population of less than 700,000, and it has a certain small city ethos. Most of the leaders know each other and see each other often. Conflict is uncomfortable to maintain. Issue-oriented groups within the city generally have small budgets and limited staffs, hardly the resources for waging a struggle for or against community control. There are no organizations in the education field with strength comparable to the United Parents Association or the Public Education Association in New York.[35] The difficulty in raising issues is compounded by the fact that neither the *Globe-Democrat* nor the *Post Dispatch* has a full-time education editor or even a regular education column. Education stories rarely receive front page coverage, and when issues are reported at all, they are rarely followed up. Sustaining opposition to the school establishment is thereby made more difficult.

Perhaps for these reasons, the principal innovator in St. Louis school policies has not been a politician, party, or pressure group, but a foundation. For several years, the Danforth Foundation, whose original income was derived largely from the St. Louis-based Ralston Purina Company, and whose principal interest is education, has launched project after project to improve the St. Louis schools. These efforts are designed to increase curriculum innovation and citizen participation. Some programs have met with enthusiastic responses from the school board. Many others have been accepted only after there seemed to be no way compatible with good public relations to turn them down. In its support of community schools, the Murphy-Blair experiments, the Community Conference on St. Louis Schools, the 1971 Spring Retreats, the Confederation of Alternative Schools, and many other projects, the Danforth Foundation has proved to be the only organization with the staying power and the leverage to induce the sytem to change. In the long run, however, foundations are better at raising public consciousness than in forcing change in a particular direction.

The school leadership, using the electoral system and the Citizens Committee for Quality Education, has a formidable ability to resist sharing power. Any election that is non-partisan, at-large and held at times when little else is on the ballot is ideally constructed to preserve well-financed incumbents. Furthermore, the anti-corruption, anti-political origins of the Committee, together with its support in the media, give it a powerful symbolic advantage. Even if one has legitimate policy differences, it is difficult to campaign against a man of such unquestioned intelligence and integrity as Daniel Schlafly. It is doubly difficult, when as in many one-party governments, the incumbents co-opt the issues of the challengers. When in 1967, Reverend Carl Dudley led a liberal, labor, anti-poverty coalition on a platform of greater community participation, the Schlafly-dominated board increased the visibility of the Parent Congresses. In 1971, when four blacks complaining of the unrepresentative middle-class nature of the board ran against the slate, a black woman whose life history would have made Horatio Alger proud was added to it. The Citizens Committee won again easily.

During the 1960s in St. Louis, holding a serious community debate over school decentralization was extraordinarily difficult. In their writing about community power, Peter Bachrach and Morton Baratz have made some provocative suggestions about the role of power in curbing the issues the public considers. They believe that it is possible that an elite might limit the "scope of actual decision-making to 'safe' issues by manipulating the dominant community values, myths, and political institutions and procedures." This they say might "effectively prevent certain grievances from developing into full-fledged issues which call for decisions."[36] As their critics have pointed out, an empirical test of those assumptions would require enormous resources,[37] for a city the size of St. Louis certainly exceeding the resources of this research.

Still their insights may be useful. In this period, our research as well as that by Crain and Gittell-Hollander found that St. Louis school politics was dominated by a select group of upper- and middle-class reformers (Citizens Committee for Quality Education) with close ties to downtown business (Civic

Progress, Inc.).[38] By taking advantage of the electoral system and by playing upon the fear of politics in education, this elite has shown a formidable ability to stay in power and to limit the issues seriously debated.[39]

As this study suggests, however, the elite has not been unchallenged, nor is it totally able to control the agenda. But by gradually increasing the number of blacks in policy-making positions, and by supporting the symbol of decentralization, the elite has shifted attention from the more rigorous demands for integration or community control that would threaten its leadership. In order to avoid the conflict that has existed in other cities, most St. Louis citizens have been willing to pay the price of limited political alternatives.

The era when the amount of local participation was determined exclusively by the central board may be nearing an end. In the spring of 1971, the two members from St. Louis on the House Education Committee of the Missouri legislature began to push for legislation that would have six of the twelve members of the city's school board elected by district instead of at-large. The proposal was in line with the recommendations of the Conference on St. Louis schools. Although this change would not create community control, it was the first legislative salvo in the effort to decentralize the board politically and strengthen the role of neighborhood groups. As Representative James Conway (who represents a poor white district—the co-sponsor Deverne Calloway represents a poor black district) argued:

. . . the majority of parents and citizens are turned off concerning the board. They feel there has been little impact from parents and citizens. They feel the board has responded on a 'we know what is best' basis and that communication with the board has essentially been unidirectional.[40]

Daniel Schlafly personally led the board's opposition by marshaling his extensive contacts in the legislature to lobby against the bill. He argued that the proposed electoral system would bring back ward politics into schools and would polarize the school board. He boasted that, "We have had few of the internal cleavages for religious, political, and ethnic reasons that have marked boards in other cities." Furthermore, he pointed out that the Conway bill would do nothing to solve the system's twin problems of social imbalance and lack of funds. A better alternative, he insisted, would be the board's proposal of ten districts, based on metropolitan-wide reorganization.

The St. Louis delegation has historically been rather apathetic about the fate of the city's public schools in the often hostile legislature.[41] Consequently, almost no lobbying was done by community groups, and the hearings were not extensive. In a surprising show of unanimity, however, the Conway bill received the support of every St. Louis House delegate and passed that body easily. It also had the approval of the Senate Education Committee, but it was buried in the year-end legislative rush. ·

In the three-year period of this study, the structural reforms that the system promised in 1969 as necessary to create greater citizen participation have not occurred. The leadership has met the cry for participation with new and better forms of communication. It either cannot hear or will not accede to the demand for power-sharing. Perhaps now that it appears stymied in its attempts to pass bond issues and levy taxes, it may realize the extent to which many people of St. Louis have lost interest in hearing the system's communications.

Yet the system is changing. More blacks are in leadership positions, and there has been a noticeable increase in curricular innovation. According to a spring 1971 report, although eighth graders in St. Louis public schools were still slightly behind national averages on standardized tests, they had significantly improved their standing over 1962 scores. This development led a reporter for the *Chicago Daily News* to write, "That makes St. Louis youngsters about the smartest big-city kids in the nation."[42] Journalistic hyperbole aside, those test scores are no small achievement for a system as underfinanced and as subject to demographic change as the St. Louis public schools have been.

Test scores may not be enough, however, to resist the growing pressure for new participatory structures. The politics of participation has moved from the board and the advisory bodies it has created to the state legislature. That new politics is now in its first stages, and the outcome cannot be predicted. Judicial trends requiring more racial integration and fiscal equality in metropolitan areas may provide increased support for the board's ten-district plan. Short of a direct court order, it is hard to see the metropolitan school concept overcoming the opposition of suburban whites who would have to share their tax and school advantages and the skepticism of city blacks who would become a permanent political minority under the reorganization. Consequently, the new direction may be toward some form of community control or, at least, as the Conway bill proposes, some neighborhood representation on the board.[43] In New York and Michigan, once the legislatures intervened, the balance of power shifted away from the central school authorities toward the neighborhoods. While in both cases the outcome was a compromise, the legislatures did require that the school system's rhetoric of decentralization begin to become a reality.

# 5 Los Angeles: The Search for Power

Los Angeles has often been described as a cluster of suburbs in search of a city. The settlement pattern of the area spreads from the mountains westward to the ocean and from Santa Barbara south to San Diego. From the sunswept beaches of the Pacific to the smoggy Pasadena hills, Los Angeles is a city of restless energy, sharp contrasts, and relentless change. The city is formless and diffuse in its physical growth, and a great variety of life styles accompanies the varied patterns of physical development. Yet a certain order governs the formlessness. Culturally, the residents of southern California tend to share the belief that their part of the country promotes greater freedom, more "openness" to experience, and is more likely to provide opportunities for the fullest development of the individual personality. Living in the city cultivates the desire to share in the communal celebration of the southern California way of life.

Even poverty in Los Angeles has its special quality: the tracts of pastel single-family dwellings in East and Central Los Angeles bake in the sun, dotted with stringy palms, and crisscrossed by freeways. Angelenos were startled when the Watts disturbances ushered in the period of major urban convulsions that shook the nation in the 1960s. But in retrospect it appeared natural that the greatest expectations should be unleashed in the city of great opportunity. The official boosterism of much of the city's public life, however, has always had a certain brittle quality. Beneath the "good life" of southern California strains and conflicts have periodically erupted. Critic and admirerer alike agree that Los Angeles is a city of extremes in its political and cultural life. By the end of the 1960s, the city's underlying tensions and anxieties had become sharply accentuated as southern California became more deeply immeshed in its own brand of the urban crisis. Census data for 1970 showed, symbolically, a reversal of the net immigration into the state as a whole and especially into southern California.

The volatile character of contemporary Los Angeles politics is in part only a sharpening of traditional features. It has always been difficult for any concern to remain at center stage in public consciousness. The politics of Los Angeles is the politics of the nonpartisan West. Issues surface, temporary alliances form, energies concert and then disperse in a poorly articulated political system. The formal structure of local government has further heightened the problems posed by the political culture of the area. Independent functional bureaucracies at the county level are insulated from effective political control, and power is dispersed widely throughout the formal governmental institutions. Wilson and Banfield cite Los Angeles as an example of extreme decentralization in which:

many things are not done because it is impossible to secure the collaboration of all those whose collaboration is needed . . . Widespread apathy and indifferences among voters mitigates the affect of the decentralization of authority to them . . . the devices of salesmanship are extensively used . . . Measures are frequently compromised so as to 'give something to everybody' in order to get them accepted.[1]

The novels of Nathaniel West, especially *Day of the Locust* and *Miss Lonelyhearts,* caught the spirit of the forces that shaped the city's social and political life in the late 1930s and continue to be important features: the influx of new populations (mostly lower- and middle-class), soaring expectations, the search for community, waves of reformist commitment and militant conservatism. The urban crisis of the 1960s has added to these traditional features the rising militancy of ethnic groups combined with the important role played by the electronic media in dramatizing issues and influencing the agenda of public policy.

### The School System

The Los Angeles unified school district (LAUSD) is the nation's second largest school system with over 620 schools, an enrollment of some 800,000, and 710 square miles in area. The Los Angeles school district was created in 1853 as one of the first major programs of the new city government after Los Angeles' incorporation on April 4, 1850. Originally, the school district was designed to serve an area of twenty-eight square miles and a population estimated to be slightly greater than the 1,250 that lived in Los Angeles in the 1840s prior to the Gold Rush at Sutter's Mill in 1848. The vast Los Angeles school district of today encompasses sixty-nine identifiable communities and twenty-five incorporated cities and has a staff of more than 60,000 employees. Despite the size of the district, a notable feature is lack of cohesion and of strong central direction. The diffusion of power is evident within the district itself and also in the relationship between the city and county jurisdictions. The Los Angeles school district is one of 95 school districts in the county of Los Angeles and covers less than 18 percent of the county's area (but provides education for 42 percent of the county's children). While the school district has an area of 710 square miles, Los Angeles City has an area of "only" 463. Thus, 385,000 eligible voters in the school district are not residents of Los Angeles City and cannot vote in city elections but do have a large influence in the city's school affairs. The Los Angeles school district contains suburban areas as well as inner-city ghettos, many children of wealthy parents as well as children of the poor, white as well as minority group children. The "unified" nature of the school district is subject to recurrent pressures for subcommunity withdrawal from the system, just as political units have resisted annexation.[2] Beverly Hills is an example of a refusal to be annexed, and Santa Monica, Culver City, Torrance, and Inglewood are prominent examples of successful secessions from the unified school district.

The school district, like the city itself, is a precarious combination of unity and diversity. Centralized and decentralized elements have combined in intricate patterns. Decentralization in some sense has always been unavoidable because of the size and diversity of the district. Yet decentralization has always been feared because of the danger that centrifugal tendencies could break the system apart into parochial fiefs of unequal wealth, taxing power, and educational services.

The board of education, which appoints the superintendent and exercises ultimate executive authority, consists of seven members elected at-large in non-partisan elections for staggered four-year terms. The members are elected by numbered seats or "slots," so that candidates run for a particular position rather than as a group with the largest vote-getters winning. The electoral arrangements, like the administration of the school system generally, reflect the results of earlier reform campaigns to insulate the schools from politics and the ethnic battles of municipal government. A chief problem of the school district is whether the structure that resulted from progressive reforms fits contemporary needs. While Los Angeles' growing minorities have been represented on the board of education, there has been a considerable lag in minority placement on the teaching and administrative staffs. Changing population patterns have placed large numbers of minority children in the public schools whose personnel and style of operation have been predominantly oriented toward middle-class whites. And in Los Angeles, the demands on the public schools have been especially acute because there is no tradition, as in eastern cities, of parochial schools serving ethnic populations.[3]

The crisis that grew up in Los Angeles over school decentralization thus reflected not only the traditional problems facing the school district, but also the new and highly complex urban issues of the 1960s. Educational concerns came to be mixed in with the larger issues of residential segregation, poverty, and public order that were beginning to afflict American cities. Decentralization became a symbolic issue of great importance. For a time it seemed to unite many divergent interests under the banner of school reform. The story can be conveniently viewed in four phases: (1) the changing patterns of citizen involvement and interest group activity, triggered by the "community revolution" in minority neighborhoods; (2) the struggle to promote administrative decentralization within the institutional machinery of the school district; (3) the legislative battles over various proposed state-mandated decentralization plans; and (4) the massive decentralization "referendum" campaign of 1971 and its aftermath. The city's experience highlights some basic dilemmas facing the reformers of the large urban school system.

## Trends in Citizen Involvement and Interest Group Activity

Interest in decentralization, and in inner-city education generally, began to grow rapidly among parents and citizens groups in Los Angeles in the early 1960s.

Interest was stimulated in part by earlier debate within the school system, and in part by community groups associated with the NAACP and the Urban League. The great surge of grass roots interest in school affairs also coincided with the impact of new federal programs. The "war on poverty" and later the Elementary and Secondary Education Act, as in our other case study cities, stimulated concern with the improvement of services to the urban poor and the participation of new elites in the shaping of policy. The federal initiatives stimulated citizen involvement but also subsequently acted as a brake on the push for complete autonomy stemming from this mobilization of energies.

It is difficult to chart the full range of citizen activity and associational life that has emerged in Los Angeles school politics since the mid 1960s. Numbers alone are deceptive, but it is probable that several hundred citizens groups with an interest in public education have come into existence. Some have been rather short-lived, some have proved more durable. Some are *ad hoc* and focus on relatively narrow issues, but many have been concerned with a wide range of interests both educational and other. A pattern can be roughly discerned despite the seeming confusion and disorder of the system of interest group activity.

First, a group of "core" actors plays a major role in filtering the demands on the school system.[4] These organizations have achieved some longevity and have the resources for a sustained existence. They usually work closely with allies in some part of the formal school bureaucracy. Some of them are umbrella organizations, aggregating the interests of locally-based groups and operating on a city-wide basis; others concern themselves only with matters within a given territory. Second, the "core" actors are supplemented by "satellites" that occasionally merge with the more established groups or provide leadership and new manpower resources for them. Beyond the satellite actors are a third set of participants in school politics, fringe groups having a high rate of mortality but sometimes providing a route of entry into city-wide school politics for the ambitious individual. These groups often function at the local school level, and wax and wane depending on the quality of their leadership. In general, the Los Angeles school interest groups are not as highly developed and professionalized as those in New York, and the personal drive of the largely-volunteer leadership is frequently a decisive factor in determining a group's influence.

The role of the satellites and of the tertiary actors are particularly difficult to characterize, although an important part of the educational scene. Consider the Black Congress, formed following the assassination of Senator Robert Kennedy in Los Angeles in 1968. It had no clearly defined objectives, but enjoyed an intense period of activity until it disintegrated after a shootout at UCLA in 1969. Several persons were killed in that episode, and one of the organization's leaders, Ron Karenga, was implicated. During the time of its major activity, the Black Congress, among other things, played a part in seeking the removal of principals who were considered incompetent, generally acting as a watchdog for shortcomings in ghetto schools in central Los Angeles. The tactics employed, in the view of police and many school officials, produced near chaos in the schools. However, to many parents and community activists, the Congress appeared as a militant fighter for better schools. But it also posed a difficult problem for the militant but non-violent community activists. They could not repudiate the organization and its tactics (until after the shootout) because they feared that to do so would break ranks and play into the hands of the forces of tokenism.

The ripples that an organization like the Black Congress sent throughout the system were substantial, posing the issue of how to distinguish legitimate dissent from terrorist tactics. The police were constantly engaged in attempts to infiltrate such organizations and maintain surveillance over their activities. When the organization was infiltrated, the individuals involved often simply reappeared in other groups, which similarly held together for only relatively short periods. The disorder in Los Angeles schools in 1969 was partially caused by a variety of *ad hoc* community groups employing harassment and intimidation to encourage the removal of principals and teachers not considered "responsive." But the impression should not be left that such groups customarily used violence in Los Angeles. Most eschewed such tactics, including even militant groups that used the rhetoric of revolution. The tertiary organizations, even though short-lived, nonetheless played an important role in the emerging school politics. Many leaders graduated through the ranks of such groups into the core organizations that shaped school politics, and in any case the tertiary groups kept issues on the agenda of concern.

The organizing abilities of some activists have been impressive. Mrs. Margaret Wright, for example, became something of a legend in Los Angeles school politics when she appeared and reappeared in numerous citizens groups and confrontations with the school system in the 1960s. With prodigious energy and a flair for self-dramatization, she became a minor political force in her area. Her activities somewhat diminished after 1970, but she still appeared as a member of the Citizens Advisory Committee of the Superintendent's Decentralization Task Force in the spring of 1971. Although distinctive in her colorful and flamboyant style, she was in other respects typical of the new inner-city school activists in being a woman, hard-working, and able to devote time to civic pursuits. Women form a high proportion of the new activists—62 percent of the Community Advisory Committee to the Decentralization Task Force, and among the active members an even higher percentage. One might say that the inner city has developed its functional equivalent to the "little old lady in tennis shoes" of Orange County mythology, who is much feared and respected in suburban politics.

### The Office of Urban Affairs

To complete the story of the "community revolution" in Los Angeles school politics, it is necessary to take a detailed look at the district's major community experiments. In 1960, the Education Committee of the Los Angeles NAACP was one of the few citizen groups concerned with the quality of inner-city education. Its activities, in conjunction with the broad factors just noted, began to stir a wide base of community interest in central city schools. In 1963, the ferment within the black inner city led to a march on the board of education under the auspices of the United Civil Rights Commission, an umbrella group largely growing out of the NAACP and Urban League. The principal demand of the march was UCRU's desire to have a municipal office devoted to the problems of minority education. The board heeded this desire by subsequently creating the Office of Urban Affairs as a staff function within the school system.

As in our other case study cities that have experimented with such an office, the OUA encountered problems because it pursued conflicting objectives. It sought to keep the community "cool" while at the same time serving as a focal point for grievances against the school system. Since the community would be more fully mobilized if the OUA did its job properly, there was a tendency for demands to be more militant than the school system was prepared to meet. The result was that from the start the OUA was embroiled in controversy. Its position as a link between the "community" and school system made it a natural target for critics. Traditionalist school officials suspected that it was promoting agitation; some believed that the impulse toward greater citizen involvement in school affairs was in part generated by figures within the OUA that wished to aggrandize their own positions. On the other hand, community groups directed their fire at this office for all of the school system's shortcomings. The more militant community activists viewed the OUA as a device of cooptation designed to divert attention from fundamental issues.

Fortunately, OUA director Sam Hamerman, who headed the office in its turbulent, formative years, steered a course between capitulating to extreme community demands and catering to traditional professional sensibilities at the cost of community support. He was able to retain confidence with his different constituencies while promoting a variety of programs to increase citizen participation. It is characteristic of such offices that they eventually become staffed largely with minority group officials, and in 1970 Hamerman was replaced by his deputy, William Bailey, a black moderate who has a similar policy orientation.

The office has remained the object of both exaggerated expectations and blame. The reality has been that it began to function in a period of rising demands that it neither generated nor could wholly control. But a dialogue between community activists and headquarter school officials was established that has proven helpful in the orderly expansion of citizen involvement in the school system. The ease of access of parents and other community representatives to the OUA suggests permeability rather than the impenetrability of the Los Angeles school bureaucracy. Equally, however, the access has not produced the capacity to influence policy significantly. Instead of the system being closed and unresponsive, the school bureaucracy in Los Angeles is loose-jointed and responsive to many conflicting influences. The result has been to make it difficult to frame coherent policies and to move clearly in any direction.

## Title I Advisory Boards

The Elementary and Secondary Education Act of 1965 provided the next significant step in expanding citizen involvement in Los Angeles public schools. Advisory boards created under Title I of ESEA provided the first formal citizen role in the district. The district was divided into three zones, with an advisory board in each to assist in planning the use of Title I funds. The history of these boards has been one of growing but still limited influence in affecting school programs—a result that has confirmed neither the initial fears of some principals nor the hopes of some community activists.[5]

The initial contact for Title I boards was mainly the downtown school headquarters through the OUA. As they gradually became more active, the boards made an impact at the individual school as well. Personnel transfers, for example, have been affected through pressure brought by the Title I advisory boards. In the spring of 1970, when additional federal funds became available for summer programs, the boards exercised considerable influence in shaping the program. The boards rejected an initial proposal by the school system that would have oriented the effort toward training programs for teachers and principals of Title I schools; instead they favored a program emphasizing parent and community training programs. The board of education adopted their program after intense controversy, and the staff for the program's administration was subsequently selected by the advisory board in each area. The "bread and butter" concerns—i.e., jobs and tangible benefits, reminiscent of old-style patronage—have been a primary preoccupation of the advisory boards. Although meetings are relatively infrequent, the leaders, principally minority group women, devote considerable time to their responsibilities, and many are familiar faces at downtown school headquarters. By virtue of their expertise and hard work, a core group of knowledgeable board members can influence the planning for Title I schools.

The advisory boards, in the eyes of some principals, have provided a forum for "busybodies" to interfere with school operations. More often, board members and principals have worked together tolerably well, even though the exact power and responsibilities of the boards have never been fully defined. The perspective of the board member has tended to be that the board should have more than an advisory role. The principals, who are required under state law to be the administrative officers of the school, have sought to limit the advisory role and to define "policy" in such a way as to leave "operations" largely in their hands. Personalities of the individuals have played a part in determining the degree of friction. However, the relationships between the boards and school principals, perhaps surprisingly, have not in general been marked by much confrontation or deep-rooted antagonism. Advisory board members have not seriously threatened the role of the professional educators, but neither have the boards been without influence. Perhaps one might say that the advisory board members have acquired the limited but significant influence that middle-class whites have enjoyed in the suburbs.

The experience of the Title I advisory boards has been duplicated in several other compensatory projects attempted by the school system. The APEX Program, the Jordan and Garfield educational complexes, and the Eighteen School Project—which were stimulated by state and/or federal action—sought community participation through advisory boards working with local administrators. These boards conform to the general patterns of Title I boards in composition, style of operation, and issue concerns. Minority women are among the major activists, meetings are relatively informal and infrequent (though there may be episodes of intense involvement), and the goals are often teacher re-education and making the principal "sensitive" to minority needs.

The least successful of the three projects has been the APEX educational park near Crenshaw and Baldwin Hills. This project was also, not entirely coincidentally, marked by militant citizen activity. The area has been referred to as a "gilded black ghetto," inasmuch as the social composition has been middle-class; besides blacks, some orientals and whites have traditionally lived there. The APEX project was designed to check the slide away from a fairly stable racial balance toward an all-black neighborhood. The project has failed in that objective. APEX, after its federal funding ran out, has existed under only token district expenditures. The combination of affluent white liberals and blacks with high expectations produced the militant climate there, as well as elsewhere in the school system. In 1969, the high point of school disturbances, community pressure forced out a number of white principals who were replaced by black principals.

In the Jordan and Garfield complexes similar aims were sought with less intense conflict between professionals and the community. In the Garfield projects the boards concentrated on seeking changes in personnel, and at Jordan the principal aims were staff development, attitude change among the teachers and principals, and curriculum innovations. The Eighteen School Project concentrated on curriculum reform as the principal objective.

Although there has been little change in the formal roles of administrators and teachers in these experimental projects, there have been important informal shifts in their attitudes that have had an impact on the style of school operations. Minority group parents have tended to get respectful hearings when they complain to the principals about the school's failings. In general, the professionals, who continue to have the most powerful voice in school policy, have come to view the parents and other community activists as an important constituency; they are now officially referred to as "school support groups." At the same time, there have been costs involved in the increased citizen involvement. Attention has sometimes been diverted from fundamental educational issues toward clashes over personnel. Parent groups have sometimes been both rigid and overly susceptible to fads in their conception of good education.

Where militancy has spilled over into disturbances the costs have been high. The incidents in schools near Crenshaw and Baldwin Hills, for example, frightened white parents, and it is probable that the increased residential segregation in the area in recent years was partly caused by the actions of the militant coalition. In the view of some activists, the changes in the social composition of the neighborhood have counterbalanced the gains in school responsiveness. The experience here suggests that greater militancy may occur where liberal whites form an influential part of the radical coalition. At any rate, when group demands center on the removal of principal or staff, the conditions exist for a bitter and protracted struggle.

## The Minority Group Commissions

Another type of citizen involvement in Los Angeles is the minority-group commission. Four of these have been created by the board of education, and they have sought to exercise influence directly upon the board. The important groups are the Mexican-American Educational Commission created in the spring of 1969, the Black Educational Commission created in 1970, and the Community Affairs Committee and Asian-American Education Commission created in 1971. These groups complete the complex and overlapping pattern of citizen involvement in school affairs by giving the board its own layer of interest representation. The commissions interact with the interest groups oriented toward the Superintendent's office and with the local school-oriented advisory boards. However, the three-tiered system of interest group activity is considerably blurred by overlapping memberships and *ad hoc* alliances. Since power is dispersed in Los Angeles school politics, interest group activity is correspondingly directed toward diverse targets. All citizen groups of whatever origin or ideological hue have sought to use the news media to legitimate themselves as influentials and to shape the general climate of elite and lay opinion.

The Mexican-American Educational Commission is somewhat unusual in the context of the city's ethnic politics since it has achieved a focused thrust and a degree of organizational capacity. Usually, Mexican-American protests here have lagged behind black demands and have had a harder time in moving past unfocused discontent to effective organizational activity. This commission has concentrated its efforts largely on the special reading problems that confront Spanish-speaking students. In contrast, the Black Education Commission has had greater difficulty in defining a distinctive mission for itself and in aligning the interests of the numerous power-seeking groups, perhaps partly because more well-established civil rights groups have pre-empted many issues. The most recent group—the Asian-American Educational Commission—is less militant and serves a more diverse constituency, and one may suppose that it will have difficulty in achieving an effective program. The board has given each commission a small budget that can be used to hire an executive director and a limited number of consultants. An energetic executive director has proved to be critical for the commissions to achieve a viable role, and with opportunities expanding for the educated minority member, it has not always proved easy to recruit or retain the right calibre of person.

Several conservative groups have sought board funding and sponsorship similar to the minority group commission, but these attempts have failed. The conservative school forces, however, have remained highly active and demonstrate considerable organizational vitality. Besides the traditional PTAs and taxpayers groups interested in keeping taxes down, newer groups have sprung up with a variety of educational goals. Some, oddly, actively seek citizen support for a policy of professional dominance in educational decision-making.

More frequently, conservatives have borrowed the rhetoric of community control in calling for schools "responsive" to parents and other solid citizens and not to what they regard as dangerous fringe groups. The new conservatives usually share with many community activists in the inner city a deep suspicion of professionals and the "system." It is the system, in their view, that has been paternalistic and that has given preferential treatment to blacks and other minorities. In their distrust of the system, and in their concern with the values inculcated through public education, many conservative parents, especially those with lower-to-moderate income, share objectives similar to those of disenchanted ghetto parents.

The career of Mrs. Dolly Swift of the conservative Parents for Students organization based in the San Fernando Valley illustrates the dilemma of the conservative. Mrs. Swift ran unsuccessfully against a liberal incumbent, Mrs. Georgiana Hardy, for the board of education in the elections of May 1971. Initially, Mrs. Swift flirted with ideas of parent control in San Fernando Valley schools. She criticized the board for not being responsive enough to the parents. Later in her campaign, she took the position that the board should not be bound by parental wishes on such issues as school decentralization. This stand satisfied some constituents who viewed a powerful and authoritarian board as an effective check against the further spread of radical and racial impulses in the city schools. In the late stages of the campaign, she took the position that: "I do not support the concept of participatory democracy."[6] But this dissatisfied other conservatives suspicious of the central board, its alleged past favoritisms to minorities, and the whole idea of stronger central control. Mrs. Swift was unable to make the transition from a local candidate strong in one part of the city to a formidable city-wide candidate. The splits she helped cause in the conservative camp by her wavering on the decentralization issue contributed to her defeat.

Conservatives have been particularly critical of the board's minority commissions. Their fear has been that these efforts to encourage minority participation have played a part in school disorders and in the decline of educational standards. Despite Mrs. Swift's defeat, the conservatives won a slight victory in the May 1971 board elections and remained an important part of the pluralist pattern in Los Angeles school politics.[7]

The new patterns of community involvement have helped produce a volatile system in which many issues pass in rapid succession on and off the agenda of public concern. Indeed, it is perhaps even somewhat misleading to speak of an "agenda" since the politics of public education, like Los Angeles politics generally, is highly disorganized and fragmented. Yet there are continuities in educational politics, especially at the city-wide level. Part of the reason why issues associated with decentralization remained in the center of debate for so long is that they overlapped long-standing disputes between the "reform" orientation and the contrasting concern with keeping taxes low and preserving the traditional values taught in schools. Although at first decentralization cut strangely across the political spectrum, the fight increasingly took on the appearance of a familiar battle between reformers and traditionalists. For example, decentralization proved hard to swallow for some traditional liberal groups, such as the League of Women Voters, that have stood for the consolidation of school districts as the progressive course of action. But the League eventually came to support the idea of decentralization. The board elections in May 1971 illustrate the aspects of continuity, bearing resemblance to the elections of April 1959. The battle then was between conservative groups seeking economy along with a more traditional school curriculum versus a liberal coalition arguing for innovation and the energizing of the school bureaucracy. As formal structural change has become less important than other devices to increase participation, it has proven easier for the traditional alignments between liberals and conservatives to reassert themselves.

The participatory cast of the decentralization ideology has emerged in Los Angeles as more important than formal structural changes. This is perhaps hardly surprising, given the appeal of participation in the political culture of non-partisan California. Yet uncertainties remain. As of fall 1971, the relationship between formal administrative decentralization in Los Angeles and the techniques of citizen involvement in educational policy-making was not fully clarified. These two components of the decentralization ideology have partly reinforced each other and have partly been in conflict. Uncertainty and confusion have resulted over the question of whether the objective to be sought is formal decentralization or citizen access to a more or less centralized structure, or some combination of each. In June 1971, the board of education mandated advisory councils with some elected parent members for all city schools, but this action has not clarified the situation.

*Administrative Decentralization*

Efforts to decentralize the school system are not new to Los Angeles, for its appeal is strong. Such efforts have usually run up against the fact that the system is fragmented and only imperfectly unified. Ironically, it has proved necessary to seek greater central authority in order to decentralize rationally. Since power cannot be delegated until it is first acquired, many of the reform struggles in the past have resulted in consolidation and centralization even when the initial intent was to promote decentralization.

The Los Angeles school system must be viewed in this context of a tradition of weak executive authority in city and county administration. Reformers have sought to strengthen executive authority through such measures as charter amendments to remove the part-time lay boards that clutter the administrative process, to improve staffing, to provide more budget authority, and the like.[8] The school system shares with the regular city departments certain features of formal structure and political culture that have worked against strong executive leadership. The ultimate executive authority is a part-time lay board. The Superintendent nominally has broad administrative powers but can be effectively checked by indecision within the board. The operative ideal, reflecting in extreme form ideas implicit in American constitutionalism, seems to be that no one in the system should emerge with too much power because the concentration of power is to be feared. The result is such a diffusion of power that even the attempts to decentralize may be frustrated by the need for strong central authority, system-wide priority setting, and coherent administration.

The period of a shift to decentralization as the progressive policy among a number of school officials can be dated roughly from 1961, when several internal studies focused attention on decentralization as a means to greater responsiveness and efficiency. An in-house study by Personnel Director Arthur G. Andresen gave direction to the early concern with the problems presented by the size of the district. A second study by the firm of Peat, Marwick, Mitchell & Co. around the same time recommended dividing the district into a number of zones. Other studies subsequently made similar recommendations. Despite recommendations for certain forms of administrative decentralization, the studies envisaged a strongly centralized district with the large role for a central board and central bureaucracy. The studies set in motion a debate within the school system that began to move the policy process toward serious consideration of the issue. The early debates among the professionals concerned some of the same issues that later were rallying cries for various community spokesmen— "responsiveness," the special needs of inner-city education, cultural variety—and were marked similarly by the profusion of conflicting ideas, lack of an orderly agenda, and difficulty in formulating clear choices.

The initial discussions led to some minor steps, including creation of the first experimental school advisory committees. After the increase in citizen activity in the 1963-65 period, the school system took further modest steps toward decentralization—the most notable being the establishment of district offices along the lines recommended by the earlier studies. Elementary schools were increased from six to eight districts (and were scheduled to be expanded into twelve) and the secondary schools four (and were to be six or eight), with a field office staff in each. The field offices never exercised much authority, since the strategic issues tended to escalate to the superintendent and the board of education for consideration. The ease of access at higher levels complicated the function of the intermediate field offices.

In 1968, the system began more serious efforts to achieve greater decentralization under the impact of a growing community control movement and the increased interest in the state legislature in school reform. In 1968, the legislature adopted the Miller Education Act, which significantly reduced the specific state mandates relating to the content, objectives, scheduling, and administration of curricula. In response to the Miller Act and to mounting community pressures, Superintendent Jack P. Crowther issued Bulletin No. 19 on December 20, 1968, which announced a pilot project of thirteen (later eighteen and then twenty-four) schools in inner-city areas in which community representatives would participate in drawing up new curricula specifically tailored to local schools.

This announcement was significant, even though couched in bland bureaucratic language. Subsequently, in implementing directives of 1969, the broad idea was spelled out to mean the establishment of a School-Community Planning Council to act as an advisory body to the principals at each school in the project area. Each school was given discretion, within limits, to shift funds between budgetary categories. Thereafter, on March 6 and 12, the Superintendent mandated planning councils for all of the 559 regular schools in the system.

It is a measure of the considerable *de facto* decentralization in the system that it was never possible to determine whether these directives had been implemented. Despite elaborate guidelines generated at downtown headquarters, there were neither adequate information systems nor staff resources to determine whether the schools complied fully with the directives. Community activists, dissatisfied with their school principals, usually sought the help of allies at central headquarters and even the school board to put pressure on the local level. In this respect, decentralization required the intervention of central authority on a broader scale than before. This intervention, at least at first, encouraged a "crisis" style of decision-making. The central board and the Superintendent's office would take little notice unless a matter had reached the crisis stage, and thus the parties to a dispute at the local school level had incentives to escalate every issue.

In the fashion of President Eisenhower's efforts to find functions that could be delegated to the states, the school system also sought to identify administrative support services that could be decentralized to field offices. Public information was an early candidate, and in the fall of 1968 this function was largely removed from the central office and its personnel reassigned to four area offices. But other promising candidates proved to be few. Even public information gravitated back to the central office, since in the turbulent school atmosphere of the late 1960s, the news media wanted to get their information about the system quickly and authoritatively from a central source, and it was found that the field office operation had increased costs greatly.

So despite much brave talk about converting headquarters into a skeleton operation and taking policy initiatives in the field, little progress was made toward this goal through mid-1969. The vagueness of the plans spelled defeat for many reform suggestions almost as soon as they were formulated. Headquarters was sometimes seen as acting in a broad policy role with operations left to field offices, sometimes as a logistics arm to the field offices that would have the main policy initiative, or as some combination of both. Many ambitious ideas were seriously considered, but it proved difficult to devise a formula for decentralization compatible with the continuing need to have policy determined at headquarters. The emerging school fiscal crisis was another stubborn reality acting as a brake on ambitious efforts of this kind. Decentralization would create more jobs, the need for coordination between more administrative levels, and would inevitably mean increased costs. Unless new funds were forthcoming, the prospects for significant reform in this direction did not look bright.

Nonetheless, the debate continued within the school system. In November 1969, a meeting was held with educational authorities from across the nation to consider the future of the Los Angeles school system, including its organization. The consultants proposed major reforms, stressing the need for dramatic and far-reaching action if arthritic bureaucratic practices were genuinely to be changed. The conference focused attention once again on the issue of decentralization. The Superintendent delayed action on the proposals, however, until a pending school-bond referendum was held. To the consternation of officials, Los Angeles voters turned down the bond issue (from 1952 to 1966 the system had won every bond vote, but since 1966 no bond issue has been approved). This defeat was painful, but the "taxpayers revolt" was at this time only in its infancy. Officials were to experience later, in two frustrating defeats of a School Earthquake Safety Bond proposal in 1971, the full brunt of citizen wrath against increases in local property taxation. The defeat of the bond issue put school officials in a quandary. A plan to implement the recommendations of the consultants would have decentralized the system into eight zones. The zones were to be supplemented by one experimental high school and feeder schools within each zone responsible only to the zone superintendent and devoted to innovative education. The plan was also designed to increase efficiency and to save money. But it was a vague proposal in critical respects, including ambiguity on the key issue of how the objectives of reduced costs and of increased decentralization could both be achieved. The success of any proposal that required significant new resources was problematical.

After much inter-system deliberation, new Superintendent Robert Kelly adopted a watered-down version of the earlier proposal. This plan, even more ambiguous in its key provisions than the earlier proposal, created four zones, abolished the existing elementary and secondary area structure, unified school administration into a single K-12 structure, and provided for field offices in each zone that would, among other things, administer certain support services previously operated from central headquarters.

The new plan, announced in May 1970, stirred controversy from the start. Community groups assailed the proposed boundary lines as a means to promote segregation. Further, in a rare display of cooperation, a number of black and Spanish-speaking school activists accused the system of attempting to encourage racial tension between the two ethnic groups by putting them together in a "minority zone." A special board meeting hastily drew new boundary lines. The board of education eventually adopted a plan designed to achieve greater "racial balance" in Los Angeles schools. However, the zones were so big and each contained so many geographically dispersed communities that the effort to achieve greater racial balance was largely a polite fiction.[9]

Enthusiasm for the four-zone plan was also slight within the school bureaucracy, since budget cuts accompanying the reorganization and amounting to $2.7 million demoted or terminated 777 administrative and certificated health employees. The cuts led to a process of "bumping" in which senior employees, terminated from a higher level position, stepped down a level and bumped the occupant at that job down to another level. Those who suffered most in the process were not the higher level administrators whose jobs were terminated, but those at the lower levels of the system.[10]

Fiscal austerity and general uncertainty resulting from the mass reassignments combined to produce an unfavorable climate for the zone reorganization plan. It seems clear in retrospect that the plan stood little chance of producing significant changes in the administration of the system. But the zone reorganization plan did not even have a chance to work. By the time it was to have become operative, on July 1, 1970, new developments were already overshadowing the internal reform and were to make far-reaching action necessary. These were taking place in the state legislature, to which our attention now shifts.

## The Legislative Struggle

The prospect of state legislature action played a critical part in the Los Angeles debate over school decentralization. School officials and community activists were aware that state intervention had played a decisive role in New York City and Detroit. The orchestration of efforts either to block or to promote school decentralization for Los Angeles was influenced at nearly every step by the changing fortunes of the idea in the state legislature. Legislative interest reached a peak in the 1970 session, when a decentralization measure actually passed the legislature only to be vetoed by Governor Reagan. Although new legislation was passed (and again vetoed) in 1971, the momentum behind the push for system-wide, state-mandated decentralization had dissipated considerably. The legislative activity, however, spurred the Los Angeles city school system to new levels of effort toward administrative reform. The school system's past efforts, including the four-zone plan, were largely superseded in the process. And, while the prospects for sweeping legislative reform were dim at the moment, the legislative struggle had created both a reservoir of suspicion of the school bureaucracy and a core group of legislators who assumed the role of attentive critic of the professional school establishment.

School decentralization was first seriously debated in the California legislature in the aftermath of the Ocean Hill-Brownsville controversy. On the surface, the debate revolved around many of the same issues as in New York, but in important respects the California context was different. The example of New York, and later Michigan, did not provide unambiguous "lessons" for the California legislators; predictably, perhaps, most California observers saw in that experience evidence and support of their own positions in the local context.

One of the first decentralization bills in the California legislature was Assembly Bill No. 320, introduced on January 30, 1969 by Assemblyman William Greene (Democrat, Los Angeles). The Greene bill called for the creation of autonomous experimental school districts in the inner cities of Los Angeles and San Francisco, with control to be exercised by elected community boards in each district. The districts were modeled somewhat on the three experimental school districts in New York City. The bill put special emphasis on contracting out educational functions to private learning and consultant firms, universities, and state colleges. The community boards, if dissatisfied with the formal school system, could simply avoid the professional educators by securing professional services via a contract. Greene's bill did not stand much of a chance at this time. It was opposed by the school system, was not endorsed by the Democratic leadership, and Greene as yet had no effective allies.

A more moderate bill, Assembly Bill No. 2118, the Self-Determination in Education Act of 1969, was introduced on April 8, 1969, by Democratic Assemblyman Leon Ralph, who, like Greene, was black and from Watts. The Ralph measure was co-sponsored by fifteen other legislators, including Democratic Assembly leader Jesse Unruh. The bill provided for designating certain schools in ghetto areas that fall below established performance levels as "self-determination schools." These schools were to become independent districts where parents could choose to send their child rather than to the regular school. Self-determination schools would be run by a non-profit educational corporation responsible to a local governing board that, in turn, was to operate under the overall but ill-defined direction of a state official. Parents were to pay for the educational services through state-supplied vouchers, an experiment to be funded separately from the regular school budget.

The school system opposed the voucher concept but did not strongly oppose the Ralph measure because its funding would be independent of and represent an increment to the regular school budget. Nor did it enthusiastically support the proposal. The official reaction was that the professionals could "live with" the bill provided that it was suitably amended. They accordingly concentrated lobbying efforts in the summer of 1969 on securing amendments designed largely to clarify lines of authority between self-determination and regular schools, and to establish tighter fiscal accountability over the self-determination schools.

The Ralph bill was amended frequently during the summer, and sometimes the original intent was scarcely recognizable. It eventually found its most serious critic, however, not in Los Angeles school lobbyists, but in rival Democratic Assemblyman Greene. Greene's staff and many of his supporters in Watts were angered by what they regarded as Ralph's efforts to gain prominence in education legislation. They felt that Greene had a longer-standing concern for education, especially as a spokesman for ghetto education. But more importantly, Greene forces saw the Ralph bill as leading away from decentralization and community control by centralizing power still further through greater state intervention in school administration. Moreover, they considered the self-determination school proposal merely a token measure involving a few schools and not basically changing the regular system.

There was little chance for a compromise between the two forces. Feelings ran strong, as they distrusted each other's motives. A worrisome factor to the Ralph forces was the alliance beginning to emerge between Greene and Senator John Harmer (Republican, Glendale). Harmer, a conservative Republican with a suburban constituency, had been deeply interested in urban education for some time and was an influential member of the Senate Education Committee. His embrace of decentralization stemmed from the traditional ideology of local autonomy, state's rights, and fiscal conservatism. This growing alliance between the old political Right and the new political Left, united in their distrust of centralized bureaucracy, seemed ominous to the moderate liberals supporting the Ralph bill.

The result during the 1969 session was that the Ralph and Greene forces neutralized each other and so prevented the adoption of any bill. The Democratic leadership, fearful of civil strife over control of ghetto schools between opposing minority factions, withdrew its support of decentralization legislation. Delegates not from Los Angeles were generally unwilling to enter into a local fight which promised them few political dividends. What did emerge from the 1969 session, however, was a Joint Committee on Reorganization of Large Urban Unified School Districts empowered to spend $50,000 to study the subject. This represented a victory for liberal Democrats and conservative Republicans who believed that urban education had failed and was in need of drastic remedies. The alliance between Harmer and Greene was consummated with the appointment of Harmer as chairman and Greene as vice-chairman of the Joint Committee. This assertion of leadership by the Harmer-Greene forces after the failure of the Ralph bill meant that for the next year bills to decentralize the Los Angeles school system would largely dominate the school reform agenda of the legislature.

Although its legislative mandate was worded so as to avoid constitutional prohibitions against special class legislation, the Joint Committee from the start focused its attention exclusively on Los Angeles. In November 1969, Harmer and Greene selected Arthur D. Little, Inc., as consulting firm to execute the study. Arthur D. Little seemed a good choice because it had recently completed under OEO sponsorship a study of community control experiments in urban education that concluded that, of four models of school reform under discussion, "the model of change which holds the most promise at present is Local Community Control."[11]

The ADL study team began its work by defining the issues in such a way as to predispose the study in favor of decentralization. The objective, as it explained later in its report to the Joint Committee, was to seek "effective representation of educational needs . . . in very large urban school districts characterized by minority group concentrations" and to this end to identify "the decision-making prerogatives in the principal administrative functions which should be decentralized to support the desired representative process. . . ."[12] The ADL study might be termed an example of research designed to buttress a policy position.[13] The research was carried forward over the winter and spring and included extensive consultations with educational interests in Los Angeles. Meanwhile, Harmer and Greene planned strategy for their campaign to secure passage of the Joint Committee's school reorganization bill, Senate Bill No. 242, introduced on January 28, 1970 and referred to the Senate Education Committee.

While they were orchestrating their efforts, the school system announced its four-zone plan designed to blunt legislative support for the Harmer-Greene measure, but it did not succeed in building up any legislative momentum against sweeping reform. The response of many legislators attentive to the matter was that the district's plan amounted to "too little, too late," and that the administrators had underestimated the intensity of legislative discontent with the system's performance.

The events of the 1969-70 school year, if anything, had improved the chances for a sweeping reform. The school system had not been rocked by the explosive disturbances of the previous year, and thus legislators fearing potential disorder under decentralization were somewhat reassured. A dramatic six-week teachers' strike in the late spring, which under different circumstances might have been a troublesome factor for decentralization proponents, had not resulted in a strong teachers' stand against decentralization. The union movement in Los Angeles is underdeveloped in comparison to New York City, where UFT strength prevented the creation of autonomous districts with full personnel powers. The union movement among Los Angeles teachers will have to overcome two obstacles: the Winton Act, a self-imposed handicap that was lobbied through the state legislature in a previous period to keep out the American Federation of Teachers; and also the anti-union climate in Los Angeles. The strike by the United Federation of Teachers of Los Angeles, a recently-formed merger of the California Teachers Association and National Education Association, was only 55 percent effective at the start; at the end only about 45 percent of the teachers were still out. The strike weakened the UTLA and slowed the trend toward consolidation of teachers unions. The UTLA later adopted a confused and wavering attitude toward decentralization. In any case, by the time the Joint Committee released the ADL study findings on June 2, 1970 and began a big push for S.B. 242, the weakened teachers union offered no serious opposition, and conditions looked promising for some kind of decentralization bill.[14]

Senate Bill No. 242 was, however, to face a bruising and protracted legislative struggle. Opponents of the measure quickly mobilized and fought hard at every stage in the legislative process down to the day of adjournment. The opposition was led by the Los Angeles school system. Board members, the Superintendent, and other school officials, plus the legislative liaison office, battled S.B. 242 in the press and legislative committees, making intensive efforts to "educate" the legislators. The school system's all-out opposition helped to water down the bill, but the school system was not the most influential critic. More significant was the opposition of civil rights groups, including the NAACP, the Urban Coalition, and The American Civil Liberties Union, concerned about the effects of the measure on integration. Also opposed were the classified unions (plumbers, electricians, non-teaching school employees) that might be affected by the hiring practices of the proposed local boards. The state-wide California Teachers Association was opposed, as at times was the local United Teachers of Los Angeles. But the UTLA adopted a peculiar stance, agreeing with decentralization "in principle" but withholding comment on the bill, then shifting to outright opposition to it, and then finally swinging back to general endorsement in its final form.

There were virtually no lobbying efforts by citizen groups on behalf of the bill. Senator Harmer, who acted as main floor leader of the bill, was able to steer it through the various committees by simply amending the measure whenever strong objections were raised.[15] The bill encountered its most serious opposition in the Assembly Education Committee, where it finally passed by only one vote. The coalition of conservative Republicans and liberal Democrats was instrumental in securing the bill's passage. On August 21, 1970, the final day of the 1970 legislative session, the Harmer-Greene forces rounded up the necessary forty-one votes to pass the measure in the Assembly and secured the Senate's concurrence in the Assembly amendments in the hectic closing hours of the session.

The bill's passage had not been easy, for at one point Assemblyman Greene was on the verge of defecting from the coalition because of the intense opposition of civil rights groups. But he returned to the fold after the adoption of amendments designed to placate the civil rights opposition. Harmer acquired a new close ally in Senator Mervyn Dymally (Democrat, Los Angeles), the only black in the California Senate, who became a strong supporter of the bill. The L.A. county delegation was split on both the Senate and Assembly side; only five of the twenty-four Assemblymen representing the Los Angeles school area voted for the legislation. The objectives of the conservative Republicans and the liberal Democrats who secured the bill's passage were not entirely compatible, but they were united enough in their distrust of the school bureaucracy and in their desire for new (or new "old") solutions to win a major legislative victory. In the end, it was the determined advocacy of a few legislators, combined with the fact that the issue did not reach the proportions of a major party battle, that led to the bill's passage despite strong interest group opposition.

The bill's adoption was not, however, a clear-cut victory for the decentralizers, since many of the crucial issues were merely deferred while a commission would "study" the possible reorganization of the Los Angeles school system. But the language of the bill implied more than study. It left a strong impression that a decentralization plan would in fact be drawn up. This plan would constitute the agenda for future legislative consideration and would very likely have stronger political support.

Attention then shifted to Governor Reagan, whose approval was uncertain. The Governor had previously expressed his support of decentralization, but his Department of Finance was unfavorably disposed to it. Governor Reagan was deeply angered at a coalition of ten liberals, including Senator Dymally, who had been instrumental in defeating his favorite bill that session, a tax reform measure. On September 20, 1970, Governor Reagan vetoed the education bill, noting "overwhelming opposition" from those "most concerned with education in Los Angeles," and saying that it "would frustrate what the people of Los Angeles have determined to try as their own effort at decentralization." He also observed that "the study required . . . has been so prescribed that it may well be difficult to arrive at any other conclusion than the organizational framework which is in essence dictated by the Bill."[16] With the veto of S.B. 242, the legislative momentum behind decentralization was greatly reduced. However, the participatory concept still had vitality, as shown by the successful effort of Senator Dymally to steer a new bill requiring elected school councils through the legislature in the summer of 1971. Dymally, increasingly the principal legislative spokesman for minority educational needs, had strong backing from a newly-formed Citizens for School-Community Councils, the Black Educational Communion, and other groups upset at what they considered the failure of the district to implement fully its own decentralization plan. Governor Reagan vetoed the bill on much the same grounds that he had earlier vetoed S.B. 242. Again, the opposition of the school bureaucracy and city-wide groups was instrumental in the veto. The failure of community-control advocates to force radical changes in the school system structure probably has signaled the abandonment of further efforts in this direction for the near future at least, although the discontent with school performance remains intense among many legislators and militant community groups.

## The Aftermath: the Decentralization "Referendum" Campaign

Although legislative initiatives to restructure the schools had failed, and the system had apparently demonstrated the ability to mobilize opinion on its behalf, the narrowness of the escape was apparent to key school officials. Some new allies, in fact, had joined the decentralization forces as a result of the legislative battles. Most important, perhaps, the 1970 legislative fight had softened the NAACP's stand on decentralization and integration. Black legislators persuasively argued that segregation was a phony issue, since integration was not a reality, and that therefore the interest of minority groups should shift toward quality education and toward control of educational services by those who understood the special needs of minority students.

With these factors in mind, school officials in the fall of 1970 were apprehensive about the future. The full extent of disaffection with the school system had finally penetrated official thinking. The need for something more fundamental than another modest tinkering with formal structure was widely felt. After anxious discussion in the fall of 1970, Superintendent Kelly decided to re-establish the staff study committee that had produced the four-zone plan the previous year. It was augmented with new members with a view to recommending dramatic new decentralization initiatives. The board of education at the same time created an *ad hoc* committee of Board President Julian Neva and two members, Arthur Gardner and Robert Doctor, to work with the superintendent's committee in formulating the new plans. In December 1970, the board converted its staff committee into a formal Office for Decentralization Planning. In the meantime, after extensive search, the board chose Dr. William J. Johnston, their Assistant Superintendent for Adult Education, as the new superintendent to succeed Robert Kelley in January 1971. Chosen in considerable part for his record in community relations, Johnston was made director of the Office for Decentralization Planning to give it prominence and stature with the public and legislature.

The plan evolved was a characteristic Los Angeles invention: a massive campaign would be launched to elicit staff, community, and group sentiment on desirable next steps in decentralization. The plan was similar to a phase of Philadelphia's experience but was even more elaborate and far-reaching in its efforts to "let the people speak" on decentralization. The aim was to hold something like a giant referendum on the issue, from which would presumably emerge a plan with a broad base of support. The people having thus "spoken," the state legislature would find it difficult to overrule the will of the local community. One might suspect in this strategy of policy-by-plebiscite a de-Gaulle-like manipulative intent. But in this case the strategy of massive consultation arose naturally out of the Los Angeles political culture and the demand for participation then in the air.

The campaign, from December 1970 to February 1971, resulted in a jumble of decentralization proposals being presented by the Office (renamed the Task Force on Decentralization) to the board in late February 1971. The campaign was characterized by a great—and sometimes bewildering to the citizen—surge of activity to elicit community involvement. Public hearings were held at various schools, conducted by members of the board and school staff, to solicit views of individual citizens. Such hearings were generally informal, with a battery of speakers asking questions and making observations. Hearings were also held at which the various associations of teachers, staff, and other school employees testified. Three additional days of public hearings were held with community organizations at which the Task Force members heard testimony from twenty-four groups. Other phases of the Task Force's activities included: a questionnaire survey of all school employees (over 52,000 questionnaires were mailed and 29 percent of them drew responses); interviews with school officials, students, and parents; discussions with a community and a staff advisory committee; a three-hour "phone-in" of questions and answers by the board president and the superintendent-elect; and a saturation radio and television campaign. Finally, in late January 1971, the crowning move involved distribution of more than 700,000 copies of an elaborate questionnaire to citizens on their reactions to alternative decentralization plans.

The mass mailing illustrates the shortcomings of the referendum approach to complex issues. First, the questionnaire was so poorly drawn that it was almost doomed to fail. Citizens were asked to indicate whether they "agree" or "agree in part," or "disagree" with a long list of verbose questions on school administration and politics. The categories were not clearly differentiated; they could not "scale" properly to produce reliable measures of intensity of feeling; and they were bound to produce highly ambiguous policy implications. Further, the wording of many questions was such that the response was virtually predetermined.[17]

However, the technical deficiencies of the questionnaire design should not conceal the larger point. The real difficulty lies in attempting to frame policy on the basis of referendum techniques. Survey responses can give only gross indications of general public sentiment on simply worded questions of preference. The process of defining the "will" of the public cannot be viewed as a matter of discovering what is "out there" at a given moment, but rather as an interaction over time with the public in which leadership and good staff work contribute to an effective dialogue. The mass questionnaire was a costly experiment that did not yield clear results despite the 130,471 usable returns in a computer tabulation prior to drawing up the decentralization proposals.

The proposals presented to the board of education by Superintendent Johnston represented a miscellany of items in which every group involved in the process of formulation got something of what it wanted. The 26-point plan, in part, called for: abolition of the four zones and division of the district into ten local units; establishment of three largely autonomous experimental areas; enlarging the board and changing its manner of election; a pre-kindergarten program; greater budgetary flexibility for local schools; special benefits to teachers under certain circumstances; greater community participation in local school decisions; and changes in central office organization (some in the direction of greater centralization and consolidation and some toward decentralization). To implement the proposals, changes in state law would be required that the board was urged to sponsor. The board quickly adopted the less controversial items but deferred action on the more sensitive issues. Meantime, Senator Harmer introduced a new version of his bill and announced that the legislature would act within sixty days unless the board enacted all of the decentralization proposals and put the plan into "meaningful" action.

The critical issues gradually narrowed down to two: the reform of the board itself and the nature of parent participation in local schools. At the end of March 1971, the board sought to resolve these issues by voting to retain its present structure (seven members elected at-large for staggered terms) and to adopt a "local option" plan. By this plan, staff, parents, students and other community people at each school could decide on what form of school-community advisory committee they wished. This did not fully resolve the issue. Controversy arose in the fall over whether schools could continue with existing councils or were required to replace them with new ones.[18] The problem was that most councils in "Anglo" areas had a fairly congenial relationship with local administrators, whereas continued frustration with achievement levels in minority areas led to continuing and even increasing demands for greater control over educational policies.[19]

The large-scale decentralization campaign and the responses by the board brought a "peaking" of the decentralization issue. The tone for the decentralization campaign seemed to be set by one parent who remarked at a public hearing: "We want to take part, not take over." The decentralization effort, for all its lack of dramatic output, at least served as a consensus-building process in which large numbers of parents and community groups could participate. The position of the community control proponents was weakened as a result of the campaign. Many parents felt that some, if not all, of the major goals of decentralization had now been accomplished. There was, however, a significant difference between minority areas and the Anglo majority. The stubborn issues of improving educational performance in ghetto schools remained and parental dissatisfaction continued.

Other events also reduced the importance of these issues in the city's educational politics. The major earthquake that struck Los Angeles in February 1971 became a dramatic symbol of the fiscal crisis confronting the district. It forced the closing of many schools and so focused attention on their dilapidated physical condition. When the bond issue failed by 0.1 percent in May 1971 to achieve the necessary two-thirds vote required under state law, the district's financial plight became clear. Internal school conflict waned as the recognition grew that external enemies and fiscal crises posed major threats for the district. It would be misleading to suggest that the drive for wider participation simply disappeared as the system entered into new crises of major proportions—the impulse toward greater parent involvement and decentralization remain vital issues. Clearly, however, a new phase was taking shape that placed these issues in a broader perspective.

**Conclusion**

The new phase taking shape in the educational politics of Los Angeles reflects the basic trends affecting many local governmental units across the country: financial crises, growing militancy of public employees, and the disparity between tax capacity and service needs in the distribution of people and economic activity between inner city and suburb. Combined with these developments, which appear to call for the rationalization of governmental structures along the lines of greater consolidation of functions, is the opposite drive toward wider participation and citizen involvement in decision-making and the delivery of public services.

If California reflects national trends, it also has unique features that complicate the problem. Nonpartisanship has left a legacy of distrust of representative government and an infatuation with direct democracy. In practice, however, popular participation often means episodic surges of citizen activity that are ineffective and easily manipulated. The consolidation of functions and rationalization of structure in the direction of metropolitanism runs up against the fact that Los Angeles earlier consolidated many functions, but did so in a way that strengthened specialized bureaucracies at the expense of general purpose units of government. The weakness of executive authority, and the enfeeblement of general purpose units of government *vis-à-vis* the functional bureaucracies poses special problems for the reform of any part of the city's government and tax structure.

The *Serrano v. Priest* decision by the California Supreme Court on August 30, 1971, has added a further dimension to school politics. The court held that the system of financing public schools in California based on local property taxes was unconstitutional as it "invidiously discriminates against the poor because it makes the quality of a child's education a function of the wealth of his parents and neighbors."[20] It found that the great district variance in resources available for each pupil did not afford equal educational opportunity. The implications of the decision were potentially far-reaching, and the full impact on the Los Angeles school system could not be easily predicted. But it seemed likely that some new state aid formula or state-wide or metropolitan-wide property taxation system would have to be developed to provide a minimum level of assistance to the local districts. Earlier in the 1971 legislative session, a state property tax plan was defeated that would have provided another $30 million to the Los Angeles school district.

Even if a new state plan were soon adopted, numerous refractory issues would likely remain to occupy the attention of state and county officials as well as the professional educators before the complexities produced by the *Serrano* decision could be fully resolved. Could municipalities or local school districts levy property taxes in excess of a state-required minimum for all schools? If so, would the sense of "relative deprivation," which gave rise to the Serrano litigation and similar cases across the county, be eased or exacerbated? Nor was it clear that a uniform state standard would greatly benefit inner-city education when the needs of poorer outlying rural areas were worked into the system.

"Control" of the schools could remain at the local level even under a system of raising taxes on a state-wide or county-wide basis, but one would also imagine a parallel upward shift of decision-making in school affairs. How parent participation might be affected by such changes could not clearly be foreseen. What seemed clear, however, was that the stakes of the game were now higher and that solutions to the strategic issues of school policy and finance could not be found at the local level. Inevitably, policy initiative would tend to shift to larger governmental units with wide powers and a broad tax base. Other than local officials would necessarily be deeply involved in determining the future of Los Angeles schools. In this context, effective central leadership, rather than more decentralization and lay participation, seemed to be the most urgently needed capacity in that system.

By 1972, the problems facing the Los Angeles school system had worsened and the future remained uncertain. Superintendent Johnston was still strongly committed to the decentralization plan drawn up in 1971, and parts of the plan had been in effect for the previous school year. The budget crisis had caused many proposals to be shelved. Any part of the decentralization plan that required additional funds, such as the program for pre-school children, was abandoned. The school system faced a chronic budget deficit. For the first time in recent history, total enrollments dropped in Los Angeles schools, reflecting the general economic distress of the region caused by the decline in the aerospace industry. Few signs indicate that educational politics of Los Angeles in the late 1970s will be less turbulent than in the previous decade. The root problems remain of improving the minority schools, especially those for children of Spanish descent. As external pressures mount, the system may benefit from a closing of ranks internally and a better relationship, born of mutual crisis, between professional and lay activist.

# 6 Washington: The Politics of Class and Race

## Basic Dimensions of Local Governance

Throughout its history, Washington D.C. has been influenced by the special pressures and circumstances stemming from its status as the nation's capital. The unusual governing arrangements that have evolved to administer the District's affairs must be understood in this light. There are no elected city officials in the District of Columbia,[1] few prizes of office, weak party structures, and limited citizen interest in local politics. The city is governed by a commissioner-council form of government, which was proposed by President Lyndon B. Johnson in 1967.[2] The commissioner (called the Mayor) and members of the council are appointed by the President and confirmed by the Senate. Since 1970, the District has elected a non-voting member of the House of Representatives, and since 1964 the citizens of the District have voted in Presidential elections.

Besides the formal institutional arrangements, the status as capital city has had an imprint on local politics in numerous ways. A recurrent theme in the District's political history is the concern with physical security and order at the seat of federal government. From the time in June 1783, when the Congress, then convened in the Pennsylvania State House, was besieged by a mutinous band of revolutionary militia agitating for overdue pay, the principle was firmly accepted by national officials that the national government ought to enjoy "an exclusive jurisdiction" at the seat of government and not be dependent on lesser jurisdictions for public order.[3]

When the constitution was adopted, Article I, Section 8 gave to Congress exclusive jurisdiction over district affairs. The Congress has been little inclined since then to relinquish its powers over District affairs despite continuing pressures for greater home rule for the District.[4]

Another aspect of Washington's political history has been the notion that the capital city should be a "showcase" for the nation. This feeling, which has waxed and waned, has led to periodic efforts by national officials to give Washington the means to achieve important national objectives. In the early days of the republic, there was a belief that the capital should blossom into the economic, social, and cultural center of the nation—in the manner of London or Paris. Although this dream foundered, hopes rose for the political leadership role of the city. In 1867, a Congress dominated by Radical Republicans granted Negro suffrage in the District to make the District an example for the South. A great revitalization of the city's parks, streets, and public works began in 1871

87

under a new territorial form of local government, only to be abolished three years later when the price-tag shocked the Congress. Today, the relations between the numerous interested federal agencies and the District are vastly more complex. The House and Senate District of Columbia Committees have had a difficult task in retaining their control over legislation affecting the city. Other committees, in league with the federal bureaucracy and clientele groups, have attempted to extend their jurisdiction in District matters.

But perhaps the most important effect of the federal role is the stunted local civic life and leadership patterns. Whatever else it implies, federal dominance has inhibited the full development of the local political system. The Congress exercises, actually and potentially, greater influence in District affairs than does the typical state legislature in municipal matters. It is not unknown for a builder, aggrieved by an adverse zoning decision, to appeal his case directly to the House District of Columbia Committee. The staff resources of Congress, greatly exceeding those of state legislatures, provide the opportunity for detailed interventions across the full range of District administration. The result is not merely the absence of electoral participation in local government, but also the failure to develop local political elites. Participation is limited by the pervasive belief that any important development may simply be taken out of the hands of local leaders. No local political class has emerged because there are few prizes of electoral office or channels of advancement to potential national prominence within the local arena. This has continued despite the addition of the non-voting delegate to the House of Representatives and the creation of the office of Mayor, although there have been efforts to build grass-roots political organizations around these offices. The "real" life of Washington to most district residents is still the activities of the federal government. Power, money, ambition, and the high stakes of national politics act as magnets drawing the attention of the media and the citizenry.

Demographic trends highlight a further dimension of Washington's politics. A population decline in each of the last two census periods, representing a total decrease of 5.8 percent from 1950 to 1970, was caused chiefly by white out-migration. Whites fell from 517,865 (64.5 percent of the total) in 1950 to 345,263 (45.2 percent) in 1960 and 209,272 (28 percent) in 1970. Despite this District decline from 1950 to 1970, the Standard Metropolitan Statistical Area grew considerably in the same period. As was true in most American cities, the city grew not in the core but on the periphery after World War II. Washington leads all major U.S. cities in its percentage of blacks (except Newark) and in its ethnic separation—blacks in the central city and whites in the suburbs. Most of the suburban increase was in the white population. The 1970 census figures show a continued concentration of the metropolitan area black population in the central city, with the surrounding suburban population chiefly white, but there has been an interesting shift. The percentage of metropolitan area blacks living in the central city declined from 83 to 76 percent. The remaining whites in

**Table 6-1**

**Population Shifts in the District of Columbia and Metropolitan Region, 1950-1970**

|  | 1950 | 1960 | 1970 |
|---|---|---|---|
| Washington, D.C. | 802,178 | 763,956 | 756,510 |
| Metropolitan Washington | 661,911 | 1,237,941 | 2,104,613 |
| Total | 1,474,089 | 2,001,897 | 2,861,123 |
| Washington, D.C. |  |  |  |
| % White | 64.5% | 45.2% | 28.0% |
| % Black | 35.0% | 53.9% | 71.1% |

Washington consist mostly of the unmarried and the aged, military and diplomats frequently reassigned, and federal employees recruited from all over the country. These characteristics have reinforced the tendency toward a lack of involvement in the civic life of the District. The white elites with long-standing family ties in Washington have tended to be more deeply involved in the social and cultural life of the city than in its local politics.

Although the local politics of Washington have become increasingly domi-nated by blacks, sharp class differences among blacks should be noted. The character of black in-migration into the city has shifted, as fewer now come from Maryland and Virginia and more from Deep South states. Also, more recent immigrants have been poorer and so have helped to create the social problems evident in high crime rates, poor school achievement, ill health, and poverty. Established black elites of the integrated and cosmopolitan world of Washington society tend to be only peripherally related to the issues of local politics. Their interests, reflecting their class, parallel those of the white elites rather than of the poor blacks. Thus the politics of Washington, D.C. reflects not merely a poor, largely black inner-city surrounded by middle-class white suburbs, but also deep class divisions within the black population.

**The School System**

In 1938 a staff study for the President's Advisory Committee on Education reached the following conclusion:

In general, social and economic conditions in the District of Columbia are those recognized as favorable to schools and education. There are abundant indications that a relatively high average level of culture prevails . . . Economic resources are ample to support a good school system. Moreover, because of the stability of the federal government, these resources are not so susceptible to depressions as are the economic resources in other communities.[5]

In the changed climate of the postwar period, that conclusion seems quaintly archaic. Today, the school system of Washington, D.C. is the focal point for most of the problems of class and race that affect the city. Whereas blacks did not become a majority in the city until the late 1950s, they became a majority of the school enrollment in 1951. In 1960, when the black population constituted 53.9 percent of the city's total, the figure for school population was 79.5 percent. By 1970, 95.4 percent of the total public school enrollment of 142,899 was black. Of the "others"—6,643 (4.6 percent)—about 600 were oriental and 700 Spanish-speaking. School enrollment of all races reached its peak in the fall of 1969 and has since declined. Just as the racial shifts in the city's population became evident initially in the school system, the class issues that cut across racial lines also became apparent first in the school system. The "tracking" system, unequal assignment of experienced teachers, and other factors reflect segregation by class as well as by race.

The recent history of the District's educational politics reflects the struggle, amid deteriorating conditions, to achieve racial integration, equality of opportunity, and quality education. The usual pathologies of inner-city education—absenteeism, low scores on standardized national tests, problems of teacher recruitment and motivation—have been present, and they are aggravated by the District's special problems. The demands on the school systems have risen, as parents have considered improved educational opportunities central to the strategy for breaking out of the cycle of poverty. Ironically, by most quantitive measures of "inputs"—class size, per pupil spending, graduate degrees held by teachers—there has been considerable improvement in the D.C. school systems over the past fifteen years. But these factors have not resulted in improvement of student achievement. Many black elites have been sending their children to private schools. Sometimes this can go to extreme lengths; parents will judge that a private school is a "good school" on the most slender evidence. The fears, expectations, and hopes of the complex mixture of Washington's black population form an important part of the reality of the city's educational politics.

Rapid change has been another component in Washington school politics. The changing social composition of neighborhoods has resulted in the "tipping" of the schools from integrated to all-black, or from middle-class to low-income black. Judicial intervention has been another source of change. The famous Dunbar school, once an elite institution for the black intelligentsia, deteriorated within the course of several years after the *Bolling vs. Sharpe* desegregation decision.[6] The *Hobson vs. Hansen* decision in 1967, which outlawed "tracking" in the District's schools, triggered major changes in many schools.

In 1968, Congress adopted Public Law 90-292 which provided for an elected board of education for Washington, D.C. Previously, Congress had granted Federal District judges the authority to appoint members of the school board. The judges used informal quotas in allocating those seats; from 1906 through 1961 three of the nine members were black and from 1962-1966 there were four blacks. In June 1967, the federal judges for the first time gave the school board a 5-4 black majority. Declaring that "the education of their children is a municipal matter of primary and personal concern to the citizens of the community" and that "the school is a focal point of neighborhood and community activity," the 1968 Act gave "the citizens of the nation's capital a direct voice in the development and conduct of the public educational system." For the first time in the century, District citizens participated in an electoral process at the local government level. The energies displaced from a non-existent local politics into the educational arena has added intensity to battles over educational politics.

## School Desegregation

### Bolling vs. Sharpe, 1954

The District of Columbia maintained a rigidly segregated school system prior to the *Bolling vs. Sharpe* decision in May 1954. Although the school system was administered in theory under one board of education and Superintendent of Schools, schools were in fact divided into Division 1 for white pupils and teachers and Division 2 for black pupils and teachers.[7] A black assistant superintendent was responsible for supervising Division 2, but subject to the overall authority of the white-oriented board of education and superintendent. The black assistant superintendent had a considerable degree of autonomy, but perpetually sought more, for the major decisions were in fact made by the board and the Superintendent. There was little communication or exchange of activity between the two systems; even interracial athletic and forensic competitions were forbidden. The black schools of Division 2 were inferior to the white— larger classes, more pupils per teacher, poorer physical plant, narrower range of vocational courses, and lower expenditures per pupil. In 1969, the Strayer report, a survey on the District's schools, exhaustively documented the failings of the segregated system.[8]

Friction over school segregation increased in the early 1950s as the black expansion put pressure on white schools. There was often increasing enrollment at black schools while enrollment at neighboring white schools declined, leading to demands for the transfer of white schools to the black school system. Such a transfer would take place when the white school was so underpopulated that its maintenance as white could no longer be justified. Interest group protests against segregation also began to mount in Washington in the early 1950s. The NAACP and the Urban League were the leaders, supported by such white groups as the American Friends Service Committee, and Anti-Defamation League of B'nai B'rith, the Americans for Democratic Action, and numerous church councils. It is noteworthy that the impetus for change in segregation practices did not come from members of the board of education or school employees who were blacks.

Indeed, many black teachers and principals, benefitting from school segregation, were ambivalent about major changes in school administration.

In late 1952, the U.S. Supreme Court agreed to hear *Bolling vs. Sharpe* as a companion case to *Brown vs. Board of Education of Topeka, Kansas.* The D.C. case had to be separately litigated since its schools were covered not by the Fourteenth Amendment but by the Fifth Amendment to the Constitution. With that court action, accompanying an increased pace of civil rights activity, integration had begun to seem likely. The school board anticipated movement toward integration and began some planning for the changes in administration that would necessarily follow. However, public hearings held in December 1952 evoked scant citizen interest. Thereafter, the board did not assume a leadership role in preparing for the eventual transition to desegregation. Reluctance to offend the Congress, with Southerners heavily represented on the House and Senate District of Columbia committees, appeared to tie the board's hands.

On May 17, 1954, the Supreme Court handed down its historic decisions on the school desegregation cases. The District government moved swiftly, under pressure from the White House and the court order, to desegregate the schools. When District commissioners met on May 18, Commissioner Spencer reported that President Eisenhower expected the District to serve as a "model" for the country in making an orderly and prompt transition to a desegregated school system.[9] In late May, the school board did adopt a plan that called for carrying out the court decision when school opened in September 1954, with the process of desegregation to be completed by the following September.

The integration of the District's schools was accomplished with surprisingly little opposition and almost no disorder. There was some dissension, however. The NAACP and ADA criticized the school board's original plan as being too gradual, and one citizens association attempted to fight the desegregation effort, to no avail, by court action. In early October, white students staged a brief strike at Anacostia and McKinley High Schools that spread to several other schools. Within a few days, however, the effort ended, and the schools were back to normal. By November 1954, over three-fourths of the District's 41,000 white students were attending schools with blacks, while about two-thirds of the 64,000 black students attended schools with whites.

The relative success in achieving a rapid and orderly integration of the District's schools, however, had unintended effects that over time served to intensify some of the system's problems. As noted above, the Supreme Court in *Bolling vs. Sharpe* had insisted on neighborhood schools, which led to the rapid deterioration of such elite academic high schools as Dunbar into low income slum schools. More basic, perhaps, school desegregation accelerated the migration from city to suburb of many white middle-class families with school-age children. Other whites who remained in the District sought transfers for their children to schools with low black enrollment. Many remaining whites (and some middle-class blacks) transferred their children to private schools. A report by Professor A. Harry Passow of Columbia Teachers College noted that 17 percent of the college-educated black parents and over a third of the college-educated white families sent their children to private and parochial schools. Many more parents, white and black, had thought of private schools but were deterred for various reasons.[10]

In 1956 the school system embarked upon a new program, the track system or "ability grouping," designed to allow students with similar academic achievement to work together regardless of race. Under the track system, students were assigned to one of four curriculum tracks: honors, college preparatory, general, and basic. Under this program, some integration existed in the honors and college tracks, but the general and basic tracks were overwhelmingly made up of black students from low-income families. The amount of desegregation achieved in the honors and college tracks varied with the location of the school. The track system was implemented for all grades in the senior high schools in 1958 and was shortly thereafter introduced into the elementary and junior high schools.[11]

The track system had numerous critics from the start, and opposition increased in the early 1960s as some of the consequences of tracking became evident. Some civil rights and education groups saw in this a new way of reinstating racial segregation and hence providing inferior education to most blacks. The track system seemed undemocratic to critics who argued that ability grouping should be replaced by heterogeneous grouping with individualized attention given to every student.

## The Hobson vs. Hansen Decision, 1967

In July 1966, civil rights activist Julius W. Hobson brought a class action suit against Superintendent of Schools Carl F. Hansen, the board of education, and the District of Columbia judges (who appointed the board). He charged that the system unconstitutionally deprived the poor and black school children of equal educational opportunities afforded to the white and more affluent students. Hobson, moreover, contended that the inequality resulted from adherence to the neighbordhood school concept, the track system, unequal faculty assignments to schools, and optional school zones for some students. Judge J. Skelly Wright of the U.S. Court of Appeals upheld Hobson in *Hobson vs. Hansen*.[12] In a lengthy decision, the court ordered the board of education, among other things to: abolish the track system; develop a pupil assignment plan in accord with the court's directive and not based solely on the neighborhood school concept; provide transportation to children who wished to transfer from overcrowded to under-utilized schools; abolish optional school zones; and achieve full faculty integration.

The decision stands as a significant event in the history of public education in the District. This is not because the case decisively resolved a series of outstanding issues and set a clear course for the future evolution of the schools—for it did not achieve these purposes.[13] Rather, the decision is important because it set the stage for the major battles that followed by highlighting the central issues. The leading figures in the city's educational politics from 1967 to 1971 also emerged from the case and its subsequent impact on the schools.

Judge Wright's decision might be summed up by saying that he sought three goals: desegregation, quality education, and equality of educational opportunity. Three major figures became publicly identified with each of these goals. Judge Wright himself became the symbol for a continuing commitment to desegregation, the petitioner Hobson became the symbol of equal opportunity and the spokesman for poor blacks, and Mrs. Anita Allen, newly appointed board member, became symbolically linked with the cause of quality education. Mrs. Allen, as a member of the first D.C. school board with a black majority, helped carry the vote to implement the Wright decree and to order Superintendent Carl F. Hansen not to appeal the decision. This took place on July 1, 1967—the day she took office. Hansen subsequently resigned, and was followed by several successors whose weakness left a leadership vacuum in the school system. Mrs. Allen attempted to fill this vacuum through her leadership on the board, but a collective body meeting infrequently could not provide vigorous executive authority. Hobson's role was mainly as gadfly and outside critic of the system, although he served for one year on the board in 1968 when he became the first elected local official in the District in over a century. Like many middle-class reformers, Hobson was hampered by his failure to develop strong ties with the constituency he sought to represent. In the 1969 school board election, he was defeated for re-election by Exie Mae Washington, a former washerwoman who was elevated to leadership status through the poverty program. Hobson had been also hurt in his efforts to stimulate change in the schools because of the weakness of the school bureaucracy and the absence of a strong executive to respond to his pressures. In short, it proved difficult to achieve simultaneously the three goals sought by the Wright decree; indeed, in the conditions of the late 1960s, satisfactory achievement of any of the goals appeared beyond reach.

Although *Hobson vs. Hansen* had sought desegregation—and by 1967 the concept of integration was widely accepted in the District and had few serious opponents—the decision helped make the issue less important. The elimination of the track system contributed to the flight of white children from the schools. At the time of the decision, the racial composition of the schools was approximately 92 percent black, and with a further increase of that number, desegregation—for practical purposes—became unattainable. That integration had become a less pressing issue seemed to be symbolically confirmed when the board of education released the findings of Passow's comprehensive study of its schools. In a section entitled "Integration in the District Schools," the Passow Report concluded that:

When a school system is more than 90 percent pupils of one race, to speak in any ordinary sense of integration, desegregation or racial balance on a system-wide scale would be pointless.[14]

However, the report did recommend some limited measures to reduce racial isolation in the District schools.[15] But the prospects for any large-scale efforts to "mix" students from the District with students from the surrounding suburban schools in extra-curricular or other programs did not seem promising. Merger of the District's schools with other school systems in the wider metropolitan area to achieve racial balance seemed an unlikely prospect. Strong opposition to busing could be anticipated, and the special constitutional status of the District also complicated the question of metropolitan-wide consolidation of government functions.[16]

## Decentralization

The decentralization issue, as it emerged in the District during the late 1960s, must be seen in the context of the general trends outlined above. Failure of desegregation to produce improved school achievements, especially for the majority of the District's poor black children, led to frustrations that were reflected in the decentralization movement. But, as in our other case-study cities, the impetus for decentralization also came from outside the system through federal government and foundation efforts.

### Model School Division

The first decentralization experiment involving the District's schools was the Model School Division established by the board of education on June 17, 1964, in the ghetto surrounding Cardozo High School. The selection of this area as the "target" for a concentrated community action program, including the Model School System as one major focus, grew out of studies conducted by Washington Action for Youth, an arm of the President's Committee on Juvenile Delinquency. The project was funded by the Office of Economic Opportunity and administered through the United Planning Organization in the area; the federal funding later lapsed and the District school system had to assume the program's cost.[17] Community participation was built in through a system of advisory boards, but the administration of the program has remained with an assistant superintendent of the D.C. school system designated as head of the Model School Division. Despite some confusion in the division of authority among the local schools, the assistant superintendent in charge of the project, and the D.C. central office, the Model School Division has not developed along the lines of community control concepts. The project remained an example of a centrally-administered experimental program with elements of administrative decentralization in program planning and operation.

## Adams-Morgan

A more significant project is the Adams-Morgan experiment launched in 1967 in the area north of DuPont Circle and east of Connecticut Avenue. The Adams-Morgan neighborhood covers about three hundred acres and has 24,000 people ranging from welfare recipients to the affluent. Since World War II, most residents have been black and poor, whereas before the war, the area was primarily white and exclusive, with a black poverty pocket. The neighborhood "tipped" rapidly following the war, and about half of the large homes were converted to rooming houses and tenements serving a somewhat transient black population. About one-third of the population has remained white, although those served by the Adams and Morgan elementary schools—the neighborhood is named for the two elementary schools located there—are overwhelmingly black and poor.[18]

The immediate origins of the Adams-Morgan program grew out of overcrowding and deteriorating physical conditions at the schools, which led a group of mothers to organize a protest meeting with school officials in the fall of 1965. This group subsequently formed an alliance with the Adams-Morgan Community Council, a neighborhood-based civic association established in 1959, to seek the improvement of the neighborhood schools. The Adams-Morgan Community Council, dominated by whites and middle-class blacks, shifted the issue from mere overcrowding and the poor physical conditions of the school buildings to a concern with curriculum and educational philosophy. Liberal whites on the Schools Committee of the Adams-Morgan Community Council, including Christopher Jencks, now at the Harvard Graduate School of Education, the two co-directors of the Institute for Policy Studies, Marcus Raskin and Arthur Waskow, and their wives were active members who played an important role in shaping the program that evolved at the Morgan School.

A group from the School's Committee met in 1966 with Superintendent Carl F. Hansen to discuss the idea of a community-controlled school (reportedly no parents of Morgan children were present).[19] The Antioch-Putney Graduate Center in Washington, D.C. appeared a logical choice as a potential university sponsor for the program, since the director of the Center and director of the board of Antioch College had been attending meetings of the School Committee of the Adams-Morgan Community Council. Antioch College agreed to act as the sponsor for the project, with Marcus Raskin playing a leading role in arranging for Antioch's participation.

In the fall of 1966, members of the Adams-Morgan Community Council's

School Committee plus the Antioch staff drafted a proposal to include the Adams and Morgan schools in an experimental program under the administration of Antioch College. Superintendent Hansen asked for certain changes in the proposal; he wanted the project limited to Morgan School for the first year of operation and then, if successful, extended to Adams School (in 1969 Adams became a separate, community-controlled school with a board of its own). In Spring 1967, a new proposal was developed, and on May 17, 1967, the D.C. Board approved the new proposal authorizing Antioch to assume responsibility for administering the Morgan School.

Strains and stresses soon developed in the relationship between Antioch and the Adams-Morgan community. From the start, many black parents with children in Morgan School were uninterested in progressive curriculum reforms and held "traditional" views about what schools should do for children—children should learn to read, write, and behave properly. Their main concerns had centered around overcrowding and the dilapidated physical condition of the building. The liberal curriculum reforms of the Antioch proposal—open classroom, abolition of grading, team teaching, learning teams instead of regular classes—made parents uneasy. Over the summer, some members of the board of Antioch began to have second thoughts, and they suggested postponing the demonstration project for one year. The Adams-Morgan Community Council rejected the one-year postponement and, somewhat reluctantly, Antioch agreed to begin the project.[20] Evening orientation sessions held in August for parents and the new Antioch teachers to explain the new curriculum and teaching methods produced more conflict than understanding, leaving a high level of tension which carried over to the opening weeks of school.

In September, the school principal, Kenneth W. Haskins, a former social worker hired by Antioch College, arrived to assume daily management of the project. Elections were also held for the fifteen-member community school council (later called the Community Board). After a rocky start, and despite the firing of an Antioch staff administrator by the community council in the fall of 1967 and a decision by Antioch to cut back on its administrative support, the project survived and even achieved limited success during the first year. Haskins provided strong leadership and formed an effective alliance with Bishop Marie Reed, chairman of the elected Community Board.

Haskin's leadership, by bringing various factions to work together, kept under control the tensions resulting from the loose structure and innovations in the school. Educationally, the project experimented with team-teaching, abolition of formal classes and the substitution of informal learning groups, elimination of the usual classroom discipline, decorum, and grading, and a very loosely structured learning environment. Children were free to move from group to group guided by their interests. There was a strong emphasis on affect and pride in the curriculum. "Our one rigidity," the first Annual Report of Morgan School stated, "was and will continue to be . . . that subject material will not be used to insult, belittle, or degrade our children or their families." The project received national publicity and was heralded as one of the most innovative school experiments in the country. Achievement test scores in reading showed some improvement in Morgan's first year, absenteeism was reported down, and as an index of student support for the school, the number of broken windows fell slightly.

In April 1968, when it became clear that the arrangement with Antioch was unsatisfactory to all parties and could not be renewed, the Morgan Community Board presented a proposal to the D.C. Board of Education calling for community control over the Morgan School. The push for community control also meant the break-up of the alliance between white liberals and black parents of the Morgan school. Most of the approximately twenty white children who enrolled in the Morgan School during 1967-68 withdrew at the end of the school year, and many enrolled in private schools the following year.

The Morgan Board's proposal for community control ran into further difficulties in the summer of 1968. An opposition group, the Adams-Morgan Federation, sprang up out of the old Adams-Morgan Community Council, which had by now followed the pattern of the ephemeral neighborhood interest group and disappeared. The Federation opposed the Morgan Community Board's proposal, urging that the school be returned to the control of the D.C. Board of Education.[21] On June 26, 1968, Superintendent William R. Manning said at a press conference that the Morgan School Board would be reduced the following year to an "advisory" status and that the "serious division in the community" was one of the factors in his decision.[22] A group of about 70 Adams-Morgan residents staged a sit-in in his office later in the day.

The atmosphere surrounding the future of the Morgan experiment continued to heat up when on July 17, 1968, the D.C. Corporation Counsel tentatively ruled that the Morgan School Board could not have the increased independent powers it had requested in its April 4 proposal. Even earlier, on January 13, 1968, the Corporation Counsel had declared that "public officials or bodies may not, without statutory authorization, delegate their governmental powers." But he had seemed to leave open the door for decentralization experiments by also stating that "there is nothing in the statutes which would prevent the board of education from seeking and acting upon the opinions, views, advice, and recommendations of citizen groups of an advisory nature, so long as the ultimate authority over educational matters in the public school system remained in the board of education." The Corporation Counsel reasoned in its July opinion that the specific requests for physical autonomy and complete control over personnel were powers that the D.C. Board of Education itself did not fully possess and therefore could not delegate.

More serious, perhaps, the D.C. Board was split over the wisdom of accepting the fragmentation of authority that seemed to be implied in the Morgan proposal. One view, represented forcefully by Mrs. Anita Allen, was that community control was counterproductive to the goal of improving the education of black children. Since there was, in effect, community control of the whole district, why bother with tiny fragments of power over individual schools or sub-districts? This position was unacceptable to Morgan School activists, who did not trust the central leadership even if it were black. The tradition of class divisions within the black community, and the history of an imposed black leadership lacking any clear ties to the grass roots level, helped make the opposing positions irreconcilable.

The intense pressures from the Morgan community ultimately forced the D.C. Board of Education to acquiesce to its demands. A meeting of the D.C. Board of Education held at the Morgan school and attended by a group of some 350 residents on July 18, 1968, proved to be the turning point. The following day a fuzzy compromise was announced in which the Morgan Board was in effect granted its demands within a framework of delegated powers and vaguely subject to the ultimate authority of the D.C. Board of Education.[23] The Morgan Board thus won community control but in the process paid a price: the D.C. Board and the school system did not identify with and felt no stake in the success of the Morgan project.

The philosophy of Haskins—now the pivotal figure in the Morgan experiment—moved in the direction of the separatist and nationalist tradition of black political thought in America. His strategy was to attract additional federal funding and other sources of funds to build a base that would be useful in various ways. Beyond being a superior educational facility, the community school would serve as an employment agency, a political machine, the social center of the neighborhood, and a center for learning useful job skills.

One problem with experiments such as Morgan is their vulnerability to loss of key personnel. In the first two years of the Morgan project, with Haskins as principal and the experiment singled out by U.S. Education Commissioner Harold Howe for praise, the school succeeded in attracting Federal and private foundation grants on a substantial scale.[24] Whether the increased funding resulted in educational improvement is difficult to say. At any rate, Principal Haskins left Morgan School in June 1969 to take a fellowship at the Harvard School of Education. A few months later, Bishop Marie Reed, local community leader and president of the Morgan Community Board, died. With Haskins and Reed gone, the difficulties mounted and whatever gains had been achieved were largely lost. John Anthony, named principal to succeed Haskins in the fall of 1969, was essentially uninterested in Haskin's curriculum reforms, and he abandoned most of them. At the same time, he sought to build on Haskin's ideas of a power base and patronage center. Bitterness and dissension grew in the Morgan Board. Personal feuds and complaints about lack of educational achievement increasingly divided the Morgan Board.[25] As an example of this strife, Miss Jeanne Walton, Board Treasurer, delivered a scathing attack on principal Anthony and other members of the board at a meeting on March 25, 1970. She began by noting that:

. . . there are many enemies of community control of schools. Some of them are elsewhere in this country: some are in Washington, D.C.: some are in this community: but the most dangerous ones are sitting on this board.

She added that, "Many people on this board do not want open meetings because they do not want the staff and the community to know what they're about," specifying:

. . . the vice-chairman of this board, the principal and their allies continually conspire to control the school and to keep information from other board members, including the chairman. . . .[26] Certain members of this board . . . dreamed up a scheme to use Follow-Through funds and Follow-Through staff to run a restaurant . . . The bitterness and envy and corruption of some of the members of this board have touched our staff and our children. Interns are frightened, anxious, insecure. Teachers are angry and depressed, and ready to resign, children are tense and belligerent.

The feuding on the Morgan Board was climaxed two months later by the bitter campaign for the board elections. Principal John Anthony and community teaching aides actively compaigned for the winning slate of what might loosely be called educational "conservatives" against the "progressives." The issues in the campaign were difficult to identify with any clarity. In part, the charges of corruption and "bossism" figured in the lines of division; in part, the issues of educational reform, especially the disputes between the adherents and opponents of Haskins' ideas, were involved; and in part, it was a simple matter of the "outs" against the "ins." There was a good deal of confusion and some surprises. Among the defeated candidates, for example, was the wife of George Wiley, leader of the National Welfare Rights Organization, who had the advantage of a recognized name. The election appeared to be in the venerable American tradition of "vote early, vote often." There was suspicion of widespread irregularity in election administration.[27] Since the estimated eligible electorate was 10,000, and there were no registration rolls or proof of eligibility required at the several polling places, the chances for abuses were considerable. The election completed the transformation of the Morgan School from one of the most educationally innovative in the nation to one that is largely conventional. "The black mamas triumphed," as one D.C. school official characterized the situation, "and the reformers fled."[28]

Since then, the school has been run as a tight oligarchy built around the board and the school principal. Participation has been generally limited to those parents who are on the board or who are paid to work as teaching aides or in some other capacity for the school. On several occasions the Special Projects Division of the D.C. Board of Education considered dissolving the Morgan experiment and assuming direct control over the school, but on each occasion drew back from the move. There has been—besides a measure of indifference to the fate of the project—a fear of tangling with a group that has shown formidable organizing capacities.

By most criteria, the Morgan experiment has not been a success. The hope to stimulate greater parental participation in the school has not been realized. Few parents even visit the school. Electoral participation in the school has varied from a high of 4 percent to a low of less than 2 percent of the potential voters. Thus, in the board election of May 1971, only 137 of 10,000 eligible neighborhood residents turned out to vote. Moreover, turnover on the Morgan Community Board has been high, with only a small activist group maintaining any continuous involvement. The turnover from 1968-69 to 1969-70 was 69 percent, and from 1969-70 to 1970-71 it was 50 percent.[29] The squabbles within the community even slowed progress toward agreement on a site for a new school that had been promised the community for some years, and it was not until June 1972 that the school's construction was finally begun.

Second, educational performance has slid back to the standards of most schools in poor neighborhoods. Morgan's average scores on reading achievement tests, after the improvements in the spring of 1968, have dropped for sixth graders to where they usually had been—about two years below norms.[30] Scores for third and fourth graders, the other groups regularly tested, held better until September 1970, when tests were given during the first week of the term. The results for all grades were low, but the average grade for fourth graders was eight months lower for the same children than when they were in third grade a year before.

Further, the trend toward fewer broken windows at Morgan and its annex, once cited as indicating gains under community control, has been reversed. In 1966-67, before community control, the D.C. school system's Office of Building and Grounds recorded 200 broken windows at the Morgan school and its annex: in 1969-70, the figure fell to 136 broken windows; but for the first eleven months of 1970-71, there were 579 broken windows.[31] No reliable figures have been kept on losses due to theft and vandalism, but the problems are so serious that most moveable equipment is kept overnight in a locked storeroom. Student absenteeism averages about 10 percent daily, better than at some schools in poor neighborhoods, but slightly above the city-wide average for elementary schools. Teacher turnover has been unusually high, and many of the newer teachers, hired by the Morgan Board on a recruiting trip through the South, are themselves deficient in written and spoken English.

Third, beside failure to meet purported objectives of adult participation and child achievement, questions of financial accountability and propriety have arisen in the Morgan project. U.S. Comptroller General Elmer B. Staats has observed, in a discussion of revenue sharing, that only a limited number of states have minimally acceptable audit capacities.[32] It is perhaps hardly surprising that a community board dominated by non-professionals and with limited staff should have difficulty in developing an effective system of financial management. But that there has been an absence of effective fiscal management seems beyond dispute. It involves: minor nepotism (the principal's wife on the payroll as a secretary); patronage (doling out jobs as teachers aides to the faithful); irregularity (failure to hold elections to the Policy Advisory Committee of the Follow-through Program as specified under federal regulations); conflict-of-interest (the former Morgan Board chairman hiring Afram Associates to "help strengthen parent involvement" and being hired a few weeks later by Afram as "a parent stimulator" at $6,500 a year); and mismanagement (the principal drawing night school pay for work not performed, the hiring of fifteen community interns never authorized in the budget provided by the D.C. school system). The case of the fifteen interns, perhaps the most spectacular irregularity that came to light, was regarded by higher-ranking D.C. school officials as equally the fault of headquarters and its weak system of fiscal controls for allowing the interns to get on the payroll in the first place.

Despite the difficulties with the project, Superintendent Hugh J. Scott decided in early 1972 that the Morgan School experiment would continue the following year but would operate "within a framework of more effective centralized budget control."[33] One should perhaps guard against overgeneralization on the basis of the Morgan experiment. Just as a "success" at Morgan would not have shown the general utility of the community-control concept in urban education, the lack of success might be argued as not proving much either. The Morgan experiment faced many problems, but it is difficult to tell which were critical. Yet in some respects—in funding, favorable media attention, a high level of outside interest—the conditions at Morgan were favorable and not easily duplicable elsewhere. The Morgan experiment highlights the extreme difficulty of achieving in poor neighborhoods the major goals sought by community control—greater parental participation and community involvement in the school, improved education, and accountability to a broad cross-section of the community.

### The Anacostia Community School

The Anacostia Community School Project, which grew out of a March 1968 Presidential message, became the District's largest experiment in school decentralization. Located in Southeast Washington and physically separated from the rest of the city by the Anacostia River, this project included eight elementary schools and three secondary schools with an approximate total enrollment of 13,000 students. In a number of ways, the experience of the Anacostia Project paralleled, only on a larger scale, the evolution of the Morgan Project, and its fate was similar. Several of its features, however, suggest an additional line of analysis.

Like the Adams-Morgan area, the Anacostia section has a predominately black population characterized by poverty, high unemployment, inadequate social services, high transient rates, and low pupil achievement in the schools. But, unlike Morgan, Anacostia has some black middle-class children and parents who have not completely abandoned the public school system. Anacostia also is something of a "natural" community. Cut off from the rest of the city by the river and with a population estimated to be some 130,000, the area has enjoyed some measure of organizational life, a network of churches and other voluntary associations, and an economic base. These factors helped to give the Anacostia project an advantage over Morgan in the range and quality of community leadership that could be drawn into the effort. In fact, the project has had a higher calibre of leadership than Morgan on both the community board and among school staff aides, while enjoying a relatively high degree of stability and continuity in its leadership.

The most important feature, however, is the direct involvement of the federal government in the creation, funding, and management of the effort. Although a recurrent theme in this book is the role of the federal government in seeking change at the local level, the Anacostia Project is special among our case studies in the degree of federal involvement it illustrates. As such, this case offers a sobering glimpse of the difficulties involved in a federally created and managed project at the neighborhood level.

The Anacostia Project had its origins in October 1967, when an inter-agency memorandum was circulated to a number of federal bureaus calling for new ideas for a dramatic demonstration project in urban education. In August 1967, President Johnson had launched the Fort Lincoln Project in Washington, D.C. as the start of a national program of surplus land development in the cities.[34]

President Johnson, conceiving of Washington as a program model for the nation in coping with urban ills, had instructed his aides to direct attention to this possibility. The preliminary screening of ideas produced in tentative outline what became the Anacostia Plan, along with other initiatives in urban education. Subsequently, on November 1, 1967, a working group under the chairmanship of Harold Howe, Commissioner of Education, with James Gaither of the White House staff as a member, was created to sift the ideas, refine them, and come up with a workable plan. The staff work was done mostly by a few officials in the Office of Education's Bureau of Elementary and Secondary Education, but there was constant White House pressure for rapid progress.

As in other areas of domestic policy, it was President Johnson's "style" to reach into the bureaucracy, skim off good ideas, and make them his own priorities. Sometimes this style produced policy ideas that were inadequately staffed out at the working levels of government. The Anacostia Project was such an idea. The first public suggestion of the plan came in a special Presidential message of January 1967 on the problems of the District of Columbia. There was at this time no clear idea of the magnitude of the effort, its exact objectives, what area would be chosen for the demonstration project, or how the project would be administered. The problems were still not worked out when the President formally launched the program in another public message on the District of Columbia on March 13, 1968.[35] President Johnson proposed "a major model school experiment in the District, embracing a significant area of the city." To support the program, the President made a budget request for $10 million in the 1969 budget for the Office of Education. With this level of support envisaged annually for the next five years, the effort was to become "a beacon to the school systems in the other cities of the nation." The President's message was filled with the ideology of participation and the virtues of the community school concept.

In April, the OE officials, including consultant Mario Fantini, then of the Ford Foundation and an influential spokesman for the decentralization effort underway at the time in New York's Ocean Hill-Brownsville, selected Anacostia in consultation with local leaders as the site for the project. The effort was orchestrated by OE officials, with the D.C. school officials and community spokesman playing only a minor role. The extent to which the Federal government directed the effort is indicated by the tenor of a memorandum from OE official John F. Hughes to Commissioner Howe in April 1968:

... it is important that Manning [the D.C. Superintendent of Schools] make the right moves between now and the school board meeting of April 25 ... Also, I think it important that Manning touch bases with the important leaders and organizations in D.C. in regard to the Nickens and Fantini appointments to be sure there is no reaction.
I have advised Superintendent Manning in these terms and he seems agreeable. However, I think it would be important for you to continue the holding of his hand during the coming week to be sure all the proper moves are made.[36]

The D.C. Board of Education made the final decision in selecting Anacostia as the site for the demonstration project at this April 25, 1968 meeting. The project got underway in the summer of 1968 with a series of intensive workshops involving staff, outside consultants, high school students, parents, and other community residents. Out of this grew twenty-four proposals that formed the basis for the first year's operation of the project. The initial thrust of the effort was toward improved reading (and the training of community residents to assist with the teaching of reading), and toward increased community participation in the school through the development of policy-making community boards.

Difficulties began to develop, however, when the project was scarcely underway. Congress balked at the magnitude of funding for the project and eventually scaled the $10 million request down to a $1 million appropriation. Commissioner Howe, at the first signs of trouble, had written to Congressman William Natcher (Dem., Kentucky), Chairman of the House Appropriations Committee on the District, assuring him that the project "meets all of the usual review requirements of the Office of Education including criteria for evaluating educational significance and effectiveness, and review by a panel of specialists who are not federal employees . . ." and ". . . will adhere to all legal and administrative requirements to assure that the project meets all quality standards which are applied to research and demonstration projects approved for funding under Title IV of the ESEA."[37] But Natcher and Congress were unconvinced, and in scaling the project down called into question a critical assumption on which the planning had been proceeding. There were some delays at the start of the project, but the first phase of the OE grant was awarded to the Anacostia Community School Council in February 1969 for the reading program, and a community participation component was added in June 1969. The delay in the transfer of federal funds, causing some phases of the effort to start late in the school year and others to be postponed for a year, was only a harbinger of other difficulties to come.

Throughout its history, the Anacostia Project suffered from a lack of consistent attention on the part of federal officials and from frequency changes in key personnel. The project was shifted from OE's Bureau of Elementary and Secondary Education to OE's National Center for Educational Research and Development, and finally to a new Experimental Schools Division. In the process, Anacostia school officials had to deal with new people from OE and with new conceptions of educational policy, not to mention shifts in policy orientation and personnel that began when the Nixon administration assumed office in 1969. The results were damaging for the project—inattention from federal officials, uncertainty in levels of funding, unanswered phone calls, confusion, and an assortment of other administrative difficulties. Delays in getting federal monies already appropriated were common. Communication between the Federal government, the D.C. Board of Education, and the Anacostia Project management was deficient. The appropriation for the project jumped 100 percent for fiscal 1971, for example, to the surprise of local officials. Hasty improvisations in program design resulted. No stable expectations were created, and the Federal government's intervention was enough to prevent real autonomy at the project level but not enough to supply real leadership.

Finally, on October 13, 1971, Robert B. Binswanger of OE wrote to William S. Rice, director of the Anacostia Project, to announce that the project would be terminated at the completion of the school year. Binswanger, in an earlier internal memorandum that provided the basis for the decision, laid equal blame on the Anacostia Project Offices, the D.C. Headquarters, and the Office of Education for the project's failure. In reviewing the evidence, he noted,

. . . It becomes increasingly evident that all three sources of responsibility share in the failure of the project to meet its objectives . . . the role of the Office of Education *vis-à-vis* the Anacostia Project was never sharply defined . . . A form of dependency relationship was established which made it extremely difficult for the project to act independently. Overprotection crippled the evolution of responsibility . . . The Office of Education is at fault for the general administration of the Anacostia Project.

He criticized the D.C. school system for:

. . . a hands-off-policy by both central administration and board. And thus the Anacostia Project or items directly related to it were rarely a topic for discussion at the highest councils of the public school system. It is clear that the central administration failed to provide the project with the support and assistance that it required. . . .

He relied heavily on an HEW audit (which stated that $118,777 of project funds had been misappropriated in the six months audit period) as evidence of lack of effective management in the Anacostia Project offices. The memorandum concluded that:

"the original mandate of the Anacostia Project is no longer viable and . . . continued support of the project would not be an appropriate, productive, or intelligent disbursement of public monies. The failure of the project to produce demonstrable results in spite of the funds expended (approximately $4 million dollars) in the time involved gives little cause to believe that continuing the effort will effect successful achievement of the objectives."[38]

The federal government's action in terminating the project was in many ways like its original decision to launch it: sudden, based on unrealistic expectations, inadequately planned, stimulated by currently fashionable bureaucratic ideologies, and lacking in thorough knowledge of local conditions. The "evaluations" relied upon to justify the decision did not always prove what OE claimed, and some of the implicit assumptions of what kind of evidence would be required to justify continuation of the project were highly unreasonable. Yet on the central points the OE decision was hard to challenge. The case that could be made for the project's continuation was weak. As to participation, there was little evidence of substantial parent involvement in the schools. Aside from the 200 paid community reading assistants, few parents visited the schools or took an active part in their management. Also, electoral participation was low. Despite an intensive campaign in the fall of 1969 to register voters, publicize the community school board elections, and create widespread community awareness of the project, the turnout was disappointing—only 437 parents and community residents voted after 6,005 had been registered by the Westinghouse Learning Corporation, the contractor that organized the elections. This amounted to a turnout of 6 to 7 percent of the registered electorate after a saturation campaign conducted by the elections contractor (which included press releases, radio broadcasts, the distribution of 60,000 flyers and notices, and the hiring of high-school students as community canvassers). This compares with the turnout of approximately 10 percent of the registered voters in the area for the 1969 D.C. school board elections and 20 percent of the registered voters in Ward 8 (the larger area in which the Anacostia Project is located) in the 1964 presidential election. The large number of candidates (392) running for a total number of 241 school board positions on the areawide board and individual school boards undoubtedly helped to confuse the voters. The basic pattern of low turnout in small constituency elections, however, would likely have not been greatly altered by simpler electoral procedures.

Nor were the elected boards as active as they might have been. The boards elected in November 1969 atrophied as attendance at meetings dwindled, fewer meetings were held, and the core group of activists shrank in numbers. The ambiguities in the division of responsibilities between the areawide board, the local school boards, and the project's administrative staff were never satisfactorily resolved. The experience with the participatory side of the effort proved so discouraging that no elections were held in 1970, even though various board members had been elected only for one-year terms. In November 1971, after OE had announced its termination of federal funds, elections were again held as part of a strategy to reverse the OE decision on appeal and convince federal officials that a broad base of popular support existed in the community for the project. Even though the voting age was lowered to sixteen, and 100 students were hired as "roving ballot boxes" to collect votes around the neighborhood, the turnout was again light. There was also a strong suspicion of irregularity in election administration. At any rate, OE remained unmoved.

Second, the project could present only slender evidence that student achievement had significantly improved. There was some slight indication that the "cumulative-deficit" phenomenon sometimes observed in ghetto children had been partially reversed among fifth graders; and comprehensive reading scores for all grades showed slight gains. But the data were limited and selective and did not make a powerful case.

Third, the project was also unable to demonstrate that it had established an effective system of financial accountability. Although there was no indication of the extreme irregularities characteristic of the Morgan Project, Anacostia's management lacked professionalism in budgetary matters and gave no indication that it could meet minimum standards of financial accountability in the foreseeable future. The HEW audit showing a misappropriation of $118,777 of federal funds for non-project purposes for a six-month period in 1971 suggested the extent of the difficulties. The dependent relationship that prevented the development of meaningful autonomy and strong management was maintained to the last when Anacostia had to ask for OE guidance in the preparation of its appeal to the new Commissioner of Education, Sidney Marland, Jr.

In December 1971, when Commissioner Marland upheld Binswanger, the first major school demonstration project officially came to an end.[39] Marland compromised, however, to the extent of a vague promise that new funds would be available for another effort focusing on the same area under "considerably more supervision from the Office of Education and the D.C. school system."[40] The current Anacostia community school board could play an active role in planning and giving support to the new project, but for the new effort, which Marland suggested might be the first of forty or fifty such efforts in other cities around the nation, "local involvement is the word rather than governance."[41] The fate of the 200 paraprofessionals in the project was unresolved, as were the exact operating responsibilities of OE and the D.C. school system.

Although they terminated the Anacostia project, OE officials nevertheless believed, in the words of Binswanger's staff memorandum of September 30, 1971, that the effort was "conceptually sound, well-planned and a product of tremendous community interaction." Hence it was decided that the same concept should be tested again, in Anacostia and elsewhere, only with new personnel, more central supervision, and larger funding. The reality is rather different; the goals of the project were too grandiose, the basic conception vague, and the difficulties of a direct federal managerial role inherent in a neighborhood level project were not appreciated.

## Equalization

Decentralization emerged as an issue in Washington, D.C. at a time of rising frustrations over the failure of desegregation efforts to produce quality education, especially for poor and black students. In turn, as people became disillusioned with decentralization as a reform strategy, demands for equality in educational expenditures emerged as a major new issue. These demands for equality have further diminished the appeal of decentralization, for strong central authority in the school system seems necessary to implement the requirements of equalization in funding. It would be a mistake, however, to see a simple evolution from the disillusionment with decentralization to the emergence of spending-equalization as a reform strategy. The lawsuits seeking equality in spending in Washington and elsewhere arose from a different source, mainly a group of public interest lawyers across the country who were previously not deeply involved in educational politics.

A suit brought by Julius W. Hobson, the original plantiff in the class action which led to the 1967 *Hobson v. Hansen* decision, crystallized the issue in the District. Hobson was assisted in bringing the suit by a group from the Howard Law School who had been active in the field of poverty law. The new action was brought as an amended motion both for further relief and for enforcement of the original *Hobson v. Hansen* decree. The decision, handed down on May 25, 1971, by Judge Wright, was one of the first in a series of significant equal protection cases concerning public school finance.[42] Repeating the dictum that "figures speak and when they do, courts listen," Judge Wright found that figures on pupil-teacher ratios, average teacher costs, and teacher expenditures per pupil in the predominantly white area of the city, west of Rock Creek Park, compared to the area east of the Park "make out a compelling *prima facie* case that the District of Columbia school system operates discriminatorily along racial and socio-economic lines."[43] The court directed that "per pupil expenditures for all teachers' salaries and benefits . . . shall not deviate by more than 5 percent from the mean . . . at all elementary schools in the District of Columbia school system." The standard of per pupil expenditures for teachers' salaries was used because the court found that it was impossible to equalize all school costs. Some variations in expenditures, relating to maintenance cost, the age and size of school plants and their cost of operations, rates of vandalism, and other factors, were truly beyond the control of the school system's management. The court ordered an elaborate system of reporting to establish compliance with its decree.

The ruling illustrates the complexities in trying to achieve equality even within a single district. Thus, even the concept of equality is difficult to define satisfactorily. Recognizing this fact, the decision left room for exceptions to the standards in the case of educationally deprived, mentally retarded, physically handicapped, or other "exceptional" students.[44] In the course of the lengthy process of argument and exchange of memoranda by counsel, Judge Wright repeatedly found himself in the position of having to arbitrate difficult questions of statistical interpretation, which he sometimes resolved by "common sense" or by reverting to "straightforward moral and constitutional arithmetic.[45] Unfortunately, "straightforward moral and constitutional arithmetic" does not always provide clear and unambiguous answers to difficult policy issues. The decision posed the problem of "leveling down" as against "leveling up." That is, would the poorer schools in the district be brought up to the level of the best schools, or would the equalizing process merely succeed in hurting the best schools? If the latter, would the flight of the remaining middle-class pupils from the public schools be hastened? There is little reason to assume that the Congress or the District government would appropriate more funds for education so that the quality of the poorer schools could be upgraded without harm to the better schools. The possibility also exists that the equalizing requirement, on the assumption of fixed resources, could result in less compensatory funding to the most needy schools.

The opening of the school year in September 1971 was delayed by one week as the school administration sought to comply with the court order. After preliminary projections of the District's elementary school enrollment, the administration shifted some 300 teachers within the system in an effort to achieve compliance. However, sharp disparities appeared between projected and actual enrollment when complete figures became available later in the fall. Drop-outs in the middle of the school year further confused matters, so that the teacher reassignments at the start of the school year did not achieve the intended effect. A review of the situation in February 1972 showed that more than half of the District's 136 elementary schools were not in compliance with the court order.[46] In light of this evidence, Julius Hobson was threatening to return to court for a finding of contempt, and to ask that the operation of the school system be turned over to an outside "master" or "czar" who would "run everything until it is in compliance."[47] School officials contended that it was impossible to keep the system constantly in compliance because too many changes were taking place. High-ranking school officials talked vaguely of a "permanent floating pool" of experienced teachers who would rotate in and out of schools across the city as one possible solution—hardly, it would seem, educationally ideal.

On May 1, 1972, the D.C. school board reassigned 120 teachers to bring all elementary schools back into compliance with the 5 percent limit set by Judge Wright. In the late spring of 1972, the ultimate effect of the equalizing order could not be clearly foreseen. Hobson and school officials were attempting to work out an acceptable plan of compliance as an alternative to new court action. But previous events provide a basis for making certain tentative observations. First, the order will likely have the effect of centralizing rather than decentralizing power in the school system. Judge Wright's decision chided school officials for deficiencies in the information system required for effective management, and the data requirements implied by the court order seemed likely to give top management more leverage to implement its priorities. The teacher reassignments implied by the court order weaken the individual principal's role in personnel matters and strengthen that of the Superintendent. Community preferences at the neighborhood and the individual school levels will become less important as the energies of central administration are devoted to devising District-wide guidelines on pupil-teacher ratios and resource allocation. In Julius Hobson's view, the quest for equality might put an end to talk of community control, for only a strong central administration can devise and implement a workable program of allocating school resources equally across the District. Although he often railed against "unresponsive administrators," Hobson always believed that the function of citizen involvement was to force the professionals to do a better job. "I wouldn't know a good curriculum if it came up and hit me in the eye," he has said.[48] In theory, equalization could be combined with local control (or widened community participation). But in practice, fiscal control and policy control have usually not been easily separable. As state legislatures around the country attempt to equalize fiscal disparities between school districts, for example, it is likely that the state's role as an educational policy-maker will become more important. As the arena of the conflict widens, teachers unions and other established interest groups will be the critical actors, with a lesser role for neighborhood-level citizen groups.

Second, judicial intervention in the school finance issue may lead to a series of legal and constitutional issues of even greater complexity than the "reapportionment thicket" of a decade ago. Judge Wright wrote a careful opinion rejecting plaintiff's original contention that all school costs should be equalized on a per pupil basis. But this and other rulings across the country seemed to provide a basis for further challenges both as to the scope of public expenditures requiring equality and the geographical unit involved. Equality could be demanded of other school costs or of public services other than education, and that would pose formidable problems for the courts. "Equality" could require compensatory treatment for the poor taxpayer or special privileges for the rich taxpayer under various reasonable assumptions. Or the schools of the District of Columbia might be judged to require equality with the outlying suburbs in a metropolitan system of school finance.

The effect of the equality rulings on past desegregation efforts remained one of the most difficult questions. Judge Wright was prominently identified with the cause of desegregation since the original *Hobson v. Hansen* decision; but now, paradoxically, his new ruling might signal the abandonment of desegregation in favor of fiscal equality between segregated schools. The Nixon Administration announced in the spring of 1972 that it sought "equality education" and "equal educational opportunity" within the context of a "neighborhood school system."[49] Should the Supreme Court and other federal courts accept the goals set forth by President Nixon, the movement to achieve fiscal equality might end the drive toward desegregation that marked the era of judicial activism in the past two decades.[50]

## Summary

The educational politics of Washington, D.C. has seemed in some ways to reflect the broad trends in the country as a whole over the past decade. First there was a period marked by a preoccupation with desegregation efforts. Then, as legal desegregation failed to achieve integration or quality education for poor black children, the demand grew for wider citizen participation and "control" of local schools. But control over unequal resources seemed a bad bargain, and attention focused on equal educational opportunity and financing. Emphasis shifted from attacking the idea of professionalism toward holding the professionals "accountable," measuring performance, and securing quality education.

The special elements in the District's situation, however, should not be overlooked. The absence of local self-government, the central city's declining and changing population, and the ubiquitous presence of the Federal government continue as distinctive influences in local affairs. Events in the District will continue to mirror high-level shifts in policy by executive officials and be shaped by the suspicions of hostile congressional committees. It would also be misleading to think of desegregation, decentralization, and equal educational opportunity as separate and discontinuous stages. The slate is never wiped clean in history, and in fact there is considerable overlapping in the policy objectives and administrative practices pursued in the three endeavors. The present agenda of educational politics in the District consists largely of efforts to sort out the conflicts, ambiguities, and linkages among desegregation policies, community involvement, and the objective of fiscal equality. Desegregation, while it is no longer as salient an issue as it once was in view of the overwhelming black school population in the District, has not been abandoned as a policy goal, especially on the part of the highly educated and upper-income blacks who live in Washington's integrated upper-class society and form part of the city's natural aristocracy.

Decentralization, although not in the original community control version such as in the Morgan or Anacostia schools, still has wide appeal among parents and has been officially endorsed by the school administration. Hugh J. Scott, a black educator from Detroit who in 1969 became the third D.C. superintendent since Hansen's resignation, announced his opposition to the concept of community control not long after assuming office. In his view, community control would be "the worst thing that could happen to the city school system." There should be:

... more community involvement in the schools, but not control. I don't support having local school boards across the city. I don't want enclaves of weakness and strength where the strong get stronger and the weak weaker. The school system is so disorganized and divided now that we must pull together. [The School System] needs strong leadership from downtown.[51]

In May 1971, Scott elaborated his proposal for administrative decentralization within the framework of an overall reorganization of the D.C. school system. Essentially, Scott's strategy was to subordinate the decentralization proposal to a broader reorganization that would strengthen the superintendent's budgetary and managerial powers. In theory, community involvement in the schools would increase, but within the context of citizen access to a strengthened and more efficient school bureaucracy.

The goal of educational opportunity presented a new challenge to school officials. Although in some ways the court order might be seen as working against the goals of both desegregation and decentralization, the official view of the school system was that the various objectives were compatible and should each be vigorously pursued. Added to this complex mixture is the concept of "quality education," which has been variously interpreted as either a synonym for equal opportunity or a revival in a new guise of the old system of "ability grouping" ruled unconstitutional in the original *Hobson v. Hansen* decision. Moreover, the D.C. school system, like those of other big cities, faces a fiscal crisis. The problem is made especially acute by declining school enrollments and congressional determination to check the rising costs of local public services.

Superintendent Scott, faced with an unenviable task, attempted to bring an energetic leadership to the school system that was not in evidence since the Hansen's departure in 1967. Scott spoke at hundreds of community meetings, building a constituency and giving a visible presence to the school cause. He made enemies on the board, however, and increasingly experienced conflict and frustration in his dealings with the board. Finally, in January 1973, he announced that he would not seek a renewal of his contract. Whatever Scott's shortcomings, the constraints on effective leadership in his case were formidable. The superintendent functions within a constitutional system that puts him at the mercy of often hostile congressional leaders, and he has no constituency that he can mobilize to bring pressure on Congress. Court orders have left little room for the selection and transfer of teachers according to well-developed educational priorities. A worsening fiscal crisis meant shrinkage of programs and fewer resources for experimentation. The middle-class migration to the suburbs continued and pupil performance worsened while demands on the system rose.

In these circumstances, the superintendent is a political bird of passage. His fate is as luckless as that of most big-city mayors. His main strategy is to look good if he can while holding off catastrophe and hoping for a more glamorous opportunity. He is tempted to appeal to the "audience"—the informal body of opinion in the Federal government, foundations, and the universities that judges one's record and influences one's career—rather than to the "constituency" served.[52] Some of Scott's critics said that he was too much the politician, evading issues, postponing hard choices, making big promises, and blaming others when problems did not get solved. But if progress is to be made in coping with the massive problems of Washington's schools, the skills of the gifted politician—managing conflict, inspiring confidence, quieting fears—will surely be essential. Forces external to the system will of course partly determine whether the District schools will be a "showcase" for the nation or a source of national embarrassment. But strong leadership within the system will still be necessary.

# 7

## Detroit: Do the Nays Have It?

Most of the great American cities had racial skirmishes during the 1960s, but Detroit had a war. Four years after the riot that lasted five days and killed forty-three people, block after block in the heart of the city lay empty of all but rubble. Fraying campaign posters plastered against the remnants of buildings seemed to be the only signs of life. The great expressways furrow through the neighborhoods as though the only thing the powers-that-be can agree upon is that Detroit is a very good place—to get in and out of quickly.

On the surface, at least, Detroit entered the 1960s with a sense of optimism. The city had a young, energetic mayor whose political style and Irish heritage seemed to be the right combination for insuring Detroit's place in the "New Frontier" federal urban programs.[1] Locally, the engine of the city's economy, the automobile industry, was flourishing and providing high wages and benefits to both black and white workers.[2] Detroit had had a history of racial problems, but the third of the city's population that was black had some significant political representation. During the 1950s, blacks became an essential part of the liberal-labor-black coalition that moved into power with the election of Jerome Cavanaugh in 1961. Detroit also had two black congressmen and in 1969, Richard Austin, a black accountant, came within 6,000 votes of becoming mayor.[3]

The same liberal-labor-black coalition also controlled Detroit's school politics by consistently winning the non-partisan at-large elections for the city's seven-member school board. In 1966, the board promoted Norman Drachler, who represented the values of the coalition, to the superintendency. Born in the Ukraine, Drachler was Detroit's first Jewish school head, and his administration was characterized by sensitivity to the needs of minorities and passion for racial equality.

One of his initial moves was to cut class size drastically in the elementary schools in ghetto neighborhoods.[4] Under Drachler and his predecessor, the Detroit schools were the first in the nation to require the use of readers that included pictures of Negroes and when no Negro history book could be found on the market, the system created its own. Detroit also had one of the first and most effective requirements of fair employment practice for those doing business with the schools. By instituting special recruiting drives and promotion procedures, the system greatly increased the percentage of black staff.[5] By 1970, Detroit had a higher percentage of black teachers (42 percent) and administrators (38 percent) than in any other major city. Pupil integration was a much more difficult problem, however. Although the system was committed rhetorically to integration, it did alter some attendance zones to preserve predominantly white schools to keep neighborhoods from tipping. Despite a substantial number of vacant seats in inner-city schools, white students were not bused. Consequently, the percentage of black students attending schools whose student body was 90 percent or more black rose slightly throughout the decade to 75 percent in 1970. Still, professional staffs with the cooperation of the teachers union and supervisory association were integrated, even balanced, in most schools. Every high school had at least some black students.

Preserving even that degree of integration required constant administrative effort and political energy. The city's non-white population grew from 16 percent in 1950 to over 43 percent in 1970. Since nearly 50,000 white students attend Catholic parochial schools, and since the black population is younger, black students became a majority of the public school population as early as 1962. Integration was further complicated by the fact that Detroit has the highest percentage of individually-owned homes of any large city. These homes often represent the lifetime savings of the blue collar Poles, Southern whites, and blacks who hold the mortgages. Their neighborhoods tend to be racially, even ethnically, exclusive, and residents regard the schools as the symbolic and tangible anchor of social stability.

Neighborhood homogeneity is such a prized commodity partly because of the history of labor violence and racial friction in the city's consciousness.[6] The 1943 race riot was described as "open warfare between Detroit Negroes and the Detroit Police Department."[7] Throughout the 1960s, arrests in black neighborhoods were accompanied by hostile crowds, but no major violence occurred. The incident that triggered the 1967 riot was a police raid on a "blind pig," a black after-hours bar and gambling spot, but the "causes" of the conflict went deep into the racial politics of housing, employment, police, and schools in the city.

After the smoke had cleared, the Detroit establishment gathered its members to decide the city's future. The New Detroit Committee was formed with the participation of most of the city's economic elite. An impressive series of programs was announced to improve the condition of blacks and also of downtown businessmen. But it is not clear that everyone believed Detroit had a future. The city spent more than $100 million to redevelop a 75-acre riverfront area into a Civic Center containing a sports arena and convention center.[8] But in 1972, acres of valuable real estate above Grand Circus Park stood vacant, and in the heart of the business district stores were empty. Headlines were more likely to announce the departure than the arrival of a business. The threat of William Clay Ford to move the Detroit Lions to a suburban site in Pontiac was particularly symbolic, but fiscal statistics may be more telling. During the 1960s, the total assessed valuation in the city fell by almost half a billion dollars. Building permits declined by one-third.[9]

What can be seen in the cold language of an assessor's computer printout can also be felt on a warm summer night strolling down Woodward Avenue. Although it is the main shopping street of the city, after dark it is so deserted that even this New Yorker felt unsafe. One wonders whether Detroit may not be the first major city that the white establishment will abandon. Between 1960 and 1969, the city's population dropped from 1,670,144 to 1,476,400.[10] This decline was a commonplace urban trend in the 1960s, but Detroit's loss of 325,000 whites placed the city near the racial tipping point. Forty-three percent of the city is now black and that percentage has been increasing by about one percent a year. Consequently, the movement of even the smallest business to the burgeoning satellite cities of Dearborn, Livonia, Southfield, and Pontiac sends tremors through the remaining whites. Every issue is examined by both blacks and whites for its effect on the city's delicate racial balance. Some struggle to preserve it; others are seeking to profit by its demise. In this context, school decentralization becomes a central issue in determining the fate of the fifth largest city in the country.

## The Detroit Schools

In Detroit, as in most American cities, the pressures for centralization and decentralization have created constantly recurring issues in educational politics.[11] After the victory of the free school ticket in the election of 1842, public education was permanently established in the city. The schools were governed by a board composed of two members elected from each of the city's six wards. In 1881, the board was reformed to take "schools out of politics," and elections were held on an at-large basis. Politics did not disappear, however, and in 1889 the ward system was reinstituted. It persisted until 1917, when, ostensibly to take the schools out of politics again but actually as a result of the school's role in the effort to Americanize immigrants, ward elections were dropped in favor of a seven-man board elected at-large. This arrangement survived until the decentralization of 1970.

If political centralization characterized the governance of Detroit schools during most of the modern period, administrative decentralization was a matter of constant experimentation. Elementary schools were first divided into districts in 1956. Then, on recommendation of Superintendent Samuel Brownell, two administrators were appointed on a trial basis to run unified (high school, junior high school, and elementary school) districts in 1957. This arrangement was designed to expedite central office decisions and to provide liaison, but it involved little local autonomy.

The next year, a Citizens Advisory Committee on School Needs, chaired by then automobile executive George Romney, and coordinated by then little-known school official Norman Drachler, was established. Their report begins:

Those of us who have been fortunate to work on this report are particularly aware that present deficiencies in the Detroit schools result as much, if not more, from the lack of citizen and parent interest as from other influences that confront us with a growing educational crisis.[12]

Consequently, the Commission proposed the establishment of eight elected regional advisory commissions and a central commission composed of their representatives. The school system responded by creating nine districts for administrative purposes; but the advisory commissions were never instituted, and little actual power was transferred.

In 1967, another reorganization elevated the status of the district administrators by changing their titles to regional superintendents. Theoretically, they were to exercise more autonomy, but in fact their power largely depended on individual aggressiveness and connections. District boundaries were also redrawn at this time in an unusual way. Predominantly white areas were paired with black areas within the same district, even though they were not contiguous geographically. This was an attempt to create interracial extracurricular activities and staff planning, although the separated districts did not permit much mixing of students in the classroom.

This pattern also did not achieve much functional decentralization. The regional superintendents had little or no staff, and they did not encourage community participation that might have generated demands they could not fulfill. Furthermore, the Superintendent's open door policy for community groups had the unintentional effect of undermining the regional superintendents. The non-contiguity as well as the racial and economic diversity of the districts also reduced the feeling of "community" and hampered organization. Concern with decentralization, however, particularly the extreme community-control versions, was not a salient issue. The liberal-labor-black coalition that governed the city and the school system was still committed to centrally-directed integrationist goals.

As was true of other school systems, integration was proving an elusive goal, so criticism of the schools began to shift to other issues. Throughout the 1960s, a series of commissions documented the ills of the system.[13] In the city, drop-out rates reached 19 percent, which was relatively low. But employers were becoming skeptical about the level of competence signified by diplomas from these schools. One survey in 1963 found that only one-third of the *top 20 percent* of the graduates of six black Detroit high schools were gainfully employed or in college. The fact is that in Detroit unemployment for black high school graduates was as high as for black elementary school graduates.[14] The school system responded with new curricula, new personnel programs, and more integration, but there was little tangible improvement and whites kept deserting the city for suburban schools.

It is not hard to see why—even in non-racial terms. Thirty of Detroit's schools were built during the administration of U.S. Grant, and 20 percent were over fifty years old. Class size in Detroit averaged 32.4 students, while in suburban Wayne County the figure was 26.2 The suburban schools spent on the average $300 to $500 more per child than the city schools, although the Detroit school board estimated that it cost at least twice as much to educate a ghetto child. Detroit's disadvantage was in part created by the Michigan state legislature, which by 1964 was providing $51 per child more to suburban school systems than to the city.[15]

The school system's dilemma was compounded by an increasingly tricky political situation. It might have been expected that those middle-class whites who chose to, or had to, remain in the city would become ardent supporters of an improved public school system. Even if age or religion prevented a family from directly benefitting through public school attendance, good schools would certainly seem to be an asset in protecting property values and maintaining racial peace. The white homeowners did not see it that way. Overwhelmingly they turned out to defeat the annual millage proposals that were the lifeblood of the schools. Although in most black neighborhoods the voters supported the schools on money issues, generally the turnout was not high enough to create a city majority. The public schools, then, became increasingly dependent on the poorest, least powerful segment of the Detroit population. As the leadership moved to reward that constituency and to equalize opportunities, the white middle class became even more alienated.

As the shrinking property tax base and lost millage elections made the situation more desperate, the Detroit schools turned to Federal and state sources for financial help. When not enough was forthcoming, the Detroit Board of Education as an official body sued the State of Michigan in 1968, challenging the whole school revenue system. The board also sought to work out cooperative agreements in the metropolitan area that might have led to consolidation with suburbs. None of these efforts was very successful. As Superintendent Drachler wryly noted, "Our suburbs would sooner unite with Canada."

Given this stalemate, then, it was inevitable that there would come a time of challenge to the liberal formula of integration and money as the solution to educational problems. After the 1967 riots, it seemed clear to many that there would never be enough of either commodity to improve the schools. Suspicious and fearful blacks and whites began to look for new solutions.

## The Decentralization Legislation

The 1969 Detroit decentralization law has a mixed ideological heritage. It was sought for motives that were almost wholly political or purely educational, fiercely conservative or ardently liberal. On one hand, the law appealed to those blacks and whites who, if they could, would build a Berlin Wall between their communities, and to those leaders for whom such situations offer enticing opportunities for setting up racial fiefs. Yet for others, decentralization was looked upon as the key that would create the parental participation necessary to remove the rigid regulations and inept administrators locking the door to educational progress. It was not a stable or even a majority coalition; but when it fused temporarily, it was victorious.

One of the first and most visible advocates of the community-control version of decentralization was the Reverend Albert Cleage, Jr., a black Congregationalist minister. Renaming his church from the Central United Church of Christ to the Shrine of the Black Madonna he had become a major spokesman for the black theology movement. Cleage is definitely not an example of someone who, disillusioned with integration, then accepted community control as the only other alternative. Instead, he affirms, "I did not have a philosophical commitment to integration at any point."[16] To promote the concept of black control of black schools, Cleage formed the Inner City Parents Council and in June 1967 made the first formal demand for such control to the school board.

Since the board was still firmly committed to integration, not much attention was paid to Reverend Cleage's separatist pleas, but community-control notions soon began to appear in the Michigan legislature. In 1968, two "community-control" bills were introduced by Detroit legislators. Representative Jack Faxon, who represented a white home-owners district, offered a relatively moderate proposal that would have created new regions, each with its own elected school board but operating within the policies set by an enlarged central board. The Faxon proposal was overshadowed by a bill that James Del Rio, a black Democrat with a poor ghetto constituency, had introduced. This bill would have divided Detroit schools into sixteen districts, each with its own tax base and as independent as the other 650 school systems in the state. The districts were to be based on census tracts with specific lines established by the Wayne County Superintendent of Schools. In support of his bill, Del Rio insisted that the Detroit Board of Education "has been more responsible for riots than all the white racism in America. They have not produced an employable product and young people have to steal because they can't find work."[17]

The bill was so politically impractical that Del Rio may have introduced it for its symbolic value or for publicity. It was opposed by the whole of the civic and public school establishment as well as by most black groups, including the black newspaper, *The Michigan Chronicle*. But despite the fact that its only public support came from Albert Cleage and a few other separatists, the Del Rio bill was given a favorable report by the House Education Committee. Later, when put to the test of a floor vote, it did not survive, and Faxon's bill was killed in committee. Nevertheless, these bills signaled a change in the politics of school decentralization. The arena for decision-making had shifted from the Detroit school system to the Lansing legislature, and the community control concept had found surprising support.

During the next year, the debate over community control rose to the top of the agenda among black groups. A city-wide Citizens for Community Control was organized and held a series of conferences. The conferences were given an emotional lift by the struggle in Ocean Hill-Brownsville that was making national headlines. Several of the participants in that dispute, including Rhody McCoy, came to Detroit to present their side of the story.

Sentiment for community control was also growing among the more established black groups. The Detroit NAACP, one of the largest chapters in the nation, had been trying for several months to reconcile its traditional commitment to integration with the growing interest in decentralization in the black community. The problem also troubled the national organization. During its 1969 national conference, held in Mississippi, the delegates adopted a carefully worded resolution supporting decentralization. That helped to solidify support in the Detroit chapter, and on April 8, 1969, the chapter presented a decentralization proposal to the school board.

The NAACP plan as it finally developed was based on the concept of a community-centered school defined as a "school in which community people exercise the decision-making roles and control the institution."[18] To implement this plan, each of the elementary and intermediate schools in the system was to have a separate elected board. Students and faculty would be represented on the board, but the majority would be parents. These boards would have almost complete personnel and budgetary power, including the right to engage in performance contracting. Each senior high school—there are eighteen—and its feeder schools would be grouped together and governed by another layer of boards, the Constellation School Boards. These boards, composed of delegates of the individual school boards, would have the power to operate the high schools, administer federal and state aid programs, procure maintenance and repairs, coordinate services, and arbitrate problems among the local boards. Finally, the superintendent and central board would be kept to recruit teachers, prepare curriculum materials, select sites and plan for school housing, negotiate system-wide collective bargaining contracts, operate special and technical schools, and evaluate schools and programs. In addition, the central board was to be "charged with the implementation of the 1954 Supreme Court decision relative to racial imbalance in the school system." If the NAACP was aware of any potential conflict between its decentralization plan and its integrationist goals, the proposal made no mention of it.

The three-tier NAACP plan was thus clearly a compromise, falling far short of the community control the separatist Reverend Cleage urged and yet substantially redistributing power from the central board toward the neighborhoods. The organization's integrationist goal remained. The plan insisted that, "Urban schools should make all efforts to accommodate the mixing of ethnic and socio-economic groups" and charged the central board with that mandate. But even the NAACP thought the time had come for tougher rhetoric. In a speech to the school board accompanying the decentralization plan, they declared:

We cannot permit the continuation of an education system that is not accountable to the community it purports to serve. The day has come when black Americans will no longer stand idly by and see their children become the sacrificial victims of an archaically structured bureaucratic school system. Nor will we continue to tolerate the twin evils of segregation and domination by the insensitive majority.

These are our schools. They must now operate under our sanctions.[19]

Within the board itself, there was considerable support for some kind of decentralization. Abe Zwerdling, the board president, suggested that citizens committees be elected in each high school district to act as liaison between the neighborhoods and the central board. But deeply committed to integration, Zwerdling was afraid to go further in power-sharing. In 1968, a black attorney, Andrew Perdue, was elected to the board and became a spokesman for more complete community control. In the middle was Superintendent Drachler, who believed in decentralization as a democratic principle, but was still uncertain about the form most beneficial to Detroit. Lacking a consensus, the board continued its experiment with giving district administrators more atuonomy, set up a task force to advise on further decentralization, and even negotiated with some local elected councils on personnel changes.[20] But no overall board plan emerged.

In the meantime, the decision had shifted to the state legislature. Although the Del Rio and Faxon bills were reintroduced, attention in the 1969 session focused on a bill authored by Senator Coleman Young. Senator Young's sponsorship of decentralization substantially altered the symbolism and the status of the issue and of its supporters. Although his proposal was not in its details very much different than the Faxon bill, Coleman Young was the state Democratic National Committeeman and the leader of the black legislators.

It was Young's intention to avoid the controversy that had attended the passage of the New York Decentralization Law. First, unlike the New York bill, which was fought over line by line and finally emerged as a complicated sixty-four page law, Young's measure filled only one page. Its main features were:

1. Creation of seven to eleven new regions of 25,000 to 50,000 students in each;
2. Each region to have its own 9-member board and to elect a person to serve on an enlarged central board;
3. The regions to have the power, "subject to guidelines established" by the central board, to:
   a. determine their budgets based upon central board allocations;
   b. determine curriculum and testing and the use of educational facilities;
   c. hire regional superintendents from central board lists and have the power to fire them;

d. employ and discharge, assign and promote all teachers and other employees, subject to review by the central board.

Like the New York legislation, Young's bill did not create community control. The policy discretion of the new local boards would be subject to central board review. But unlike New York, the regions were to be directly represented on the central board, and thus the central review powers might be modified over time. Young felt that this was at least a good beginning toward decentralization.

As a former employee of the UAW and the Public Employees Union, and as a leader of the Michigan Democratic party, however, the senator wanted particularly to avoid the kind of conflict with labor that decentralization has fomented in New York.[21] The Detroit Federation of Teachers (40 percent black), in opposing the Del Rio bill, had taken a negative, if cautious, position toward decentralization. President Mary Ellen Riordan had declared:

Local commumity groups need to be more actively involved in their schools. But I do not believe in complete local control, including hiring and firing of teachers. Problems of inadequate financing and teacher and class room shortage would not be helped one single iota. As matter of fact, a local board would have fewer resources and less ability to resolve the problems. Local control would result in local union negotiations which would make it difficult to maintain basic good curriculum, salary, and teaching conditions throughout a large city like Detroit. The basic issue in local control is the level of achievement of the youngsters. A change in who controls the schools won't change the achievement level unless the other problems are also resolved.[22]

Consequently, the Young bill included from the beginning a prohibition against any regional action violating existing contracts and left collective bargaining to the central board. At the insistence of the DFT lobbyist, even more protections guarding rights of transfer, tenure, seniority, and other benefits for teachers were added to prevent regional abrogation or modification.

The other potential source of opposition was the Detroit Board of Education itself. In retrospect, its leaders and their Lansing lobbyist say they could have killed the bill. Given the lack of organized support and public knowledge about the bill, that hindsight judgment is probably correct. But the board had no consensus except to be vaguely in favor of more participation, and Young's proposal was clearly better than Del Rio's or others that might yet appear. So after gaining the concession that all guidelines would be centrally determined, the board declared its neutrality and decided to stay out of the debate.

Actually almost no debate ever took place. Most of the action on the bill was taken during the summer months, when it was difficult for school-oriented organizations to maintain watchfulness, let alone mount a campaign. The hearings, such as they were, were held in June, though no public announcement of them was made. Only the board and the·Detroit Federation of Teachers appeared. Organizations such as the NAACP, the PTA, the Urban League, and union or business groups did not testify, principally because of the timing of the hearings and their inability to take positions on the bill.

Given this apathetic political environment, the bill passed the Senate easily (25 to 5) with little debate. In July, it passed the House by a vote of 83 to 18. Republican Governor William G. Milliken, with no particular enthusiasm, signed the measure (Act 244) into law on August 11.

The legislative politics of decentralization in Michigan, then, were quite different from those in New York. In the Empire State, the controversy mobilized every interest group concerned with education, and intense lobbying almost paralyzed the legislature for a year. The law that emerged was a collection of detailed but ambiguous compromise. Yet, although there has been much litigation, it was a settlement of sorts. None of the contending parties has been eager for another round of the uncertainties and cost of a new legislative struggle. In Michigan, no pre-passage struggle took place, and thus few organizations were aware of the stakes involved in decentralization. Because there was no political mobilization and little legislative struggle, the major policy questions were decided after the law was enacted.

What did Act 244 really change? As students returned to school in September, the functional consequences of decentralization seemed rather obscure. Detroit, after all, had had administrative districts for some time. The newspaper headlines that greeted the Act were generally routine. A few blacks grumbled that the Act was only a token gesture toward genuine community control, while some conservative whites saw it as yet another accommodation to black militants. Serious public consideration of the issues raised by decentralization was yet to come.

## The New Regions

The first major decision that had to be made under Act 244 concerned the shape and character of the new regional districts. The Act merely specified and there had to be between seven and eleven districts with at least 25,000 and not more than 50,000 enrolled students. The nature of the districts had important educational and political implications in Detroit. In addition to their function as educational planning areas, the district lines would also determine the racial and ideological characteristics of those elected to control the regional boards and those represented on the reconstituted central board. Furthermore, the board's attorney declared that the regions must conform to judicial rulings on one-man-one-vote apportionment and on integration. The eight-district pattern already in Detroit was not considered suitable, because these districts, not being contiguous, were inappropriate for an experiment with community control.

The first step taken by the board was a contract with Wayne State University

Professor August Kerber to gather election and population data in computerized form so that the political consequences of districting could be ascertained. This statistical task was fairly easy because demographic data for each precinct had been developed for the Gribbs-Austin mayoral election. Several neighborhood groups also used computer data to promote their version of community control. Six plans were eventually developed by the Kerber team for a closed session of the board's legal staff. The number of districts in the plans ranged from seven to ten, but more importantly, they varied greatly in the amount of integration likely to occur and in the probability of black control over regional school boards and black representation on the central school board. Table 7-1 illustrates the racial implications of two of the proposals. In Plan A, which provided the most integration, black students would have been a majority in every district. In Plan D, however, whites would have controlled at least three districts, but at the cost of considerable *de facto* segregation. Actually, several of the plans were only theoretical alternatives, since they contained features that were probably illegal according to Act 244's requirement of 25,000 students per district, the one-man-one-vote principle, or integration decisions.

The board's discussion indicated that it was very far from consensus on any of the plans, and so it decided to release them to the public for a series of hearings. At the time the plans were released, the Board President Remus Robinson told the press that the plans were merely "some examples of the kinds of boundaries decisions that could be made. None of them is the final plan of the board. Before we decide on the boundaries, we may even add another one."[23] Dr. Robinson's *caveat* was lost, however, on the throngs of citizens who crowded the nine public hearings on the plans. They could read the maps with the racial statistics figured to a tenth of a percentage point. The implications for their children's schooling seemed clear. Overwhelmingly both black and white parents argued for the plans with the most compact, racially homogeneous districts.

Even in groups that had traditionally supported integration, the board found little support. An NAACP spokesman declared that, "Consideration should be given to those areas where a sense of community prevails. This decentralization bill is not a vehicle for integration." The largely black First Congressional District Democratic organization put it more bluntly: "Redistricting must guarantee black control of black schools." Even with purposeful racial gerrymandering, however, such a goal would have been nearly impossible. There were many more black students (65 percent) than black voters (44 percent) in the city. Blacks could not hope to control every school with a black student majority in a one-man-one-vote election. Furthermore, the immediate conflict between integration and community control was obvious. The more integrated the districts, the more likely whites were to win the elections.

The hearings proved to be a shock to the liberals on the board. The new President of the Board, A.L. Zwerdling insisted:

**Table 7-1**
**A Comparison of Two Proposed Plans for Decentralizing Detroit Schools February 28, 1970**

| | | Plan A | | |
| --- | --- | --- | --- | --- |
| Region | Population | Pupils | % Negro | % White, Others |
| 1 | 166,509 | 32,352 | 54.7 | 45.3 |
| 2 | 212,206 | 39,066 | 52.3 | 47.7 |
| 3 | 254,030 | 43,695 | 53.9 | 46.1 |
| 4 | 215,658 | 43,248 | 71.4 | 28.6 |
| 5 | 218,495 | 35,726 | 58.9 | 41.1 |
| 6 | 218,712 | 37,517 | 66.4 | 33.6 |
| 7 | 218,280 | 40,015 | 73.2 | 26.8 |
| Average | 214,777 | 38,802 | 61.7 | 38.3 |
| Range of Deviation | 87,971 | 11,343 | 20.9 | 20.9 |
| Average Deviation | 14,654 | 3,090 | 7.5 | 7.5 |

| | | Plan D | | |
| --- | --- | --- | --- | --- |
| Region | Population | Pupils | % Negro | % White, Others |
| 1 | 166,868 | 31,453 | 71.5 | 28.5 |
| 2 | 172,786 | 33,817 | 70.9 | 29.1 |
| 3 | 263,730 | 48,581 | 66.2 | 33.8 |
| 4 | 164,245 | 27,577 | 22.0 | 78.0 |
| 5 | 139,333 | 27,073 | 66.1 | 33.9 |
| 6 | 159,486 | 25,586 | 43.1 | 56.9 |
| 7 | 196,929 | 39,257 | 90.4 | 9.6 |
| 8 | 240,063 | 38,275 | 48.8 | 51.2 |
| Average | 187,930 | 33,952 | 61.7 | 38.3 |
| Range of Deviation | 124,397 | 22,995 | 68.4 | 68.4 |
| Average Deviation | 34,233 | 6,064 | 16.4 | 16.4 |

Source: Detroit School Board Statistics as reproduced in the Detroit NEWS, March 4, 1970.

[Decentralization] is not going to end racial isolation. But if we drew boundaries that put blacks into one region and whites into another there could never be any integration. We would have frozen things.[24]

The rest of the board was not so certain, and it seemed unlikely they could agree on any plan. Consequently, on March 9, Superintendent Drachler called together staff from the Housing and Human Relations Departments and expressed his concern that regions might be created that would lock out the possibility of integration. He suggested that they might take Plan B2 and change the junior high school feeder patterns for the high schools from a north-south to an east-west direction. As he surmised, this would increase integration, but it also meant increased busing. After some intense internal politics on April 7, the board, in a 4 to 2 vote, adopted Plan B2 as Superintendent Drachler had modified it.

Although, as Table 7-2 shows, the plan would have substantially increased high school integration, it was still clearly a compromise. In half of the twenty-two high schools, the junior high school feeder patterns would be changed, but students already in high schools would not be affected, and younger siblings would be able to join older brothers and sisters in their high school when transferring from junior high school. About 3,100 additional students or almost 5 percent of all high school students would be bused in the first year. At the plan's maturation, about 12,000 would have been involved. Actually, about 25,000 Detroit students generally rode public transportation to school anyway. Many of these were black students attending open enrollment schools in white neighborhoods, although whites also commuted to attend the prestigious Cass Technical High School and other special schools. But this busing was voluntary, aimed at facilitating a student's choice of school. The feeder pattern change, on the other hand, meant that some parents who had made substantial financial sacrifices to pick a certain neighborhood because of the local school might no longer be able to send their children to that school. An

**Table 7-2**
**April 7 Board Plan and School Racial Composition (Plan B2 Revised)**

| School | Percent of Blacks 1969 | Plan Fall '70 | Plan Fall '71 | Plan Fall '72 |
|---|---|---|---|---|
| Western | 38.6 | 39.2 | 44.6 | 51.0 |
| Southwestern | 87.7 | 71.3 | 60.8 | 53.0 |
| Cody | 2.1 | 9.7 | 20.9 | 31.3 |
| Mackenzie | 91.6 | 83.8 | 78.9 | 69.9 |
| Redford | 2.2 | 11.4 | 20.5 | 29.2 |
| Cooley | 57.5 | 53.0 | 49.7 | 42.6 |
| Ford | 12.4 | 16.3 | 26.5 | 31.3 |
| Pershing | 57.5 | 50.9 | 46.5 | 41.8 |
| Osborn | 15.1 | 22.6 | 32.7 | 45.8 |
| Kettering | 89.3 | 81.3 | 73.9 | 65.1 |
| Denby | 3.1 | 19.3 | 36.2 | 53.9 |

Source: Detroit School Board Statistics as reported in the Detroit FREE PRESS, October 15, 1970.

entire neighborhood that once commanded a premium of several thousand dollars a house because of its local school now felt property values threatened. Furthermore, this busing proposal meant that for the first time whites would be sent to predominantly black schools. With the national and local press constantly reporting school violence, and with the national administration increasingly critical of busing, white parents began to look for ways of opposing the board.

Even before the April 7 meeting, forceful opposition to the board's attempt to combine decentralization and integration had emerged. When one of the dissenters on the board, Patrick McDonald, released a copy of the plan to the papers, Detroiters awoke to Sunday morning stories about the board's sweeping integration plan. By Monday, white parents at some junior high schools had organized a student boycott. That evening a white-dominated Citizens Committee for Better Education was formed to fight the plan. On Tuesday evening, when the board was formally to adopt the boundaries, white parents flooded into the meeting and almost disrupted the vote.[25] Most of the witnesses were against the plan, but the board had already committed itself. Board member McDonald, however, vowed to continue to fight. Addressing the white parents jammed into the lobby outside the chambers, he reminded them of the provision in state law for the recall of public officials.

Since the linking of decentralization to further desegregation was an obvious recipe for controversy, why did the board run the risk?[26] There are several hypotheses in Detroit political circles. The most cynical insist that the board, which had never been very enthusiastic about decentralization in the first place, saw in Plan B2 a way to kill Act 244 itself. This seems not to have been the case, because the most ardent supporters of decentralization on and off the board were willing to accept B2. Another view is that board attorney George Bushnell convinced the board of the legal necessity of furthering integration as a phase of decentralization in order to withstand probable court tests. Bushnell did work on Plan B2, but the board's majority had been long committed to integration, anyway. The most persuasive theory is that Zwerdling and others on the board were afraid that decentralization would alter school politics in Detroit so much that, without the new school boundary lines, the integrationist cause would be lost.

With an idealism touched with arrogance and naivete, they chose to confront increasingly hostile public opinion on the issue. After the decision, Superintendent Drachler wrote his staff:

America has been willing to deprive itself of billions of dollars to travel 250,000 miles in space to reach the moon. I am confident Detroiters will be willing to accept the idea of traveling one or two extra miles to school for the sake of a better education for our young people and for a better future for our city.[27]

## The Legislative Counterattack

Even before the districting decision became public knowledge, the dormant opposition to Act 244 awakened in Lansing. Representative Daisy Elliot, a black legislator who felt that the Act did not provide enough community control, proposed delaying its implementation for a year. E.D. O'Brien, whose earlier sponsorship of decentralization was overshadowed when Coleman Young took up the issue, now called for a referendum on Act 244. In the Senate, Raymond Dzendel, an early opponent of decentralization, took the opportunity to argue for repeal.

The main concern of decentralization proponents was that the DFT, with the backing of other unions, might move to support one of those bills.[28] Although the teachers apparently had written strong safeguards in Act 244, decentralization made union leadership uneasy. Would there be a future move to substitute regions for central board bargaining? If so, the affiliates of the Michigan Education Association or some new black caucus might win negotiating rights in a region. Would decentralization strengthen school critics who might pressure to increase accountability measures and diminish job security? Finally, some wondered why the DFT had accepted what union colleagues had fought so bitterly in New York.

The DFT Executive Board was deeply divided. Zeline Richards, a black vice president, was ardently for decentralization and campaigned publicly and independently to save Act 244. Many black members probably agreed with her. But another black vice president, John Elliot, testified before the Senate Education Committee that two-thirds of the teachers in a DFT poll were either for repeal or referendum. Like most in-house polls, one may have doubts about the sample and the way the question was worded, but it seems likely that decentralization was unpopular among the union rank and file. When DFT President Mary Ellen Riordan appeared to support the referendum alternative, which everyone conceded would kill decentralization, Coleman Young responded furiously:

The original decentralization bill was amended wholesale last year just to meet the complaints of the teachers. Now you do this. This is a stab in the back . . . I know they are worried about their prerogatives, but their prerogatives have to be secondary to the interests of the people. Besides, Act 244 gives the teachers all the protection they need.[29]

Throughout the month of March, the executive board wavered. Then in April, when the board's districting decision changed the issue from decentralization to integration, the union had little choice but to move formally at least to support the board.

Within days after the board's decision, members of the city's delegation in Lansing were bombarded by protests. The board was prepared for some objections, but it was startled by the vehemence of the popular response and by the hostile legislative mood. In addition to the earlier bills for postponement, referendum, and repeal, Representative Joseph Hunniger proposed a general investigation into the operation and management of Detroit schools. Several hearings were called and legislative reconsideration of decentralization began in earnest.

The board's exposure of its own internal divisions did not contribute to solving the problem. At a hearing of the House Education Committee, five board members testified—often with intense emotions. Andrew Perdue a black board member, charged:

Those who oppose Act 244 and the changes in feeder patterns are taking a racist and bigoted view. If you take action on it [repeal], you are demonstrating your weakness in responding to a racist and lawless element of the Detroit community.

White board member Patrick McDonald responded to the charge of bigotry:

It takes one to know one. What right does that gentleman [Perdue] have to look into peoples' minds and call them racists and bigots? The legislature is the last resort of the people to have this corrected. If this plan goes through, it will make Detroit a disaster area.[30]

The board's opponents could not muster much consensus either. The legislature was unable to act effectively to overturn either decentralization or desegregation. A bill to delay decentralization passed the Senate on a voice vote on March 26, but two weeks later the Senate decided to support outright repeal instead. In the House, the bill for referendum passed by a vote of 63 to 31 on April 7, 1971. Neither House could agree with the other.

Consequently, the decentralization opponents turned toward a different strategy. A new plan was proposed that created eleven regions with boundary lines based on the districts for state representatives and that incorporated protection of neighborhood schools. The new central board would be made up of eleven members from the districts and four incumbents. The three incumbents who would have been eliminated from the central board—not so coincidentally—had voted for the feeder change. This plan had considerable political advantage. Using election districts as the boundary lines for the new school districts would strengthen the hand of local political organizations in influencing school politics. The plan's opponents quickly labeled the concept a "return to the ward system." As is typically true, these districts were somewhat gerrymandered to create racial or class homogeneity in order to protect incumbents; so the use of election districts would not further integration—quite the contrary. By using the neighborhood school concept, not only would white schools be preserved, but whites might possibly control a majority of the eleven school districts.

Much to the surprise of the city's political and educational establishment, the 11-district plan sailed through the Senate 31 to 2, but then its opponents mobilized. Organizations like the PTA, the DFT, and the Organization of School Administrators and Supervisors, though internally divided and unenthusiastic about Act 244, realized the threat to integration in the legislative mood and came to the board's defense. Less equivocally, the AFL, UAW, ACLU, and Metropolitan Detroit Council of Churches backed the board's action. Messages (some solicited) from such notables as James E. Allen, U.S. Commissioner of Education, Theodore M. Hesburgh, Chairman of the U.S. Civil Rights Commission, and James S. Coleman, author of the famous report on educational equality, came in supporting the board. An Ad Hoc Citizen Committee for Detroit Public Schools, composed of citizens from liberal, labor, black, and religious groups, organized to oppose the 11-district proposal. They argued that since election districts had little correspondence to school attendance sites, there would have to be massive transfers of children if parents were to be able to vote in the same districts in which their children attended school. Furthermore, additional districts would increase administrative costs and at the end of its statement the coalition noted the plan would decrease integration.

Nevertheless, despite the opposition of both the Democratic and Republican party leadership, the bill passed the House 67 to 25. The Detroit delegates split 11 to 11; all nine blacks were in opposition. To take effect by the opening of the school year, however, the bill had to pass by a two-thirds majority, or 74 votes. Realizing the harm that the 11-district bill might cause to education, Republican Governor Milliken was reluctant to sign it. On the other hand, there were a lot of Republican votes among the feeder change opponents. To save face, then, the Republicans saw to it that it failed to obtain the necessary two-thirds vote and thereby permitted the Governor to avoid the issue.

Indecision in the legislature added to the racial polarization in the city. The black establishment (the NAACP, Urban League, and Trade Union Leadership Conference) supported the board, but the separatists did not. Albert Cleage declared:

The black community will not accept any integration scheme as a substitute for community control of schools. We do not object to white parents controlling predominantly white schools and we intend to control predominantly black schools.[31]

In the white neighborhoods, there was intense political mobilization. Representative E.D. O'Brien called for student strikes and massive letter-writing campaigns. He urged:

Even the lower elementary students should take the time to write the Governor. Every weapon the Governor receives is a weapon in the hand of the community. The time to fight is now.[32]

At one high school in O'Brien's district, students responded with a "Keep Denby White" sign and hoisted a Nazi SS flag.

Most adult activity, however, focused on the snowballing campaign to recall the board's integrationist majority. Although at first poorly organized, neighborhood leaders were convinced that busing had little support in the city or anywhere else, for that matter. Ironically, on the same day the board made its decision to change feeder patterns, a Gallup poll reported national attitudes on busing. In answer to the question "In general do you favor or oppose the busing of Negro and white school children from one district to another?", 11 percent were in favor, 86 percent were opposed and only 3 percent had no opinions.[33]

In Detroit and elsewhere, opposition to busing seems to be a curious combination of outright prejudice, rational self-interest, and fear. It is risky to speculate on the precise mixture of those motives in a particular population. Given Detroit's violent history, racial hostilities and prejudices are an unescapable ingredient in its politics. The fact that Detroit is still largely a city of single-family homes and strong neighborhood attachments also contributes to the feeling against busing. And then there is fear—rational or irrational, it exists. A letter printed in one of the white neighborhood newspapers illustrates the fine line between racism and fear in the reaction to busing.

### Open Letter to Denby and Redford Area Parents

Now you parents and homeowners FINALLY know what to expect in the next few years in your area. I am in deep sympathy.

My family has experienced this in the last decade in the 6 Mile-rd—west of Greenfield area and at Cooley high school. The only difference being, the entire operation was handled more secretively by our Detroit Board of Education.

Look forward to your students:

1) Having books stolen.
2) "Losing" money in purses.
3) Held in a corner until money is given.
4) Threatened not to come to school.
5) Having hair cut off.
6) Having college required classes cancelled (not enough students).
7) Clothes damaged from food thrown in lunchrooms.
8) Cancelled classes (false fire alarms, etc.).

Get used to this new lower form of affluent society—or move *NOW* as fast as you can to salvage your investment and your sanity.

The bitterness of what I have had *FORCED* upon me in the last decade will remain forever.[34]

Whatever the mixture, racism and fear are a potent political force. As the summer approached that marked the first anniversary of Act 244, no one could be certain whether decentralization, desegregation, or the liberal-labor-black coalition that dominated the school board would survive the controversy.

## The Office of School Decentralization

Long before the controversy over Act 244 began, the board became aware of the enormous complexity of implementing decentralization in a system with 18,000 employees, 290,000 students and a budget of $216 million. Because of the unusual technical and political skills needed, the board decided to create an independent agency to do the work. Since Act 244 provided no state funds for this task and local funds were already committed for other purposes, money had to be raised privately. In October 1969, the board asked the Ford Foundation for help in preparing for decentralization. The Foundation, which at that time was supporting the establishment of participatory devices in education across the country, responded with a $360,000 grant. These funds made it possible to set up the new Office of School Decentralization (OSD).

To free the agency from the vested interests of the bureaucracy and to enhance its credibility with the community, all staff were recruited from outside. The chief coordinator, Lawrence Doss, formerly directed the Detroit data center for the Internal Revenue Service and had connections with the Black Economic Development Group, an association of businessmen. A systems analyst, Doss was one of three men responsible for designing the Automatic Data Processing System of IRS. The two assistants in the office were chosen for their expertise in the other areas necessary to development of decentralization. Malcolm Dade had been the deputy chairman of the Democratic State Central Committee in Michigan, and Delmo Della-Dora was coordinator of federally-funded educational programs in Wayne County. The task of OSD, then, was to mesh the talents of a systems expert, a politician, and an educational administrator to change the governing structure of the nation's fifth largest school system.

When OSD began its work in January, 1970, it defined for itself three tasks: development of guidelines that would allocate power between the central board and the regional boards; implementation procedures; and long-range systems designed to insure good management in the new structure.[35] While letters and resolutions praising or damning the district boundary changes were being produced all over the city, OSD went quietly about the business of preparing alternative sets of guidelines for the board. Since there were bills calling for repeal of the decentralization law in the legislature during the whole period of preparation of the guidelines, there was a certain Kafkaesque quality about OSD models of organizational change, decision flow-charts, and careful time schedules. Nevertheless, OSD's decision to ignore the legislative combat and to persevere in grinding out alternative guidelines was the only practical thing to do.

The task was enormous. First, it was necessary to document the current personnel, budget, and contracting procedures in the system. Many of these procedures were not written down, at least not in any comprehensive form. In the typical centralized bureaucracy, there is a continuity of personnel through apprenticeships and orderly promotion ladders. The lack of codified procedures may then be tolerable because officials "know" what has to be done, but in a decentralized system it is essential to have clear-cut written procedures. Consequently, OSD entered a series of contracts to get help with this work. The management consulting firm of Price Waterhouse was hired to create a comprehensive description of the essential processes of the central staff and to recommend changes for the central and regional boards. Graham Finney, former deputy superintendent of the Philadelphia schools and the drafter of the original OSD funding proposal to Ford, assisted in identifying the issues for the guidelines. A team of four Wayne State professors of educational administration, headed by Carrol Munshaw, worked out a system of alternative policies.

The character of the guidelines was a crucial part of decentralization policy, because Act 244 appeared to give the regions broad power, "subject to the guidelines" established by the central board and the collective bargaining control. For each issue, OSD articulated three alternative guidelines, placing power in the hands of the central board, the regional boards, or on a shared basis. The options were spelled out as follows:

| | CENTRAL | CENTRAL/REGIONAL | REGIONAL |
|---|---|---|---|
| Personnel Management Procedures | The central board shall determine the procedures for handling personnel management. | The central and regional boards shall jointly determine the procedures for handling personnel management. | Each regional board shall determine its own manner of handling of personnel management assigned to its region and the central board shall do the same for its directly employed personnel. |

After considerable staff modifications of the Finney and Munshaw proposals, some tentative guidelines were released to the public for comments. They covered these areas: curriculum and instruction, administration, student and community relations, and long-range and current planning information. Within these areas, the staff formulated ninety-nine separate issues.

Then OSD began an extensive consultation process. Because the staff believed that the rationale of decentralization was to create greater participatory democracy, consulting panels were established for students, parents, and school personnel. Each panel was selected in a different way. For the student groups, a representative from each high school was chosen by its student government or by the principal. Rather than depending on the official school parent organizations, which were regarded by some as too pro-school system, eighty-eight parents were selected at random in an elaborate process that involved weighting the school's enrollment. All fourteen bargaining units in the system, except the Teamsters and the Machinists (whose interests were peripheral), were represented on the employees panel. Members of the school system's executive staff were polled separately. In addition twelve neighborhood meetings were held and 1,500 questionnaires sent to community group leaders.

The decision to involve such a large number of individuals and organizations created some risks. By drawing so much attention to the proposed decentralization changes, the staff might have inadvertently increased the opposition to decentralization itself or created an unwanted polarization about some issue. Outweighing that danger, however, were the staff's ideological commitment to participation and their hunch that the guideline discussions would be a useful support-building device. OSD also recognized that the potential opposition of traditional interest groups would be minimized since their voices would be drowned out by the other panelists.

How functional was this experiment in administrative restructuring through participatory democracy? Among both parents and students, there was skepticism about how seriously their opinions would be taken, and consequently there was a high degree of turnover on the panels and in some cases an obvious lack of sophistication. Nevertheless, by June 1970, when the board was to consider the guideline alternatives, the staff had prepared a 305-page document, "Working Reaction Draft of Decentralization Guidelines," tabulating the panels' responses to the ninety-nine issues. On sixty-four issues, there was consensus (usually for the shared power alternatives), and on twenty-seven more every group agreed except the students, who wanted a larger role. On eight issues, the panels were divided. In each of these, the consensus was for power shared by the center and the regions, but in personnel matters the school employee representatives opted for central board control. On the issues of selecting textbooks and reporting on student progress, both parents and students wanted regional board power. These are not unimportant issues, and one may also question whether general agreement to share power between the center and the regions was really a choice or a decision to defer choice, but participants in the process of drafting guidelines took a pragmatic perspective. There was little conflict and considerable overall consensus. Consequently, OSD suggested that the board might tentatively adopt those guidelines on which unanimity or near-unanimity existed and then move to the remaining questions.

When the tentative guidelines were presented in June, however, the board saw itself in a position in which it might have to oppose a policy choice "agreed to unanimously" by groups of students, parents, and school employees. The board proved stubborn, and the rational systems approach began to retreat before the real world of politics. Some board members challenged the representativeness of the panels OSD had used, and so an elaborate justification of the sampling method had to be prepared. Furthermore, representatives of the teachers and administrators who had participated in the OSD process criticized some of the results. Some of the issues were not resolved to their satisfaction, but it was also true that the internal politics of the DFT and OSAS demanded that their leaders have special status in drafting the guidelines.

The board, afraid to stimulate any more controversy over decentralization, decided to postpone consideration of the guidelines until the DFT and OSAS could formulate alternatives. The task of redrafting the guidelines was also taken out of the hands of the more independent OSD and given to Superintendent Drachler's staff liaison on decentralization, Mary Brand. A new committee almost wholly representative of the school establishment was then set up to work on the guidelines. Eventually, they mailed a "Public Reaction Draft" to 3,800 concerned citizens for comment. The guidelines[36] were then finally adopted by the board with little debate on October 26, 1970.

The main change wanted by the two employee organizations was a reduction of the power of the regional board over the high schools and over all personnel evaluation. The DFT and OSAS lost on the high school issue, though the powers of the central board as conflict arbiter in personnel matters were further articulated. Even if the establishment committee produced somewhat the same results as OSD's community participatory process, it seemed important to the board to be deferential to the employee groups. During the summer of 1970, however, the controversy over decentralization had spread far beyond the school establishment.

## The Recall Campaign

The same week in June when the board was supposed to be concentrating on the proposed guidelines, petitions were filed with the city clerk asking for the recall for the four board members who had voted for the decentralization-desegregation plan in April. Two weeks later, the Michigan legislature replaced Act 244 with a new law designed to placate the enraged white neighborhoods. The anti-busing movement in Michigan had gained its first of many victories.

The new law, Act 48, strengthened the neighborhoods in several ways. First it mandated the creation of eight regions instead of seven and gave authority to draw the new district lines to a special gubernatorially-appointed commission. The legislative mandate to the commission was "to enable students to attend a school of preference . . . ," and in cases of insufficient school capacity to give priority "to those students residing nearest the school." In short the board's integration program was repealed. The law also shortened the term of the regional board members from four to two years, decreased their number from nine to five, and provided for a small per diem allowance. Under Act 48, the person receiving the highest vote in the region automatically became the chairman of the regional board and the region's representative on the central board. After weeks of indecision in the face of considerable constituent pressure, the legislature was relieved to pass the bill—in the House by 93 to 1 and in the Senate by 30 to 0. Blacks, including Coleman Young, went along because decentralization had been saved and because the NAACP was confident it could get the integrationist feeder patterns reinstituted by the courts.

The Governor's Boundary Commission—two whites, a city councilman and a Wayne State professor of law, and one black, a clergyman—agreed from the outset that integration would not be a goal of the new plan. In theory, political control was to be divided equally between blacks and whites, four districts for each group. In two week's time, they had worked out a plan that kept closely to existing school boundaries and avoided changes in feeder patterns.

The state legislature clearly had hoped that Act 48 would end the integration controversy. The Act specified that any pending recall petitions could be withdrawn within ten days after the Act's passage, but the furies in the neighborhoods could not now be quieted. The move to recall board members was the first in the 128-year history of the school system. An earlier attempt to recall Mayor Jerome Cavanaugh had failed to garner enough signatures. Lacking support from either political party, any major group, or the media, it seemed unlikely that the newly-organized Citizens Committee for Better Education (CCBE) could succeed in recalling board members. It was an amateur, low-budget effort from the beginning.[37] Led by Aubrey Short, a Chevrolet metallurgist and father of eight, CCBE avoided the downtown media and relied on neighborhood shopping papers for publicity and on local schools and churches for meeting places. At first, the recall petitions were seen mainly as a device for focusing public opinion on the legislative campaign. Recall petitions make all politicians uncomfortable and give protestors leverage, but CCBE became determined to oust the integration foursome on the board.

Petitions began to pile up. On June 15, seventy-five persons, mostly housewives, carried twenty-four boxes of them to the city clerk. The goal of 114,000 valid signatures was reached, and the recall was placed on the August 4 primary ballot.

While the recall advocates were expanding their organization in the white neighborhoods and establishing contacts with some black leaders, the threatened board members and their allies seemed deep in a curious malaise. Some felt that whatever the outcome of the recall balloting, it could be overturned in the courts. Several suits were initiated, but four days before the election the Michigan State Court of Appeals ruled that recall would appear on the ballot. Abe Zwerdling, the integrationist leader on the board, never really believed in the legal strategy, but he was so saddened by the recent death of UAW labor chief Walter Reuther that he was unwilling and unable to rally support. Others were drained and divided by the ongoing legislative struggle. Both the Detroit *Free Press* and the Detroit *News* joined to oppose recall, but its opponents never really mobilized their strength.

Primaries and recall elections especially favor organized groups. Only 32 percent of the eligible voters came to the polls on election day; 60 percent of them supported recall. In black neighborhoods, not only was the turnout slightly lower, but in some areas almost half the voters neglected to pull any lever on the recall question. The turnout in white neighborhoods was higher, as expected, but more important to the outcome was that almost all whites voted on recall—and voted yes. As Superintendent Drachler was quick to note, and as Table 7-3 illustrates, the middle-class white neighborhoods that had been saying no to increased school support were also saying no to integration—perhaps for the same reasons. They had broken the liberal-labor-black coalition's hold on the central school board, and they now turned to organizing for the new regional and central board elections.

**Decentralization at the Polls**

The weather was cloudy, threatening rain, as Detroiters went to the polls to elect a Governor, a Senator, and new representatives in Washington and Lansing. Also on the ballot were candidates for the central school board and, for the first time in history, candidates for regional school boards. Although Republicans had conceded the failure of Lenore Romney's challenge to incumbent Senator Phillip Hart, they were waging a tough campaign to protect Governor William Millikin against Sandor Levin, the first Jewish candidate for statewide office. Further-more, Proposition C, a proposed constitutional amendment that would invalidate the recently-passed state aid to parochial school program, proved to be one of the most emotional issues in Michigan's history. A large turnout seemed likely.

In fact, almost 62 percent of Detroit voters went to the polls. At least 30% voted for the central school board candidates, and at least 24% marked their ballots for the regional elections. When one compares these figures to the 14 percent turnout in New York City's first decentralized school election, the consequence (in terms of voter participation) of holding school elections on regular election days is apparent. On the school section of the ballot, the voter had to choose three names from the eighteen listed who were running at-large and five names for each region. In Region 4, thirty-six candidates turned out, although the average was about twenty-four. Racially mixed neighborhoods tended to produce more candidates (average twenty-seven) than predominantly black (nineteen) or white (nineteen) areas.

Since most of the 186 regional candidates running were new to politics, their first task was to find recognition among the voters. The board's original proposal to Ford Foundation had asked for $100,000 to conduct voter education and to

**Table 7-3**

**Neighborhood Attitudes toward School Finance and School Integration in Detroit**

| Neighborhoods Defined by High School Constellations | School Finance[1] | | | School Integration[2] | | |
|---|---|---|---|---|---|---|
| | Average % Votes Cast of Total Registration | Average % Opposing Increased School Taxes Who Voted on Question | Average % Blank Ballots[3] | Average % Votes Cast of Total Registration | Average % Favoring Recall of Integrationist Board Members Who Voted on Question | Average % Blank Ballots[3] |
| High School Constellations 75% or more white (N=4) | 81 | 74 | 13 | 37 | 84 | 12 |
| High School Constellations 25 to 75% white (N=9) | 78 | 63 | 36 | 31 | 60 | 31 |
| High School Constellations 25% or less white (N=8) | 77 | 43 | 47 | 31 | 37 | 39 |
| Grand Mean | 79 | 62 | 32 | 32 | 60 | 28 |

[1] Millage Vote, November 5, 1968.
[2] Recall vote August 7, 1970. The smaller turnout for the recall vote compared to the millage vote is in part caused by the fact that it was held on an August primary date rather than on a November regular election date.
[3] Voters who voted in this election but not on this issue.

Source: Calculated from statistics supplied by the Detroit school system.

operate a two-week institute for candidates, but that section was not funded. Meetings to introduce candidates were poorly attended, and the city newspapers confined themselves to printing two-sentence biographies of the candidates. The contests for major offices dried up campaign funds and tied up potential workers, so that the principal means of establishing an identity was to obtain endorsements. Some candidates were endorsed by local politicians or neighborhood celebrities, but most attempted to obtain organizational support. Although several candidates were blessed by clergymen, the churches made no systematic effort to influence the election. Perhaps their energies were diverted by Proposition C. Individual parent, homeowner, and block associations backed some candidates. Political clubs were active and twenty-four candidates had party endorsements (almost all Democratic), but only seven won. Indeed, one candidate was endorsed by both parties and still lost. In a few instances party support proved valuable, but generally the parties were otherwise occupied or ineffective and did not greatly influence the regional board elections. On a city-wide basis, two other organizations had greater impact—the UAW-CAP and the Citizens Committee for Better Education.

Unions have long been a major political force in Michigan politics.[38] In presidential election years, Democratic candidates traditionally open their campaigns with a Labor Day address to union families massed in Cadillac Square. The party's dependency on organized labor in Michigan is probably greater than in any other state, but in Detroit the non-partisan structure of city elections has diluted union influence. Still, politicians attempt to clear most issues with labor, and the Metropolitan Detroit AFL-CIO, the UAW, and the DFT are often active and prominent in supporting liberal educational goals. Labor was an important component of the Serve Our School Committee that had successfully functioned as a screening panel and supporter of liberal candidates in the last two decades. In the case of Abe Zwerdling, who had been associate general counsel of the UAW, it was Walter Reuther himself who had convinced Zwerdling to run and provided the campaign support necessary for his victory.

Not surprisingly, then, after the recall, the liberals looked to the UAW's Committee on Political Action for help in the school elections. The UAW could not fully respond, however. Its priorities were the gubernatorial and senatorial contests, and the sagging national economy had depleted its campaign chest. Walter Reuther's death had left the leadership somewhat disorganized and possibly less fervent about integration than before. Nevertheless, though the UAW did not recruit candidates, it did endorse a city-wide slate of thirty-five candidates. The DFT, the AFL-CIO, and the Teamsters also supported candidates. The union endorsements often overlapped, but no unified labor slate ever existed. More important, no attempt was made to work with civil rights groups and others to replace the now defunct Serve Our School Committee. But even fragmentary support was better than none. Marvin Pilo estimates that the various unions spent about $15,000 on the school board elections and provided some important publicity for candidates.

The Citizens Committee for Better Education found the momentum it had gained in the recall campaign a valuable asset. Election committees were established in regions where the CCBE had strength, and elsewhere liaison was set up with such black leaders as Reverend Albert Cleage, Representative James Del Rio, and Bob Johnson, the director of the Detroit Education Association. Screening panels ranging from small committees to the 35-member Denby Council in Region 7 were established. According to the CCBE, the criteria for endorsement were support of high academic standards as the primary educational goal and opposition to busing. Overall, twenty-three candidates received formal CCBE endorsement. The organization had little money (Aubrey Short claims that only about $1,000 was spent), but it could print campaign materials (over 200,000 slate cards were distributed), provide mailing lists and campaign workers. In a neighborhood-based election, this kind of assistance can be crucial.

Notable absentees from the election were the traditional civil rights groups and other black organizations. There was no deliberate boycott such as occurred in New York, but neither was there much campaigning or endorsing. The few candidates who received the endorsement of radical black groups all lost. Black leaders cannot fully explain this lack of effort, except to suggest that the suddenness of the election and the complexity of the procedures made it difficult to organize ghetto residents.

When the votes were finally tallied (a matter of considerable suspense when Detroit's new punchcard system broke down), one black and one white candidate not affiliated with any particular slate led in the polling for the central board slots with over 70,000 votes each. In the contest for the third position, a white housewife endorsed by the CCBE just edged (600 votes) a black executive of the Michigan Civil Rights Commission. Although the UAW-CAP organization elected fifteen regional members to the CCBE's twelve, in five of the eight regions the CCBE candidate obtained the highest vote. These winners therefore became the chairmen of those regional boards and their representatives to the central board. The new CCBE members and their incumbent allies had obtained a working majority on the central board. The defeat of the liberal-labor-black coalition was clear.

For black advocates of decentralization, the regional board election in Detroit, like the district elections in New York, once again failed to produce the desired results (see Table 7-4). Under the old structure, blacks constituted 45 percent (three of seven members) of the central board. After the 1970 election, they were halved to 23 percent (three of thirteen members), their lowest percentage in fifteen years. On the regional boards, only twelve of forty members are black, despite the fact that two of every three students in the public schools are black. As in New York, the first decentralized election resulted in white boards controlling the education of black students. In Region 8, for example, 93 percent of the students are black, but whites will control the new board 3 to 2.

But viewing the election in these terms is too simple. For one thing, as was

Table 7-4

**Racial and Organizational Identifications of the Winners of the 1970 Detroit Regional School Board Elections**

| Region | % White Public School Students | % White Board Members | % CCBE Endorsed | % UAW-CAP Endorsed |
|--------|-------------------------------|----------------------|-----------------|--------------------|
| 1 | 12 | 20 | 40 | 0 |
| 2 | 29 | 60 | 40 | 40 |
| 3 | 40 | 80 | 0 | 60 |
| 4 | 42 | 100 | 40 | 20 |
| 5 | 6 | 40 | 0 | 80 |
| 6 | 53 | 100 | 60 | 0 |
| 7 | 65 | 100 | 60 | 40 |
| 8 | 7 | 60 | 0 | 60 |

Source: Racial data comes from in-house studies of the Detroit Public Schools. Information on candidate organizational affiliation comes from a pre-election survey by the League of Women Voters and from interviews with CCBE and the UAW-CAP.

true in New York, when one considers the racial identities of the eligible voters rather than those of the students, the results were not so disproportionate. It is estimated that almost 65 percent of Detroit voters are white, so the fact that 70 percent of the newly-elected regional board members are white is not extraordinary. Furthermore, there are other bases of representation than race. Polish-Americans, who constitute 15 to 20 percent of the electorate and who had been previously unrepresented on the central board, won four seats. Whereas the old central board had no women, six women were elected to the new board. There is also more occupational diversity on the new central board. However, contrary to the hopes of decentralization advocates, very few blue collar or "poor people" were elected to regional boards.[39] On the pre-recall central board that was elected at-large, four of the seven members lived in one high school district. Under decentralization, every area of the city will be represented on the central board.

As important as the socio-economic background of the new board members are their attitudes on school policy. It was not possible to interview all forty regional board winners, but almost all candidates did respond to a four-item League of Women Voters questionnaire, and their answers were published before the election. Table 7-5 reflects the results. The League's sense of propriety apparently prevented it from asking about such volatile issues as school busing, but the answers to the four questions that were asked present a surprising picture. Only on the question of stationing a police officer in the school was there any substantial difference between white and black winners. Obviously, that is a highly symbolic issue for blacks, but 68 percent of the white winners also agreed that it was a bad idea. On the issue of regional versus central board

**Table 7-5**

**Issue Orientation of the Winners in the 1970 Detroit Regional School Board Election**

| Questions | White (28) | Black (12) | UAW-CAP (15) | CCBE (12) | Other (13) |
|---|---|---|---|---|---|
| 1. Do you favor pub-lication of test scores for individual schools? (% voting yes) | 91* | 78 | 86 | 100 | 80 |
| 2. Who should have the MOST responsibility for selection of principals? (% voting region rather than central) | 91 | 90 | 93 | 100 | 87 |
| 3. Shall the regional Boards allocate extra funds to schools with the largest number of students who are read-ing below grade level? (% voting yes) | 85 | 100 | 91 | 60 | 100 |
| 4. Shall a police offi-cer be present in each junior and senior high school? (% voting no) | 68 | 100 | 91 | 50 | 80 |

*Percentages are of those answering the question.

Source: Data comes from a pre-election survey of the League of Women Voters.

power, the white and black percentages are nearly identical in their preference for regional predominance.

Another way to examine the issue orientations of the new board members is to compare the position taken by those affiliated with various slates. When one compares the two dominant slates, those of the UAW-CAP and the CCBE, the differences are not as great as one might have predicted. Although the UAW-CAP slate is considerably more in favor of redistributing funds in aid of disadvantaged students and opposed to policemen in schools than is the CCBE slate, both of those positions found great support in the CCBE slate as well. That 60 percent of the CCBE winners favor additional funds for the low-reading-score schools (predominantly black inner-city) was not expected. On the other two questions, releasing test scores and regional selection of principals, the UAW-CAP and CCBE candidates are both overwhelmingly in favor (CCBE winners in fact are 100 percent on both items). The consensus on these questions suggests a non-racial hypothesis about the effect on political recruitment of school decentralization.

Clearly, decentralization in Detroit produced a large number of new school activists. Among the winners are more women, more ethnics, and more white homeowners than before. What distinguishes these new activists, however, is not their social backgrounds but their suspicion of the central school administration and educational professionals generally. One might have imagined that decentralization elections in Detroit would have produced sharp racially-linked ideological conflict in school politics, but that apparently did not occur. Instead, the conflict is more likely to be between the new school activists of either race and the educational professionals and their allies who have traditionally made school policy. When asked what CCBE's other objectives were in addition to halting school busing, Aubrey Short's answer was one that might be echoed in many ghetto neighborhoods: "End Tenure."

### Decentralization—The First Year

On January 1, 1971, decentralization began a new era of Detroit school politics. The newly-elected central and regional board members took office and started searching for their respective sovereignties.

Almost immediately, the central board replaced James Hathaway and chose Patrick McDonald as its President. The selection of McDonald, the representative of the white neighborhoods who had been censured by the old liberal board, was the first clear indication of the consequence of the election. A few weeks later, the second predictable outcome occurred. After thirty-four years in the school system, Norman Drachler announced his resignation to accept the leadership of the Ford Foundation-funded Institute for Educational Leadership at George Washington University. Abe Zwerdling had earlier left for Washington to become General Counsel of the Federation of State, County, and Municipal Employees.[40]

The changes of leadership wrought by decentralization may be the most apparent, but in the long run subtle shifts in structural relationships and system policies may be more important. Not only are these sometimes difficult to trace, but it is not always clear whether they are the result of decentralization or of some other forces working within the system. Some of the more significant developments can be examined, however.

### *Integration Policy*

Even before the new boards took office, for example, their alternatives on integration policy were substantially restricted by the federal courts. As soon as the recall results were in, the Detroit NAACP moved to invalidate the neighborhood schools section of Act 244 and to return to the recalled board members' integration plan. On October 13, the U.S. Sixth Circuit Court of

Appeals agreed that a state legislature could not overturn a local school board's integration efforts and remanded the case to District Court Judge Stephen J. Roth for hearings on an appropriate integration plan.[41] Judge Roth gave the board (then composed of the four gubernatorially-appointed members who replaced the four recalled members and three incumbents) twelve days to suggest alternatives. After a period of intense internal discussions, the board submitted three plans to the Court. One was the old April 7 feeder change plan; another was a dual enrollment option requiring all students to take some courses in a second (presumably more integrated) school. Neither of these plans were politically feasible so Judge Roth reluctantly accepted a magnet school program sponsored principally by Patrick McDonald and ordered it implemented for the fall 1971 term.

The magnet school plan is based on the theory that a specialized or enriched school curriculum will attract students from families otherwise skeptical about integration. Detroit's version of the plan involved pairing a predominantly black region with one predominantly white and then designing a new curriculum for several high schools within the two regions. For example, in Regions 2 and 3, special programs in the performing arts, vocational education, science, and business education were established in four different schools. A similar approach had worked at Cass Technical High School in Detroit, where a special curriculum drew students from throughout the city to an integrated, high quality program. The other magnet feature envisioned was a new middle school (grades five to eight) in each region. In Detroit, as in most cities, the junior high schools have become the most troublesome schools in the system. It was hoped that a new grade format and a smaller school size (limited to 500 students) might create that most elusive goal of "quality integrated education."

Unfortunately, whatever the magnet school's pedagogical virtues, the time was past when any voluntary attendance plan would greatly increase integration in Detroit. After the schools opened in September, Judge Roth reviewed the integrating effects of the magnet plan and found them unsatisfactory.[42] In a decision that had national political repercussions, he suggested that the only solution might be cross-busing between the white suburbs and Detroit, or even that it might be necessary for the state to create a single metropolitan-wide school district that would have the effect of creating financial as well as racial equality. As the Judge acknowledged, despite serious efforts by the Detroit school system to integrate in the 1960s, there were by 1971 twenty-two more all-black schools than there were ten years earlier. Judge Roth blamed school zoning patterns, housing and financing policies and even blacks themselves who, he noted, "like other ethnic groups in the past, have tended to separate from the larger group and associate together."[43] Whatever the Judge's rationale, there was some logic in his remedy. Whereas the Detroit schools were now 65 percent black, the surrounding counties—Wayne, Oakland, and Macomb—average only 3 percent black students.[44]

Ironically, this cross-busing "solution" was advocated by both the NAACP and CCBE, if for different reasons. The NAACP supported it philosophically, while the CCBE saw it as a useful tactic to build a coalition with suburban whites to end all busing. Such subsequent political events as Senator Robert Griffin's (R-Mich) sudden sponsorship of a constitutional amendment barring busing, Governor George Wallace's smashing victory in the Michigan Presidential primary, and perhaps even President Nixon's hardened position against busing can be attributed partly to the shock waves that followed the Roth opinion.

At this writing, the challenge to Judge Roth's latest opinion *is* being heard by the Sixth Circuit Court of Appeals. The only thing that is clear is that neither the central board nor the regional boards would have any final discretion in pupil integration policy. That issue would be decided in the courts and legislatures.

### Education Policy

The magnet school plan was adopted before the boards chosen in the decentralized election took office, but the regions were put in charge of implementing it. Some of the regions were less ideologically committed to the concept than others, but the main problem was lack of money. There was no new money for the magnet school program—or any other additional program for that matter—and the central board found its deficit greater than usual. There were cutbacks throughout the system. Region 1 voted not to set up any magnet school in order to dramatize its financial problem. Generally, budgetary restrictions cramped any educational goals the regions wished to pursue. In the Spring of 1971, students closed schools in three regions to protest budget cuts and school security measures. In their first confrontation with school unrest, the regional boards found it impossible to act. Finally, the central board had to step in.

As in New York, the problem of legitimacy has proved worrisome for the new boards. Much to their surprise, they quickly became viewed as a part of the school establishment. Furthermore, they threatened channels of access and influence that other neighborhood groups had established. When told that the regional board now had the authority to screen administrative appointments, one member of a neighborhood group responded:

You come by with some old two-by-four guidelines. Well as long as we pay your salary, you're gonna recognize us and if you don't, I'm gonna get your job! Now you go ahead and do your thing and just let us do our thing![45]

To improve communications and legitimacy, several of the regions set up councils of neighborhood organizations and individual parents that participated in considering personnel and curriculum decisions.

The CCBE has been kept very much alive by NAACP litigation. Aubrey Short claimed a membership of 60,000, representing some 168 community groups in 1971.[46] The organization, which sometimes represents itself as "we the white people of the city of Detroit" or "the conservatives who work for a living," has a 13-member board of directors and a $2 membership fee. It fully intends to contest future school elections, but it has not really attempted to keep active liaison with those it endorsed on the various boards, nor can it function with any party-like discipline. The CCBE's preoccupation with integration has also limited its efforts to influence other education policy, but it is still potentially the most influential pressure group in Detroit school politics.

No new liberal coalition has emerged to replace the defunct Serve Our School committee and to challenge CCBE. Many white liberals are very pessimistic about the future political consequences of decentralization. Yet, although discouraged by the first election, some moderate blacks want to give decentralization more of a chance. A few black activists have obtained policy-making jobs with the regional boards. In the two regions that blacks control, some feel that they are shaping the black future—a feeling that too often eludes blacks in America. Finally, the demographers say Detroit will have a black majority before the end of the decade, and so black politicians believe their electoral positions must improve.

## Structure and Personnel Policy

One consequence of decentralization is that the Detroit schools have had to gather more information about themselves and take modern management methods seriously. Several feasibility studies examining various forms of PPBS, information retrieval, and accountability were initiated and completed by OSD and its successor. The paradox is that, while decentralization requires new management techniques for administrative efficiency and to avoid conflicts over equal treatment among the regions, politically it creates competition for authority that is antithetical to the techniques. It is not clear how this paradox will be resolved in Detroit now that implementation of most of the techniques has been hampered by lack of money and instability in top administrative offices.

Nor is it possible to evaluate what the eventual role of the regional boards will be. In the first year, most of the changes they made were largely symbolic, like the decision reached by Region 4 to reject John F. Kennedy or Louis Armstrong as a school name in favor of Ivan Luddington, Sr. Mr. Luddington, it seems, was a beloved local newsdealer who gave schools books and shelves.[47] Lacking money, legitimacy, and established procedures, the regional boards found it difficult to function. Furthermore, their internal structures and their relationships with the central board were not clear. The political role of the regional board chairman was ambiguous. As highest vote getter in a region, the chairman was not necessarily representative of the other board members—which sometimes created internal conflicts as well as dissension over the votes cast by the regional chairman as representative on the central board. Several regional board members attempted to force their chairmen to act as a delegate, but the central board attorney ruled that the chairmen—when voting on the central board—were free agents. Some regional board members then set up a caucus of regional boards to attempt to gain broader powers and to have a voice in the selection of the new Superintendent. Also a bill was introduced in Lansing that would require the region's central board representative to be elected by the regional board, but the legislators were in no mood to tamper with Act 48.

Replacing Norman Drachler as Superintendent was the central board's foremost personnel task. Given the system's political and racial hostilities, its fiscal deficits, the impending judicial mandates, and perhaps decentralization itself, it proved almost impossible to find a "big league" school administrator who would take the position. A year after Drachler's resignation, no new Superintendent had been installed.

The CCBE's threat to abolish tenure has not been carried out,[48] but the board did try to shorten the contract terms of 1,000 administrators from three years to one year.[49] Since that violated the OSAS collective bargaining agreement, the board was rebuffed. It then settled for a review of the eighteen top administrators who were not covered by collective bargaining, and it has been attempting to work out new evaluation procedures for other personnel.

Each regional office will have a staff of sixty to seventy persons, and state law requires that existing central board employees be given preference in hiring. Many did not want to transfer, but eventually some 280 people—mostly attendance officers, school-community relations agents, and school social workers—were moved. All of the incumbent regional superintendents were placed, though several were not expected to keep their jobs. But there have been no racial or ideological purges. For one thing, the decentralization law clearly protected employee rights, and the specter of Ocean Hill-Brownsville made everyone cautious. In Region 3, black parents succeeded in ousting the acting superintendent and in gaining *de facto* control over the selection of new principals. The OSAS threatened a strike, but no one forced the confrontation, and a compromise was reached.

*Decentralization In the Balance*

It is, of course, impossible to detail or even to know of all the complex and subtle educational changes that occurred in the first year of decentralization in Detroit. Most professional observers, however, have focused on the political impact of decentralization on race relations and integration, and their judgments have been negative. In an article first published in *The Public Interest* and later widely reprinted by the United Federation of Teachers, William Grant, Education Editor of the *Free Press* argued:

> The national importance of Detroit's experience with decentralization lies in the conflict which developed between decentralization and integration . . . in Detroit the process of decentralization produced severe racial polarization and a backlash vote which put a conservative school board in office. The blacks who pressed for decentralization were the losers; they ended up with less power and less influence than they had had before decentralization . . . the "peace of reconciliation" that Alan Altshuler envisions as the ideal outcome of decentralization has yet to descend upon Detroit.[50]

One can agree with Grant's factual assessments of the politics of decentralization in Detroit and yet question the perspective he uses for judgment. Although decentralization did provide political means for driving out the liberal coalition that governed the Detroit schools, it was not responsible for initiating racial polarization or killing integration in the city. The enduring nature of racial conflict in Detroit is abundantly evident in the city's history. Decentralization, or more precisely the policies chosen to implement it, led to a referendum on busing, but that vote merely articulated attitudes that had existed in Detroit for some time. Much of the change in racial attitudes occurred before decentralization moved onto the political agenda and is probably more attributable to the Detroit riots and national events. According to surveys conducted in 1971 by Joel D. Aberbach and Jack L. Walker, integration was a principle still publicly affirmed in the city.[51] Only 34 percent of the whites and 8 percent of the blacks would admit to preferring school segregation, but among blacks the level of commitment to integration had significantly declined. In 1967, 66 percent of the blacks were willing to risk violent demonstrations to secure integrated schools, but by 1971 the percentage had fallen to 29. Concurrently, about one of every five blacks moved from unequivocally affirming an integrated society to preferring something "in between" integration and separation. Many of these blacks favored community control. This shift may have been the reason why even in high school constellations with overwhelmingly black student bodies 37 percent of the voters favored recalling the integrationist board members (Table 7-3). The Aberbach and Walker survey does not show a comparable shift in white attitudes away from integration, but that it did take place is clear from other political evidence.

In short, although decentralization may prove to be a structure in which those opposed to integration are more accurately represented than before, it is not at all certain that there was or will be in the near future a consensus that would permit a centralized school system to encourage further integration. As important as the opportunity for interracial educational experience is, it may be that for now we shall have to judge both centralized and decentralized school systems on other criteria. A comprehensive study of Detroit's elementary schools that was begun before decentralization but reported in February 1971 said, "We find a headquarters-centered system, with too much responsibility flowing upward and not enough downward."[52] The survey authors, eight nationally-respected educators, recommended giving each elementary school within the regions considerable autonomy. The decentralized regional boards, councils, and *ad hoc* groups has already increased participation in school politics in Detroit,[53] but it is far too soon to tell whether it will improve the achievement of disadvantaged children or alleviate the alienation of white middle-class neighborhoods.[54] These, too, are important goals.

Aberbach and Walker, however, make another charge against decentralization. They claim it is not what a majority of Detroiters wanted as a school structure, and their survey reported in Table 7-6 supports this position.[55] Indeed, when analyzed by educational level, college-educated blacks were the only group with a clear-cut majority in favor of decentralization.[56] That this group possessed the educational, political, and race consciousness that led it to support decentralization is quite interesting, but not surprising. They, after all, would have the skills to capture the new leadership positions created. That decentralization should have become policy at all, given its lack of general support, requires more explanation.

The Aberbach and Walker survey provides no evidence about the relative strength of attitudes for and against decentralization. It is commonplace, however, in politics that a passionate minority can outwit and out-muscle an apathetic majority. In 1969, given the failure of the public school establishment to fulfill black educational aspirations, black leaders as diverse as Reverent Albert Cleage of the Shrine of the Black Madonna and Dr. Jesse Goodwin of

Table 7-6
**Attitudes Toward School Decentralization in Detroit by Race\* (1971)**

|  | Racial Group | |
|  | Whites | Blacks |
| --- | --- | --- |
| Single City-wide Board: | 50 | 64 |
| Decentralized Boards: | 37 | 29 |
| Don't Know/No Answer: | 13 | 7 |
| Total | 100% | 100% |

*The question was: "There's a lot of controversy these days in Detroit over the way the public schools should be organized. Some people believe that the schools will pay more attention to the needs of parents and students if each area in the city elects its own separate school board; others believe that the system would be more efficient and cheaper to operate if it remains under the control of a single, city-wide school board. Which way would you prefer: separate area school boards or a single, city-wide school board?"
Source: Joel D. Aberbach and Jack L. Walker, "Citizens Desires, Policy Outcomes, and Community Control." Institute of Public Policy Studies Discussion Paper No. 29, 1971, p. 8.

NAACP became committed to some kind of decentralization. When so prestigious a politician as Coleman Young sponsored the idea, no one wanted to oppose him. Anyway, Act 244 was little more than an open-ended mandate to the Detroit school board to speed up the decentralization process it had already begun. The board believed it had the lobbying strength to kill the bill, but it chose not to, since it was ideologically committed to some kind of decentralization and Act 244 let it make the critical decision. Other potential actors remained uninvolved. In the two-year controversy, Mayor Gribbs made almost no public comment about school politics (except to support aid to parochial schools) and played no behind-the-scenes role either. Neither political party became active, nor did any of the other major figures in Michigan politics. Few of the voluntary agencies interested in education had positions on decentralization, because the passage of Act 244 in the summer months had caught them unprepared.

If decentralization was passed in a sort of political vacuum, the board policies implementing the law eventually heightened public interest to the point of backlash. As public concern grew, however, the organizations that traditionally articulate and shape educational policy were unable to function. The city has no citizen education organization like the Public Education Association in New York, and its parents associations are comparatively weak. The Detroit PTA, which has been losing members to independent groups, was never seriously consulted during decentralization policy development. Unable to bridge the gap between its white and black constituencies on either decentralization or recall, it played little role. Similarly, the Detroit Federation of Teachers leadership, which was inclined to follow the lead of fellow unionists in New York, was never able effectively to oppose decentralization because of the large number of blacks in the organization. Furthermore, both Act 244 and Act 48 guaranteed all union rights. While black leaders uniformly supported decentralization as a symbol, the integrationist-separatist ideological dichotomy made it impossible for them to agree on implementation. In the media, the liberal *Free Press* was inclined to be sympathetic to decentralization as a new reform, while the conservative *News* was skeptical, even hostile, from the beginning. With the traditional educational leadership and organizations divided, the board's integrationist districting policy mobilized neighborhood whites. Using *ad hoc* groups, a recall campaign, and an almost populist appeal, they captured much of the decentralization structure in the first elections. Decentralization may have been a black symbol, and in the future it may be a black asset, but some whites have found that they can profit from it. Whether decentralization, then, is a recipe for accommodation for urban blacks and whites, and whether that accommodation will be benign, may well be first tested in Detroit.

# New York: Breaking Up the Bureaucracy

Considerations of decentralization in New York are inextricably linked to the sheer size of the city. Although its geographic growth ended before the twentieth century, and although today it ranks only sixth in land area, New York's supremacy in population has never been challenged by any of the newer cities. Indeed, if New York's boroughs were individual cities, Brooklyn would be the third most populous in the country, Queens fourth, Manhattan sixth, and the Bronx eighth. Although no real New Yorker ever goes there, the other borough, Staten Island, is still larger than Dayton or Albuquerque.

The size of the school system and its problems, of course, reflect the magnitude of the city. If the 1,100,000 students in the public schools were citizens of a separate city, it would be seventh largest in the country. The city's Catholic school system enrolls more students than all but two other public school systems in the country. New York's teacher organization, the United Federation of Teachers, is the largest union local in the world. Its public school budget in 1972 was $1.5 billion, more than the total budget of half of the states. New York schools spend more money for erasers than Cincinnati does for books.

The importance of school politics in New York is not just a matter of size. The historic leadership role of some New York schools and educators and the city's dominance of the national media are as significant. But are the events that have characterized school decentralization in New York precursors of some national trend, or are they merely reflections of the city's unique dimensions? Both theories have their supporters. Fred Powledge, writing on the plight of urban government, looked first to New York because:

... whatever happens in New York City, as atypical as it is, is going to happen sooner or later in other cities. If the police and firemen strike in New York, they will soon strike in Detroit and New Haven, the same goes for battles over school decentralization, the future of the telephone system, transportation network, etc.[1]

On the other hand, James Reston editorialized:

The life in New York is not a typical but a special case in America. It has frightening and even tragic problems between the majority of the Jewish teachers in the public schools and the majority of Negro pupils. It thinks it leads America, and that it represents America's problems, but it is probably the most unrepresentative community in the entire United States.[2]

Whoever is right, the fate of school decentralization across the country will be substantially affected by the images and realities of the politics of school decentralization in New York.

## The Formation of School Government

Unlike cities farther West, where public school systems were established almost as a matter of course, the existence and governance of public education in New York was a matter of great controversy.[3] The first schools in the city were founded, funded, and operated by religious groups for the members of their denominations and by charitable trusts for poor children.[4] By 1805, state funds were granted to each of these private systems, but the arrangement proved unsatisfactory. Some fraud occurred, but more important, the private schools were unable to cope with the tides of immigrant children flowing into the city. By 1840, less than half of the city's children were attending schools of any kind, while upstate 94 percent were enrolled in the new public school systems.[5]

Proposals to create a single publicly-controlled school system in New York City provoked considerable acrimony. Protestants were generally supportive. They were fearful for the civic welfare if large numbers of immigrants remained illiterate, and they knew that common schools would reflect Protestant cultural biases if not their explicit doctrines. Catholics were just as determined to preserve public funds and religious control for their schools. These issues were not just matters of nineteenth century sectarian rivalry. The debate involved fundamental questions of the degree of cultural and administrative diversity in education. It was a significant episode in the continuing controversy over the school's socialization role as manifested in struggles over centralization and decentralization.

Governor William H. Seward took a decentralized approach and argued:

The children of foreigners, found in great numbers in our populous cities and towns, and in the vicinity of our public works, are too often deprived of the advantages of our system of public education, in consequence of prejudices arising from difference of language or religion. It ought never to be forgotten that the public welfare is as deeply concerned in their education as in that of our own children. I do not hesitate, therefore, to recommend the establishment of schools in which they may be instructed by teachers speaking the same language with themselves and professing the same faith.[6]

To implement this goal, his superintendent of public schools, John C. Spencer, offered a compromise. A board of elected commissioners would be created to set and implement general standards, but they would distribute public funds to the trustees of the individual school who would operate those schools and make religious policy. In language that anticipates some of the modern arguments for educational vouchers, Spencer theorized:

A rivalry may, and probably will, be produced between them, to increase the number of pupils. As an essential means to such an object, there will be a constant effort to improve the schools, in the mode and degree of instruction, and in the qualification of the teachers. Thus, not only will the number of children brought into the schools be incalculably augmented, but the competition anticipated will produce its usual effect of providing the very best material to satisfy the public demand. These advantages will more than compensate for any possible evils that may be apprehended from having schools adapted to the feelings and views of the different denominations.[7]

When the proposal met with resistance in the city, however, Catholics grew impatient and Bishop Hughes made a fatal tactical error. Four days before the election of 1841, he decided to field his own slate of candidates for the state legislature. They lost, and the reaction was such that at the next session of the legislature an elected board of education for the city was established. But instead of supervising denominational schools as Spencer had proposed, common schools were organized in each ward, and state law forbade public funds from going to any school "in which any religious sectarian doctrine or tenet" was taught.

For both sides, the outcome in New York eventually became decisive. New York's law barring sectarian teaching in public schools was adopted by other states and finally received ratification as the national standard by the Supreme Court in 1963.[8] Most Protestants gradually accepted non-sectarian public schools, but Catholics decided to continue their parochial schools. That pattern exists today as does the religious bitterness that underlies much of New York's educational politics.

If the law of 1842 established a non-sectarian public school system, it was by no means a centralized one.[9] In each of the ten wards then existing, two Commissioners were elected to a central board, but the schools were actually managed by two locally-elected Inspectors and five Trustees. The Inspectors acted as administrators, while the Trustees hired teachers, selected school sites, and set the curriculum.

This arrangement did not prove stable, and by 1851 the partisans of centralization were successful in giving the central board sole power to expend funds and in establishing the position of City Superintendent with the authority to set standards for teachers. Gradually, the Mayor also increased his power over the schools by winning the right to appoint the Ward Inspectors in 1864 and five of the then twelve city school Commissioners in 1869. At the behest of Boss Tweed, the state legislature reduced the fiscal autonomy of the schools, and eventually the independent board of education was replaced by a Department of Public Instruction that functioned as part of the municipal government. The victory of the centralists appeared to be complete.

Whatever noble goals of efficiency and equality motivated this change, control of patronage was the most tangible incentive. When in 1873 corruption scandals toppled Tweed, the centralized structure of school governance collapsed as well. For the next two decades the ward system functioned much as it had before.

## The Reform Victory

By the 1890s, however, it was apparent that ward control was creating serious management problems and that the schools were failing to keep up with the growth of population. To the blue-ribbon reformers of that period, enamoured of non-partisan civil service ideals, the solution was more centralization. Several panels of distinguished citizens made such a recommendation. For one thing, they suggested that the ward system was so complicated that it

. . . results in inefficient action, protracted delays, always vexatious and, at times, almost disastrous, and renders it almost impossible to fix responsibility where it justly belongs.[16]

Since most teachers had obtained their positions through political relationships, they opposed centralization as a threat to job security. Ironically, eighty years later, the United Federation of Teachers would also oppose decentralization to preserve job security.

The centralizers won, however, and the Charter of 1898 re-established the leadership of the City Board and Superintendent. Still there were great variations in methods of appointing staff, in salaries, in curriculum and in school organization among the boroughs. Consequently a Board of Examiners that would function to set criteria and test all prospective teachers was created. After two years experience with it, Superintendent William Maxwell decided that teachers would not only have to pass the examination, but they would be appointed in order of their standing on the eligibility tests. He wrote that the advantages

of this wise and progressive legislation are, that members of the School Board and the Board of Superintendents are relieved from the political and social pressure brought to bear by candidates and their friends to secure favorable consideration for appointment; that trained teachers are relieved from the degrading necessity of soliciting appointments or promotions; and of resorting to all kinds of wire pulling to secure their objects; and that, in short, the appointment and promotion of teachers have been taken out of politics and placed on a merit basis.[11]

Political and social pressure were not, of course, completely eliminated,[12] but the civil service, non-partisan meritocratic impetus continued to increase. Borough school boards and superintendents were eliminated in 1902. In their place, forty-six local school boards were created "to keep the schools close to the people." Appointed mainly by the borough presidents, they were given clerical help, the responsibility to report on school conditions, and the authority to dismiss local school personnel. As the central bureaucracy increased its jurisdiction, the local boards gradually lapsed into desuetude. The Board of Examiners especially extended its authority. During the depression it developed ever more elaborate tests to screen out the hordes of job applicants and to protect the civil service rights of job incumbents.

In 1917, the number of city board members was reduced from forty-six to seven, still to be appointed by the Mayor. Since the positions were not salaried and had little patronage connected with them (indeed New York school boards were usually not able to obtain even minimal staff resources), the Mayor had a relatively free hand in appointments.[13] The board had to be "balanced," however, particularly among religious groups. A sort of religious party system had grown up within the school bureaucracy—the Jewish Teachers Association and the Catholic Teachers Association were thought to be highly relevant organizations in personnel decisions. In 1943, the board membership was increased to nine, allowing the Mayor to grant de facto equal representation to the three major religious groups.

## The Dominance of 110 Livingston Street

By the 1950s, the public schools had evolved a stable, some would say almost impermeable, governance system.[14] Mayors could exercise some leverage in appointments to the board, but members served seven-year terms, and they could be removed only after formal charges and hearings. When some were removed in 1961 after evidence of extensive corruption, the state legislature established new selection procedures. Boards were to be chosen from nominations made by a screening panel composed of presidents of universities, civic associations, and educational organizations. This reform definitely improved the stature and character of board members and gave certain groups more access to the system, but it reduced the political accountability of the board to the mayor.

Although some board members were well connected in city politics and therefore personally had some political power, the board as a whole had only limited authority. It could appoint the Superintendent, but its choices were circumscribed.[15] In the history of the school system, not until 1958 did a Superintendent come from outside the system. Furthermore, although the Superintendent, the deputy, and the eight associate superintendents served technically for six-year terms, they were by custom reappointed automatically and could be removed only after formal charges and hearings. Except for the Superintendent, then, all the administrators down to the elementary principal had formal or informal tenure.

Being a product of the bureaucracy often meant that the Superintendent was more its captive than its leader. The Superintendent could nominate the deputy and associate superintendents who formed the board of superintendents, but after their appointment he often became merely the chairman of that board, casting one vote in ten. Sayre and Kaufman report that:

... For more than forty years successive boards of superintendents have patiently instructed Superintendents in the limits of power, the risks of innovation, and the necessities of unanimity if the Superintendent is to bargain successfully with the Board of Education. In the closed world in which these ten school officials operate, each familiar with the values and aspirations of the others and accustomed to mutual accommodations, the strongest inclinations run toward minimal changes in institutional habits. Even bold and energetic Superintendents quickly learn how inelastic is their organizational environment.[16]

Even if a Superintendent or board wanted to make significant changes, the personnel procedures were a formidable barrier. No teacher or administrator could be appointed without passing the written tests and the interviews of the Board of Examiners. These five men, permanently tenured veterans of the system, controlled the criteria for all professional school positions. After passing the examinations (in the case of administrators often after expending substantial sums in time and money in taking cram courses from other administrators), candidates were placed on a personnel list and could be appointed only in rank order. This system did succeed in preventing the most obvious incompetents from working in the schools, and patronage was eliminated. Clever or influential district superintendents also managed to make the procedures more flexible than they looked, but overall the personnel decisions were often irrelevant to the needs of both community and employee. Principals who spoke Yiddish were sent to schools where the parents spoke only Spanish, while schools in Jewish neighborhoods were given Irish principals. Most importantly, black and hispanic teachers and particularly, administrators, were almost totally excluded by the examinations and related procedures. In 1967, New York ranked twenty-two out of the twenty-nine largest cities in percentage of black and hispanic teachers.

The personnel system was almost exclusively an insiders' arrangement. Although in almost every other field New York's rewards and problems have long been a magnet for the nation's best talent, in public education a distinguished career in another city or state or field meant nothing until one passed the proper examinations and was placed on the list. Once given a position, however, the job and the promotion ladder was secure. A few teachers lost their licenses when the system capitulated to the McCarthy hysteria in the mid-1950s,[17] but dismissals for poor performance were almost unheard of. Personnel deficiencies were handled by shifting job assignments—usually by kicking incompetents upstairs. Guidance departments in some schools were composed of teachers who had to be removed from the classrooms, while sections of 110 Livingston Street were made up of administrators who had been rescued from the field to save their superiors from embarrassment. This naturally lowered the morale in the system and led to some incredible bureaucratic mix-ups.[18]

Stories about the inefficiency, the calculated indifference of the public employees of 110 Livingston Street are legion among New Yorkers. It was believed to be easier to have an audience with the Dahlai Lama than to see some school officials. Emissaries from the mayor's office found it impossible to obtain the most basic data on the schools. Until recently, the payroll office routinely did not answer its phone.

There were potential points of leverage within the system. Unlike Detroit or St. Louis, the New York schools are considered fiscally dependent. That means that rather than raising money through tax levies or bond issues ratified in special referenda, the schools must seek approval of their budget from the Mayor and the Board of Estimates. Dependency does not necessarily mean accountability. After 1962, the schools received lump sum appropriations, and funds could be generally shifted from one program to another without further outside review.

The budget itself was put together at 110 Livingston principally by the Office of Business Affairs and arrived at by a process that was more cumulative than analytical or priority-setting. The budget was based largely on formulas or ratios that could be implemented as populations shifted, and it provided for automatic increases to take account of inflation and wage settlements. One consequence was that in 1966 the student per capita expenditure in New York City was $960 compared to $506 in Detroit and $502 in St. Louis.[19] The actual allocation of funds for particular schools and programs was a bit of a mystery even to those most responsible. In 1967, the president of the board of education, an intelligent and skilled lawyer, remarked:

Only two people know where the money goes [at that time $1.4 billion] —God and Ferris [John J. Ferris, the director of the school budget], and when Ferris dies, God will know a great deal more than He does now.[20]

Since the board had no staff and the Mayor no serious commitment to monitoring the funds, the influence that might have existed in the budgetary process was dissipated.

Unlike other cities, New York has been blessed with competent lay groups that might have made the system more accountable. Although some groups, such as the Citizens Union and the Citizens Committee for Children, frequently take positions on school affairs; and other organizations, such as the civil rights groups, are active on special issues; two associations, the United Parents Association (UPA) and the Public Education Association (PEA), have had the most influence.[21] Both had slots on the screening panel for board members, for example.

The UPA theoretically represented public school parents throughout the city, but most of its 400,000 membership and particularly its leadership come from middle-class Jewish neighborhoods. Its political style was generally to back liberal candidates and causes within the system. It moderately supported integration and vigorously opposed aid to private schools. This approach gave UPA a kind of influence and access, but it also tied the organization closely to the system. The UPA stood for reform but not for fundamental restructuring.

The PEA is not a mass membership organization. Founded in 1895 as a part of the civic reform movement, it has remained a small elite group financed by its trustees and foundations. Mostly old line WASPs or German Jews with business, law, or financial backgrounds, the PEA Board pursued policies of protecting the schools from partisan interests while expanding their social services. Because of its prestige, its links with other educational interest groups, and its staff, PEA's public reports and informal contacts often affected policy. It was finally successful in 1958 and 1961 in influencing the system to hire a Superintendent from the outside, but overall it was too well connected with the city's establishment and too ideologically committed to the non-partisan civil service good government ethos to really rock the boat.

Vestiges of the nineteenth century ward system, the local boards survived, but as "obscure political honorary societies."[22] Their members continued to grace ceremonial occasions, and their names were inscribed on school building plaques, but their powers had been whittled away. After the scandal of 1961, the law reorganizing the central board included a provision "for revitalization of the present system of local schools boards." So the old system of fifty-four boards, each with five members, was changed to twenty-five and later to thirty-one boards, with nine members each.

But what had really changed? The selection process became more elaborate and ostensibly more representative. Replacing the borough presidents was a screening panel, half of which was controlled by officers of parent organizations and half by community leaders. These panels could recommend and rank nominees, but the central board made the final choices. The painstaking selection arrangements might have indicated that the local boards were to be given real power, but in fact they could act only as liaison between the community and the central board, a task that often proved to be as fruitless as it was thankless.

Yet the local boards were able to recruit surprisingly competent people. One of them was author Martin Mayer, who served as chairman of the board on Manhattan's east side. If an active citizenry could have successfully improved public education through those local boards, it should have been able to do so in that well-to-do cosmopolitan community. But in a 1967 *Saturday Evening Post* article, Mayer wrote what proved to be an epitaph for these powerless bodies:

To say that my five years were a complete failure would be unfair to the hundreds of people who worked so hard with me on the many things we tried to do. But the fact is that the schools in my district are still in trouble, that the programs of most children have changed little, that the quality and performance of the teaching staff have not noticeably improved. I cannot imagine any other potentially useful activity into which I could have put 2,500 hours (my wife says 5,000) and seen so little result.[23]

From this brief history, it is obvious that the tug of centralization and decentralization has long been a part of the politics of education in New York City. As contexts, ideologies, and rewards have shifted, so have the positions of the actors as they have sought advantages in the restructuring of the system's governance. By the early 1960s, however, it appeared for a time that the pendulum had stopped at centralization. Over the years the system confronted real problems in corruption, political favoritism, McCarthyism and fiscal uncertainties, but its response had become increasingly single-minded. School decisions, its defenders argued, should be made by and evaluated by professionals who in turn are certified and chosen by professionals. Lay participation should be confined to persons of impeccable credentials who are committed to the system, and their role should only be advisory. The politics of the city as a whole might be pluralistic, as Sayre and Kaufman found it, but Marilyn Gittell described the educational subsystem as "narrow, convergent, and dominated by a consensual elite." In the mid-1960s, however, two sometimes conflicting forces emerged, the United Federation of Teachers and the black and Puerto Rican groups, that could not be contained within the status quo.

## The Challenge to Bureaucracy

Historically, the number and diversity of New York's teachers led them to create a wide variety of associations. By 1900, it is estimated that there were more than 160 such groups organized by geography, subject matter, school division (elementary, high school, etc.), ethnicity and religion.[24] However useful as social clubs and discussion forums, their very numbers left teachers fragmented and unrepresented regarding the major issues of school policy. Their long struggle for unity and collective bargaining is an important factor in the teachers' response to decentralization.

The teachers union movement in New York began with the chartering of an American Federation of Teachers (AFT) chapter in 1916.[25] The organization grew slowly, but by the 1930s it was plagued by bitter factional battles between socialist and communist adherents.[26] Although each side had similar educational programs, their conflict over the external relationships of the union precluded much teacher solidarity. After World War II, the development of the Cold War and McCarthyism destroyed the communist faction, and the socialists (Teachers Guild) emerged supreme.

Still, many teachers gave their primary loyalty to groups like the High School

Teachers Association (HSTA), and status differences as well ideological divergencies continued to prevent unity. While other public employee organizations were achieving some economic gains, the relative financial condition of teachers worsened.[27] Finally, in 1960, the HSTA joined with the Guild to form the United Federation of Teachers (UFT), a local of the AFT. The following year, the UFT petitioned for a referendum on collective bargaining that passed easily, and months later the union won a smashing victory in the election for bargaining agent. After decades of fierce internal struggles, teachers in the largest school system in the country were finally represented by one organization.

Yet the UFT was not in a very strong position. Only about 15 percent of the teachers had agreed to dues check-off. There was no precedent for collective bargaining with the school board, and public employee strikes were illegal in New York. In 1962, after salary negotiations broke down, union leadership was seriously divided over the risks and ethics of striking. But at an emotional membership meeting, the sentiment on the floor was so strong that a decision was made to strike. The next day 22,000 teachers stayed home or picketed. The board responded by obtaining an injunction prohibiting the strike, and union officials called it off after one day. The leadership's face-saving rhetoric was not very impressive to the teachers, but when Governor Rockefeller suddenly "found" an additional $13 million in state aid for salary increases averaging $1,000 per year per teacher, the potential of collective bargaining was readily apparent.

The 1962 strike and wage settlement was the turning point. After that, the UFT grew steadily, and today it is the largest and most powerful teachers union in the country. The long years of factional struggle and insecurity have left their mark, however. While the membership and leadership of the union are unusually liberal and intellectually oriented, its most serious collective bargaining demands have been the very traditional union goals of organizational maintenance, job security, wages, and fringe benefits.

The union's principal proposals for educational reform were the so-called More Effective Schools (MES), which were incorporated into the 1967 contract. The MES approach involves placing the most disruptive and slowest learning students in special schools and providing them with elaborate and expensive compensatory education. Whether the MES program has been successful has been the subject of considerable academic and political debate,[28] and the only thing that can be said for certain is that the union is convinced that more money and more teachers are a more effective solution to educational achievement than administrative reform or further redistribution of power. While the UFT has altered the old policy process by vigorously representing teacher interests, overall it has been system-supporting rather than reformist. As teachers have become a policy partner in the system, the gaps between their interests and the interest of parents appear to have grown.

Doubts about the union's benign influence were voiced, particularly by the leaders of the black and hispanic communities whose children were enrolling in schools in increasing numbers. As a symbol of political and economic opportunity for Southern blacks and the main port of entry for Puerto Ricans and others from the Caribbean area, New York has had historically large numbers of the groups now called minorities.[29] But they made up only 27 percent of the city's total population in 1960. In the public schools, however, the percentage of minority group students by 1960 was 52 and growing rapidly. The only districts with white student majorities were on the fringes of the city.

This trend was caused principally by two factors. Between 1950 and 1960, 1.2 million whites, mostly middle class, left New York to be replaced by 400,000 often poor members of non-white minority groups.[30] This population flow was part of a national pattern, but what was unusual was the intense desire of the remaining whites to place their children in private schools. Even with the outflow of the white middle class during the 1950s, the city's private schools grew twice as fast as public schools, until by 1960 they enrolled about one of every three children.[31] Some of this increase occurred in the traditional Catholic schools, but there was even a faster growth of new Jewish schools and non-sectarian college prep schools. The motives for this growth were diverse and rooted in the racial attitudes and parental ambitions of thousands of families, but the political implications were fairly clear. Public education had always been part of ethnic politics in New York. The severe imbalance in the ethnic makeup of the student bodies and the leadership of public education was an obvious problem. In 1967, 11 percent of the teachers and less than 2 percent of the administrators were black or hispanic. From the minority perspective, it was one thing for the white middle class to flee the city or seek refuge in private education, but it was indefensible for them to continue to try to control public school policy and jobs. Yet the examination systems, tenure, and other union contract provisions were formidable barriers to any rapid personnel changes. The Board of Examiners, the UFT, and the Council of Supervisory Associations (administrators) did finally agree to a bit more flexibility in selection procedures, but it was too little, too late.

The failure of the system to adapt to the ethnic and class changes in its client population might have been more tolerable if it were evident that the merit procedures were producing quality education. During the 1960s, substantial numbers of New Yorkers, influenced by the media and less subjective evidence, became convinced that quality was declining. Whether they were scurrying frantically on the East Side to get their children into the acceptable nursery school that would lead to the right prep school that would lead to an Ivy League admission, or whether they were listening in the slums and *barrios* to the whispers becoming shouts alleging educational genocide, New Yorkers had lost faith in public education.

To some extent, this apostasy is part of the nature of the city. New York easily absorbs its successes and relishes its failures.[32] The Bronx High School of

Science is probably the finest single urban public high school in the country, but its achievements create little civic pride. Stuyvesant has produced the best high school mathematics team nationally for several years and Boy's High some of the country's leading basketball players. But almost no native New Yorker knows about these mathematical prodigies and the Kangaroos play their home games in a gym that would embarrass an Indiana village. Perhaps because school funds do not depend on referenda-determined tax levies or bond issues, the system provides no regular reports or journals to advertise its successes. Albert Shanker, the UFT President, has taken to purchasing weekly space in *The New York Times* to comment on school news from a union perspective, but 110 Livingston Street does not favor its constituency with any more printed information than absolutely necessary. Consequently, as the mass media and intellectual critics relentlessly expose public school failures, the system remains mute about the successful teachers, the curriculum innovations, and the achieving students that other systems would boast about.

None of this is to suggest that the very real problems in the city's schools could have been or should have been solved by better public relations. But establishing the precise degree of success and failure in the schools is a very difficult task. Though the New York schools have been the subject of several extensive reports by educational consultants, these documents have focused on the organizational and administrative defects in the system and have said little about academic achievements.[33] Similarly, data on that facet are only fragmentary in the booklength critiques of the system by Rogers and Gittell. Even the Bundy panel, which might have considered a serious evaluation of the academic performance of the schools a necessary precondition for making its recommendations for reform, declined to take responsibility for this task. It noted instead that "advice and testimony . . . from hundreds of parents, other citizens, teachers, and other professionals give witness to the decline of educational effectiveness."[34] The panel did cite some comparative evidence on New York's schools; but in the few instances where the panel cited actual data, it ignored the complicated issues of evaluation.

Five years later, however, the Fleischman Commission produced a sophisticated analysis of the performance of the city's public schools.[35] By graphing student reading scores, it found that instead of following a normal bell-shaped curve, the scores tended to cluster in two groups in sort of an **M** shape. In one group, those reading significantly above grade level were mostly white students; those in the below-level group were the minority group students. The Fleischman Commission report concluded that ". . . there are two public school systems in New York City, one that teaches children to read and one that doesn't." As white students have left the city or the system, the percentage of poor readers has increased. Overall school attendance has relatively declined,[36] and the dropout rate of entering high school freshmen has gone up from approximately 34 percent in 1966 to 47 percent in 1971. Although board of education policy has reduced the discrepancy between the number of experienced teachers in white and non-white schools and instituted numerous compensatory programs, the massive academic failure of black and hispanic children continued.[37] Their parents and community leaders, ever more aware of the social economic and political cost of that failure, naturally believed that the situation was intolerable. Whatever rationale administrators and social scientists might produce to explain the situation, in human terms it was indefensible. If the system could not educate their children, then the system would have to be broken up.

## The Decentralization Experiments

From the time of the final decline of ward governance of the schools to the modern period, there have been numerous reports on New York's public education lamenting the movement toward centralization and proposing various means of increasing citizen participation through decentralization.[38] Some were widely discussed; none were implemented. Of course, even a bureaucracy as large and tenacious as 110 Livingston Street could not make every decision, and energetic local administrators often carved out some autonomy for themselves. After World War I, Leonard Covello attracted some publicity when he turned Benjamin Franklin High School into a community school by introducing Italian into the curriculum and setting up other programs to help immigrants adjust to their new culture.[39]

A more formal experiment, the Bronx Park Community Project, was sponsored by the Public Education Association, Teachers College, and the City Superintendent. The project, begun in 1949, was designed to find out:

What degree of local autonomy for relatively small population groups within large city school systems is needed to provide a productive relationship between school and public? Is it realistic to hope that the public and the school staff will embrace an opportunity for exercising local autonomy.[40]

Located in a white middle-class neighborhood of 141,000, the project was intended to involve parents and community groups in school activities and in defining school problems. Since all published reports were written by the project's sponsors, retrospective evaluation is difficult. The authors seemed pleasantly surprised that the citizens showed interest and behaved constructively. But despite elaborate election procedures for the Community School Committees, the project's powers were strictly advisory. In today's terms, the project was more public relations than politics. At any rate, after three years it disappeared for lack of further funding.

By the 1960s, Leonard Covello and the Bronx Park were merely quaint curiosities for parents who felt increasingly frustrated by the general unresponsiveness of specific policies of the system. Protest tactics began to escalate.[41]

Demonstrations frequently turned into boycotts or sit-ins. More than 140 incidents of assaults against teachers were recorded each year from 1965 to 1967, and the CSA began to keep track of the growing number of teachers and supervisors who were forced to quit or into early retirement. Vandalism, which destroys millions of dollars of school property each year, rose, and there were even isolated instances of firebombing. Not all of the protests came from ghetto dwellers. In 1964, white neighborhood groups sponsored a boycott to protest school pairing that was 27 percent effective; a year earlier, the City-Wide Committee for Integrated Schools had managed to keep 45 percent of the city's students out for a day.[42] Whatever the source of the protest, the system was clearly in trouble.

*The Origin of the Experiments*

Riots in other cities and the rising tension in New York school politics led educators and politicians alike to view with considerable anxiety a controversy that flared up in 1966 in an East Harlem school. The new I.S. 201 was planned to be a showcase school. Its architecture won prizes for innovation and its educational programs were geared to the special vocational, recreational, and ethnic needs of its ghetto neighborhood. The hand-picked faculty was experienced and racially balanced. Although a white principal had been designated to lead the school, his assistants were to be two Puerto Ricans and one black. Despite these plans, however, neighborhood leaders complained that the site of the school doomed it to be segregated and thus of doubtful quality.[43] They demanded that white students be bused to the new school, but the board's response was to send invitations to 10,000 white families living across the East River in Bronx and Queens to consider I.S. 201. Not surprisingly, none volunteered.

When a joint meeting of the Harlem Parent's Committee and EQUAL, a sympathetic white organization, gathered to review their failure to achieve the integration of the school, the thinking of the blacks underwent an important shift. According to one parent who attended the meeting:

Isaiah Robinson suggested, almost as a joke, that since white children would not be sent into Harlem schools and black children were not being invited downtown in any meaningful numbers, maybe the blacks had better accept segregation and run their own schools. A jolt of recognition stung all of us: Isaiah's joke was a prophecy. It is hard to get across the sudden sadness we all felt. We had worked together for a long time, blacks and whites. We were close, loving friends. Now we had to agree to separate because the society would not recognize our marriage and one way or another, the black children had to be legitimized.[44]

At subsequent meetings, parents and leaders from the I.S. 201 neighborhood developed the first comprehensive community-control program in New York by proposing a representative parent-community council with the power to hire and fire teachers and to share in the development of curriculum standards and evaluation.

When negotiations with the board achieved nothing, local groups delayed the opening of the school. Then in September, the push for community control took a more provocative turn. Demonstrators from the neighborhood—joined by Harlem CORE, SNCC, the Black Panthers, and the Black Muslims—challenged the appointment of the white Jewish principal, Stanley Lisser, and demanded that a black male be selected. The school's integrated faculty, the UFT and the CSA supported Lisser, who had been picked because of his knowledge of black history. But his position was untenable and he eventually resigned.

As the media began to publicize the story, the aspirations of the I.S. 201 parents, if not their specific demands, attracted sympathetic interest from politicians like Senator Robert Kennedy and Mayor John Lindsay, from school reform groups, and even from the board itself. At that time, several new appointments had produced an unusually liberal and competent board majority. Frustrated by their inability to reform the system from the top, they had moved to increase administrative decentralization. In 1965, the board had considered and rejected the idea of decentralizing by borough.[45] Instead it decided to phase out the high school, junior high school, and elementary school divisions at 110 Livingston Street and place all schools under the authority of district superintendents. The board moved to further implement that policy in 1967 by granting these superintendents small discretionary sums to use for maintenance and supplies as well as an increase in their authority over curriculum and staff.[46] The local boards were for the first time given office space, though not staff or support services. The new guidelines also required that these boards be consulted on a wide range of matters, including selection of local administrators, but they were granted no binding authority. Most important, the board requested the Superintendent to recommend several experiments "to find means of strengthening decentralization by deepening and broadening the relationship of the communities to schools." It was understood that I.S. 201 would be one of the experiments. The board created a committee headed by John Niemeyer, president of Bank Street College, to advise them and evaluate the projects. About the same time, Mayor Lindsay appointed a panel chaired by McGeorge Bundy, president of the Ford Foundation, to make recommendations on further decentralization. Serious consideration of school decentralization was now irrevocably on the public agenda.

## The Demonstration Districts

Of the seven demonstration projects proposed, two involved minor adjustments of administrative patterns and never amounted to much. Disagreements among community groups on Manhattan's West Side prevented the creation of a consensus proposal, so the *Joan of Arc* demonstration project was unfortunately never approved. Despite the turbulence of politics in that neighborhood, the area is integrated racially and economically and has an abundance of indigenous leadership. The three demonstration districts that were approved took place in three of the most deprived and politically-troubled neighborhoods in the city.[47]

So much has been written about I.S. 201, Two Bridges, and Ocean Hill-Brownsville, that no comprehensive chronicling of their politics is necessary or possible here.[48] Still, some of the events and actors there shaped the decentralization law of 1969, and the historical and theoretical significance of the three experiments should be acknowledged.

**Planning Processes.** Although groups in the districts had previously made proposals for more autonomy, planning began in earnest in the summer of 1967. The catalyst was the board's resolution and Ford Foundation grants totalling $135,000 to local pro-decentralization groups in each district. The money and the opportunity to shape the future of school educational and hiring policies touched off struggles among political factions, anti-poverty groups, and parent associations. Eventually, relatively stable councils were formed that included UFT representatives as well as university consultants.[49] As the plans developed in each district, so did the desire for community control. In the end, all plans followed the Ocean Hill-Brownsville model calling for the election of a district governing board that would choose a project administrator. These boards and their administrators would then make the personnel, curriculum, and fiscal allocation decisions for the district. The relationship of the districts to city-wide personnel and testing standards was purposely left ambiguous.

After the plans were drawn up, negotiations were begun to obtain the central board's acceptance. But no time schedule nor approval process had been specified, and meetings were informal and sporadic. The board balked at granting the autonomy the districts demanded and urged revision of the plans to insure more representative elections and better fiscal procedures. The board approved the district plans only in principle. Without a formal charter, the demonstrations suffered a fatal loss of legal authority.

Part of the board's reluctance was due to the increasing hostility of the school employee unions to the demonstration enterprises. As the schools were ready to open in 1967, the UFT launched a city-wide strike for higher wages, smaller classes, more MES programs, and more teacher authority in dismissing disruptive children.[50] From the union's point of view, the latter three issues were evidence of its concern for educational quality as well as teacher benefits, but from the minority groups' perspective, the strike threatened the future of the demonstration projects. Furthermore, it seemed to them that not only had the white teachers failed to teach their children, but that now by labelling them disruptive, black and Puerto Rican youth could be barred from the schools. Consequently, the I.S. 201 Planning Board opposed the strike and warned teachers who participated that they would be "re-evaluated" if they attempted to return after the settlement. Earlier, some UFT officials and teachers had favored the demonstration either because of generalized pro-minority group liberal attitudes or because they hoped for a teacher-parent coalition against the bureaucracy. But by trying to force teachers to choose between the strike and the community, the planning board confirmed all of the union's worst fears about decentralization. The strike was settled after fourteen days. The central board halted attempts to screen returning teachers, but one by one UFT personnel began to leave the demonstrations. Some were pressured to go; others thought the project should choose its personnel. The Planning Board's action had publicized the goals of community control and won some support, but it had created an irreparable breach with the union.

**Elections.** From the district's viewpoint, the primary task was of consolidating support in its neighborhoods and creating the semblance of legitimate government. Elections were scheduled, and for the first time in the modern era New Yorkers had the chance to vote for a "school board." The central board had expected to establish or at least approve election procedures, but the projects could not afford to and did not want to wait. Given the confusion over nominating and balloting arrangements, the erratic nature of previous political participation in these neighborhoods, and the ambiguous authority of the new boards, the electoral conditions were hardly optimum. Yet the turnout of one-quarter to one-third of the eligible parents was better than most school or special elections.[51] There were some irregularities in the voting, and the Niemeyer Committee recommended that "one-third of the members of each board stand for re-election as soon as possible . . . to restore community confidence."

**Operations.** The district boards, however, felt the best way to gain community confidence was to show some educational progress, and so they plunged into the task of managing the demonstration projects. Their first problem was to find acceptable administrators. At the time, there were no black male principals or district superintendents in the entire city.[52] Furthermore, the boards wanted administrators who had innovative attitudes, confidence in the learning ability of minority group youngsters, and loyalty to the project rather than to 110 Livingston Street. All these factors dictated that the boards would have to go outside the regular appointment process, and this necessarily meant that each appointment would be subject to unusual scrutiny by the UFT and the CSA. The project leaders attempted to clarify their authority by gaining an agreement with the State Education Department to create the post of demonstration principal requiring state rather than city certification. The CSA objected and went to court, but the agreement was upheld. Altogether nineteen major administrative appointments (fourteen principals and five project administrators) were made by the projects. Most of them were from minority groups but Ocean Hill-Brownsville went out of its way to select some non-black principals.

It was one thing for the governing boards to write letters appointing administrators, but it was quite another to obtain cooperation from the rest of the system. Some claimed that the lack of cooperation stemmed from ethnic hostility, but it is more likely that most of the problems were caused by the threat these appointments raised to the established promotion ladder and by the limited experience of the new administrators. In any event, salaries went unpaid, supplies undelivered, and telephone calls unreturned. Those in the demonstration projects became convinced that 110 Livingston Street and its allies wanted them to fail.

When questioned later, governing board members said that they had spent 50 percent of their time on matters of survival and only 5 percent on educational philosophy. Still, the districts did experiment with some newer educational concepts, although no comprehensive program design emerged.[53] Part of the problem was the conflict between those who saw in the demonstration districts an opportunity to socialize students in ethnic solidarity and those who pursued more conventional academic goals.[54]

Even with the best of leadership and the most coherent philosophies, schools are not changed rapidly from the top without the cooperation of teachers. Consequently, attention was soon focused on the competence and loyalties of the teachers in the projects. From the teacher's viewpoint, the confusion over legitimate authority and curriculum goals and the willingness of the project leaders to suspend or reverse the system's traditional defenses against parental accusations were menacing. There was also the matter of professional pride. The demonstrations after all, were based on the assumption that those who had been in authority in the schools had failed, and it was not easy to accept decisions of boards of uncertain legality and competence—less than 10 percent of their members were college graduates. Still, the projects had no difficulty recruiting new teachers, many with liberal arts degrees from the best colleges. The new teachers, motivated by a specific commitment to educating the disadvantaged or by a desire to avoid the draft through a teaching deferment, often clashed with the older school personnel.

Finally, in May 1968, the Ocean Hill governing board decided to make an issue over the control of personnel. Thirteen teachers and six administrators were summarily transferred by the board and reassigned to 110 Livingston Street. Actual dismissals in the New York system are rare—in a five-year period only thirteen of 60,000 teachers—but threats of termination proceedings that force resignations and negotiated transfers between districts were more common. These transfers were not approved by the Superintendent, and the unions have argued they were in fact dismissals without due process. The motives and the merits of these cases have been argued passionately and *ad infinitum*[55] and need not be discussed here. Suffice it to say that many believe both sides welcomed the test of strength.

The immediate result of the muscle-flexing was a series of three strikes as well as massive publicity campaigns by the adversaries waged with tactics and rhetoric unprecedented even in New York politics. Martin Mayer wrote at the time:

The New York teachers' strike of 1968 seems to me the worst disaster my native city has experienced in my lifetime—comparable in its economic impact to an earthquake that would destroy Manhattan below Chambers Street, much worse in its social effect than a major race riot.[56]

As in most wars, neither side won a complete victory. The old personnel system would never again be as rigid as it once was, but the demonstration districts were doomed.

**Evaluation.** The Decentralization Act of 1969 (described in the next section) eventually eliminated the demonstration projects as separate entities by deliberately setting higher minimum population requirements than could be met by the demonstration districts. Nevertheless, there has been considerable interest in evaluating the political and educational consequences of their brief existence.

Given the special purposes of the demonstration districts, some evaluators have insisted that conventional measures of their effectiveness are inappropriate or even unfair.[57] Ocean Hill became a sort of Mecca for visiting educators and journalists. Several of them, observing the *esprit de corps* among the surviving staff and the bright new curriculum plans, concluded that achievement scores were certain to rise. The Institute for Community Studies later searched for harder data and found some encouragement in the fact that reading scores remained stable in I.S. 201 and Two Bridges while declining in the rest of the city (primarily because of the strikes).[58] On the other hand, Diane Ravitch, writing in *Commentary*, argued that—compared to other Brooklyn and ghetto schools—reading scores in Ocean Hill fell substantially between 1967 and 1971. Nat Hentoff, in an article called "Mugging a Corpse," countered by reminding her of the unusual disruption of learning and school organization in the districts and of the fact that the children had not taken standardized reading tests for three years and thus may have lost some test-taking skills.[59] Given these factors, further debate about the effect of the demonstration districts on student achievement seems pointless.

At any rate, the demonstration leaders stressed that their mission was the political reform of the schools, not pedagogical innovation. Community participation, not compensatory education, was the goal.[60] By this measure, the demonstrations achieved some success in recruiting new people to policy-making positions. Only 20 percent of the new board members had professional occupations, 40 percent were employed by anti-poverty organizations or as paraprofessionals, and 22 percent were housewives. Over 85 percent were public school parents. Board membership was an important impetus for political and vocational mobility for some. Among parents as a whole a belief grew that the community had increased its influence over the schools, and their feelings of alienation toward school authorities and teachers declined. Of course, the cast of characters had substantially changed in these districts, and some of the project leaders had become figures of considerable fame—even of heroic stature. This was true of Rhody McCoy of Ocean Hill-Brownsville:

McCoy became a national black figure overnight, whose doings were regularly followed by both the white and black press. He received innumerable awards from black groups. His very name was used as advertising copy in a national magazine (*New York Magazine*). He was in demand as a guest speaker and signed several contracts with a large publishing company to write educational books. A survey by Louis Harris and Bert Swanson showed him to rank third as a black leader in the nation.[61]

Black preachers, politicians, and revolutionaries have received this kind of attention in the city before, but never a black educator.

It is difficult to generalize from these occurrences, however. The events that gave rise to and characterized the demonstration districts are probably unique. In particular the projects were able to attract the short-run support of allies that might not have been ordinarily available. Journalists and university educators were useful; but two supporters, foundations and anti-poverty groups, were absolutely essential.

The Rockefeller, Carnegie, New York, Field, and Episcopal foundations all provided some funds for the demonstration projects, but the key, financially and politically, was Ford. During the first I.S. 201 controversy, two Ford staff members visited the neighborhood to talk to the parents and returned impressed with their cause. McGeorge Bundy and other foundation officials played a role in convincing the central board to establish the demonstration. According to the Foundation's 1968 report, it granted nearly $1.4 million, "primarily for technical assistance to parent and community-centered groups who have been given greater authority in running the schools." The sums given to the districts for planning and holding the elections[62] have already been mentioned, and their importance cannot be underestimated. They got the projects going and lent them legitimacy.

Later, the districts were given funds to hire paraprofessionals who were used by some governing boards for both their educational impact and their political ties with the community. Also critical were the grants given the Institute for Community Studies at Queens College. The Institute, directed by one of the most prolific and persuasive spokeswomen for community control, Professor Marilyn Gittell, provided assistance to the districts on legal, budgetary, public relations, and educational resource problems.[63] Most important, its staff publicized the districts' cause, providing sympathetic and influential evaluations of the political processes and educational consequences of decentralization.

A lot of good and considerable mischief can be done with grants of $1.4 million. Foundation officials now concede that some mistakes were made.

During 1967-68, for example, one appointed board in Manhattan found itself in a contest within a foundation-financed protest group. Although the regular and appointed board was liberal, pro-decentralization, and ethnically balanced, funds from Ford (chanelled through the Institute for Community Studies) and from the Field Foundation were given to the West Side Committee for Decentralization to finance elections and to hire community organizers with the aim of challenging the authority of the regular board. Bitterness grew in a conflict over the right to appoint a junior high school principal, and the regular board found its meetings disrupted and its business difficult to conduct. When the funds ran out, the Committee disappeared.[64]

The other non-system source of money and manpower for the demonstration was the anti-poverty organizations in each district.[65] These agencies had been organized in the city's poorer neighborhoods before the decentralization controversy. Like their clients, they generally supported integration as the educational remedy. Since an important reason for the creation of these agencies was the belief that powerlessness was an essential cause of poverty, it was inevitable that anti-poverty groups would become involved in the community control controversy.[66]

After their initial confrontation at I.S. 201, HARYOU-ACT, one of the two anti-poverty agencies in Harlem, held a community-wide conference to publicize the demands of the parents. From then on, the agency was deeply committed. As one participant remembers it:

When (Livingston) Wingate was the head of HARYOU-ACT, any group fighting an issue could get services. During the I.S. 201 struggle, he provided sound trucks, pickets, the use of office machines, and secretaries.[67]

Many of the key I.S. 201 leaders were staff members or paid consultants of MEND, the other Harlem agency. During one of the strikes, Humberto Cintron, its Executive Director declared:

Everyone seems to forget that it was the teachers who were the villains in this drama. If East Harlem is to be the next battlefield in this war for community control let the ground rules be perfectly clear. MEND will stand behind I.S. 201 come hell or high water and if the City of New York chooses to give its police protection to the striking teachers rather than to the schools, the parents and non-striking teachers of East Harlem, then as we say in the vernacular ****** [68]

During the strikes, both anti-poverty groups organized alternatives to the schools the UFT closed and provided additional staff to those that stayed open. In Two Bridges, anti-poverty and foundation money was joined to create the pro-decentralization group.[69] Originally, the Parent Development Program (leadership training for poor people) was funded by OEO; but as its original grant expired, it turned to Ford. The foundation, seeing a chance to launch decentralization in a multi-ethnic neighborhood, urged PDP to expand its focus and to become the nucleus for a demonstration district. The grants were made, but PDP, though influential, was never able to dominate the planning council or the demonstration. The multi-ethnic character of the district led to fierce power struggles and eventually to a leaderless stalemate.

In Ocean Hill-Brownsville, the anti-poverty agency, the Brownsville Community Council (BCC), was most responsible for conceptualizing an independent school board for the area and for negotiating a Ford demonstration grant. During the strikes, the BCC aided the local governing board with the tools of modern confrontation (soundtracks, mimeograph machines, etc.) to consolidate the support of the parents. The Brownsville Parent Association became a delegate agency of BCC. There was some criticism of these activities in ghetto communities. The New York City Commission on Human Rights reported:

Domination by community action groups has caused resentment among many parents, especially those active in the parents associations who feel that the parent members should come from the PAs. The parents distrust control by these groups and feel that politics and personal gain rather than education are uppermost among their motives. This has raised charges from parents that the boards are not representative of the community and that parents have a small voice on them.[70]

The demonstration districts, however, could not have survived at all without the support of the anti-poverty organizations. Reciprocally, the school confrontations enormously enhanced the visibility and popularity of the agencies in the poorer neighborhoods.[71] When the political establishment also came to that realization, the process of dismembering the anti-poverty program began.

In evaluating the demonstration districts, one can not overlook the enormous amount of conflict that they caused or had visited upon them. Clarifying that distinction and assigning blame has preoccupied many other writers; but here we are more concerned with examining the consequences of the conflict.

Conflict can, of course, be a necessary and even creative part of politics— loosing new energies, redressing old grievances. From the Institute of Community Studies perspective:

The community groups that nurtured the concept of community control viewed the system as a protagonist from the beginning. They initiated the experiments in order to change the school system; they had no intention of accepting things as they were. . . . Once you establish institutional change and a redistribution of power as a primary goal of the participants, however, it is difficult to imagine any community strategy which would not have ended in conflict. From the point of view of evaluation, the action of the districts which were labeled "disruptive" may well have been the means for producing change and must therefore be viewed as essential to goal fulfillment.[72]

Surveys show that the parents in the districts were not nearly as angry about the schools or as ideologically militant as either the supporters or opponents of decentralization made them out to be.[73] Initially, being pro-decentralization was an acceptable position within the UFT. But suspicion on both sides quickly drained the reservoirs of good will. The combination of inexperienced community leaders and insecure union officials; the mossbacks at 110 Livingston who discredited central authority; the separatist firebrands who exploited the tensions inherent in the experiment; and finally the bungling by "responsible" leaders led to political disaster.

Murray Edelman suggests in *Symbolic Uses of Politics*[74] that people and groups who cannot hope to understand the complex issues and events of modern politics fasten onto symbols to create identification. The demonstration districts, particularly Ocean Hill-Brownsville, created potent symbols—among the most polarizing in the city's history. Militant rhetoric and ethnic power struggles make good copy and TV filmclips. Day after day during the 1968 strikes, the front pages and the six o'clock news were filled with images of lines of police struggling to protect teachers from angry community residents, and non-striking teachers from those aggressively manning the picket lines. Shouts and curses—"kikes, nigger lover, scab"—quickly create symbolic identification that overwhelms rational consideration of the restructuring of school governance. For the minority group leaders and their allies in the foundations, universities, and media, the demonstrations became a crusade against everything that was reactionary and racist in urban politics. For the teachers, white municipal workers and government officials, and their allied ethnic and religious group members, the demonstrations threatened all the status and stability that hard work and bargaining had won for them. For a time, it seemed that the numbers, skills, and energies of those in the uncommitted center would be too few to effect any compromise. But even at the height of the strikes, a more carefully articulated approach to decentralization involving new legislation was being developed.

## The Legislative Struggle over Decentralization

During the spring of 1967, city-wide school decentralization first began to be seriously considered. The board, embarrassed by the sympathy the I.S. 201 parents had received and by its own inability to make the bureaucracy responsive, moved to give local boards more consultation privileges and to establish demonstration districts. The confrontation at I.S. 201 also led the city's liberal press and politicians to reassess their traditional commitment to central as against local authority. Decentralization became an abstract good that even the UFT could support. Only the question of actually redistributing power seemed to remain. That question, however, led to a controversy quite unprecedented in American educational politics.

### The Bundy Panel

Ironically, the event that led to the first legislative proposal went almost unnoticed. Budget director Fred Hays had determined that, if the state school funds coming to the city were calculated on a borough-by-borough basis, the amount would be substantially increased. State aid allotments are dependent on real estate assessments. Manhattan's extraordinarily high property value consequently had the effect of lowering the overall amount of money coming from the state. Mayor Lindsay, willing to try any gimmick to obtain more state funds, petitioned the legislature in February 1967 to adopt the Hays formula.

Requests for additional state funds are so commonplace in New York that The *Times* gave the Mayor's speech page 38 coverage.[75] But the legislature was in a surprisingly receptive mood. It accepted the proposal, which amounted to an extra $108 million—with one string attached. The law required the Mayor to prepare a comprehensive study "to foster greater community initiative and participation in the development of educational policy."[76]

The motives of the men who conceived this arrangement were varied and complex. House Speaker Anthony Travia regarded the "study" language as more of a suggestion that a mandate, but Senate Majority Leader Earl Brydges had long believed the city schools should be governed on a borough basis. Commissioner of Education James Allen also saw the legislation as an opportunity to move toward decentralizing the system. As for the Mayor, his willingness to claim intellectual paternity for school decentralization has waxed and waned with his political goals. It is clear that he was genuinely concerned over the gulf between 110 Livingston Street and his minority-group constituency, and that he was seeking levers to change more than the funding of the system.

Given that intention, it was obvious that the study could not be done by the Mayor's staff even if that were logistically possible. Consequently, the Mayor decided to create an independent study commission and asked McGeorge Bundy, the new head of the Ford Foundation, to chair it. Lindsay knew that the Foundation was generally sympathetic and had the staff and other resources to operate the commission. The others on the panel were Mitchell Sviridoff, head of the city's Human Resources Administration, Francis Keppel, former U.S. Commissioner of Education, Antonia Pantoja, President of Puerto Rican Forum, and Benetta Washington, Director of the Women's Training Center of the Job Corps and wife of the Mayor of Washington, D.C.

The panel was, then, ethnically and sexually balanced, but there was no respresentative of the school establishment. The board of education was already angry that the legislature had given the reorganization task to the Mayor, and its members began to raise the old specter of political interference in education. Finally Board President Alfred Giardino was invited to join. Though he was personally sympathetic to more decentralization, neither he nor the board ever really approved of the goals or operation of the panel. In the end, he was the lone dissenter to the report.

The panel knew that it had only about six months to make recommendations. That fact and a low $50,000 budget precluded it from doing any basic research.[77] The panel held hearings and meetings with interest groups; it also sent out questionnaires, but mostly it worked to hammer out compromises on the tough political questions involved in the move toward decentralization.

November 9, 1967, the panel released its 119-page report. It recommended that the city's public schools be reorganized in a "Community School System, consisting of a federation of largely autonomous school districts and a central educational agency." The thirty to sixty districts would be governed by 11-member boards—six members selected by parents and five by the Mayor. Each district would have policy responsibility for all regular schools within its boundaries. So long as state standards and existing tenure rights were preserved, districts would have the authority to make all personnel decisions. A city board selected by the Mayor or nominated by community boards (the panel could not agree) and a city Superintendent would continue to exist but their functions would be dramatically reduced. Essentially, their task was to operate the special schools, collect school funds and determine the lump sum allotments to the districts, promote integration, and provide certain other centralized services at the district's request. The transition phase was to be monitored by the State Commissioner of Education.

There was a certain paradox in the Bundy recommendations. If implemented, they would have led to more community control of education in New York than in any other large city in the country. Yet, by ending the traditional isolation of the Mayor from New York school politics, the panel might have created a powerful new centralizing force in City Hall. The paradox was temporarily resolved for the panel members because Mayor Lindsay was at that time committed to decentralization. But the abstract question of where the centralizing, integrating function should be placed in an overall decentralized system is one of the most difficult for policy planners to solve.

Board President Giardino's dissent in the report was short and rather *pro forma*, but the whole board issued an official rebuttal the same day the report was released.[78] Noting that it had been committed to further decentralization since the previous spring, the board conceded that existing staff procedures were inadequate and that local boards needed to be strengthened (above all be given the right to hire district superintendents). It therefore asked for legislative powers to carry out these goals believing decentralization could be accomplished through delegation. But the board rejected the creation of "full-blown, autonomous, fragmented, parallel school districts," and it was irritated over the role the panel gave the state and the Mayor.

Neither the UFT nor the CSA welcomed the panel's report. Since the panel's proposals jeopardized the examination system and the career ladders on which most incumbent administrators had prospered, CSA members had solid pragmatic grounds for their opposition. The UFT, however, took a more ideological stance. Sandra Feldman, the decentralization expert on the UFT staff, agreed that the school hierarchy was "archaic, ineffective," and that "the long-needed break-up of the unresponsive school bureaucracy is coming." But she feared that decentralization would impede further desegregation and distract attention from the problems of overcrowding and insufficient resources in the system.[79] No matter how much "control" poor communities had over their school, they could not integrate or raise funds themselves, she argued, and decentralization might permit the affluent to evade their responsibilities. Furthermore, the Bundy panel had suggested not very subtly that the UFT might itself be decentralized with local leaders arranging "hours and working conditions with community board and superintendents."[80] While the union did have some decentralization in its administrative structure, union leadership had long feared that decentralizing the system ultimately might lead to district-by-district negotiation and, worse, separate bargaining units (some of which might be controlled by the NEA or groups like the Afro-American Teachers Association). Consequently, though the UFT still professed an interest in decentralization, it did not believe communities should have any additional power over teachers.[81]

*The Legislative Process—1968*

The panel's report was cheered by the UPA, many local boards, and, most importantly, Mayor Lindsay. His task was to take the document and turn it into legislation. The bill that emerged from his staff followed the Bundy proposal in many aspects, with three important exceptions.[82]

1. Selection procedures for the central board were to be generally the same as for the then current system.
2. High schools were to remain under the jurisdiction of the central board.
3. Teachers would still have to pass a local qualifying exam administered by the central board (not the Board of Examiners).

The Mayor had sought a compromise, but had not engaged in the necessary negotiations. The draft pleased very few and served to alienate him from the community control constituency that he might have led. Furthermore, state legislators for whom this was the first exposure to the problem were shocked at the length and complexity of the proposal. Governor Rockefeller and the legislative leadership became very wary of taking any firm position.

Consequently, the role of designing a legislative response to the proposal was assigned to Senator John Marchi, Chairman of the City of New York Committee and later John Lindsay's conservative opponent in the 1969 Republican mayoral primary. Marchi, who represented Staten Island, had previously supported school reorganization, but seeing a chance to lead the growing go-slow-on-decentralization coalition, he introduced his own legislation modeled after the central board proposals.

Since it appeared that a stalemate might develop, Commissioner Allen began to develop his own plan for the State Board of Regents. The Regents plan (as it became known) began by requiring the replacement of the incumbent city board of education with a new 5-member board appointed by the Mayor. This board would then have the mandate to decentralize the system into fifteen districts plus a limited number of experimental areas (the demonstration districts). These local boards would have the same kind of authority as fiscally-dependent school boards had in the rest of the state and eventually would be elected by all district voters. The size of the districts (about the same as in Pittsburgh or Cleveland), it was felt, would insure against their capture by racial extremists or parochial interests and would encourage the development of professional rules and standards.

The legislature now had six major alternatives to consider (proposals from Bundy, Lindsay, Marchi, Regents, UFT, and CSA)[83] in addition to variations proposed by the many other interested organizations and individuals. As the several coalitions expanded their alliances and articulated their grievances, the lobbying grew more intense. Governor Rockefeller made an attempt to mediate, but finally the legislature followed its customary pattern—when faced with controversy—of delaying the ultimate decision. It passed Senator Marchi's temporizing measure expanding the city board from nine to thirteen members and giving the Mayor four new appointments. The reconstituted board was then empowered to adopt decentralizing measures for the following year, subject to the approval of the Board of Regents, and to prepare a comprehensive school organization plan for the 1969 session.

*The Legislative Process–1969*

During the summer following the legislative action, a dispute broke out over the attempt of the Ocean Hill-Brownsville governing board to transfer nineteen teachers. The divisions in the central board between the pro-Lindsay (pro-decentralization) members and the more establishment-oriented members was such that for several months no president could be chosen. Nor was the board able to agree on a plan to enforce Judge Rivers' decision that the teachers had been deprived of due process and had to be given back their jobs. Consequently, the UFT struck three different times, and by the time a settlement of sorts was reached, the atmosphere surrounding the decentralization issue was poisoned. As one legislative staff person expressed it, "The difference between the 1968 and 1969 session was the difference between disagreement and real rancor!" As strikes polarized feelings between blacks and Jews, one of the strongest liberal coalitions in the country was shattered. The UFT ended its criticism of the "archaic, ineffective" school bureaucracy and gave up its abstract commitment to decentralization to form an alliance with the CSA and the Central Trades

Labor Council (the school custodians had been invaluable allies in padlocking the schools during the strikes). Bruised from the demonstration district debacle and facing re-election, Mayor Lindsay declined further leadership of the decentralization forces. The school board, with its new majority of pro-decentralization members, was barely able to agree long enough to produce the plan required by state law. The final document contained four different concurring opinions and three dissenting opinions. The board's vice president, black minister Milton Galamison, disowned the plan saying:

At best the proposal is designed to patch up a school system which cannot be patched up. At worst, in the process of clinging to all the liabilities of the present structure and in keeping control of the major power functions, this proposal is a betrayal of most of the change for which the people have spoken.[84]

With the city's leadership paralyzed, responsibility for reorganizing the nation's largest school system returned to Albany. The state legislators, who had hoped that an agreement could be worked out among the contending parties in the city that would require only minor modification, were not pleased to find the decentralization issue threatening to engulf the 1969 session. Again the Board of Regents, using their expertise and prestige in the role of honest brokers, submitted draft legislation. The bill was an amalgam of earlier proposals and attempted to give the local boards enough autonomy to create diversity and innovation while leaving to the central board the last word on budgetary matters, collective bargaining, capital construction, and personnel appeals. The decentralization groups were pleased. Several major political leaders flirted with support of the Regents' proposal, but learning of the union's opposition to it, they backed off.

Then a new stage of the legislative process began. Albert Shanker and the Democratic legislative leadership began personal negotiations. At first, the venture seemed promising, since the union and the party had close ties and presumably were better able to resolve differences. But when the liberal wing of the party (Manhattan white and minority-group legislators) saw the agreement ensuing, they denounced it as a sellout abandoning the principle of community control.

With the Democratic party in disarray, the issue thus finally and ironically fell to the Republicans to settle. Their constituencies, mostly upstate and suburban, were not particularly interested in reorganizing the city's schools, except to be certain it did not cost too much and that black militants did not take over. Governor Rockefeller, however, had substantial support among minority groups, and he instructed his staff to work out a new settlement.

It was now obvious that the forces both for and against decentralization were strong enough to veto each other. With logistical support from the anti-poverty organizations[85] and ideological backing from considerable segments of the liberal press and civic organizations, the decentralization advocates were formidable, if not always united. Yet the unions and their allies consistently had the upper hand. Not only did they have more of the raw materials of political power—money, campaign support, constituencies readily mobilized for picket lines and bus trips to Albany—but the symbolism surrounding decentralization (black vs. white, dissenter vs. established authority) also helped influence the legislature. Furthermore, the controversy and stalemate benefited the unions. They could live with the status quo, and sooner or later public interest in decentralization would wane.

Consequently, although the Republican leadership kept in touch with all relevant groups, the key negotiations were with the unions and the few Republican legislators from the city, most of whom were quite conservative. The remaining issues to be solved were the selection of the central board, the status of the Board of Examiners and existing personnel system, control over maintenance and construction funds, and the future of the demonstration districts. In the end, the unions-conservative coalition won in most areas.[86] The power of Mayor Lindsay over the city board was reduced. Overseeing decentralization was entrusted to a so-called interim board having one member chosen by each of the five borough presidents. After the interim period, five members were to be elected by each borough and two chosen by the Mayor. The Board of Examiners and its paraphernalia was preserved, as were tenure and all other job perquisites specified in the contract. But the system of ranking candidates for supervisor was abolished so that local boards could hire anyone who was on the eligibility list. Furthermore, districts whose students ranked in the bottom 45 percent on city-wide reading tests could hire any teacher who had passed the National Teachers Exam with an average score or better. This was to give minority group districts more flexibility in finding teachers of their own ethnic background. The districts would also control promotions, though inter-district transfers (the Ocean Hill-Brownsville fiasco) were forbidden and intra-district transfers subject to careful regulation. The city board also retained control over capital construction, except that community boards were to be consulted throughout and were empowered to select the architect and to spend up to $250,000 for maintenance without special approval. Finally, the demonstration districts, which were of great importance to minority groups, were to be disbanded when the new boundary lines were drawn.

A few days after the details were settled, the bill went to the legislature where—with an enormous sigh of relief—it was passed in one day by the Senate 48 to 9 and in the Assembly 125 to 23. Almost all the no votes were cast by the ardent community control advocates (though many minority group legislators supported the legislation). In the city, the community-control advocates greeted the measure with scorn or chagrin. Their goal of nearly autonomous districts had not been achieved, and they had lost on most of the symbolic issues. But it was incorrect to say, as some did, that the legislative changes were meaningless or irrelevant to the need for redistribution of power and more lay participation. Though the legislation was full of delicate compromises and was even contradictory in places, at its heart were the new community school boards, which for the first time had been given definite powers over personnel, expenditures, and curriculum. In time, the legislature's general intention to decentralize would be turned into concrete policies by statutory interpretation and by the behavior of the new boards and central authorities.

## The Implementation of the Decentralization Law

Despite the three-year legislative contest and the extraordinary detail in the 64-page act finally passed, some important issues were left unresolved. The three most important decisions preceding the implementation of decentralization were the creation of district boundaries, the development of operational guidelines, and the arrangements for the community school board elections. Those tasks also confronted Detroit as it decentralized, and a comparison of the decision-making processes and results in the two cities is instructive.

### District Boundaries

In both New York and Detroit, districts with limited administrative functions already existed when the decentralization laws were passed. These districts appeared to have little political significance, or citizen identification, however, and politicans in neither Michigan nor New York took them very seriously. During both legislative struggles, districting proposals were made that would have radically altered the size, shape, and political character of the existing city districts. In the end though, the decentralization laws in both cities set some restrictions on the new districts and then turned the task of creating precise boundaries over to the city boards of education.

In New York, because of the legislative desire to eliminate the three demonstration districts, the restrictions in the law were much tighter than those in Michigan. The New York legislation specified that there could be no more than thirty-three and no fewer than thirty community districts. There was to be a minimum of 20,000 elementary and junior high school students in each district. That meant that the total adult population of each district would be about 250,000. The Bundy proposal had suggested as many as sixty districts, but the specific antagonisms toward the demonstration projects, a general fear that extremists might dominate other small districts, and a desire to limit administrative costs led the legislature to reject smaller districts.

An important factor in the legislature's stance was the adamant opposition of the UFT and the CSA to small districts. In part, this was a pragmatic position. If, from a union perspective, decentralization had objectionable consequences, then sixty districts were surely worse than thirty. But the position was also a reflection of the inbred character of New York teachers and administrators and the stereotypes they held about local control elsewhere. In response to an interviewer's question about the role of local school boards, Albert Shanker, UFT President replied:

I'm not much one for local school boards or local communities. I don't believe very much in the warmth of the little Mississippi or Alabama town. I never felt that the small town was a warm place for me or for members of other minority groups. I've always felt that the big city was a much warmer place, and that because of its cosmopolitan nature and its multiple groups, each with the power to check other groups from doing certain things wrong, the bigness of our country, the bigness of our cities, is something I felt much more positive about. My own feelings are that small communities, small school boards, really cannot provide the necessary variety of educational programs. They can't provide a proper base of financial support. And the smaller the community and the school board, the greater the likelihood of bigotry and provincialism.[88]

The problem of drawing boundaries for the new decentralized districts was first faced by the Marchi Law's reconstituted 13-member board. As required, that board issued a tentative plan for decentralization. The board's cautious attitude was evident from the plan's preface:

The board of education has developed a plan which would effect the transition to a community school district system with the least possible uncertainty and with necessary policy safeguards and fiscal controls.

Thus, this plan will not change any pupil's school. Each New York City public school pupil would attend the same school on the effective date of this plan that he previously attended.[89]

As in Detroit, the boundary question was the most controversial on the agenda. Seven hearings were held, but the board, though legally committed to thirty districts, decided to put off specifying the boundaries. Within the plan, however, was a statement of the board's districting philosophy. The "basic building blocks of the community school districts" were to be the intermediate or junior high schools and their feeder elementary schools. In clustering these building blocks into districts, the board said it would be guided by:

1. The special and common educational needs of the communities and children involved, transportation facilities, and existing and planned school facilities;
   a. Suitable geographic size for efficient policy making and economic management based on experience in New York City and throughout New York State;
   b. Convenient location for the attendance of pupils;
   c. Reasonable number of pupils; and

2. Relationship to geographic units for which New York City plans and provides services.[90]

Conspicuously absent was any declaration about the districts' relationship to integration, except that each community board would have responsibility for reviewing and modifying attendance zones within its district to comply with civil rights law. Unlike Detroit, New York made no serious attempt to use district lines to further integration, although some claimed that destroying the demonstration projects was necessary to stamp out separatism.[91]

By the time the tentative boundary lines were to be published, the 13-member board had been replaced by the 5-member (so-called) interim board. This board had sent out 3,000 questionnaires to individuals and groups soliciting views on district patterns. The 50 percent response rate was then computer-analyzed and, according to the board (no breakdowns were ever published), the response overwhelmingly favored minimal change.

However convenient "minimal change" might be for parents, the major beneficiaries were incumbent district administrators and board members whose established political contacts could be maintained. From the board's perspective, district stability was a welcome respite amidst the controversies decentralization has created.

Thus the chance to totally re-examine the districts in the light of the new demands of decentralization was passed on. When one attempts to discover the rationale behind the then existing district lines that proved so attractive to the board, it turns out to be impossible to push back the curtain of failing memories and administrative clichés. When the fifty-four district system was created in 1927, many of the boundaries followed health district lines. The consolidation of 1965 was intended to give every assistant superintendent a single district, but the new district lines were drawn by headquarters staff after little consultation with the public. Of course, those districts were not intended to play a very important role.

In any event, the board decided to make no district alterations in Queens (by choice) and in Staten Island (by law). In the Bronx and Brooklyn, where the former districts were too large, a new district was carved out in each consistent with the principal of "minimal change." Actually, the new Brooklyn district was created by adding twelve schools to the eight in the Ocean Hill-Brownsville district, thus overwhelming the constituency of the governing board there.

In Manhattan, however, the problem was not so simple. Not only did two of the demonstration districts exist there, but the six regular districts, depleted by the loss of child-bearing families, no longer had the stipulated minimum enrollments. Reduction in the number of districts always creates political problems. Some hoped that if an exception were made for Manhattan, the demonstrations might be revived. Others saw the possibility of establishing a Puerto Rican district in east Harlem if six were permitted in Manhattan. Several groups argued that redistricting would jeopardize the fragile integration arrangements at some schools.[92] Finally the Board appealed to the state legislature to allow an exception for Manhattan. Although the other boroughs protested, the legislature agreed so long as the demonstrations were eliminated.

Generally then the new district boundaries turned out to be quite similar to the old lines. The demonstrations, particularly Ocean Hill-Brownsville, protested their demise

Despite the wedges people try to forge in our community and decisions of the politically-motivated interim Board of Education, we parents will control these eight schools despite any 'legal' decision to return our children to their former state. Mr. McCoy and our eight principals will stay here as long as we desire.[93]

But after the elections their money and authority ran out, and their supporters once again became a pressure group within the system.

## Elections

The problem of selection procedures for local boards has created a dilemma for community control advocates. On one hand, they have wanted to emphasize the similarity in authority and autonomy of neighborhood boards to the typical American local school board. On the other, they have been reluctant to adopt the small-town and suburban pattern of open school board elections. In such areas, public school parents are usually a majority or near majority of the voters and in either case they usually possess about the same ethnic and class backgrounds as non-parents. But in the larger cities, with their higher proportions of non-parents, and private school parents, public school parents may be a minority of the electorate. Moreover, they are usually more black and lower class.[94] Consequently, by weighing parental votes disproportionately or excluding non-parents altogether, methods have been sought to insure that these parents (the intended beneficiaries of community control) would in fact dominate the neighborhood boards.

There is a contradiction in these two community control goals, because to the extent the neighborhood boards are given the authority to be "real" governing bodies, the more likely it is that they would be covered by judicial one man-one vote rules which would nullify any parental advantage. The community control theorists attempted to solve the problem by arguing that, since their boards would not have taxing power, they could give parents disproportionate power in selection of the board.[95] Existing law is not on their side. The Supreme Court has not confronted the particular question of decentralized school boards in urban school elections, but it has been striking down barriers to voting in school board elections.[96] In 1968 it used school boards as an example of local governmental units in which election districts are bound by the one man-one vote rule.[97] In 1970, it applied that principle to elections for governing boards of public junior colleges. Justice Hugo Black's majority opinion declared that a state was free to select members of an educational board by appointment rather than election, but "once a state has decided to use the process of popular election. . . we see no constitutional way by which equality of voting power may be evaded."[98]

## Procedures

The problem of representation on the new school boards had been fiercely debated in New York since the time of the Bundy panel. The pro-community control forces advocated a structure that preferred parents, while those opposed insisted on broader representation. The Bundy report found a compromise calling for an 11-member board with six positions to be filled by parent elections and five by mayoral appointment. The Albany legislature, unwilling to strengthen Mayor Lindsay's role and worried about the complexity and legality of the Bundy proposals, decided to require direct elections.

In addition to stipulating nominating procedures, voter eligibility, and the time of the election,[99] the other important decision the legislature made was to accept the proportional representation system of counting the ballots. In 1937, New York began an experiment with PR as a method of election for the city council, but it was abandoned in 1945 when it resulted in the election of two Communists, and generally fragmented the traditional Democratic party major-ities.[100] Proportional representation has always had a champion in George Hallett, the legislative director of the Citizen's Union. He and friends in other educational groups made a personal lobbying effort that sold PR to the legislature on the basis that it would insure the representation of minorities or, alternative-ly, that it would prevent control of the districts by extremists. The only decision left to the interim board was whether the community boards should have a minimum of seven or a maximum of fifteen members. In order to facilitate PR, the board finally agreed on nine members.

The electoral arrangements ran into immediate trouble. The district lines had been fixed on December 22. Registration of voters was to take place from January 2-16, and the election was to be held on January 27. The deadline for nomination petitions was only nine days before the election. Since these were the first official school board elections in the city's modern history, they would have been difficult in any event, but the election procedures came close to creating chaos.

In order to add some rationality to the election and possibly to influence its outcome by stimulating parent participation, the Ford Foundation funded voter registration and education efforts. Money also came from the New York Urban Coalition, and eventually $60,000 was spent to get out the vote in a campaign through the media and some 3 million fliers and pamphlets.[101] Community meetings and speakers bureaus were organized by the Proportional Representation Educational Project, headed by a UPA official. Another organization, the Coalition for an Effective Community School System, represented forty city groups sympathetic to decentralization. They attempted to mobilize the parent vote, while pressing for election reforms. The registration drive was not, however, very successful in finding additional parent voters.[102] Though it cost over a million dollars, only 40,461 additional voters were registered, and nonparents outnumbered parents five to three.

More ominous was the tactical and ideological split that developed in the pro-community control forces. Despite misgivings about the law and the election procedures, the predominantly white Coalition was held together by the belief that the arrangements should be given a chance, and that if the pro-community control voters stayed home the new machinery would be captured by their opponents. Others, mostly Puerto Rican and black groups, were so disillusioned with the legislative process and fearful of the elections that they advocated a boycott. The potentially powerful United Bronx Parents Association declared:

We refuse to participate in an exercise in futility. Our children are facing real and terrible problems in their schools every day. We cannot afford to waste time playing games which pretend that change is taking place—when in fact, nothing is changed and our children are still being crippled.

False reform is the enemy of true reform. We refuse to implement this unfair, immoral, retrogressive law because:

*The local school boards will be powerless.*
*The Election Procedures are undemocratic.*
*The District Lines are illegitimate.* [103]

Finally, however, the board did agree to postpone the election until March to decrease the confusion and permit more campaigning.[104]

Except for Isaiah Robinson, the black member from Manhattan, the board of education did relatively little to inform voters or increase turnout. The Board of Elections that was supposed to manage the affair was totally unprepared for PR, and an unusual number of improprieties were alleged in the balloting and the complex counting.[105] Still, 279 candidates were eventually certified winners. The decentralized era in New York educational politics had begun.


*Outcomes*

Shortly after the election, representatives of the Coalition met to discuss a report on the outcome gathered by the United Parents Association and the Institute for Community Studies. From their perspective, the news was grim. In the demonstration districts, the electoral system had produced boards dominated by lower-class and minority-group public school parents. Since city-wide public school enrollment was increasingly from the lower classes and minority groups, the community-control advocates had intended that city-wide decentralized elections would have the same result in poor neighborhoods. But as their reports showed, the new board members were likely to be neither lower-class, nor minority-group, nor necessarily committed to public schools. According to Boulton Demas, who analyzed the election for the Institute, the profile of the typical board member was "a white male Catholic, professionally or technically trained, with two children and living in his district for about nine years."[106] Looking at these results, Maurice Berube, the co-director of the Institute declared ". . . the community school board election was a disaster unparalleled in the history of the New York City school system."[107]

The results are, of course, considerably more complicated than that, but, as in Detroit, districts with overwhelmingly minority-group student populations produced white-dominated boards. There are several explanations for this phenomenon. The simplest is that in an election open to all citizens, it is to be expected that a representative result would reflect the ethnic proportions of the populace at large rather than of public school pupils or even of their parents. As Table 8-1 shows, whites won 72 percent of the seats, blacks 17 percent, and those of hispanic descent 11 percent. When one compares these results to the 1970 census data, which shows that the total city population is 64 percent white, 20 percent black, 13 percent Spanish, and 3 percent others, and when one considers that the non-white population is likely to be younger and otherwise not registered to vote, it is evident that the election results come close to reflecting accurately the ethnic proportions of the city's adults.

In most public school elections, parents are more likely to vote than non-parents, but it is not clear that that happened in New York. In some neighborhoods, the boycotters influenced minority-group parents against voting. In District 9, the center of United Bronx Parents activity, the turnout was only 7.2 percent; in central Harlem District 5, the turnout was 5.6 percent; and in the Ocean Hill-Brownsville District 23 it was only 4.6 percent (Table 8-1). Even excluding those three districts, the turnout in the five most white districts was 19 percent, while in the five districts with the most hispanic residents it was 11 percent, and in the five with the most blacks it was 9.8 percent.[108] Actually, the city-wide voting average of 14 percent, compared to turnouts in anti-poverty and Model City elections, was fairly good. But in those elections, white middle-class voters are excluded by income qualifications or geographical restrictions, so that even with relatively low voting rates, minority groups still control the boards.

In addition to the boycotts and the traditionally low levels of political participation in ghetto neighborhoods, the lower-class voter faced some addi-

**Table 8-1**
**Ethnicity and the 1970 New York School Board Elections**

| District | % Voting | % Pupil Population | | | | Elected | | | |
| --- | --- | --- | --- | --- | --- | --- | --- | --- | --- |
| Manhattan | | H* | B | W | O** | H | B | W | O |
| 1 | 15 | 71 | 15 | 9 | 5 | 3 | 0 | 6 | – |
| 2 | 9 | 31 | 13 | 37 | 19 | – | 1 | 7 | 1 |
| 3 | 8.3 | 31 | 50 | 18 | 1 | 2 | 1 | 6 | – |
| 4 | 9 | 65 | 33 | 2 | – | 4 | 2 | 3 | – |
| 5 | 5.6 | 16 | 82 | 1 | 1 | 2 | 7 | – | – |
| 6 | 12.9 | 38 | 36 | 25 | – | 1 | 1 | 7 | – |
| Bronx | | | | | | | | | |
| 7 | 9.8 | 66 | 32 | 2 | – | 5 | 2 | 2 | – |
| 8 | 13.6 | 42 | 30 | 28 | – | – | 1 | 8 | – |
| 9 | 7.6 | 40 | 45 | 15 | – | 3 | 4 | 2 | – |
| 10 | 15.2 | 22 | 21 | 57 | – | 1 | – | 8 | – |
| 11 | 12.2 | 12 | 33 | 55 | – | – | 1 | 8 | – |
| 12 | 7.3 | 57 | 38 | 5 | – | 2 | 1 | 6 | – |
| Brooklyn | | | | | | | | | |
| 13 | 7.8 | 22 | 73 | 5 | – | 1 | 3 | 5 | – |
| 14 | 17.3 | 63 | 27 | 10 | – | 2 | 1 | 6 | – |
| 15 | 14.3 | 49 | 17 | 34 | – | – | – | 9 | – |
| 16 | 7.9 | 31 | 60 | 9 | – | 2 | 5 | 2 | – |
| 17 | 8.0 | 19 | 69 | 12 | – | – | 3 | 6 | – |
| 18 | 17.6 | 7 | 31 | 62 | – | – | – | 9 | – |
| 19 | 19.3 | 33 | 50 | 17 | – | – | 2 | 7 | – |
| 20 | 15.1 | 10 | 11 | 79 | – | – | – | 9 | – |
| 21 | 18.1 | 8 | 11 | 81 | – | – | – | 9 | – |
| 22 | 18.8 | 2 | 9 | 89 | – | – | – | 9 | – |
| 23 | 4.9 | 28 | 71 | 1 | – | 2 | 6 | 1 | – |
| Queens | | | | | | | | | |
| 24 | 15.5 | 16 | 13 | 71 | – | – | – | 9 | – |
| 25 | 19.3 | 4 | 9 | 87 | – | – | 1 | 8 | – |
| 26 | 22.0 | 2 | 13 | 85 | – | – | – | 9 | – |
| 27 | 16.5 | 4 | 28 | 67 | – | – | – | 9 | – |
| 28 | 12.4 | 6 | 41 | 53 | – | – | 3 | 6 | – |
| 29 | 16.6 | 4 | 57 | 39 | – | – | 2 | 7 | – |
| 30 | 13.7 | 14 | 20 | 66 | – | – | – | 9 | – |

**Table 8-1**(cont.)

| District | % Voting | % Pupil Population | | | | Elected | | | |
|---|---|---|---|---|---|---|---|---|---|
| | | H* | B | W | O** | H | B | W | O |
| Richmond | | | | | | | | | |
| 31 | 20.2 | 3 | 8 | 87 | – | – | – | 9 | – |
| Totals | – | – | – | – | – | 30 | 47 | 201 | 1 |
| Averages | 14.0 | 25 | 34 | 40 | 1 | 11 | 17 | 72 | 0 |

Principal Sources: United Parents Association (Sylvia Deutsch) and New York City Board of Elections (George Hallett).

*H is an abbreviation for Spanish-speaking residents.

**O refers to residents of Oriental dissent.

tional handicaps in the election structure. The election was non-partisan and, as E.C. Lee and others have pointed out, this favors middle-class voters.[109] The nomination process, which required only 200 signatures, produced more than 1,051 candidates. Since few of the candidates had district-wide reputations, the voter had to exert a special effort to inform himself or depend on slates to select candidates. Assuming the necessary pre-polling place calculations had been made,[110] the voter had to find and then rank his choices on a ballot containing an average of thirty-four names. In addition, to the disadvantages the PR system caused for lower-class participation, it does not seem to have produced the minority representation it had promised. Blacks were unable to elect any board members in ten districts in which they had ten percent of the pupil population; hispanic voters were similarly shut out in nine districts. Whites, on the other hand, had a representative in all but one district.

Candidate slates existed in both Detroit and New York, but PR made them much more necessary in the latter election. While slates were endorsed by anti-poverty organizations, civil rights groups, civic associatons, and political clubs, the important slates were those of parent associations, school employee unions, and religious groups.

Since the community boards were to have personnel power, both the UFT and the CSA were vitally interested in who the new members would be.[111] Yet it would have been inappropriate for CSA members to run, and the UFT leadership was ideologically opposed to teachers assuming "management" functions on the boards, so both organizations sought influence through endorsements. In most districts, screening panels were set up and candidates were asked to appear to make statements and to be questioned. The "right" answer varied by district but usually it was necessary to be specifically in favor of collective bargaining and professional rights and generally unsympathetic to community control and Mayor Lindsay. The Institute also implied that the unions aligned themselves with religious groups throughout the city to control the election.[112] Since the UFT had long been one of the fiercest opponents of aid to parochial schools in the state, that would have been an unholy alliance indeed. The union denies the charge.[113] In some districts, the union, seeking candidates cool to community control, found that all such candidates were also church endorsed, but there was no formal alliance. Only about 12 percent of the winners had both union and religious endorsements, while almost 19 percent of the winners shared union and parent association endorsements.

Still there were objections to union campaign tactics from some parent groups. According to one writer:

The union spent great amounts of money printing propaganda, putting out expensive mailings, and arranging parties, teas and receptions so that candidates sympathetic to them would be identifiable.[114]

Zealous teachers were not always able to maintain their campaign neutrality within the public schools. The union did send out letters to teachers and other allies throughout the city indicating its endorsements. But it claims that only $30,000 was spent on the campaign, and that it was rather disappointed in the lack of interest shown by teachers in these elections. One leader lamented that even an average turnout of teachers could have carried one district that later turned out to be troublesome.

In Detroit, religious organizations generally did not participate in the school board elections, but the long history of religious rivalry over New York schools, together with some immediate religious fiscal and ideological goals, produced an extensive political effort by Catholic churches and Orthodox Jewish synagogues.[115] Monsignor Eugene J. Malloy, the secretary for education of the Diocese of Brooklyn, discussed Catholic attitudes:

It has been said in the past that the Catholic people of the city, who represent more than 40 percent, were not sufficiently interested in public education because there was a large Catholic school system educating about 400,000 children.

Now I think that was an exaggerated charge, I think our Catholic people were always interested in the public school system and . . . have been denied adequate representation.

As you know, the local school boards were appointed . . . on the basis of screening panel recommendation. . . . And the screening panel in most districts consisted of the presidents of the public school PTAs.

Now I can tell you, because I was deeply involved for 10 years, that they used as a criterion whether you and your children went to public schools. This effectively made it impossible for any Catholic people to choose, for reasons of conscience, to send their children to a religiously-oriented school to offer their services or their help. . . .

In addition to that, once we began to have federal aid under Title I where children in parochial schools had rights under the law, there was a very great interest in putting someone on the local board who could explain what the situation was. I would say there's been a great deal of frustration because for five years we've believed they wouldn't listen. And they wouldn't grant the benefits. . . .

With this background of frustration, one can see how, given the opportunity for the first time to elect school boards, it is only natural that the Catholic people would take a great interest in some kind of representation. . . .

I think that whenever you lock people out—and Catholics were discriminated against as far as sitting on local school boards—and then give them a chance at a free election, they're going to react strongly.[116]

No one will discuss the amount of money spent by the Catholics or the exact pattern of their city-wide political coordination, but some idea of their campaign can be gathered from a few of the districts. Congregations rooted in neighborhoods make an ideal communication network for this kind of an election. In District 30, one parish held a candidates night at which only the pro-parochial school aid candidates were permitted to speak. Videotape and closed circuit television were used to spread the word among other parishes. Finally, before the election, priests in the district endorsed candidates and warned that their election was necessary to prevent parish elementary schools from closing.

In District 26, a letter was used to get across a similar message.

Parish Council
Our Lady of the Blessed Sacrament

March 6, 1970

Dear Parishioner,

The Parish Council, Holy Name Society and Rosary Society of Our Lady of the Blessed Sacrament Parish have ratified the endorsements of the Interfaith Council and urge you to vote for these candidates in the order of your preference.

The Community School Board elections are extremely important to all members of the community—whether your children attend public or parochial school—or whether you have any children at all. It is not a public school board that is being elected, but a **COMMUNITY SCHOOL BOARD.**

This Community School Board will:

1. Administer all State and Federal aid to parochial school children. Examples:
   a. Under the present law—textbooks for parochial school children in grades 7 to 12.
   b. Title I, II and III—Federal Aid Programs.
   c. Any aid that the legislature may in the future see fit to give to parochial school children.
2. Have authority to introduce or not introduce as it sees fit, the busing of public school children from one neighborhood to another for integration purposes.
3. Have jurisdiction in public schools over the following: Sex Education Programs, Narcotics Prevention Programs, Curriculum, Selection of textbooks, Hiring of School Superintendent, and teachers, and many other powers.

All of these functions of the Community School Board will have a direct effect on the entire community in which we live.[117]

The letter included a list of candidates endorsed by the Interfaith Council of Non-Public Schools of District 26 and instructions for manipulating the proportional representation system. It was signed by the Chairman of the Parish Council and the Presidents of the Rosary and Holy Name Societies.

Actually, the local school board's ability to aid or influence parochial schools was so circumscribed by federal and state law and court rulings that their immediate authority in this area was minimal. Still looking to the future and to broader political goals, the Church felt it important to make a serious effort to elect candidates. In the two districts cited, at least half of the winners had church endorsement and 70 percent supported increased aid to parochial schools.

Organization of public school parents for the election centered around the parent associations.[118] Each school is supposed to have such a group, but in fact many are moribund or exist mainly on a piece of paper in the principal's vest pocket. In a few neighborhoods in Brooklyn and Queens, strong parent groups do exist, but they are quite conservative and are not supportive of decentralization. The rest of the schools (about half of the total) have parent associations affiliated with the more liberal United Parent Association (UPA).

It was UPA's task to rally public school parents to defend their interests in the decentralized election, but the assignment was difficult. In the past, UPA has supported issues but not specific candidates, and it found itself without the philosophy or machinery to change its role in the election. So UPA did what it could. It helped with parent registration and set up a voter information campaign on PR. It also urged local PAs to endorse candidates supporting the principle of parent participation, having experience in public schools, and being opposed to or opposed by parochial schools. When some PAs were intimidated by principals from using their bulletin for campaign purposes, the UPA intervened to stop the censorship. Still, with almost no money and little central direction, the campaign effort of the public school parents was minimal.

The slate affiliations of the winners are listed in Table 8-2.[119] The results appear to show that the success of candidates endorsed by unions and religious groups was greater than that of parent association candidates, but analyzing this election in terms of slates is quite difficult. Almost two-thirds of the winners had multiple endorsements. About 45 percent of the winners endorsed by the UFT or religious groups were also supported by parent associations. Candidate-initiated coalitions, which existed in many districts, also confuse the interpretation of the election. Furthermore, some endorsements meant very little to the candidates and in some instances were not even desired. Still, PR and the general anonymity of most candidates made it very difficult to run as an independent or without endorsements. (Only about one-quarter of the winners ran without any

Table 8-2
**Elected Local School Board Members and State Affiliations\***

| District | Public School Parents | Religious Organizations or Private School Parents | UFTA or CSA | Civic or Political Organizations | Civil Rights and/or Poverty Organizations |
|---|---|---|---|---|---|
| 1 | | 1 | 7 | | 2 |
| 2 | 5 | 3 | 4 | 5 | |
| 3 | 4 | 1 | 5 | 5 | |
| 4 | 3 | 5 | 1 | | 3 |
| 5 | 1 | 1 | 4 | | 1 |
| 6 | 1 | 1 | 4 | 1 | |
| 7 | | | | | |
| 8 | 2 | 1 | 1 | | 1 |
| 9 | 2 | 3 | 7 | 4 | 3 |
| 10 | 5 | 9 | 5 | 5 | |
| 11 | 7 | 5 | 3 | 4 | 2 |
| 12 | | 1 | | | |
| 13 | 2 | 1 | | 3 | 4 |
| 14 | 1 | 2 | 1 | 1 | 1 |
| 15 | 5 | 3 | 4 | 5 | |
| 16 | 2 | | 4 | | 1 |
| 17 | 1 | 2 | 4 | | |
| 18 | 4 | 2 | 6 | 3 | 1 |
| 19 | 2 | 1 | 2 | | |
| 20 | 4 | 8 | 3 | 3 | 1 |
| 21 | 5 | 2 | 5 | | |
| 22 | 2 | 3 | 4 | | |
| 23 | | | | 9 | |
| 24 | 3 | 1 | 3 | | |
| 25 | 4 | 8 | 4 | 5 | 3 |
| 26 | 5 | 5 | 4 | 1 | 1 |
| 27 | 2 | 1 | 2 | 2 | 2 |
| 28 | 6 | 9 | 6 | 1 | |
| 29 | 3 | 7 | 4 | 3 | |
| 30 | 6 | 4 | 2 | 2 | 3 |
| 31 | | 3 | 2 | | |
| Total | 87 | 93 | 101 | 62 | 29 |

\*180 of the winners were endorsed by more than one slate. If the slate endorsements were in the same category (civil rights groups or anti-poverty—column 5) it is listed only once. If the endorsements were by slates in different categories, they are listed separately.

slate endorsement.) As Table 8-3 shows, slating was used more often in white than black districts, possibly because the former had more of the organizational skills necessary to manipulate PR. But the table also indicates that slates were most important in districts with racially mixed school populations. In those districts, whites may have thought it particularly necessary to coordinate to control the outcome.

Most important is the question of the cohesion or discipline in the slates. They did not caucus before or after the election, and there is little evidence that systematic liaison between those endorsed and their sponsors was maintained. Furthermore, as Table 8-4 shows, the slates were by no means cohesive in their educational policy choices.[120] Civil rights and anti-poverty organization-backed winners were almost unanimous in wanting to give the districts the right to appoint staff, while other slates were divided. Religious and private school slate members were unsurprisingly much more favorable to aid to parochial schools than others. But on the questions of community board and central board relations, selection of a community superintendent, and integration, the slates differed little.

**Table 8-3**
**Slate Success in Community School Board Districts Classified by Race (% of winners endorsed by a particular slate)***

|  | Public School Parents | Parochial School or Religious Organizations | UFTA or CSA | Political or Civic Organizations | Anti-Poverty or Civil Rights Organizations |
|---|---|---|---|---|---|
| Predominantly white Districts (60% or more white students) N=10 Winners=90 | 39 | 41 | 39 | 19 | 12 |
| Districts 25 to 59% white students N=8 Winners=72 | 47 | 53 | 43 | 30 | 4 |
| Districts 1 to 24% white students N=13 Winners=97 | 14 | 15 | 30 | 19 | 13 |
| *Total | 31 | 34 | 37 | 22 | 10 |

*Where multiple endorsements of a candidate existed, each endorsement is counted separately in this table, if this slates are in different categories or columns.

**Table 8-4**
**Slate Attitudes (Winners Only) Toward Educational Policy in 1970 School Board Elections (% Agreeing with Policy Statements)**

| | Public School Parents N=87 | Religious Organizations or Private School Parents N=93 | UFT or CSA N=101 | Civic or Political Organizations N=62 | Civil Rights or Anti-Poverty Organizations N=29 |
|---|---|---|---|---|---|
| **1. Relation of community board and central board** | | | | | |
| a. The central board should have the basic responsibility for all schools and the necessary authority to exercise that responsibility. | 2 | 5 | 2 | 5 | 0 |
| b. The community board should have the basic responsibility for the schools under its jurisdiction and the necessary authority to exercise that responsibility, but certain limited powers should remain central. | 82 | 85 | 83 | 79 | 75 |
| c. The community board should be independent and have the same autonomy and status as any school board in the state. | 16 | 10 | 15 | 16 | 25 |
| **2. Selection of community superintendent. In choosing a community superintendent, which of the following candidates would you choose?** | | | | | |
| a. A candidate who has excellent educational experience and ability and is fair on sensitivity to the conditions and needs of the community. | 47 | 49 | 61 | 61 | 47 |
| b. A candidate who is excellent on sensitivity to the conditions and needs of the community and has fair educational experience and ability. | 53 | 51 | 39 | 39 | 53 |

3. Staff selection. With the stipulation that all teachers and supervisors must meet basic New York State licensing requirements,

| | | | | | |
|---|---|---|---|---|---|
| a. The appointment of staff for the Community School Districts should basically be controlled by a central examination and assignment procedure. | 42 | 46 | 45 | 44 | 7 |
| b. Appointments of staff for a Community School district should be controlled primarily by the community board and community superintendent. | 58 | 54 | 55 | 56 | 93 |
| 4. Aid to parochial and private schools | | | | | |
| a. There should be public subsidy for parochial and private schools at the same level as for public schools. | 4 | 10 | 6 | 7 | 11 |
| b. There should be some public subsidy for parochial and private schools but at lower levels than public support for public schools. | 27 | 60 | 30 | 31 | 26 |
| c. There should be noneducational aid to parochial and private schools confined to fringe services, such as transportation and hot lunches. | 40 | 19 | 37 | 26 | 37 |
| d. There should be no aid to parochial and private schools. | 29 | 11 | 27 | 36 | 26 |
| 5. Integration | | | | | |
| a. Integration in New York City schools is no longer a desirable goal. | 2 | 2 | 0 | 9 | 0 |
| b. Though school integration is a desirable goal, conditions in New York City are such that it cannot have a high priority. | 67 | 78 | 71 | 58 | 78 |
| c. The community board must take the initiative to ensure maximum integration. | 31 | 20 | 29 | 33 | 22 |

Source: Compiled from PEA and League of Women Voters Survey. No answers not included.

Ethnic and occupational-class identities may be as important as slates in determining policy attitudes. Table 8-5 displays these relationships. Not surprisingly, black and hispanic winners were more favorable to abstract community-control concepts (Question 1) than whites. This minority group-majority group division is also reflected in the matter of staff selection (Question 3). The central examination and assignment system was thoroughly discredited among minority groups, but it is equally important to note that 54 percent of the white winners also believed in giving the community boards personnel powers. In choosing a community superintendent (Question 2), however, the hispanic winners (68 percent) were more impressed by expertise than either whites (57 percent) or blacks (47 percent). (Possibly this is a reflection of the traditional hispanic view of authority.) Similarly white and hispanic winners were more likely to favor aid to parochial schools (Question 4), which no doubt reflected the number of Catholics in these two groups. On the issue of integration (Question 5), blacks and hispanic winners were twice as likely to regard integration as a serious goal, though most of the few separatists were black. Interestingly enough, all the separatists apparently were professionals. On the other questions, occupation seems to make little difference, after one takes into account the ethnic proportions of each profession.

Many voters chose candidates by slate, ethnic, or even occupational identifications without knowing what their individual policy positions were. But a few voters may have been motivated mainly by policy issues. Whether voter choices are purposeful or inadvertent elections do influence policy alternatives.

Table 8-6 shows the choices that were made. The overwhelming number of candidates chose the middle ground on the abstract question of community control (Question 1), and that was apparently the voters' position as well. The voters were more likely to prefer candidates who, in choosing for Superintendent, would rate expertise more highly than community sensitivity as a qualification (Question 2).[121] Indeed, incumbent board members who stood for re-election were twice as likely to win if they took that position (Question 3).

Candidates who took a moderate stance on integration (Question 5) were preferred by the voters. The non-incumbent winners were less in favor of taking the initiative on integration than either incumbent winners or losers. Candidates who supported more aid to parochial schools (Question 4) were also the voters' choice. Four times as many incumbent winners as losers favored such aid, and the new recruits to board membership (non-incumbent winners) were the most ardent parochial school advocates.

This analysis creates a picture of the election results that is somewhat different from the view taken by the Institute and the Coalition. The Institute's perspective was based on the community control ideology that minority group parents should control minority group schools. The election did not produce that result. The major groups in the Coalition had been the dominant forces in the screening panels that had recommended city and local board members in the old system. They had used their power to select pro-intergrationist and anti-private school candidates. Since the new board members (non-incumbent in Table 8-6) recruited through the new election process were less sympathetic to those positions, the Coalition naturally was disappointed.

If one views the election outcomes less ideologically, however, the fact is that the winners were ethnically representative of the city's voters. The consensus profile of the new board members—"white male Catholic, professionally or technically trained with two children"—is a profile similar to that of other legislators in the city. Indeed the city council (1970) with two blacks and one Puerto Rican was much less ethnically representative than the new school boards. The winners' attitudes of slightly less sympathy toward integration as a priority and more support for parochial schools are consistent with recent trends in the city (and in the state and nation, for that matter). So again the outcome seems to be representative.

When one analyzes the positions held by the new board members on the issues most directly related to community control, it is hard to see the election in the Institute's words as "a disaster unparalled in the history of the New York City school system."[122] As Table 8-6 shows, 97 percent of the new board members said they favored giving the community boards basic or exclusive decision-making powers. On the key issue of personnel powers, a clear majority of the election winners favored giving them to the community board. As in Detroit, then, the decentralized electoral process resulted in a loss of power for the liberal school establishment. But the board members recruited to school politics by this means were more representative of the city population than those selected by the old system and in their own way advocates of more community control.

## Decentralization in Operation

Even before the election of the CSBs, the 1969 decentralization law had effected major changes in the leadership of the school system. The act required the replacement of the then mayorally-appointed board with an interim board composed of appointees of the five borough presidents. That board was supposed to function for a year, until a new board including one elected member from each of the five boroughs plus two mayoral appointees took office in the summer of 1970. In addition, the law changed the title of the administrative head of the system from Superintendent to Chancellor, and it was understood that the incumbent head would be retiring. In both cases, the legal changes were more than cosmetic or nominal.

With the responsibility of selecting the five members of the interim board, the law had given the borough presidents appointment with more visibility and potential power than any they had exercised in decades. At first glance, it

**Table 8-5**

**Educational Policy Attitudes of Winners Classified by Ethnicity and Occupation in 1970 Community School Board Elections (% Agreeing with Policy Statements)**

| | White (n=199) | Black (n=47) | Hispanic (n=32) | Professional (n= | White Collar (n= | Blue Collar (n=14) |
|---|---|---|---|---|---|---|
| **1. Relation of community board and central board** | | | | | | |
| a. The central board should have the basic responsibility for all schools and the necessary authority to exercise that responsibility. | 4 | 0 | 0 | 3 | 3 | 0 |
| b. The community board should have the basic responsibility for the schools under its jurisdiction and the necessary authority to exercise that responsibility, but certain limited powers should remain central. | 87 | 59 | 64 | 79 | 83 | 75 |
| c. The community board should be independent and have the same autonomy and status as any school board in the state. | 9 | 41 | 36 | 17 | 14 | 25 |
| **2. Selection of community superintendent. In choosing a community superintendent, which of the following candidates would you choose?** | | | | | | |
| a. A candidate who has excellent educational experience and ability and is fair on sensitivity to the conditions and needs of the community. | 57 | 47 | 68 | 55 | 60 | 69 |
| b. A candidate who is excellent on sensitivity to the conditions and needs of the community and has fair educational experience and ability. | 43 | 53 | 31 | 45 | 40 | 31 |
| **3. Staff selection. With the stipulation that all teachers and supervisors must meet basic New York State licensing requirements,** | | | | | | |
| a. The appointment of staff for the Community School Districts should basically be controlled by a central examination and assignment procedure. | 46 | 9 | 14 | 38 | 41 | 29 |
| b. Appointments of staff for a Community School District should be controlled primarily by the community board and community superintendent. | 54 | 91 | 85 | 63 | 59 | 71 |

4. Aid to parochial and private schools

| | | | | | | |
|---|---|---|---|---|---|---|
| a. There should be public subsidy for parochial and private schools at the same level as for public schools. | 7 | 14 | 11 | 7 | 10 | 14 |
| b. There should be some public subsidy for parochial and private schools but at lower levels than public support for public schools. | 51 | 33 | 63 | 50 | 58 | 71 |
| c. There should be noneducational aid to parochial and private schools confined to fringe services, such as transportation and hot lunches. | 26 | 28 | 11 | 27 | 12 | 7 |
| d. There should be no aid to parochial and private schools. | 16 | 24 | 16 | 16 | 20 | 7 |

5. Integration

| | | | | | | |
|---|---|---|---|---|---|---|
| a. Integration in New York City schools is no longer a desirable goal. | 2 | 14 | 0 | 0 | 7 | 0 |
| b. Though school integration is a desirable goal, conditions in New York City are such that it cannot have a high priority. | 77 | 41 | 52 | 70 | 61 | 67 |
| c. The community board must take the initiative to ensure maximum integration. | 22 | 45 | 48 | 30 | 32 | 33 |

Source: Compiled from PEA and League of Women Voters Survey. No answer not included.

**Table 8-6**
**Educational Policy Attitudes of Participants in 1970 Community School Board Elections (% Agreeing with Policy Statements)**

|  | All Candidates (n=1034) | All Winners (n=279) | Incumbent Winners (n=68) | Non-Incumbent Winners (n=209) | Incumbent Losers (n=47) |
|---|---|---|---|---|---|
| 1. Relation of community board and central board |  |  |  |  |  |
| a. The central board should have the basic responsibility for all schools and the necessary authority to exercise that responsibility. | 3 | 3 | 3 | 3 | 4 |
| b. The community board should have the basic responsibility for the schools under its jurisdiction and the necessary authority to exercise that responsibility, but certain limited powers should remain central. | 80 | 81 | 78 | 81 | 77 |
| c. The community board should be independent and have the same autonomy and status as any school board in the state. | 17 | 16 | 18 | 16 | 19 |
| 2. Selection of community superintendent. In choosing a community superintendent, which of the following candidates would you choose? |  |  |  |  |  |
| a. A candidate who has excellent educational experience and ability and is fair on sensitivity to the conditions and needs of the community. | 52 | 57 | 63 | 56 | 30 |
| b. A candidate who is excellent on sensitivity to the conditions and needs of the community and has fair educational experience and ability. | 48 | 43 | 37 | 44 | 70 |

3. Staff selection. With the stipulation that all teachers and supervisors must meet basic New York State licensing requirements,

| | | | | | |
|---|---|---|---|---|---|
| a. The appointment of staff for the Community School Districts should basically be controlled by a central examination and assignment procedure. | 34 | 38 | 32 | 39 | 12 |
| b. Appointments of staff for a Community School District should be controlled primarily by the community board and community superintendent. | 66 | 62 | 68 | 61 | 88 |

4. Aid to parochial and private schools

| | | | | | |
|---|---|---|---|---|---|
| a. There should be public subsidy for parochial and private schools at the same level as for public schools. | 6 | 8 | 3 | 10 | 0 |
| b. There should be some public subsidy for parochial and private schools but at lower levels than public support for public schools. | 40 | 51 | 43 | 57 | 32 |
| c. There should be noneducational aid to parochial and private schools confined to fringe services, such as transportation and hot lunches. | 28 | 24 | 28 | 24 | 32 |
| d. There should be no aid to parochial and private schools. | 26 | 17 | 9 | 18 | 36 |

5. Integration

| | | | | | |
|---|---|---|---|---|---|
| a. Integration in New York City schools is no longer a desirable goal. | 6 | 3 | 3 | 3 | 4 |
| b. Though school integration is a desirable goal, conditions in New York City are such that it cannot have a high priority | 61 | 68 | 56 | 71 | 57 |
| c. The community board must take the initiative to ensure maximum integration. | 33 | 28 | 41 | 25 | 39 |

Source: Compiled from PEA and League of Women Voters Survey. No answers not included.

appeared that they had succumbed to the long-standing religious-ethnic quota system of city politics. The Jewish borough presidents in Brooklyn and Queens appointed Jews; the Catholic member was selected by the Catholic borough president of Staten Island; while the black borough president of Manhattan and the Puerto Rican borough president of the Bronx chose a black and Puerto Rican respectively. But that kind of ethnic and religious representation is not without its strengths, given the political problems the schools faced, and the particular members chosen were not without qualification.

## The Chancellor and the Bureaucracy

If the ethnic, religious, and educational backgrounds of the interim board members were fairly predictable, the characteristics of the new Chancellor turned out to be a complete surprise. Indeed, if one could have enticed Jimmy the Greek to quote odds on the possibility that the interim board would choose a white Congregationalist from Vermont who finished near the bottom of his high school class; who did not graduate from Farmingdale State Teachers College until he was 32; who began his educational career in a one-room school house at $13.00 a week; and who had no really urban administrative experience—a small wager might have permitted a comfortable early retirement.[123]

To be sure, the board did not look first to Harvey Scribner, the Vermont State Commissioner of Education. The Board's initial consensus was that only a Chancellor with national stature and proven ability to manage unweildly bureaucracies could make decentralization work. Robert McNamara would have been ideal, but since he clearly was not available, the Board toyed with such names as Arthur Goldberg, Sargent Shriver, Ramsey Clark, James Webb, Sol Linowitz, Willard Wirtz, Chester Bowles and Ralph Bunche. None of them was very interested, except Shriver, who was seeking gainful employment at the time. But he dropped out of the running to explore the possibility of running for the Maryland governorship. Then the board turned its attention to local political figures and state commissioners. Those names, however, tended to attract vetoes from several of the groups concerned about the selection. Finally, two months after he had submitted his application, the board chose Harvey Scribner.

This description of the vagaries of his selection process is not intended to denigrate Mr. Scribner whose quiet commitment to integration and innovation eventually convinced the Board, but it does indicate the rather unusual problems that confronted the Chancellor when he took office. Scribner was little known in the city, and he was obviously not the board's first choice. Most important, although the law specified that the Chancellor was to be chosen "as soon as possible," the process in fact took fourteen months. By the time he was finally installed, many of the important decentralization policies had been established, and the interim board had become accustomed to exercising administrative powers. Thus, although the statute had intended to focus central authority in the Chancellor's office, the interim board has been aggressive in maintaining and expanding its role.

In the decentralized system, the Chancellor has three main responsibilities: (1) to operate the high schools; (2) to enforce central authority where appropriate, adjudicating conflicts among the local boards; and (3) to supervise personnel practices. In carrying out these assignments, the executive, legislative, and judicial roles often overlap.

There are essentially three different kinds of high schools in the New York public system; elite academic high schools with city- or borough-wide enrollments; vocational schools ranging from the High School of Performing Arts to the High School of Printing and neighborhood comprehensive schools. The high schools were exempted from the CSB's jurisdiction because of the multi-district enrollment patterns in the academic and vocational high schools, and because the problems in the comprehensive schools seemed likely to swamp the fledgling local school boards. The decentralization law makes it possible for the Chancellor to turn the high schools over to the CSBs in 1973, but there has been little public support for that option, and it seems unlikely.

The high schools vary enormously in quality and student constituencies, but if they have one thing in common it is their size. Several enroll more than 5,000 students. Most American high schools have been affected by the rise of drug abuse, racial tension, teenage crime, and the intense alienation, apathy, or activism of many students; but all these problems are magnified in the large urban high school. Chancellor Scribner has therefore moved to reduce the scale of educational institutions and hopefully the problems as well. Mini-schools and street academies have been established. One of the most troubled high schools has been reorganized on a house plan, and many others boast annexes where students who need more personal attention or experimental curriculums can be placed. The new high schools will be built for smaller enrollments.

While nothing in the decentralization law mandated smaller schools—and indeed central authorities rather than the CSBs have taken the lead in their establishment—the decentralization movement may have sensitized people to the importance of creating a human scale in institutions in order to increase participation and identification. At least that philosophy commends itself to Harvey Scribner, who has been very much committed to the decentralization concept. Its implementation, however, has not always been easy.

Probably the greatest potential bone of contention between the CSBs and Scribner has been in the area of personnel selection. The law permits CSBs to assign teachers to a particular school, but the Chancellor assigns teachers to each district, though he is supposed to honor CSB requests for specific persons. The old Board of Examiners system of eligibility lists ranking teachers has been maintained. To give black and Puerto Rican schools the flexibility to recruit from outside the city, however, any school which ranks in the bottom 45 percent on city-wide reading scores can choose any teacher who has made an average score or better on the National Teachers Examination. As a generalization, there has been little conflict over the assignment of teachers, although the Chancellor has had to restrain some districts from attempting to make personnel arrangements that would violate the UFT contract.

The selection and assignment of supervisors has been a more controversial matter. The most unambiguous power given to the CSBs was the authority to appoint the district superintendent. Although there have been intra-district conflicts about particular choices, with one exception they have not included central authorities. But the selection of building principals has stirred considerable controversy within the districts and has pitted the CSBs against the CSA and other defenders of the old order. To reconcile the old Board of Examiners eligibility lists and the anticipated demand of the CSBs to appoint their "own" principals, the statute cleared the existing list by giving the 106 members on it automatic appointments. That gave the CSBs several options. They could appoint someone on the new eligibility list or persuade a principal to transfer from another school. Or the CSBs could hire an auxiliary or acting principal and make him *de facto* principal. Many boards, especially those interested in principals from minority groups, took this option; but it had an obvious disadvantage in terms of the status and salary of the person chosen. Consequently, in 1971, two acting principals—one who failed the Board of Examiners test and another who refused to take it—challenged the examination system on the grounds that the results were racially discriminatory. They won a smashing victory. Not only did Judge Mansfield agree that the tests were *de facto* discriminatory, but required that the new procedures be more adaptable to the Community School Board type of administration.[124] At this point, Chancellor Scribner played a key role in defusing the ethnic aspects of the issue. He not only supported the decision, but he successfully urged the school board not to appeal it.

Though the Chancellor has consistently supported the concept of decentralization, his role in enforcing central board policy and in hearing appeals from CSB action has often led his office into confrontation with one or another of the local boards. Most of the appeals have not been on issues of great principle. Often it is simply a matter of forcing a CSB to abide by its own rules when it has found it convenient to act privately or informally. The other major area of appeals concerns personnel action; in such cases, the Chancellor has to find a way to honor contracts and yet move toward decentralization.

If the Chancellor's powers have in many respects been expanded, those of bureaus at 110 Livingston Street have been curtailed. To take just one example: under the old system, the Division of School Planning and Research was almost wholly responsible for the much criticized school building program under decentralization; but now the CSBs have the power to propose sites directly to the City Site Selection Board and to choose an architect from those on a city list. The law also gives the CSBs greater influence in proposing capital projects and approving architectural plans.[125] All of these powers are shared. They are not community control, but they have broken the pattern of bureaucratic monopoly.

## The Interim Board

For more than a year, the interim board ran the New York City schools without a Chancellor. After Scribner's appointment, they continued to dominate several areas of policy. They divided their labor in two ways. On issues concerning a particular borough, the board tended to defer to the member from that borough. Each member also had a functional specialization as well—i.e., Murray Bergtraum, collective bargaining; Seymour Lachman, student rights. The board presidency has been rotated, and the members tend to regard their positions as a full-time responsibility. Unlike previous boards, the interim board has insisted that each member have a personal staff. Given the complexity of the task of decentralizing an institution as large and badly managed as the city's schools, these working arrangements might not seem unreasonable. The board's critics, however, contend that it has not really wanted to decentralize power as the law intended.[126]

Under the 1969 Act, the board's curriculum and personnel powers were reduced, but it maintained major budgetary authority.[127] Under the old system, the board had actually turned over budgetmaking to the central administrative staff, principally the Bureau of Business Affairs. Lacking its own budget experts and unwilling or unable to use modern technology, the board had little to say in determining priorities. Budget decisions tended to be incremental and did not reflect overall policy directions. The combination of decentralization, a fiscal crisis, and the interim board's activist ideology, however, has resulted in a decline of the central bureaucratic role. The board has had to devise fiscal policy in three areas: (1) allocation of state and local funds; (2) distribution of Title I funds; and (3) reform of the budgetary process.

Under the old system, most state and local money was allocated to schools on the basis of equalizing student-teacher ratios. In part, this was done to fulfill the class size requirements in schools under UFT contract; but it had the effect of favoring middle-class schools, which had many high-salaried experienced teachers, or ghetto schools in which teachers were given more preparation periods. Several CSBs objected and insisted on equal funding for each district—partly as a principle of decentralization and partly as an expedient to increase their share of the pie.

Instead of turning to the administrative staff, the board hired a management consultant firm, to work out a new allocation formula.[128] The law required the creation of "objective formulae" that would "reflect the relative educational needs of the community districts to the maximum extent feasible." An interpretation of "educational needs" that would have redistributed money from the middle- to the lower-class districts would have caused considerable political controversy and violated the staffing ratios in the union contract. Consequently, the formula the board finally adopted combined several compromises. Ninety-five percent of all instructional dollars were allocated to the districts on a per capita basis, with compensatory factors for differences among districts in student ages, teacher salaries, and Title I schools. The other 5 percent was allocated to districts on the basis of the proportion of students who were retarded in reading by a year or more. Considered as a whole, the formula has only a slight redistributive effect.

In the struggle over federal Title I funds, the question was not just over *which* districts would get *what*, but over the authoritv of the CSBs in spending these funds. Title I funds are intended to provide diverse compensatory programs for disadvantaged students. Under the old system, a substantial proportion of this money was used to underwrite the cost of union-sponsored MES schools. In the 1969 contract, the board had agreed to continue twenty-one of these schools and begin ten more. The schools generally served poorer children, but they were located according to available space and some of the poorest districts in the city had none. These districts were not eager to have "their" Title I money spent in other districts and some CSBs were opposed to MES schools and the UFT involvement.

The board attempted to solve the problem by spending the money in two ways—$58.5 million for mandated services (MES schools and programs for non-public schools and open enrollment students), and $16.25 million for CSB discretionary purposes. Naturally, the CSBs were displeased, and District 3 went to court and obtained a temporary injunction against the allocation of Title I funds. During the lengthy legal maneuvering, however, the board obtained a ruling from the City Corporation Council that the MES language in the contract was not binding. Fortunately, Congress also substantially increased the amount of Title I funds, so the board was able to fund the mandated program and the district proposals as well. In the long run, however, the CSB had won a victory. According to the court, after the formula was determined, the CSBs had the right to set up their own Title I programs with only very limited review power given the Chancellor.[129]

Though the interim board had been aware of the problems in the budget-making process for some time, it was still shocked to discover in February 1971 that it had spent $40 million over its budget. A report of a subsequent State Senate investigating committee noted that, although the board's budget was equal to that of the twelfth largest corporation in the world, it conducted its business "in the same manner as the Mom and Pop grocery store, where bills are paid out of the cash box and totaled at the end of the year."[130] These problems had existed long before decentralization, but the existence of community districts complicated fiscal management because they were supposed to play a role in budget proposals, and because it was difficult to keep them from filling allocated positions even if the system as a whole was running a deficit.

To balance its budget, the board took several steps. First, it forced the layoff of about 5,000 teachers—mostly those with substitute licenses and those with little seniority. Since this system disproportionately affected minority-group teachers, several districts demanded the autonomy to decide who should be laid off. District 3 went to court again, but this time it lost when the court held the proper appeal would be to the State Commissioner of Education.[131] When that appeal was taken, the Commissioner upheld the board. A longer-range solution to budgetary problems is being sought by improving management procedures. The payroll has been computerized, and a position control system and an expenditure reporting system have been instituted. To help the CSBs make budget proposals and to keep track of expenditures, business managers have been appointed by each district.

In the first two years under decentralization, then, fiscal policy-making has undergone some changes. The central board has asserted itself and the bureaucracy has declined. Allocations are made by district rather than by school, and this has caused some shift of funds. The districts have been given some control over Title I funds, and that discretion will probably increase. Overall, however, the kind of flexibility that formerly resulted from loose management has been reduced, and the CSBs have not developed the capabilities to have a more systematic influence over budgetmaking. Though by law the CSBs do submit budget requests after district public hearings, the approval process involves the Chancellor, the board, the Mayor, the City Council, and the Board of Estimate, and thus the CSBs have little influence over the final outcome. For that reason they have attempted to control Title I funds and to reduce the personnel requirements placed on them by collective bargaining.

*The Community School Boards*

It is doubtful that most of the CSBs could have handled more budgetary responsibility had it been offered. Most of the members (75 percent) are new to school boards and the Decentralization Act, the UFT contract, and the city's politics of education generally create a very complex environment in which to function. After the first two years, more than 20 percent of the board members have resigned. Some have quit for a variety of personal reasons, but others to permit the appointment of minority group members in districts where few were elected.[132]

As required by the Decentralization Act, each CSB has adopted bylaws and selected officers. In procedures and agendas the boards might resemble school boards everywhere.[133] The usual conflicts with other agencies in the system will be discussed elsewhere. But there is one problem that has plagued these boards more than typical smalltown boards. It is the question of their legitimacy and their obligation to delegate powers to parents.

Any new legislative body will have some problems of legitimacy, but the CSBs have had some special difficulties. The ambiguities in the law have been a handicap, but in some districts the fact that board members are white and parents are mostly not has made matters worse. Added to that is the general ethos of decentralization, which is sometimes suspicious of any authority and demands a degree of participation inconsistent with the need to arrive at some decision. This situation is made more complicated when many of the participants lack the skills and emotional attitudes necessary to function in formal meetings. Several boards have had severe problems in keeping order, and one suspended its meetings for a time until police protection could be had. On the other hand, the existence of the CSBs has tended to dissipate some of the hostilities felt against the larger system, and central board meetings have not been disrupted nearly as often as before decentralization. Perhaps, in the long run, one of decentralization's greatest contributions is that now there really is someone to complain to about the many injustices in the system. The board members sit and listen with worried faces and try to understand and try to find a remedy. It is a privilege residents of smaller places take for granted.

According to law each CSB must create a parents association if none existed and some boards have gone further in setting up advisory committees and liaison with individual schools. Still, many boards are conserving their still uncertain authority and have not seriously involved parents in decision-making.

The greatest issue between the CSBs and their constituencies has been over administrative appointments, particularly at the building level. In a few cases, the CSBs have deferred some of their personal powers to parent associations. In District 6, the PAs are permitted to interview all candidates and then submit a a list of the top three to the CSB for its choice. In District 24, the personnel committee is composed of one board member, two UFT representatives, two CSA members, and as many parents as would like to join. So far, the parents have been rather apathetic. In most districts, however, the boards have done the screening and then "consulted" with PA leaders. When a PA in District 19 was unsatisfied with the quality of the consultation it sued. The court ruled, however, that the law did not require a parental role in personnel selection.[134] Still, many boards are finding that placement is easier if the PA approves, and the expectation of a parental role seems to be growing.

The CSB communicates with the interim board in two different ways.[135] A Consultative Council was initiated by Murray Bergtraum when he was President of the Board. It meets once a month to mediate the problems between the central board and the CSB. The CSBs also have their own organization, originally called the Confederation of Local School Boards. Recently, however, that name was changed to the New York City School Boards Association, a name designed to indicate the parallel between CSBs and boards in other parts of the state. Only two-thirds of the boards are members, however, and the Association's budget of a little over $10,000 does not go very far. Thus far, the CSBs have rarely united to demand anything from the interim board. In many instances, the districts do not have common interests, and the CSBs are still individually testing the limits of their power.

### The New Balance of Power

Although local politicians have sometimes been drawn into disputes in the districts, neither the state nor the city government has been an active participant in major decentralization issues. State officials are waiting for the recommendations of the Fleischman Commission (see next section) before suggesting revisions in decentralization. Mayor Lindsay regards decentralization as one of his major accomplishments and said so during his brief campaign for the presidential nomination. But his administration has generally avoided involvement in subsequent operational decisions. Of course, he no longer appoints members to the board and so has less influence on school affairs.

The non-school agency with the greatest influence on the operation of decentralization has been the courts. In decentralization's first two years, there have been thirty-one major cases involving allocation of power within the system. Judicial appeals are frequent in instances of major structural revision, but they have been particularly critical in New York because of the ambiguity of the original law and because previously existing procedures have been abolished or lost their legitimacy. In general, the courts have favored a "federal" system granting specific powers to the CSBs where the law so indicates, but granting residual powers to central authorities, especially when due process has been involved.[136] It seems likely that an increased judicial role is an inevitable consequence of decentralization.

Though the enactment of the decentralization law has not resulted in much parental power, and though the CSBs have not yet fully developed, the decentralization movement has achieved some success in dismantling the bureaucracy. The influence of 110 Livingston Street on the day-to-day operation of the schools has decreased. The Chancellor is an outsider who is publicly critical of bureaucratic control of schools. The board has its own staff and is willing to bypass the bureaucracy for analysis of major system problems. There is not much room for promotion in the declining bureaus at headquarters. For the ambitious young administrator, the action now is in the districts.

## Decentralization: Pro and Con

Some of the functional consequences of the structural changes wrought by decentralization have already been discussed. Evaluations of its overall impact have been as fiercely debated as were its origins.

Experience with decentralization did not improve Albert Shanker's attitudes toward it. "Decentralization," he argues, "is like a Banana Republic revolution. The pictures of the leaders change, but life on the plantation is the same."[137]

More surprisingly, his opinion was joined by Kenneth Clark, the noted analyst of race relations:

My assessment of the consequences of decentralization as of now is quite different from my anticipation of two, three years ago when we were fighting for it. I personally do not see evidence that decentralization has resulted in increased quality of education for the children in the schools. I do not see that . . . the local boards have concentrated on . . . [educational] quality as much as they have concentrated on power, actions, and control of finances.[138]

Reacting to Clark's pessimistic appraisal, Mayor Lindsay insisted that decentralization had brought "a new vigor to the whole process of achieving quality public education."[139] While Chancellor Scribner suggested that observers should:

. . . keep in mind that decentralization is only two years old. It is unreasonable to expect overnight changes. One must ask how effective in the area of learning programs was the centralized system before decentralization.[140]

The Chancellor is surely correct that a complete evaluation of decentralization is not yet possible, but some of its effects can be discussed.

*Academic Achievement, Curriculum Policy,*
*and Pupil Policy*

The Bundy panel began with these sentiments:

The first premise of this report is that the test of a school is what it does for the children in it. Decentralization is not attractive to us merely as an end in itself; if we believed that a tightly centralized school system could work well in New York today, we would favor it. Nor is decentralization to be judged, in our view, primarily by what it does or does not do for the state of mind, still less the "power," of various interested parties. We have met men and women in every interested group whose spoken or unspoken center of concern was with their own power—teacher power, parent power, supervisory power, community power, board power. We believe in the instrumental value of all these forms of power—but in the final value of none. We think each of them has to be judged, in the end, by what it does for the education of public school pupils.[141]

In its first two years, what has decentralization done for public school pupils? The truth is that there are not even any well-informed opinions on this key question. For one thing, high schools, where tangible evidence might have been easiest to obtain, are excluded from local board control. The 1971 reading test scores from elementary and junior high schools show a slight decline, but that is consistent with the pre-decentralization trend and with demographic changes in the school population.[142] It is implausible that decentralization would have much of an impact on achievement in the first year. Moreover, community-control advocates point out that the vital link that decentralization was supposed to forge between students, parents, and professionals did not material-ize, and thus the system now in force does not provide a true test of the achievement potential of community control.

If the results of decentralization are not very discernible in test scores, curricu-lum change and student policies should theoretically be more visible. Again a true measurement is difficult. As a study for the Fleischman Commission notes:

New York City is renowned for the scope of diverse educational programs instituted in its various schools. It has a progressive educational policy concern-ing both curriculum and pupils in the last few years. One can see an open integrated classroom, a Montessori classroom, a school without walls, a Bereiter-Engleman school, the latest bilingual classroom, talking typewriters and com-puterized education, a More Effective school. In short, nearly every new educational idea has been instituted in New York City.

But then the authors concede:

Critics contend that more enterprising educational innovations are implemented on an experimental and piecemeal basis. One can find exciting educational ventures in scattered classrooms; little effort is made to translate these successful recipes into programs that might effect substantial numbers of students.[143]

There is a severe credibility problem in the field of education innovation. Substantial funds and publicity have been available to the administrators and boards that were willing to "experiment" or even to put new labels on old programs. But after a decade of these enterprises there are few, if any, that have proven widespread success, so it is difficult to evaluate the performance of the CSBs in this area.

Some new curriculum programs have been developed. Probably the most important is the promotion of bilingual education. These programs also have a political socialization and patronage significance, but in a system with more than one-quarter of a million Spanish-speaking students, they also have considerable educational potential. Other districts have moved toward open classrooms and certain of the other contemporary pedagogical reforms. But, considering the fact that two-thirds of the new board members said the schools were unsatisfactory, there has been far less educational change than one might have expected.

There are several reasons for the CSB's inaction. The most important is that they have been absorbed in other matters—particularly in establishing personnel policy and board procedures. Curriculum goals were not a part of their individual campaigns and few of the CSBs have articulated a philosophy or attempted to reach a consensus on these matters. Finally there are no clearly successful models to follow and little unencumbered money. Most of the new programs have been more paper proposals than actual reforms and where change does exist the Institute authors contend, "No pattern is emerging so that the community school board patchwork of educational innovation resembles that under the central board before . . . the 1969 state act."[144]

Like most other large cities, New York has long followed the tracking approach in arranging student curricula. In the first grade, pupils are directed to particular classes based on standardized test results and teacher estimates of intellectual ability, emotional and physical health, and social maturity. By the time the student reaches high school, five tracks are available (general, vocational, commercial, technical, and academic—college preparatory). This arrangement has some advantages. Teachers believe that it is easier to teach homogeneous classes, and college-oriented parents feel that ability grouping is the only way to insure the competition needed for college success. But at best the system is easily abused, and it has been much criticized. Existing measures of ability are often too inexact or culture-bound to allow for making decisions so crucial to a student's future. Tracking also fosters substantial inequality when, as is often the case, minority group youngsters are disproportionately assigned to the lower tracks.[145]

In the old centralized system, tracking was official policy, but after the 1969 law, Chancellor Scribner and the interim board changed that policy. The offices at 110 Livingston Street for Intellectually Gifted Classes and Special Problem Groups have been phased out, and decisions about tracking are now left to the CSBs. Given the controversy over the issue and its ethnic implications, it might have been expected to have priority on the CSB's agenda. With few exceptions, such has not been the case, and the old tracking procedures have been continued. Should the ethnic and class composition of the CSBs be changed in some future election, tracking may be subjected to further scrutiny.

Pupil policies are another area in which the CSBs might have played a large role. The size and bureaucracy of the New York schools, which created so many problems for parents and teachers, frequently caused students to be dealt with in a heavy-handed and arbitrary manner. To take the most severe problem, a study by the New York Civil Liberties Union found that almost all of the 13,000 student suspensions in 1968-1969 took place without due process. Less publicized instances of unequal discipline, censorship, and rigid student conduct codes were commonplace in the system.

Though most of the problems occurred in the high schools, the CSBs might have been a force to alleviate the arbitrary treatment of students. There is very little evidence that they moved in this direction.[146] Instead, the new policies on students rights have come from the interim board. When these policies were ignored by building administrators, who are often faced with difficult drug and discipline problems, and who find the concept of legal rights for students too mind-boggling to implement, the watchdogs were citizen pressure groups like the Civil Liberties Unions and the Queens Law Advocate Service. The CSBs, which are now the agency of first appeal for disciplinary cases in schools under their jurisdiction, and which could change attitudes toward students, have been rather cautious. While it is not surprising that many of the white church-sponsored candidates have conservative views on students, it has been a shock to community-control advocates to find out how traditional and discipline-minded many of the minority-group board members have been.

Overall in the area of education policy, whether because of a lack of money, philosophical consensus, or experience, the CSBs made little impact in their first two years. The important policies (mini-schools, modifications of tracking, and liberalization of students rights) came from a reformed 110 Livingston Street. Of course, without the 1969 decentralization law neither Chancellor Scribner nor the interim board would be in office, but the most important educational changes in the system in the first two years resulted from central initiative rather than from the communities.

## Personnel Outcomes

Grievances over the system's rigid and ethnically skewed personnel procedures had been one of the principal causes of the decentralization movement. Under the 1969 law, personnel powers were divided between the central bureaucracy and the community school boards. How has the new authority been used or abused by the local boards?

Buttressed by the Mansfield and Rinaldo decisions, decentralization has made personnel recruitment considerably more flexible. In the past, the system had made it almost impossible to recruit an established professional from another part of the country since no promise of a position could be made until the candidate passed the lengthy examinations and worked his way up the eligibility list. Some thought that, with the loosening up of the system and the extraordinary salaries in New York, a nationwide talent search would be instituted. That has not happened, though some districts regularly advertise openings in city and ethnic newspapers, presumably to stimulate wider competition for jobs.

Most white districts are still recruiting from personnel pools within the system, while some black and Puerto Rican boards have gone to the South or to Puerto Rico to find professionals of their ethnic backgrounds. Ironically, one of the major sources of minority-group personnel for the city staff has been the paraprofessional program. This program, though funded by the federal government and originally staffed by anti-poverty groups, is now organized, represented, and promoted by the UFT.

It is difficult to document the extent of personnel change in the system. Union contracts and the law itself have protected against ethnic purges if anyone had intended that. There has been an unusual turnover in district superintendents in the first two years of decentralization; eighteen of the thirty-one districts chose new ones.[147] For most of the affected superintendents, a change of political style in their districts rather than purely ethnic reasons led to resignations or ousters. One superintendent complained:

It's practically impossible to make an administrative decision. When you have to truckle to the community school board, which seems to think your professional integrity and experience and know-how is of no value, then you got to get out.

While another suggested:

There's a disillusionment among the professionals who have to stand outside Scribner's office and can't get in to see him, while a community group with a complaint can barge right in. There's a great put-down going on in this city, and the professional is the guy who's getting put down. If there's a question between a superintendent and a community group, you can be pretty sure it's the superintendent who is wrong.

In some districts, however, there is no question that white administrators and, to a lesser extent, white teachers are being replaced with minority-group personnel.[148] Generally, this has been a matter of attrition, but in the former demonstration districts, personnel policy is still a volatile matter of settling old grievances. In poorer neighborhoods, school positions are prizes well worth competing and organizing for. One new CSB member likes to publicize his calculation that the black community loses $82 million a year because black staff is not proportionate to black students.

In some districts, preferential recruitment of minority personnel is being carried out in connection with the goal of bilingual education.[149] Sometimes this recruitment is for "Puerto Ricans only." Cubans and other Spanish-speaking natives are not considered. In two Manhattan districts (1 and 3), the desire to redress previous ethnic imbalances led to the formulation of policies proposing hiring quotas based on the ethnic proportions in the student body. In both cases, protests from the UFT, Jewish, and other civil rights organizations, and the Chancellor's office caused the districts to abjure quotas formally, but some observers feel that the practice still exists.

The tight school budget and overall economic recession that came at the same time as decentralization have restricted the number of new positions in the system. But decentralization has contributed to the ethnic and geographic diversity of the system's personnel. The pace of integration of school staffs seems to have accelerated. Whether some future ethnic power struggle will encourage resegregation by using decentralization to create some homogeneous minority-staffed districts remains to be seen. In some districts, the always latent pressures to use school positions for patronage have come to the surface.[150] Generally, however, teacher aides and other supplementary personnel, evaluation and maintenance contracts are more involved in partronage than regular teacher or administrative positions. It is not yet possible to do comparisons of patronage in the old and new systems.

Most of the community-control advocates were realistic enough to pin their hopes less on recruiting new staff and more on making existing staff accountable.[151] Aware of the national interest in this concept, even the central board and the UFT have been rhetorically committed to accountability since 1970. In the preamble of the collective bargaining contract signed that year is the statement:

The board of education and the union recognize that the major problem of our school system is the failure to educate all of our students and the massive academic retardation which exists especially among minority group students. The board and the union therefore agree to join in an effort, in cooperation with universities, community school boards and parent organizations, to seek solutions to this major problem and to develop objective criteria for professional accountability.

Several of the districts have sought their own accountability mechanisms. District 9 in the Bronx had a short-lived performance contracting experiment, and District 3 in Manhattan considered conducting a voucher experiment. Probably the most controversial of the accountability devices has been the utilization of parent committees in teacher evaluation.

The central board's policy statement on parent associations stipulates that the PAs shall be told which school personnel are beginning their probationary period and be informed of the criteria and time-tables for their evaluation.[152] It also requires rating officers to consider any "valid and timely complaints" with due process for all concerned. The policy then states that the PAs shall not have rating responsibilities and that their role is only advisory. Final decisions rest with the board.

It is not clear whether the drafters of this policy had anything more in mind than sensitizing those who make tenure decisions to the occasional grievances of the schools' clientele. But several community boards decided to institutionalize the parents' role, allowing them to set up committees that may visit classes and observe and comment on teacher performance. Not surprisingly, this practice makes teachers uncomfortable, and it can disrupt the classroom and be used for harrassment. The UFT has reacted vigorously to the parent committees on both practical and philosophical grounds, declaring:

The notion that parents can determine the professional quality of a teacher's performance is blatantly false. Teaching is a profession requiring years of college preparation and skill in applying instructional systems.[153]

The UFT also established a policy urging teachers to halt all instruction in any school visited by a parent committee, and it threatened a citywide work stoppage if there were reprisals against teachers who objected to the evaluation.

This issue poses nicely the conflict between the emergent role of laymen under decentralization and the established prerogatives of professionals under the traditional civil service system.

## Fiscal Consequences

In addition to whatever political or educational costs and benefits decentralization brings, it also has some tangible fiscal effects.[154] But they are very difficult to evaluate. For example, to take a relatively simple criterion: How much does decentralization cost in additional dollars expended? The Bundy report could only predict that

The net annual cost of decentralization might be very small indeed, or it might in the long run go as high as $50 million or even $100 million a year, depending on the choices of those responsible for the new system.[155]

Several kinds of information would be needed to make a reasonable estimate.

(A) How much does the decentralized administrative structure itself cost in terms of:
   (1) Increased staff?
   (2) Board member expenses?
   (3) Additional office space, stationery, etc.?
(B) Since at least one other level of decision-making (the CSBs) and sometimes two (the PAs) are involved under decentralization, how much additional decision-making costs are involved?
   (1) If some decisions take longer to make, how many man-hours involved are salaried? How many are citizen-donated?
   (2) If some decisions are being made more quickly and more efficiently at the local level, how much has been saved by reduction in 110 Livingston Street staff, and by greater availability of personnel, equipment, and supplies at schools when and where they are needed?
(C) Since school funds pass through more hands under decentralization, has there been an increase in financial mismangement or outright graft?

Comparisons are difficult because the New York schools had a structure with district administrators and boards before the Decentralization Law. Though the old districts lacked the power of the new districts, they still showed up in some budgets. Definitive answers to questions about efficiency and mismanagement will have to await some future state investigative commission or grand jury, but some facts are available.

The new or additional money costs attributable to the Decentralization Law are fairly minimal. Each CSB has a fund of $40,000 to $50,000 for administrative expenses. They have used it mainly to hire professional help, an administrative assistant or, in some cases, a business manager or attorney. But they have not received a budget for public relations or collective bargaining positions which would have increased their political power. There has been no wholesale transfer of positions from 110 Livingston Street to the districts despite CSB pressure for more control over curriculum specialists, etc. Central board member Murray Bergtraum has claimed that several hundred positions have been cut out of the central bureaucracy, but because of inflation and expansion in other areas, the central budget is still growing. The reductions were achieved by retirement and turnover. Few, if any, professionals were forced out, but it is no longer as easy to move up or be transferred to headquarters staff.

Although it is an obviously important issue, precise evaluation of the relative costs and benefits of the decentralized decision-making process is at this point impossible to make and would probably depend overmuch on a particular evaluator's ideological perspective. Relatively hard information on the fiscal management of the CSBs does exist. The first audit statements are available and they reveal the following kinds of problems.[156]

(1) A few of the boards appear to have gone on some rather costly junkets.
(2) District 27 used funds to purchase $3000 worth of office equipment which was installed in board members' homes.
(3) Checks amounting to $6154 were allegedly forged by an employee (later dismissed) of District 23.
(4) Many of the districts did not go through the required bidding procedures for equipment, supplies, etc.
(5) About half of the districts did not keep proper expense vouchers.

The reports contain little evaluation so it is hard to guess whether the auditors considered these problems damaging evidence to the overall concept of decentralization or whether they viewed them normal for any new administrative structure. The clues suggest that most of the bidding and voucher incidents were less fraud than matters of inexperience with some CSB rebelliousness toward centrally-established procedures thrown in. Of course, carelessness and graft are not entirely novel at 110 Livingston Street or in other central agencies of the city. Only time will tell whether decentralization will have a major impact on the fiscal management of the schools, but it appears that it has already had a substantial effect on collective bargaining.

*The New Politics of Collective Bargaining*

In its recent contracts, the UFT has scored some considerable successes.[157] AFT President David Selden called the 1969-72 wage and educational policy agreement "one of the most remarkable documents in the field of education." Albert Shanker said simply, "We have negotiated the finest contract for teachers in the United States."[158] These statements appear to be more than mere organizational self-congratulation. To take salaries as one indicator: according to the PEA, in the four years since 1968 the consumer price index has gone up 24.2 percent, the average professional, administrative, and technical wage has increased 23.2 percent, while the average New York teacher's wage rose 51.6 percent. These figures actually understate the financial gains of the UFT, since they do not include the substantial pension increase in the last contract.

Several of the reasons for the teachers' bargaining success are related to the general politics of municipal unions and will be discussed in the last chapter, but the UFT negotiations have had some particular characteristics. As a newly-recognized union, its members and able leadership have been more vigorous than most. In some cases, teachers have merely gained parity with other city workers. But in obtaining their lucrative financial settlements, they have been especially benefited by the eagerness of political leaders to avoid school strikes, which have dangerous racial implications in New York. The UFT has also been aided by the fact that administrative salaries are determined according to a ratio based on the teacher scale. Thus "management" is predisposed toward wage increases. Finally, there is no balloting for school tax levies or even for city board members that would make voters more attentive to the fiscal consequences of the negotiations.

Decentralization did not change any of these factors and the 1972 negotiations might have slipped by without anything other than the usual last minute bargaining and public pressure to avoid a strike. But decentralization did change the constituency of school activists and gave them a new role in collective bargaining. The city board is still the "public employer," but the decentralization law requires establishment of "formal procedures under which the community boards will be consulted with respect to collective negotiations by the Chancellor ... on matters which affect their interests.[159] To implement this provision, the city board agreed to seat three community board representatives as bargainers and decided to caucus periodically with the Consultative Council on Collective Negotiations, to which each community board had one delegate.[160]

Generally, the community board representatives functioned as an influential counterforce to union demands. To the lower- or lower middle-class board members, school salaries already appear high, and the procedures of collective bargaining, arbitration, and elaborate grievance processes seem to conflict with their image of direct democracy.[161] Even the more professionally-oriented board members were shocked to discover that, although they were allegedly elected to make policy for their districts, 80 percent or more of the school budget consists of contract-mandated salaries. They also found that other critical educational decisions are locked into collective bargaining agreements. Of course, that is the dilemma of school boards everywhere, but these community boards were new and had no previous bargaining experience.

Consequently, the community boards took a tough stand during the bargaining. Their association demanded the right of contract ratification, though no such right technically exists in the law. Substantively, in addition to opposing the amount of UFT demand for salary increases, the community boards have vigorously objected to attempts by the union through collective bargaining to establish system-wide rules regarding ratios of school security guards, relief from non-teaching duties, preparation periods, limits on supervisions, transfer arrangements, and seniority in administrative appointments. These policies, the boards believed, should be established locally. In addition the community boards made some "blue sky" demands of their own.

The community boards' pressures on the union were supported and publicized by two important allies: UPA and PEA. Under the leadership of a new president, a black male, UPA insisted that the agenda of negotiable items be limited. Their resolution states:

The rights of parents and the managerial rights of those responsible for administering the schools cannot be bargained away under the guise of "improved working conditions" and "job security." Too often in the past items of educational policy have been traded off because they have little or no financial cost. This must stop!

We plead with all concerned to enter into contract negotiations with the recognition that just as the union fights for the very best contract it can get for its members, parents fight with equal fervor for their parent demands. Should these two goals clash, parents must not be accused of union busting. Such attacks on parents only provoke an emotional debate which beclouds the real issues. It must be accepted by all involved as a difference over issues not an attack on unionism.[162]

To implement this position, UPA urged PAs in every district to establish priorities among problems and concerns. These "parent contract demands" were then conveyed through the community board representative and by UPA staff to the city board and the union and discussed at the bargaining table.

PEA, which is not a mass membership organization, used a different strategy. Asking "Who is going to run the schools and make decisions, the UFT or the representatives of the public?," PEA has concentrated on providing research and public relations materials to counter the union.[163]

Part of the opposition to the UFT arises from grievances stemming from struggles over the decentralization law and demonstration district strikes. Since that time there have been widely-held and vocal anti-school professional feelings among other school-related groups. More fundamentally, however, decentralization and collective bargaining represent different styles of making municipal decisions. In collective bargaining policies are negotiated in closed meetings by adversarial elites representing workers and government. The general citizenry plays no direct role. Decentralization, however, represents the participatory and equalitarian (often overtly anti-professional and anti-bureaucratic) thrust in American politics.

For the first time in recent New York history, there developed a broad-based and informed opposition to the negotiating goals of a particular union. The decentralization advocates were determined not to increase the scope of collective bargaining that served to strengthen the central system and union powers. For the UFT, the 1972 contract was equally critical.[164] Inflation influenced monetary demands, but teachers were as concerned about the growth of school violence and their inability to find the conditions and time to teach effectively. From these perspectives, it was essential that they give the anti-professional biases in the community control movement no victories to feed on. Moreover, the UFT and Albert Shanker have been leaders in the state and national NEA and AFT merger movements. A generous contract was important in order to preserve that role.

The contract settlement was not reached until three days before the opening of schools. Albert Shanker called it "a fine settlement, one that we can be thoroughly proud of," but he conceded that the union had not achieved many of its demands for better working conditions and professional prerogatives.[165] A *New York Times* editorial said bluntly that these negotiations marked "the first time since the start of bargaining nearly two decades ago that the United Federation of Teachers did not strongarm the board, under threat of strike, into surrendering control over major elements of basic educational policy."[166] In fact, the contract seemed to be, in the words of one journalist,"a victory for all, compromises up and down the line."[167] Most importantly, in a post-settlement evaluation, Shanker concluded:

The fear we had that decentralization might make negotiations impossible did not come true. . . . These negotiations proved that decentralization and collective bargaining are compatible.[168]

One cannot generalize from a single contract settlement, but the inclusion of representatives of local boards seemed to add a new dimension of public participation without undermining the complex bargaining that contemporary labor relations require. A community control arrangement forcing the union to bargain with thirty-one separate boards would probably have had very different results. In some of the districts, it seems clear that strikes and considerable conflict would have resulted. The pressure on union negotiators to match gains in other districts would have been enormous. Still, some observers believe that municipal unions have become so powerful that only a radical urban decentralization can curb their power.[169] As consideration of decentralizing the whole of New York City government increases, the effect of various new structures on collective bargaining is one of the most important issues.

## Decentralization Reform

After two years of decentralization, some groups have proposed amending the original law. Sometimes this has been motivated by a desire to win back points lost during the earlier legislative struggle. Others, disillusioned by the outcome of the first election, have wanted to change those procedures. Others still have wanted to remedy the legal ambiguities that created such administrative difficulties.

The first of the many problems the legislation created was in selection procedures for replacing the interim board. That board, with its five members appointed by the five borough presidents, was scheduled to be replaced on July 1, 1970, by a board of seven members, five elected from the boroughs (one from each) and two appointed by the Mayor. Those election procedures were later ruled to be a violation of one-man-one-vote, since the boroughs are of very different sizes.[170] Consequently, the interim board has stayed on—and on. Although groups like the PEA have given considerable thought to alternative methods of choosing a new central board, each method has its disadvantages and no consensus has developed behind any proposal.[171] In the meantime, the members of the interim board have proved competent and even fairly popular, so there has been a reluctance to disturb the status quo. The legislature, eager to avoid new school controversies, has three times decided to extend the term of the interim board. Almost nobody thinks that the borough presidents should be permanently empowered to appoint central board members, however, and the problem of selecting the central board and defining its role continues to be one of the issues plaguing decentralization in the city.

Other aspects of the decentralization compromise have also been challenged. A report of the Institute for Community Studies has argued, "the 1969 decentralization law failed to grant to Community School Boards sufficient powers to operate their schools."[172] Furthermore, according to the Institute, the CSBs are not very representative and have not performed well given the powers they have had. Consequently, the Institute proposes smaller districts with simplified election procedures restricting the balloting to parents and eliminating proportional representation. If these reforms were made, the Institute feels, most central board powers could be eliminated. In short, the Institute is still committed to its original vision of community control.

The most publicized advocate of change in decentralization has been the Fleischman Commission. While its reforms are as thoroughgoing as the Institute proposals, they do not stem from an ideological commitment to community control. Its assessment of decentralization is rather cautious:

Decentralizing the governance of the elementary and junior high schools has not diminished the scale of educational problems in New York City. But it has begun to create administrative arrangements and a system of governance able to combat many problems more effectively than proved possible under the centralized administrative structure in force prior to 1969.[173]

The Fleischman Commission's recommendations for reform of the current decentralization structure are predicated upon its judgment that the state should assume fiscal responsibility for education, including basic collective bargaining. Under this arrangement, New York City would become one of thirteen regions in the state. A regional board, i.e., a central board, would continue to operate the city's high schools, provide transportation, and funds for capital expenditures. Somewhat inconsistently, with its general support of community autonomy, such a regional board would also be able to alter attendance lines and end tracking within districts to achieve racial equality. Despite these *caveats*, Fleischman recommended that the community school boards have power comparable to that of their peers in other parts of the state. Except as noted above, central board controls over personnel, curriculum, and budgetary matters would be discontinued; only state and federal standards would exist.

The Fleischman Commission felt that altering the number of districts at this time would create too much controversy, though it stated its preference for smaller districts. The CSBs would continue to be elected by all eligible voters, but proportional representation would be dropped. Instead of having candidates run in entire districts (often of more than 250,000 population), the election districts would coincide with junior high school attendance areas. This arrangement would probably increase the proportion of parents voting and thus the percentage of minority-group winners. Minority-group candidates would also be encouraged to run by allowing payment to school board members of $50 a day for up to 100 days of service.

As Manley Fleischman has conceded, the report is aimed at expressing the ideal, not necessarily the most politically feasible reforms. Some changes will probably be made in the selection system for school board members (central and local), but there is little public pressure to alter the basic decentralization arrangement radically. Partly, this is because those arrangements are fluid and complex, and interest groups are still learning how to use them. Also, there will be a new CSB election in the spring of 1973, and it may alter the balance of power. Most important, both the community-control advocates and the unions fear that if the issue goes back to the legislature, the outcome might be to create separate school systems for each of the five boroughs. This would probably be a prelude to breaking up the city into borough government. Since the record of borough administrations is largely one of patronage and parochial interests, the liberal-left forces view that alternative with extreme foreboding. Consequently, most of the public school-oriented groups have decided to live within the existing decentralization system. Changes in national or state policy on integration, or fiscal equality, or the revision of city government may eventually alter the New York school system, but for now there is a determination to make decentralization work.

# 9 Conclusion

This study has sought to provide an empirical base for a theoretical and public policy analysis of the decentralization movement in urban education. As our case studies have shown, the decentralization issue developed in very different patterns. The variety of urban governmental structures, the diversity of political actors, and the distinctiveness of local custom and ethos complicate the social scientist's quest for broad generalization. The problem is to combine historical accuracy, which often demands attention to the unique or special qualities of events, with the search for uniformities of behavior and underlying explanatory variables. Both historical accuracy and generalization are affected when the events described are as volatile and contemporary as school decentralization. Yet theory and policy alike demand attention to these events, because they have the potential for reshaping our cities and their politics.

We have tried to steer a course between too many details and vague generalities by concentrating on five cities over a three-year period. This provides a limited empirical record, but it is still possible to search for generalized findings regarding the evolution of the decentralization issue, the participants in the major conficts, and the outcomes of these struggles.

## The Evolution of the Issue

Some social scientists, for example, Munger and Martin, have created elaborate typologies for differentiating the steps in the development of an issue.[1] It seems sensible here, however, to focus on five stages of the decentralization process: placement on the agenda, reception by the educational authorities, response of the pressure groups, appeal to outside legislatures, and alteration of existing school governance.

Until the late 1960s, the agenda for structural reform of school districts was dominated by the movement to consolidate districts in rural areas. Although several academic reports had earlier called for decentralization of urban school districts, there were no significant steps to decentralize until the mid-1960s. At that time, cities such as New York, St. Louis, Chicago, Los Angeles, and Detroit moved tentatively to delegate more authority to district administrators, but there was little initial consideration given to delegating policy-making powers to neighborhood laymen. Community control was not a salient issue.

There is, of course, no definitive method of determining precisely when an

225

issue first moves into public consciousness, but it is appropriate to consider particular events or documents that symbolize public awareness. It is clear that by 1969 in all five case study cities the issue of school decentralization, including calls for community control of ghetto schools, had moved onto the agenda of public concern.

The events that prompted public consideration varied. The most readily apparent occurred in New York, where the conflict over I.S. 201—pitting black parents and their supporters against the central authorities and the professional unions—sparked intense controversy and led to the coalescing of alliances for and against community control. The conflicts in New York, particularly the Ocean Hill-Brownsville strikes, were closely watched by black leaders in Detroit. Even though black political and vocational representation was much greater in Detroit than in New York, the racial overtones of the New York strikes were the catalytic agents in black support of decentralization in Detroit. Blacks in St. Louis, however, have paid little attention to events in Detroit or New York and have not been much affected by community control or separatist movements. What consideration there has been of decentralization was largely instigated by whites, two foundation-supported reports, Carl Dudley's campaign, and the Murphy-Blair DEB. Similarly, although blacks constitute 94 percent of Washington's public school student population, white parents in the Morgan neighborhood and federal officials played an important part in raising the issue. In Los Angeles, black and brown protest groups, aided by minority legislators and by leverage afforded by federal guidelines requiring community involvement, succeeded in dramatizing the issue.

In all five cities, the school boards responded to the decentralization movement by declaring general symbolic agreement with its goals and by instituting some experiments. When the push came to a shove for decentralizing system-wide, however, as it did in every city except Washington, the boards split into racial and ideological factions. No board fully supported community control, and most board members sought to modify or defeat legislation introduced at the state level.

Similarly, the greater participation promised by decentralization attracted the symbolic support of most educational interest groups. Even teachers unions (though not administrator organizations) were sympathetic in the early stages of the discussions of decentralization. Later, as specific plans were advanced, and as the racial implications of decentralization were highlighted, the educational pressure groups were unable to take consistent positions or form coalitions. Only in New York have they played influential roles at each stage of the process.

In each city decentralization advocates found that legal requirements and political opposition forced them to appeal their case to outside authorities. Except in the special instance of Washington, where the appeals went to the U.S. Office of Education rather than to the hostile Congressional District committees, the pro-decentralization forces took their case to state legislatures. In that arena, the reaction to decentralization was by no means uniform. In Michigan, it passed easily; in New York, it was adopted after a bitter struggle; in California, it was narrowly beaten; and in Missouri, it has not come to a vote. In no state has the issue become a strictly partisan measure. Nor, with the exception of Governor Reagan, who vetoed several decentralization bills, has any governor become substantively involved. The racial and ideological forces aligned for and against decentralization in the cities were replicated in the legislatures, and the results were mixed.

Although, as we will discuss later, the decentralization movement has had an influence in the school politics of each city studied, it has achieved structural reform in only two. Although there are important differences in the selection procedures for local and central boards in New York and Detroit, their powers and problems have been similar. In neither city was community control finally established. In both, New York by law, in Detroit by guidelines, the local boards have been given certain formal powers, but they have found these difficult to exercise fully because of budget stringencies, union contracts, and lack of internal consensus. Additionally, in Detroit, education politics has been virtually paralyzed by the issue of school busing.

The different paths that the issue has followed confirms a truism about American politics: the fact that there is a local politics that is not merely the reflection of national political trends. Despite the "nationalizing" trends since the 1930s,[2] local politics in America have retained a local character. Despite the national media attention given to the dramatic events of Ocean Hill-Brownsville, the decentralization issue evolved the way it did in our different cities in important part for local reasons. Although almost all of the participants in decentralization controversies across the country were familiar with Ocean Hill-Brownsville, its significance was largely perceived in local terms, and it was used as a rallying cry tailored to the tactics of the local struggle. Indeed, our case studies suggest—but by no means conclusively show—that a partial reversal of the nationalizing trends of recent decades may have begun in American politics. While the country will not return to the sectionalism of the nineteenth century—and no local government will be able to detach itself from the wider federal context—the difficulty of solving all problems nationally may lead to a new localism in public affairs, a partial realignment of public policy issues into localized and regionalized issue clusters.

## Decentralization and Political Participation

Some of the participants and their roles have already been discussed, but it is worthwhile to single out some other actors in the process.

The leadership in school decentralization controversies generally has not come from either established politicians or from the political parties. The partial exception to this generalization is John Lindsay, who played a critical role in translating the protests of minority parents into a program for system-wide restructuring of school governance. But after his political career was almost engulfed in the controversy, he withdrew from prominent advocacy. In the other cases, despite the ideological threat that community control could pose to city hall, and despite the amount of money involved in public school budgets, parties and political leaders have rarely been central participants in the decentralization issue, becoming involved only reluctantly when the intensity of conflict made dodging the issue impossible. Their aloofness stems, in part, from the fact that there is little patronage left in the school system. They also have little legal leverage in school affairs, and important sectors of public opinion have been traditionally opposed to political interference. Now that the public schools are in so much difficulty, big city mayors have found such opposition a very convenient excuse for avoiding involvement. Also, ethnic rivalry is so intense that identification with any position can be dangerous.

While city and state politicans have been wary, federal officials in both the Office of Economic Opportunity and the Office of Education have intervened extensively in several cities to promote the idea of community control. In New York City, Chicago, San Francisco, Los Angeles, Washington, D.C., and St. Louis, neighborhood groups have been able to use their contacts in the federal bureaucracy to win a share of control over local schools. Since the amount and timing of grants under Model Cities or Title III (ESEA) depends almost totally on the attitudes of a few federal officials, the leverage of neighborhood groups with access to those officials has been considerable. Even amounts as small as $50,000 have been used to force school systems to accept citizen participation on federally specified terms. This helps explain how the decentralization issue could become a major concern even in the face of aloofness on the part of local officials. The federal intervention has, however, tended to be short-lived and episodic, characterized by intense periods of involvement and then withdrawal from the fray. In the past several years, since the advent of the Nixon Administration, the federal role as an advocate for community control has diminished greatly.

Another important supporter of the decentralization movement has been the foundations. At critical movements, they have provided the seed money, the technical advice, and the legitimacy without which the movement might have collapsed. Ford has been most influential, with grants in New York, Washington, and Detroit. Rosenberg in Los Angeles, Danforth in St. Louis, Field and Taconic in New York, and Russell Sage and Rosenberg in San Francisco have also supported decentralization projects. With an investment of $100,000 to $150,000, a foundation could create a decentralization movement of some consequence in any large city.

Locally, the school decentralization issue has been largely fought among the traditional school interest groups, emerging neighborhood leaders, teachers organizations, and the school bureaucracy. Administrators have opposed the community control version of decentralization everywhere and have been either lukewarm or ambivalent in occasionally supporting administrative decentralization plans. Public school leadership has been precarious. Not one of the superintendents in our case study cities survived the three-year period of the study. Teachers have tended to back decentralization in principle and to be suspicious or even hostile in practice. Some black teachers, however, have had firm ideological commitments or pragmatic incentives, and have supported decentralization. Generally, school-parent groups and blue-ribbon school associations have favored decentralization, though often only after overcoming internal divisions. Neighborhood leaders, black, hispanic, or white, have also tended to support decentralization in principle, though the issues of election procedures, of district lines, and of which leaders are "representative" of the community have proved deeply divisive. Since the issues of what is a "community" and who speaks for it are so difficult in the complex urban setting, the coalitions favoring decentralization have tended to be unstable.

If there was any single, dominant purpose in the decentralization movement, it was to increase participation in the making of school policy, especially by the poor and those not previously involved. In certain respects, that goal has been achieved. In general, decentralization has increased the number of participants and changed the character of successful school activists. The new activists are often upwardly mobile members of minority groups with few previous ties to city-wide politics or institutions.

Although new activists have emerged as participants in school politics, there has been no massive grass-roots citizen involvement in poor neighborhoods. Voting rates in poor neighborhoods have been low and attendance at meetings erratic. Some of this may be due to special conditions, such as the boycott by militant groups in the 1970 New York election or unfamiliarity with new election procedures. The evidence of lack of grass-roots citizen involvement is clearest where advisory councils lack formal powers over curriculum and personnel. The record is not quite so clear with respect to the boards in New York and Detroit, which have formal powers. There are some indications of greater involvement, but even here an effective link between the boards and the wider public has not developed. Observers are divided about whether voting rates will increase or decrease in future board elections, and whether other indices of participation will or will not increase, but decentralized school structures have not yet overcome the traditional barriers to political participation that exists among the poor.

On the basis of available evidence, it does not appear likely that mass citizen involvement could be induced under any imaginable system of local control of the schools. Our findings tend to be consistent with the weight of evidence regarding participation in small units of government in the rural setting—village councils, town meetings, special districts. There tends to be less, not more, participation in small units, particularly in special purpose governmental units. While participation in general is low, small groups of elites, usually representing the consensus of dominant interests in a locality, have been quite active.[3] Similarly, under school decentralization, although the rhetoric speaks of direct democracy (the "people" must decide, the "community" endorses this proposal), the new elite that has emerged to represent ghetto residents functions much like traditional elites.[4] Many of these new activists have had backgrounds in anti-poverty organizations and have used these connections as a basis for political power. This elite has been able to dominate many of the advisory groups and other participatory structures that have been set up in connection with decentralization.

Electorally, they have been less successful. Indeed, the outcome of both the first two decentralized elections disappointed the spokesmen for the poor. Although in both elections the percentage of minority group members elected to local boards was almost the same percentage as eligible minority group voters, it was far less than the percentage of minority group school enrollment. In most instances, the policies for black students will still be made by whites. But the background of the whites who gained power under decentralization was quite different from the professional-big business, liberal whites who controlled the old centralized structures. The new white activists elected to the decentralized boards represent neighborhood power bases, parishes or congregations, home-owner and taxpayer associations, and small businessmen. They are more likely to be Catholic and have strong ethnic identifications. Conservative in their attitudes toward integration and expanded public spending for public schools, it might have been predicted they would clash with the activists representing the poor.

In some districts and cities the clash has occurred and the perceived gains of minority groups has accelerated the awakening white ethnic political consciousness. Indeed, one important result of the decentralization movement has been to mobilize white ethnic constituencies that have felt threatened by the liberal-black Great Society programs of the 1960s. But the new activists, white or black, share some objectives, and their relationships have not been wholly antagonistic. The poor activists, generally black or Puerto Rican, are ethnics too; and in the era of ethnic pride, accomodations can be reached if there is respect for each other's turf. Furthermore, both groups have agreed on emphasizing discipline and mastery of traditional skills as educational goals. They also share a common suspicion of the professional prerogatives enjoyed by teachers and administrators. In collective bargaining, decentralization has given these new community activists access to and influence on contract negotiations. In the 1972 New York contract negotiations, they functioned as a counter-pressure to union demands with some success.

Although mass participation has not materialized, the participatory ethos remains the most powerful and appealing part of the decentralization ideology. Sometimes as a substitute for formal decentralization, sometimes in conjunction with it, advisory councils, paraprofessionals, community liaison workers—all manner of citizens—have come to be viewed as normal participants in school operations.

But participation does not always lead to an increase in influence. If there is a further decline in the legitimacy or autonomy of local school systems or if increased accessibility leads to the creation of perpetual stalemates, then nothing has been gained. The policy process can tolerate only so many veto groups. Still, the growth of citizen participation is a goal with widespread support among school officials and community groups. For the new activists, the call for greater participation has helped legitimate their own role in school affairs even if continuous widespread citizen involvement was never attained. School officials have found the prospect of creating a supportive clientele group appealing, especially in view of the growing fiscal crisis of the school system and the need for allies with political support. Even the teachers unions may come to see wider parent participation in a more favorable light as the lesser of several evils. Pressures for the educational voucher plan and for contracting out with private corporations for educational services may appear more threatening, so that union support for community involvement might seem a price worth paying to help forestall more radical changes.

## The Impact of Decentralization

It is difficult to generalize about the actual impact of decentralization on the schools. In some districts there have been curriculum changes, more bilingual programs, and some ethnic studies, but the reforms have been limited by lack of funding and by state curriculum standards. Some districts have begun to recruit staff outside the system and to experiment with accountability devices, but union contracts and other civil service requirements do not leave much flexibility. No significant evidence exists about the relationship of decentralization to student achievement. Cause and effect relationships will be so difficult to sort out that no such evidence is likely to appear in the short run.

Any evaluation of the impact of decentralization is greatly complicated by the effects of broad national trends. Issues of school finance and desegregation, for example, intersect with decentralization controversies, and inevitably bring dimensions of national policy into local conflicts. The Nixon Administration, although deeply committed to less federal intervention and to a strengthened role for the states and their localities in addressing the problems of the cities, has found it impossible to avoid involvement with these school issues. The school finance crisis, and in particular the tangle of issues concerning local property tax burdens and equalization of per-pupil expenditures, will be greatly affected by federal action. Federal court decisions as well as administration policy may be decisive in determining the structure of school finance and administration.

Equalization could in theory work against greater participation at the local level, insofar as guidelines and standards adopted by the state legislatures, the Congress, or the courts determine the assignment of experienced teachers, the allocation of funds for special projects, and numerous other educational policy matters. Thus there might be less scope for local influence and participation in critical aspects of educational policy.

Yet one can also imagine that fiscal equality could be combined with greater citizen participation at the local level. If equalizing formulas could be designed so as to assure fixed minimum operating revenues to either the individual schools or small districts, much like revenue sharing arrangements that call for the "pass through" of monies to local governments, there might be substantial opportunities for increased local participation in deciding curriculum, personnel, and other policy matters. Yet the complexities of devising such procedures are a principal reason why revenue sharing and tax reform measures are so difficult to legislate. Also, the complex nature of the task makes it likely that any system will require considerable administrative machinery. The operation of any new school finance system is likely to involve federal and state guidelines along with continual administrative contact between officials at the different levels of government. The extreme versions of local control are clearly ruled out in such circumstances, although other forms of citizen involvement in school affairs would still be possible.

Similarly, local integration policies will be affected by shifts in federal priorities. The decentralization movement seems to have had less tangible impact on integration than many earlier commentators feared. In most cities, the realistic possibility of integration had ended before the decentralization movement gained momentum in the late 1960s. The reasons behind the failure of integration lay chiefly with the racial demography of most large American cities. The influx of blacks to the cities and the white flight to suburbs and to private schools left the public school enrollment "too black" to be integrated. Generally, decentralized boundary lines have merely recognized the *de facto* racial situation. It is perhaps true that decentralization may have accelerated trends already present and thus further retarded the short run prospects for integration in some cities. But, equally, by giving white neighborhoods a sense of control over "their schools," decentralization in some instances may have encouraged whites to stay in the city.

Decentralization has also had an effect on the symbolic support for integration. It gave white liberals a fall-back pro-black position when the integration alternative collapsed or became too costly politically. For some blacks, community control was an ideological concept that could be used to organize their agenda when integration was no longer an alternative. Decentralization became not just a means, but a legitimate end in a pluralistic society. Control over neighborhood institutions was the way a group could create the group identity and cohesion to play pluralistic politics.

Although ideological commitment to the separatist version of community control still exists among minority leaders, the numbers of ideological purists are small, and their influence is waning. Ideological rigidity seems to be receding and a tactical flexibility, geared to the conditions faced locally, seems to be emerging among big city blacks and Spanish-speaking groups. Community control of the schools and other public institutions might be sought as a goal in Chicago or Philadelphia, where effective city-wide influence is blocked for the near future. But in cities dominated by minority groups, a different political strategy is favored. In Newark and Gary, for example, white suggestions of community control for certain neighborhoods have been blocked by black mayors. A similar pragmatic attitude appears to be emerging toward integration among minority group political strategists. Where integration appears realistically attainable, or where white allies are essential to a political coalition, integrationist appeals and tactics will remain important. The integration issue will be ignored in cases where conditions make integration unrealistic and where white support is either unavailable or unnecessary.

While the relationship between decentralization and integration has been exaggerated, the implications of decentralization for the municipal union movement have not been fully appreciated. The objective of many community control advocates, and a goal that has increasingly emerged as critical to school activists of many political shadings, is holding school personnel accountable. This often means, in practical terms, the right to hire, fire, and promote school personnel. The challenge to professionalism has not abated but has intensified in all cities where the decentralization movement was strong. In theory, one might suspect that a powerful teachers union organized on a city-wide basis would have little difficulty in bargaining with the individual boards, whip-sawing, and threatening selective strikes against recalcitrant districts. In practice, however, the local boards have seemed to be unusually tough bargainers, often seeking to undo long-standing agreements that the unions have won in collective bargaining at the city-wide level. The presence of local board representatives in the fall of 1972 at the contract negotiations between the central board and the UFT in New York City, as noted above, contributed to the stiffening of the board's position.

The local boards, because of the distrust of the school professionals, have generally appeared to be more resistant to union pressures than city-wide officials who have been afraid to incur the wrath of the increasingly militant municipal unions. Decentralization may perhaps offer what has been conspicuously lacking in most urban political systems: an effective counterweight to the growing power of public employee unions. Although the effects of a growing role for the local boards in a collective bargaining process are not entirely predictable, a likely consequence may be a toning down of union wage demands and a shift emphasis toward the preservation of job security and due process rights already won at the bargaining table.

Those whose interest in politics is broader than schools have begun to notice another potential shift in power related to decentralization. Neighborhood groups have found natural allies among the state legislators against the power of City Hall and the city school board. The combination of heightened political activity on the neighborhood level and a more active role for the state has created an intricate situation for city-wide officials. To harrassed mayors, and to city boards of education, there seems to be a potential danger of erosion of authority from below and absorption of functions by higher authority. The net result may be that, by undermining the power of traditional city authorities, important decisions will be shifted away from local constituencies to the state level. Minority groups, in particular, may find that they were in a stronger position to influence budgeting and other policies made at the city level rather than in the state legislature or state administrative agencies.

Nowhere are these intersecting trends more apparent than in New York City, where intense political battles over structural reform have continued into the 1970s. By 1972, school decentralization had become a fact of life in New York. Political attention was focused on decentralizing other city services. The rule that structural reform never has neutral political consequences was closely observed by all parties. The Lindsay administration began a modest experimental program in several districts of the city. Decentralization plans were proposed by the Bronx and Manhattan Borough Presidents, the Bar Association for the City of New York, and other groups.[5] A state study commission investigating the city also supported decentralization, and various state agencies maneuvered for a larger role in city affairs. The Fleischmann Commission studying public school finance recommended both the takeover of an important share of educational financing by the state and greater citizen participation in school affairs at the local level. The Rockefeller-Lindsay disputes had temporarily stalemated with the creation of a new charter commission to review the structure of city government and to prepare a referendum for 1973.

The outcome of this complex interplay of forces was difficult to predict, but several developments were noteworthy. As the politics for city-wide decentralization began to intensify, an interesting change of alignments took place. Mayor Lindsay (now a Democrat) and reform Democrats previously sympathetic to decentralization began to back away, while the formerly apathetic Republicans found new "good government" values in the concept. This change was particularly embarrassing to the reform Democrats, whose years of agitation against the "bosses" and unresponsive authority had helped to create a climate of distrust of traditional city-wide institutions and a feeling that more citizen participation was a cure. Now that the upstate Republicans have come to view decentralization within New York City as a means of breaking up the traditional Democratic stronghold, however, the enthusiasm among city Democrats for the concept has waned rapidly. The political task for them seemed to be to find some way to satisfy popular desires for wider participation without at the same time enfeebling the city government and especially the powers of the Mayor. The roots of this conflict lay not in antagonism between Governor Rockefeller and Mayor Lindsay, despite their occasionally colorful personal clashes, but in the issue of the future of self-government in the city and the struggle for dominance in state politics.

Some believe the conflict can be resolved by creating regional or metropolitan government. The drive toward regionalism has, in fact, flourished in the period since decentralization has been a salient urban issue. In some respects, the two strategies may be mutually reinforcing. By breaking up the big cities into units more nearly the size of the suburbs, it is hoped, the suburban fear of consolidation might be diminished and a more rational allocation of resources and responsibilities achieved. At this moment, however, no serious plans have been designed for the three-state New York metropolitan area, and no plausible formula for combining metropolitanism and decentralization has been devised.

It is a matter of some irony that the urban decentralization movement, which started out five years earlier as a black protest movement, has become an essentially conservative strategy for guaranteeing Republican hegemony in the state and fragmenting Democratic power in New York City. This perhaps implied a return to tradition, since for most of this century the ideology of decentralization has not been identified with the cause of reform in American politics, but rather with the preservation of existing values. As such, decentralization is more naturally a Republican doctrine. For the Democrats, the concept poses the risk of antagonism between elements of the New Deal coalition, chiefly labor and minority gorups, and thus of fracturing the Democratic alliance. The current weakness of the Democrats in the state to some degree may be a reflection of the internal conflicts caused by the decentralization issue. Labor, with a predominantly white ethnic constituency, has resented the efforts of party reformers to redistribute power and union jobs to minorities. The same sort of difficulties may increasingly confront the Democratic Party nationally. The poverty program in the 1960s complicated the position of many Democratic mayors and further weakened urban party structures that were already undergoing a process of erosion. As we have shown, however, it is the particular elements of a particular decentralization plan in a particular context that determines who will benefit, not the abstract concept of decentralization itself.

### The Future of School Decentralization

The speed with which community control rhetoric was adopted by minority groups and white liberals in the late 1960s made it appear plausible, for a time, that the radical versions of decentralization might become a dominant form of urban school government in the 1970s. In the light of subsequent experience, it has become apparent that the momentum of the school decentralization movement has considerably slowed, and in its more radical versions has all but disappeared.

There are several reasons why this is so. In the first place, the coalition that supported the movement was more fragile than appeared to early observers, themselves caught up in the battle as either advocates or enemies and somewhat misled by the attention the mass media paid to the issue. The volatile urban political process, in which the mass media have come to play an important role as agenda-setters, contributed to the rapid rise and fall of decentralization as a prominent public issue. Although in some cities, decentralization became a major focus of media attention during the New York controversy, it had not achieved a broad base of local support, and the issue faded rapidly as a major news item once the immediate controversy was over. This abrupt lack of media attention made it seem that the movement had run its course, which dampened the enthusiasm of its followers. As a matter of fact, some of the most significant developments in the decentralization movement have proceeded almost unnoticed by the media since the period marked by dramatic confrontations. This rather deceptive coverage by the mass media is one of the curiosities of contemporary urban politics. The erosion of the political parties, and the absence of their traditional role in an orderly articulation of the issues, has undoubtedly played a part in the emergence of a rather unstable agenda of public concerns.

Second, the money which funded the movement has all but disappeared. The Nixon Administration has tightened the purse and political strings on OEO community action agencies. As irregularities have emerged in the management of many of the experimental programs of the 1960s, there has been much less "loose money" available from federal agencies for political mobilization purposes. In the past several years, only the measure calling for federal aid to establish day care centers on a large scale has represented a significant new opportunity to create a local political base in minority areas, and this was no doubt a key factor in President Nixon's decision to veto the bill in the spring of 1972.

The Tax Reform Act of 1969, in dealing with foundations, has made them much more cautious about financing community control projects. Although the effect of the revisions in the internal revenue code has been less far-reaching than many foundation officials originally feared, the action taken by Congress has left a widespread feeling in the foundation community that community control efforts in education, like voter registration drives, created too much controversy and endangered the foundation's role in American life. There has also been an important change of view as to the wisdom of some of the early foundation efforts in the field of community control of education. The Ford Foundation, for example, which played an important role in funding community control projects in New York City and elsewhere, came to believe that some of its early activities in the field had disappointing consequences.

Furthermore, the general economic recession has limited all kinds of educational experiments and made it clear to community leaders that control of the schools carries a heavy mortgage. As the public schools have faced massive budget cuts, parents, community leaders, teachers, and administrators have had to put aside their differences to create temporary alliances. A vivid example of this was the extraordinary situation in New York City in 1971 following the announcement of a $40 million cut in the school budget by the board of education; an *ad hoc* alliance led by UFT president Albert Shanker and his former enemies among the community leaders said that it would conduct a march of one and a half million people—the largest demonstration in United States history—to city hall to protest the proposed cuts. The march was called off when an eleventh-hour solution averted the crisis.

The decentralization movement lost more of its steam as it became clear that political realities did not match the rhetoric of community control. For one thing, its advocates misperceived the character of local school government in non-urban America. Parents do not hire and fire teachers at will in Scarsdale and Grosse Pointe. Collective bargaining agreements, state regulations, and court orders cannot be disregarded in so-called independent school districts. Indeed, all school districts have lost considerable autonomy in recent years, and shared authority characterizes educational politics everywhere. Nor were the community control advocates able to predict that it is easier to mobilize the vote through the infrastructure in middle-class white neighborhoods than in the ghettos. The results of the first two elections, though not as bad as originally perceived, have had a chastening effect on those who saw decentralization as a device for creating black control of black schools.

Finally, many school systems, out of fear or agreement with the participatory ideology, have made some response to it. New participatory mechanisms have been adopted and, although these mechanisms are subtle and uneven, minority group parents often find that the system affords them easier access and a more sensitive reception than in the past. In Los Angeles, and especially in New York City, where minorities were distinctly under-represented in the administration of the school system, important shifts have begun in staffing patterns. The number of blacks and, to a lesser extent, other minorities in teaching and administrative positions has generally increased and in some instances dramatically. Paraprofessionals in some cities have acquired full status as employees of the school system.

In some schools with disciplinary or learning problems, white teachers and white principals have gradually been replaced with blacks by informal and tacit understandings as the means of buying peace and achieving the possibility for order in the schools. Many white principals have opted for early retirement rather than to fight what they regard as increasingly frustrating battles with the community. What has happened at the local level is sometimes greater than is officially acknowledged by central school administrators who are not eager to advertise their lack of effective control over the school system. Indeed, in some schools, parent associations have achieved *de facto* control over some curriculum and personnel decisions. To the extent that lack of access or participation were the problems decentralization was supposed to solve, these accommodations have decreased the pressure for further structural change.

Although the momentum of the social decentralization movement has faltered and community control proposals are currently moribund, cities other than those discussed here will eventually be considering structural reform of school governance and the decentralization option. Should they follow the pattern set in New York and Detroit? Should they adopt participatory devices short of community control? Or is there some other model that could be generally recommended?

Our case studies lead us to conclude that it is unlikely that any single model could be adopted or would be effective if implemented. The great differences in the populations and problems in America seems to foreclose such a uniform solution. Furthermore, we are skeptical about the romantic yearning for Milton Kotler's "Neighborhoood Government" and suspicious of the partisan and class interests seeking to dismantle city halls. But we are not adverse to further careful experiments with decentralization and other participatory devices. While educational policy shares with other policy areas the factors of complexity and systemic impact that might inhibit an effective role for lay citizens, it has some special characteristics as well. Unlike institutions in other policy areas, most citizens have had some sustained involvement with schools. Although that may not give them any insights into the technical problems of either budget or pedagogy, it does provide an important reservoir of intuitive evaluations and value judgments that ought to be represented in the policy process. Further, if a school system is serious, motivation often exists among parents to learn enough to participate competently in policy discussions. What is involved after all is the policy that will develop the civic attitudes and vocational options of children. Society at large has an important interest in these questions, but there is a particular stake for parents. There is nothing analogous in other policy areas to the special emotional ties and responsibility of parents for their children.

Added to this consideration is the growing desire to increase educational options, especially the variety of socialization patterns. We think decentralization is a better alternative to that end than adopting a voucher or tax credit program. The latter reduces the public accountability of schools, and exacerbates the divisions and inequalities in society.[6] Short of decentralization, some parental and student needs can be met by creating more distinctive smaller schools within the larger system. In some cities, Fantini's concept of empowering parents through petition rights might prove valuable.[7] If laws established the obligation of school systems to respond to petitions for curriculum changes and other reforms, some of the feelings of alienation and lack of communication might be mitigated. Within certain categories, minority groups could get some of their programs implemented without having to win a majority on the school board.

None of these suggestions constitutes a definitive recommendation for or against decentralization in a particular city. Here we can be more confident about the right questions than the right answers. Few large school systems, none that we studied, have effectively used contemporary techniques of public opinion polling or market surveys. Such information should not be decisive for public policy, but in a political arrangement where city board members are often appointed or elected in non-partisan, low turn-out, issue-obscured elections, these techniques can be useful in assessing the attitudes of the system's clients and in keeping minority viewpoints from being buried. Certainly, before deciding on the decentralization alternative it would be useful to know how seriously people take neighborhood and local community values compared to other identities and values. If neighborhoods are salient for citizen identity, it should also be useful to know the character and quality of education various communities want. Are these desires compatible with other broader goals of equality and integration? Indeed, what policy role do parents want? The answers to these questions surely cannot be assumed—as the community-control advocates have typically done. Rarely, however, will an opinion poll provide simple and unambiguous guides to decisions on the muddy normative issues of broad school policy.

Hopefully, we have reached the end of the panacea era of educational reform. Teaching machines, performance contracting, PPBS, educational parks, and the like may be useful in certain contexts, but they are not "the" reform. The same is true for school decentralization. We hope that this book has contributed to de-mythologizing the concept, and that it has encouraged further analysis of realistic policy options.

For those who expected profound changes from the decentralization movement, as well as for those who viewed the events reported here as almost wholly transitory, our findings will no doubt prove disappointing. The decentralization movement has been neither revolutionary nor inconsequential. The energies released in the 1960s and the powerful appeal of the participation ideology have left an imprint on America's politics. Even where institutional practices have not been permanently changed, the process of interaction between professional and citizen has been modified. But America's pluralist politics has absorbed the new activists using the traditional means of resolving conflict to answer their demands for change. The challenge of federalism in the urban context remains characterized by the search for solutions to common problems within a framework of fiscal constraint and shared powers. The 1970s will see experimentation with new forms of urban school government, including elements of both metropolitanism and community involvement at the local level. The viability of these educational experiments will have important ramifications for the kind of federalism that will develop in other public service areas, and for the wider political struggles that involve the cities.

**Notes**

# Notes

## Chapter 1

1. Samuel Beer, "Liberalism and the National Idea," The PUBLIC INTEREST, (Fall 1969).

2. Alan Altshuler, COMMUNITY CONTROL (New York, Pegasus Books 1970); Milton Kotler, NEIGHBORHOOD GOVERNMENT (Indianapolis and New York: Bobbs-Merrill, 1969), and Joseph F. Zimmerman, THE FEDERATED CITY (New York: St. Martins Press, 1972).

3. Daniel Bell and Virginia Held, "The Community Revolution," the PUBLIC INTEREST (Summer 1969), and Henry S. Kariel, OPEN SYSTEMS: ARENAS FOR POLITICAL ACTION (Ithaca, Ill.: F.E. Peacock & Co., 1969).

4. THE GOVERNMENT OF THE CITIES, Occasional Paper of the Weatherhead Foundation, New York, 1971, p. 19.

5. Walter Farr, Lance Liebman, and Jeffrey S. Wood, DECENTRALIZING CITY GOVERNMENT (New York: Praeger Special Studies, forthcoming, 1973).

6. See, *inter alia*, Committee for Economic Development, RESHAPING GOVERNMENT IN METROPOLITAN AREAS (New York, 1970); Alan K. Campbell, ed., the STATES AND THE URBAN CRISIS (Englewood Cliffs, N.J.: Prentice-Hall, 1970); and Bruce L.R. Smith and George LaNoue, eds., URBAN DECENTRALIZATION AND COMMUNITY PARTICIPATION, AMERICAN BEHAVIORAL SCIENTIST (vol. 15, no. 1, September/October 1971).

7. James Q. Wilson, CITY POLITICS AND PUBLIC POLICY (New York: John Wiley and Sons, 1968), p. 3.

8. Herbert Kaufman, "Administrative Decentralization and Political Power," PUBLIC ADMINISTRATION REVIEW, 29 (January 1969).

9. One commentator has urged that citizens be allowed to play the role of public official or to act, under proper supervision, as technical staff in complex government operations like tracking a missile at the NASA space center. See Henry Kariel, op. cit.

10. J. Clarence Davies, NEIGHBORHOOD GROUPS AND URBAN RENEWAL (New York: Columbia University Press, 1966).

11. James S. Davis, Jr., and Kenneth M. Dolbeare, LITTLE GROUPS OF NEIGHBORS: THE SELECTIVE SERVICE SYSTEM (Chicago: Markham Publishing Co., 1968).

12. Roscoe Martin, GRASS ROOTS (Montgomery: University of Alabama Press, 1964).

13. Herbert Kaufman, "The New York City Health Centers," Interuniversity Case Program 9 (University of Alabama, 1959).

14. Roscoe Martin, G.S. Birkhead, Jesse Burkhead, and Frank J. Munger, RIVER BASIN ADMINISTRATION AND THE DELAWARE (New York, Syracuse University Press, 1960).

15. See the discussion in Charles V. Hamilton, "Conflict, Race and System-transformation in the United States," JOURNAL OF INTERNATIONAL AFFAIRS (vol. 23, no. 1, 1969), pp. 106-118.

## Chapter 2

1. For a history of this development see R. Freeman Butts and Lawrence A. Cremin, A HISTORY OF EDUCATION IN AMERICAN CULTURE (New York: Holt, Rinehart and Winston, Inc., 1953), pp. 100-106.

2. For a history and description of the operation of school districts and boards a good standard source is Raold F. Campbell, Luvern L. Cunningham, Roderick F. McPhee, THE ORGANIZATION AND CONTROL OF THE AMERICAN SCHOOLS (Columbus, Ohio: Charles Merrill Co., 1965), pp. 80-109, 157-187.

3. James Conant, THE AMERICAN HIGH SCHOOL TODAY (New York: McGraw Hill Book Co., Inc., 1959).

4. The best statistical analysis of school boards is Alpheus L. White, LOCAL SCHOOL BOARDS: ORGANIZATION AND PRACTICES (Washington, D.C.: G.P.O., 1962). See also Keith Goldhammer, THE SCHOOL BOARD (New York: The Center for Applied Research in Education, Inc., 1964).

5. This myth is explored in Thomas H. Eliot, "Toward an Understanding of Public School Politics," AMERICAN POLITICAL SCIENCE REVIEW (December 1959).

6. For example, August B. Hollingshead, ELMTOWN'S YOUTH (New York: Science Editions, 1961), Chapter 6. These studies are summarized in Daniel E. Griffiths, HUMAN RELATIONS IN SCHOOL ADMINISTRATION (New York: Appleton-Century Crofts, Inc., 1956), pp. 109-110.

7. A useful symposium about the role of local boards can be found in the papers from the Cubberly Conference as reprinted in THE AMERICAN SCHOOL BOARD JOURNAL (March 1967).

8. For analysis of both aspects see Roscoe C. Martin, GOVERNMENT AND THE SUBURBAN SCHOOL (Syracuse: Syracuse University Press, 1963).

9. Raold F. Campbell, "The Folklore of Local School Control," THE SCHOOL REVIEW (September 1959).

10. Among the best critiques are Joseph Pois, THE SCHOOL BOARD CRISIS (Chicago: Educational Methods Incorporated, 1964), David Rogers, 110 LIVINGSTON STREET (New York: Random House, 1968), and Peter Schrag, VILLAGE SCHOOL DOWNTOWN (Boston: Beacon Press, 1967).

11. Luvern L. Cunningham and Raphael O. Nystrand, CITIZEN PARTICIPATION IN SCHOOL AFFAIRS (Washington, D.C.: The Urban Coalition, 1969).

12. Raold F. Campbell and Robert A. Bunnell, NATIONALIZING INFLUENCES IN SECONDARY EDUCATION (Chicago: Midwest Education Center;

University of Chicago, 1963). For an argument that local control of education was morally and politically untenable by the 1960s see Myron Lieberman, THE FUTURE OF PUBLIC EDUCATION (Chicago: The University of Chicago Press, 1960).

13. George D. Strayer, for the Educational Policies Commission, THE STRUCTURE AND ADMINISTRATION OF EDUCATION IN AMERICAN DEMOCRACY (Washington, D.C., The Commission, 1938), p. 79.

14. Paul R. Mort and Francis G. Cornell, ADAPTABILITY OF PUBLIC SCHOOL SYSTEMS (New York: Bureau of Publications, Teachers College, Columbia University, 1938), p. 100.

15. Francois S. Cillie, CENTRALIZATION OR DECENTRALIZATION? A STUDY IN EDUCATIONAL ADAPTATION (New York: Bureau of Publications, Teachers College, 1940).

16. These studies are discussed in Bureau of School and Cultural Research, HISTORICAL REVIEW OF STUDIES AND PROPOSALS RELATIVE TO DECENTRALIZATION OF ADMINISTRATION IN THE NEW YORK CITY PUBLIC SCHOOL SYSTEM (New York: The State Education Department, 1967), pp. 16-19.

17. Stokely Carmichael and Charles V. Hamilton, BLACK POWER: THE POLITICS OF LIBERATION IN AMERICA (New York: Random House, 1967), pp. 166-167. An excellent 23-article symposium of black attitudes on the questions of integration and community control can be found in EBONY (August 1970).

18. Preston R. Wilcox, "The Controversy over I.S. 201," THE URBAN REVIEW (July 1966), pp. 12-17.

19. Joe L. Rempson, "For an Elected Local School Board," THE URBAN REVIEW (November 1966), pp. 2-11.

20. Milton Kotler, NEIGHBORHOOD GOVERNMENT: THE LOCAL FOUNDATION OF POLITICAL LIFE (Indianapolis and New York: The Bobbs Merrill Company, 1969), p. 39. For a more sober view of the possibilities of neighborhood government see "Reshaping Government in Metropolitan Areas," (New York: Committee for Economic Development, 1970), and "Neighborhood's Subunit of Government? State Legislative Programs" (Washington, D.C.: Advisory Commission on Intergovernmental Relations, 1970). A useful review of these issues and a bibliography can be found in Donna E. Shalala, NEIGHBORHOOD GOVERNANCE: ISSUES AND PROPOSALS (New York: American Jewish Committee, 1971).

21. Alan A. Altshuler, COMMUNITY CONTROL OF SCHOOLS: THE BLACK DEMAND FOR PARTICIPATION IN LARGE AMERICAN CITIES (New York: Pegasus, 1970), p. 216.

22. Leonard Fein, THE ECOLOGY OF THE PUBLIC SCHOOLS: AN INQUIRY INTO COMMUNITY CONTROL (New York: Pegasus, 1971).

23. Mario Fantini, Marilyn Gittell and Richard Magat, COMMUNITY CONTROL AND THE URBAN SCHOOL (New York: Praeger, 1971), p. 251.

24. The most optimistic view of the research on this subject can be found in Carol Lopata, Erwin Flaxman, Effie M. Bynum and Edmund W. Gordon, "Decentralization and Community Participation in Public Education," REVIEW OF EDUCATIONAL RESEARCH (February 1970), pp. 135-150. See also Maurice Berube, "Educational Achievement and Community Control," COMMUNITY ISSUES (November 1, 1969), and "Administrative Decentralization Sharpens Staff Performance," SCHOOL MANAGEMENT (September 1968), pp. 45-48, 51-52. David Cohen in "The Price of Community Control" reviewed this evidence and concluded " . . . if one were to be guided solely by research on achievement and attitudes, one would not employ community control or decentralization as the devices most likely to reduce racial disparities in achievement." COMMENTARY (July 1969), p. 28.

25. For an interesting discussion of current ethnic competition, see the new introduction by Nathan Glazer and Daniel P. Moynihan to BEYOND THE MELTING POT, Second Edition (Cambridge: MIT Press, 1970).

26. Mario Fantini, THE REFORM OF URBAN SCHOOLS (Washington, D.C.: NEA, 1970), p. 52.

27. Marilyn Gittell, et al., DEMONSTRATION FOR SOCIAL CHANGE: AN EXPERIMENT IN LOCAL CONTROL (New York: Institute for Community Studies, 1971), p. 1.

28. Terry Clark, "On Decentralization," POLITY (vol. 2, 1970), pp. 508-514.

29. Suzanne Keller, THE URBAN NEIGHBORHOOD (New York: Random House, 1968), pp. 99-102.

30. Lieberman, op. cit., p. 34.

31. Fein, op. cit., p. 42.

## Chapter 3

1. The exception to this generalization might be the various federal programs aimed at requiring citizen participation among minority and low income groups. Considerable debate exists regarding the purposes of these programs. In some cities, New York, St. Louis, for example, they were important in assisting the decentralization movement. Some local groups, particularly anti-poverty organizations, thought in terms of a comprehensive community control ideology, but it is not clear that their federal sponsors ever agreed on such a goal. Discussion of these programs and their problems may be found in Kenneth Clark, A RELEVANT WAR AGAINST POVERTY: A STUDY OF COMMUNITY ACTION AND SOCIAL CHANGE (New York: Harper and Row, 1969) and Daniel P. Moynihan, MAXIMUM FEASIBLE MISUNDERSTANDING: COMMUNITY ACTION IN THE WAR ON POVERTY (New York: Free Press, 1969) and Ralph M. Kramer, PARTICIPATION OF THE POOR (Englewood Cliffs: Prentice-Hall, 1969).

2. David Rogers, 110 LIVINGSTON STREET (New York: Random House, 1969).

3. A list of some of these projects can be found in Lloyd R. Howell, "Decentralization Patterns of Action in Great Cities," NORTH CENTRAL ASSOCIATION QUARTERLY (Fall 1969), pp. 257-260.

4. Much of the data gathering and statistical analysis for this chapter was done by Marvin Pilo, a graduate student at Teachers College.

The population statistics used in this section are from the 1960 census and later projections. School data are from the Fall of 1967. They were made available by the Office of Civil Rights, HEW. The data on residential integration which compares 1940 and 1960 are from Karl E. and Alma F. Tauber, NEGROES IN CITIES (Chicago: Aldine Publishing House). Statistics on dropouts (1960) are from Robert A. Dentler and Mary Ellen Warshauer, BIG CITY DROPOUTS AND ILLITERATES (New York: Center for Urban Education, 1965). Data on vandalism (net cost per pupil 1966-67) are from Baltimore City Schools, Division of Research and Development), VANDALISM: STUDY OF SELECTED GREAT CITIES (Baltimore: mimeo, 1968). Information on school board elections comes from Education Research Service, "Local School Boards: Status and Practice" (Washington, D.C.: Educational Research Service, mimeo, 1967). Fiscal relationships are described in H. Thomas, James, et al., DETERMINANTS OF EDUCATIONAL EXPENDITURES IN LARGE CITIES OF THE UNITED STATES (Stanford: School of Education, Stanford University, 1966).

5. It might have been possible to apply factor analysis or some other more sophisticated statistical technique than was used here. But it is difficult to use such techniques in a sample of this size. Expanding the sample by including smaller cities distorts the comparisons with larger cities. Without intensive field investigation it is not very feasible to scale the cities according to the degree of school decentralization, so a simple but not very satisfactory centralized/decentralized classification was used. Finally there is the problem of the chronological match of the classification with the comparative data available from the cities. Though it is probable that these demographic or political factors do not fluctuate rapidly in large cities, there is still the problem of comparing decentralization in 1970 with a variable measured in 1965 or 1960. We think the statistical approach used here demonstrates that there are no simple statistical correlations of much importance.


**Chapter 4**

1. A description of the failure to create a limited-function metropolitan government can be found in Henry J. Schmandt, Paul G. Steinbecker, and George D. Wendel, METROPOLITAN REFORM IN ST. LOUIS: A CASE STUDY (New York: Holt, Rinehart and Winston, 1961). A Metropolitan Sewer

District and a Metropolitan Junior College District do exist and a Metropolitan Cultural District was created in 1971 to help the city keep its fine Forest Park facilities and museum open, but cooperation between city and country is otherwise quite restricted.

2. Marilyn Gittell and T. Edward Hollander, SIX URBAN SCHOOL DISTRICTS (New York: Praeger, 1968), pp. 152-164.

3. Patricia Jansen Doyle, "St. Louis: City with the Blues," SATURDAY REVIEW, February 15, 1969.

4. These statistics come from a series of annual reports on the St. Louis public schools which Superintendent Kottmeyer has titled HARD TIMES AND GREAT EXPECTATIONS, A TALE OF TWO CITIES and ST. LOUIS SCORE-CARD. Immediately after the *Brown* decision and before action by the state legislature, the reform-dominated board adapted a plan that would have created substantial integration.

5. A very laudatory description of the system's desegregation efforts is contained in THE ST. LOUIS STORY by Bonita H. Valien, a professor at Fisk University. Written in 1956 and published by the Anti-Defamation League of B'nai B'rith, this pamphlet reflects the rosy optimism of integrationists after *Brown*. One interesting facet of the system's desegregation strategy was its use of decentralization as a defense mechanism. Authority to decide the myriad transportation, curriculum problems, etc. that were created by desegregation was theoretically given to individual school principals. This approach effectively defused citywide protests. A description of a later period of desegregation politics (1963-1965) in St. Louis can be found in Robert L. Crain, THE POLITICS OF SCHOOL DESEGREGATION (Chicago: Aldine, 1968). This study also gives good marks to the system for its desegregation efforts (p. 27) though St. Louis had the lowest percentage of Negro students in integrated schools of any of eight cities he studied (p. 107). Ralph Reisner's chapter "St. Louis" in AFFIRMATIVE SCHOOL INTEGRATION: EFFORTS TO OVERCOME DE FACTO SEGREGATION ed. by Roscoe Hill and Malcolm Falley (Beverly Hills: Sage Publication, 1967) is considerably less laudatory. Reisner points out that when black students were bussed in 1962 and 1963 they were kept in segregated classrooms in the white receiving schools, (p. 55). The problem was ameliorated later by building new schools in black neighborhoods and reducing busing. In any event, since the mid-sixties, massive population shifts caused by urban renewal, expressway construction and suburban flight have substantially resegregated the schools despite limited Board efforts to the contrary.

6. The Civil Rights Commission classifies a school as integrated if it enrolls no more than 69 percent minority group students and no less than 29 percent. St. Louis GLOBE DEMOCRAT, March 9, 1970.

7. "St. Louis Ranks Worst in Survey of Liberalism," ST. LOUIS POST DISPATCH, April 5, 1970.

8. H.C. Morrison, ADMINISTRATION AND ORGANIZATION IN ST. LOUIS PUBLIC SCHOOL SURVEY (St. Louis: Board of Education, 1937), p. 49.

9. Most of the history of the reform movement comes from a memorandum that Daniel Schlafly kindly provided the author, December 15, 1971.

10. Ibid., p. 18.

11. Mr. Kottmeyer targets have even extended to such previously sacrosanct figures as Professors of Education doing field research. His sentiments were expressed thusly:

> A musky college prof flew in.
> (His teaching load was light).
> "I haven't time to stick around.
> My schedule's awf'ly tight.
> The schools here *must* be obsolete.
> I'll depart and start to write!"

ST. LOUIS SCORECARD, pp. v.-10.

12. The U.S. Civil Rights Commission criticized the St. Louis tracking system in CIVIL RIGHTS U.S.A.: PUBLIC SCHOOLS IN CITY IN THE NORTH AND WEST (Washington, D.C.: G.P.O., 1962), p. 292.

13. In 1950, St. Louis city schools received more money from the state than country schools. By 1964, city schools received $8.00 per child less than county schools despite the increasing educational disadvantage of city students and the declining city tax base, as cited in the REPORT OF THE NATIONAL ADVISORY COMMISSION ON CIVIL DISORDER (New York: Bantam Books, 1968), p. 435.

14. William S. Rukyser, "The St. Louis Economic Blues," FORTUNE, vol. 77, 1968, pp. 210-212.

15. For a discussion of the development community schools see Elsia R. Clapp, COMMUNITY SCHOOLS IN ACTION (New York: The Viking Press, 1939).

16. The Banneker district programs received an extraordinary amount of publicity. Discussions of the programs occurred in TIME, June 8, 1959, LOOK, September 16, 1961, LIFE, January 26, 1962, FORTUNE, March, 1962, SATURDAY EVENING POST, April 14, 1962 and September 14, 1963 and READERS DIGEST, March 1964, as well as in many education journals. One of the best descriptions of the program is contained in THE NEW ERA, December, 1966.

17. The St. Louis community schools have been formally evaluated by the Governmental Research Institute in two reports dated September, 1967 and May 1970. The quotation is from the latter report, p. 3.

18. Ibid., p. 66.

19. ST. LOUIS SCOREBOARD, Section VII, p. 3.

20. See the press release "Recommendations for Greater Local Participation in the Total Operation of the St. Louis Public Schools," Office of the Superintendent, January 14, 1961. This document also contains much of the earlier history of school decentralization in St. Louis.

21. Most of the historical background on the Murphy-Blair district comes from interviews with George Eberle, the director of Grace Hill.

22. Milton Kotler, NEIGHBORHOOD GOVERNMENT (Indianapolis: Bobbs-Merrill Co., 1969).

23. "The Murphy-Blair Neighborhood Residents Plan," Hellmuth, Obata, and Kassabaum Inc., 1968.

24. "What is a School Forum?" Grace Hill Settlement House (Mimeo), March, 1969.

25. "Report to DEB on Status of Community School Proposal." Murphy-Blair District Education Board (Mimeo), October 16, 1969.

26. Letter from David Colton, member of the DEB and Director of the Graduate Institute of Education, Washington University of St. Louis to Elmer Pounds, member of the St. Louis Board of Education. December 23, 1969.

27. Letter from Elmer Pounds to John Fedrick, Chairman, Model City Board, March 19, 1970.

28. Division of Evaluation and Research. "A Response to the Recommendations of the Community Conference on St. Louis Public Schools," February, 1970, p. 53.

29. Ibid., p. 26.

30. Ibid., p. 17.

31. See the press release "St. Louis School Reorganization Plan," Office of the Superintendent, June 9, 1970.

32. For a discussion of the problems in researching non-issues see the exchange between Raymond Wolfinger and Frederick Frey in the AMERICAN POLITICAL SCIENCE REVIEW, 65, December 1971, pp. 1063-1104.

33. A 240-item bibliography can be found in Willis D. Hawley and Frederick M. Wirt, eds., THE SEARCH FOR COMMUNITY POWER (Englewood Cliffs, N.J.: Prentice-Hall, 1968).

34. REPORT OF THE NATIONAL COMMISSION ON CIVIL DISORDERS (New York: Bantam Books, 1968), p. 287.

35. Gittell and Hollander also found that community organizations played a comparatively minor role in educational decision-making (p. 165).

36. Peter Bachrach and Morton Baratz, "Decisions and Nondecisions: An Analytical Framework," AMERICAN POLITICAL SCIENCE REVIEW 57, (September 1963), p. 641.

37. Wolfinger, APSR, p. 1077.

38. Crain, p. 23 and Gittell and Hollander, p. 160.

39. The consequences of elite control may not always be conservative. Crain,

who felt that St. Louis had had some early integration success, explained that achievement largely in terms of the elite nature of the Board. Robert L. Crain, "Urban School Integration: Strategy for Peace" SATURDAY REVIEW, February 18, 1967, pp. 76-77.

"What is the difference between the conflict-ridden cities and those that have made progress peacefully? The major common factor in the cities that had made progress and kept the peace is a school board made up of what we call the civic elite—community leaders or their wives who have achieved success in the business or financial world and have shown a commitment to the community by volunteering their time for civic projects. Though they are in touch with other business and civic leaders, these people are somewhat aloof from day-to-day party politics. In short, they are not aristocracy, but they have energy, skill, prestige, and considerable political independence. In contrast, the cities which have had little integration and a great deal of conflict have boards which are made up of professional politicians or of individuals whose function it is to represent the various political, religious, or ethnic factions in the community. These findings, it should be noted, operate whether the board members are appointed or elected. If the cities studied are listed in order of the number of board members who are civic leaders, and then listed again in order of their acceptance of integration, the two listings are nearly identical."

40. The Conway and the Schlafly quotations are from the POST DISPATCH story of June 7, 1971.

41. An extensive description of state politics and education in Missouri can be found in Nicholas Masters, Robert Salisbury, and Thomas Eliot, STATE POLITICS AND THE PUBLIC SCHOOLS (New York: Alfred A. Knopf, 1964), pp. 12-85.

42. Chicago DAILY NEWS, October 16, 1971.

43. Postscript: The Conway bill was defeated again in 1972. This time the city PTA, the Missouri State School Board Association, and the St. Louis Elementary Schools Principals Association joined in opposition centered around the fear of increasing partisan influence in the schools. Rep. Conway, however, believes that his measure or some version of it will continue to be politically alive in the city.

## Chapter 5

1. Edward C. Banfield and James Q. Wilson, CITY POLITICS (New York: Vintage Books, 1966), p. 111. See also James Q. Wilson, THE AMATEUR DEMOCRAT (Chicago: University of Chicago Press, 1962), and the considerably dated but still useful A REPORT ON POLITICS IN LOS ANGELES (Cambridge, Mass.: Joint Center for Urban Studies, MIT and Harvard University, 1959). See also J. David Greenstone and Paul E. Peterson, "Reformers, Machines and the War on Poverty" in James Q. Wilson, CITY POLITICS AND PUBLIC POLICY,

New York, John Wiley, 1968, pp. 267-292, Francis M. Carney, "the Decentralized Politics of Los Angeles" ANNALS OF THE AMERICAN ACADEMY OF POLITICAL AND SOCIAL SCIENCE, May 1964, Vol. 353, pp. 107-121. For an authoritative account of the governmental structure of Los Angeles, see Winston Couch and Beatrice Dinerman, SOUTHERN CALIFORNIA METROPOLIS, A STUDY IN THE DEVELOPMENT OF GOVERNMENT FOR A METROPOLITAN AREA, Berkeley and Los Angeles: University of California Press, 1963. An unusual and dramatic exchange between Mayor Yorty and Senate critics illustrates the weakness of Los Angeles city government. See FEDERAL ROLE IN URBAN PROBLEMS, Hearing before the Subcommittee on Executive Reorganization of thy Committee on Government Operations, U.S. Senate, 89th Congress., 2nd session, part 3, August 22 and 23, 1966, esp. pp. 671-673, 774-775:

Senator Ribicoff: As I listened to your testimony, Mayor Yorty, I made some notes. This morning you have really waived authority and responsibility in the following areas: schools, welfare, transportation, employment, health, and housing, which leaves you as head of the city basically with a ceremonial function, police and recreation.
Mayor Yorty: That is right, and fire.
Senator Ribicoff: and fire.
Mayor Yorty: yes.
Senator Ribicoff: Collecting sewage?
Mayor Yorty: Sanitation; that is right.
Senator Ribicoff: In other words, basically you lack jurisdiction, authority responsibility for what makes a city move.
Mayor Yorty: That is exactly it.
Senator Ribicoff: . . . I would say that the city of Los Angeles, from your testimony, does not stand for a damn thing.
Mayor Yorty: Well, it stands for a lot, We are a great city.

2. For a detailed account of the annexation process that has shaped the city's boundaries, see Richard Bigger and James D. Kitchen, METROPOLITAN LOS ANGELES, A STUDY IN INTEGRATION; II. HOW THE CITIES GREW (Los Angeles: The Haynes Foundation, 1952).

3. The lag between the ethnic composition of the student population and the staff makeup is suggested by figures from the RACIAL AND ETHNIC SURVEY, Los Angeles City Schools, Fall 1968. For example, Spanish-surname pupils constituted 21.4% of the elementary school population but only 2.0% of the teaching staff and 1.8% of the administrators. For blacks, the figures were 24.5% of the elementary student population and 8.2% of the administrators and 17.7% of the teachers. By 1971, the figures for blacks had improved slightly, while the Spanish surname situation worsened. Browns had become 25% of the elementary pupil population but were only 2.4% of the teachers.

4. The concept of "core" and "satellite" actors derives from Wallace Sayre and Herbert Kaufman, GOVERNING NEW YORK CITY (New York: Russell

Sage, 1965). The major interest groups involved in L.A. school politics include: the United Teachers of Los Angeles, and other teacher associations, supervisory and other staff associations, the PTA, Join Hands, League of Women Voters, Parents for Students, Parents for Equity in Education, Valley Education Council, People Care, the minority Commissions, Urban Coalitions, Chamber of Commissions, Urban Coalition, Chamber of Commerce and Watts Coordinating Council.

5. The experience of the Title I boards appears to parallel that of the Bay Area Community Action groups analyzed in Ralph Kramer, PARTICIPATION OF THE POOR (Englewood Cliffs, N.J.: Prentice-Hall Inc., 1969). See also Dale Rogers Marshall, THE POLITICS OF PARTICIPATION IN POVERTY (Berkeley and Los Angeles: University of California Press, 1971) for similar findings in the Los Angeles poverty program.

6. As quoted in the LOS ANGELES TIMES, May 19, 1971.

7. Conservatives won two of the three contested seats in the school board elections (incumbent J.C. Chambers defeating Mrs. Janice Bernstein, Phillip C. Bardos defeating Arnett Hartsfield, thus creating a 4 to 3 conservative edge in the full board).

8. John Bollens has noted, "having assigned much administrative responsibility to the mayor, the charter does not grant him authority equal to the assignment. His administrative authority is highly restricted and very indirect." Quoted in Francis M. Carney, op. cit., p. 112. See John C. Bollens, A STUDY OF THE LOS ANGELES CITY CHARTER, Los Angeles, Town Hall, pp. 149-187, for a detailed analysis of the weakness of executive power in Los Angeles.

9. The problem of achieving racial balance in Los Angeles schools is particularly difficult. State guidelines call for a maximum of a 15% swing for the individual school from the percentage of minority group population in the school system as a whole. With Blacks over 20%, and Anglos approximately 50% in the district as a whole, for example, no school in Watts could thus be more than 35% black. State guidelines, however, have a softening clause that permits some escape from this requirement. The standard laid down by Federal Judge Irwin Gitelson is somewhat different, calling for no school to have less than 10% minority or more than 50% minority group students. But the Gitelson decision also indicated that the Los Angeles school system could follow the state guidelines. The peculiar nature of the problem in Los Angeles is complicated by the geographic dispersion of L.A.'s population and the odd boundary lines of the unified school district.

10. One school official estimated that there were over 13,000 personnel actions resulting from the elimination of the high-level jobs and the subsequent reassignment scramble.

11. Arthur D. Little, Inc., URBAN EDUCATION: EIGHT EXPERIMENTS IN COMMUNITY CONTROL, Report to the Office of Economic Opportunity, October 31, 1969, p. 5.

12. Arthur D. Little, Inc., ALTERNATIVES FOR REORGANIZING LARGE UNIFIED SCHOOL DISTRICTS, vol. 1 June 2, 1970, section 1, p. 1.

13. See Joseph Eaton, "Symbolic and Substantive Evaluative Research," ADMINISTRATIVE SCIENCE QUARTERLY (March 1962), and also Ashley L. Schiff, FIRE AND WATER: SCIENTIFIC HERESY IN THE FOREST SERVICE (Harvard University Press, Cambridge, Mass., 1962).

14. A Los Angeles Times story reported that the "demise of the Los Angeles City School District—at least in the form it has had for 115 years—is apparently drawing near." Jack McCurdy, "LA Schools May Be Split Into 24 Districts: Legislature Appears Ready to Act," LOS ANGELES TIMES, June 7, 1970, p. 22.

15. The bill was significantly amended on April 29, June 24, July 2, July 16, July 20, July 30, and August 7. In the process, it was watered down to a study proposal.

16. Jerry Gillam, "Reagan Vetoes Bill to Decentralize L.A. School District," LOS ANGELES TIMES, September 21, 1970, p. 1. Several efforts were made to override the Governor's veto, but they were unsuccessful. Override of a gubernatorial veto is extraordinarily difficult in California, requiring a two-thirds vote of the total members of each house.

17. On the larger issues of the plebiscite as an example of democracy in action, see Leo Bogart, "No Opinion, Don't Know, and Maybe No Answer," PUBLIC OPINION QUARTERLY, 1967, pp. 331-345, and Raymond E. Wolfinger and Fred I. Greenstein, "The Repeal of Fair Housing in California: An Analysis of Referendum Voting," in AMERICAN POLITICAL SCIENCE REVIEW, 62 (September 1968), pp. 753-69.

18. "Assail School Advisory Council Policies," LOS ANGELES TIMES, November 25, 1971.

19. The dispute continued until it was apparently resolved in the fall of 1972, when the board finally decided to announce unequivocally that principals, not parents, were in charge of the schools, and to clarify other issues of parent participation left unresolved. See Jack McCurdy, "Board Ruling Near on Who Will Run Schools," LOS ANGELES TIMES, September 27, 1972, pp. 1 ff.

20. SERRANO VS. PRIEST, 5 Cal. 3rd 584: 96 Cal. Rptr. 601; 487 P. 2nd 1241. For excerpts, see CURRENT HISTORY (July 1972), pp. 28 ff.


Chapter 6

1. Except, since 1968, the citizens of Washington, D.C. have voted for the D.C. Board of Public Education as provided by Public Law 90-292, 90th Cong., H.R. 13042, April 22, 1968.

2. Reorganization Plan No. 3 of 1967, 81 Stat. 948 (1967). President Johnson decided to submit the basic structure of the reform proposed to

Congress as a reorganization plan rather than as legislation as a means of bypassing the House District Committee. See Royce Hansen and Bernard H. Ross, GOVERNING THE DISTRICT OF COLUMBIA: AN INTRODUCTION (Washington Center for Metropolitan Studies, Washington, D.C.), p. 16. The major study of the politics of Washington, D.C. is Martha Derthick, CITY POLITICS IN WASHINGTON, D.C. (Cambridge:, Mass. and Washington, D.C.: Harvard-MIT Joint Center for Urban Studies and the Washington Center for Metropolitan Studies, 1963). In some ways the authority of Congress over internal administrative affairs of the capital city resembles the power exercised by the central governments of unitary nation-states over their cities. See, for example, Samuel J. Humes and Eileen Martin, THE STRUCTURE OF LOCAL GOVERNMENT THROUGHOUT THE WORLD (the Hague: Martinus Nijhoff, 1961), pp. 1-2, 31-50, and R.M. Jackson, THE MACHINERY OF LOCAL GOVERNMENT (London: Macmillan and Co., 1968), pp. 13-16.

3. See James S. Young, THE WASHINGTON COMMUNITY (New York: Columbia University Press, 1966), pp. 13-16.

4. See Derthick, op. cit., pp. 169-178, for an analysis of the "home rule" controversy and the sources of support for and opposition to the idea.

5. Lloyd E. Bauch and J. Orin Powers, PUBLIC EDUCATION IN THE DISTRICT OF COLUMBIA, Staff Study No. 15, prepared for the President's Advisory Committee in Education (Government Printing Office, 1938), pp. 7-8.

6. Lawrence Feinberg, "Years Bring Change to Dunbar High School: 'Black Elite' Institution Now Typical Slum Facility," THE WASHINGTON POST, December 28, 1969.

7. See Derthick, op. cit., pp. 212 ff, and Carl F. Hansen, DANGER IN WASHINGTON, for a description of the segregated school system.

8. Named for Professor Emeritus George D. Strayer, Columbia Teachers College, who conducted the survey, as summarized in Derthick, op. cit., p. 212.

9. Ibid., p. 214, and Carl F. Hansen, op. cit., pp.

10. See A. Harry Passow, TOWARD CREATING A MODEL PUBLIC SCHOOL SYSTEM: A STUDY OF THE WASHINGTON, D.C. PUBLIC SCHOOLS (the "Passow Report"), Columbia Teachers College, New York, September 1967, p. 51, 71. Derthick, op. cit., p. 222, reports that 14,533 white D.C. children as of October 1959 attended private or parochial schools inside or outside of the District.

11. Hansen and Ross, op. cit., p. 19.

12. HOBSON V. HANSEN, 269 Fed., Supp. 410 (1967).

13. On the role of law generally in social change, see Frederick M. Wirt, POLITICS OF SOUTHERN EQUALITY: LAW AND SOCIAL CHANGE IN A MISSISSIPPI COUNTY (Chicago: Aldine Publishing Co., 1970). Wirt's conclusions regarding the effectiveness of law as an instrument of education change in Panola County have relevance for Washington, D.C. Wirt notes (p. 235): "thus it is that, compared to the vote, educational changes have been few under the force

of law. A decade of judicial enforcement after 1954 produced only minute change." For a highly critical assessment of the HOBSON V. HANSEN decision, see Carl F. Hansen, op. cit.

14. Passow, op. cit., p. 13. Although the Passow Report was not published until October 1967, its mainfindings were made public on June 19, the same day that Judge Wright issued his decree in HOBSON V. HANSEN. At a press conference, reported in the WASHINGTON POST, June 20, 1967, Passow said he disagreed with the Wright opinion because he did not believe that poor Negro children consistently received an education inferior to that of white or middle-class children in the District.

15. Ibid.

16. There are some instances of metropolitan cooperation in providing public services, but these are principally in the area of "hardware" rather than "software" government functions. A Metropolitan Washington Council of Government was formed in 1968, but has taken only limited steps to date toward area-wide coordination of government functions. See Hansen and Ross, op. cit., p. 26, and on the earlier efforts in metropolitan cooperation, see Derthick, pp. 225 ff.

17. Carl F. Hansen, DANGER IN WASHINGTON, ch. 8 analyzes the background of the Model School Division. In his view "among the notable big-name impositions on the Washington schools, the Model School Division has top rank for the length of pedigree of its sponsors and shortness of their patience . . . The lure of big and easy outside money led me to propose the setting up of the Model School Division. This in itself is an indefensible basis upon which to make decisions, although there is always hope that services to children through their teachers may be enhanced. But once a school system is caught up in this alluring trap, disengagement is almost impossible. Withdrawal from a wasteful program produces a flood of criticism, particularly from those elements that made the initial proposal but had no responsibility for its success. For schools and citizens, the lesson of the Model School Division is the ancient one: 'Beware of the Greeks who come bearing gifts.' "

18. According to one estimate in 1968, 98 percent of the parents whose children attend the Morgan school are black and 80 percent are poor. MORGAN COMMUNITY SCHOOL: ANNUAL REPORT TO THE COMMUNITY, 1967-68 School Term, mimeo publication of Morgan Community School Board, 1968, p. 2. The main published accounts of the origins of the Morgan experiment include Arthur D. Little, Inc. URBAN EDUCATION: EIGHT EXPERIMENTS IN COMMUNITY CONTROL, Report to the Office of Economic Opportunity, October 31, 1969; Paul Lauter, "The Short Happy Life of the Adams-Morgan Community School Project," HARVARD EDUCATIONAL REVIEW (Spring 1968): Lawrence Feinberg, "Experiment Fades: Morgan School Goes Conventional," THE WASHINGTON POST, July 6, 1971; and Mario Fantini, Marilyn Gittell, COMMUNITY CONTROL. Our account draws on these sources plus interviews.

19. Arthur D. Little, Inc., op. cit. p. 96.

20. MORGAN COMMUNITY SCHOOL: ANNUAL REPORT, 1967-8, p. 5. This is the view of events from the perspective of the Morgan Community Board. The Antioch view is rather different. As explained by Paul Lauter, the reason for seeking delay stemmed from the basic unwisdom of launching full-scale into the ambitious effort without adequate preparation. See Lauter, op. cit., pp. 239-247.

21. "Morgan School Plan Called a Failure," THE WASHINGTON POST, May 16, 1968, quoted in Arthur D. Little, Inc., op. cit., p. 100.

22. Ibid.

23. The Corporation Counsel was gotten around by his simply not being asked to rule on the agreements in question. A similar agreement was subsequently approved between the Adams Community Board and the D.C. school system.

24. In 1971 the Morgan School received more government and private foundation grants than any other school in the city. It also ranked in the top fifth among all city elementary schools in spending from the regular budget. Before the community control experiment, spending per pupil at Morgan from the regular city budget was much below the city-wide average. From 1968 to 1971, the school received $440,000 from the federal government, mostly in direct payments, bypassing the D.C. school board, for an elaborate Follow-Through Program for kindergarten, first and second graders, with $231,000 scheduled for 1971-72 under the Follow-Through grant. Morgan has also received about $100,000 from foundations, the biggest donation being $60,000 from the Ford Foundation.

25. Grant McConnell, PRIVATE POWER AND AMERICAN DEMOCRACY (New York: Alfred A. Knopf, 1966). Chapter 4 presents an extended discussion of the politics of small constituencies such as town meetings, school boards, and village councils. These typically display oligarchical characteristics, factionalism, and lack of orderly articulation of issues.

26. Statement of Miss Jeanne Walton, member of the Morgan Community School Board, at a meeting of the board and staff of the Morgan Community school, March 25, 1970, mimeo.

27. Confidential interviews with D.C. school officials.

28. Quoted in Feinberg, "Experiment Fades," THE WASHINGTON POST, July 6, 1971.

29. Compiled from a list of board members for those years obtained from the Special Projects Division of the D.C. school system.

30. Feinberg, "Experiment Fades," THE WASHINGTON POST, July 6, 1971.

31. Quoted in IDEM.

32. Anglo-American Conference on Accountability and Independence in the Modern Public Sector, sponsored by the Carnegie Corporation of New York, Williamsburg, Va., September 1971.

33. Interview, Washington, D.C., February 29, 1972.

34. Martha Derthick, "Defeat at Fort Lincoln," THE PUBLIC INTEREST, No. 20, Summer 1970.

35. President's Message on the District of Columbia, 4 PRESIDENTIAL DOCUMENTS 498, 502-03 (1968).

36. Documents obtained from L.B.J. Library, Austin, Texas, courtesy of Lawrence Feinberg, THE WASHINGTON POST, who kindly gave us access to his file on Anacostia.

37. Letter from Harold Howe to Congressman William Natcher, April 1, 1968, reprinted in the documentary file of the Anacostia Community School Project Appeal to U.S. Commissioner of Education, Sidney Marland, Jr.; copy obtained from Anacostia project offices.

38. Staff Memorandum on Overall Assessment of Anacostia Project With Recommendations for Action, September 30, 1971, by Robert B. Binswanger, in Anacostia appeal documents.

39. An elaborate campaign, including the use of "mau mau" tactics against Binswanger at a meeting where he served as the federal "flak-catcher," failed to move Commissioner Marland. Confrontation tactics seemed to have little effect at the federal level. Nixon Administration officials, despite embracing the rhetoric of decentralization, have been much less inclined to accept the legitimacy of neighborhood groups as participants in the educational policy process than their predecessors in OE. Remarks by Harold Howe, "Participation and Partnership" before the annual meeting of the Council of Chief State School Officers, Salt Lake City, Utah, November 18, 1968, reflect the enthusiasm of Great Society policy officials for the participation ethic and contrast sharply with the prevailing cautious view of the Nixon administration.

40. Bart Barnes, "Anacostia to Get New School Plan," THE WASHINGTON POST, January 2, 1972.

41. IDEM.

42. HOBSON V. HANSEN Civil Action No. 82-66, U.S. District Court for the District of Columbia. The leading cases include SERRANO V. PRIEST, 5 Cal. 3rd 584; 96 Cal. Rptr. 601: 487 P. 2nd 1241, decided by the Supreme Court of California on August 30, 1971; VAN DUSARTZ V. HATFIELD, 334 F. Supp. 870, decided October 15, 1971 by a federal district judge; RODRIGUEZ V. SAN ANTONIO INDEPENDENT SCHOOL DISTRICT, 40 Law Week 2398, decided by a three judge Federal District court on December 23, 1971; ROBINSON V. CAHILL, 287 A. 2nd 187, decided in the Superior Court of New Jersey on January 19, 1972; and SPANNO V. BOARD OF EDUCATION, 40 Law Week 2475, decided by a State judge of the Supreme Court of New York on January 21, 1972. Earlier school finance cases, McGINNIS V. WILKERSON, 293 F. Supp. 572, affd. Mem. sub. nom. as McGINNIS V. OGILVIEW, 394 U.S. 322, and BURRUS V. WILKERSON, 397 U.S. 44 involved arguments made by plaintiffs asking Federal district courts to deter-

mine the "educational needs" of students. These cases present a somewhat conflicting precedent in that they upheld state legislation and reflect a policy of judicial non-intervention. For a review of the cases, see Richard Pious, "The Judiciary and Public School Financing," CURRENT HISTORY, August, 1972. See also, "School Finance Litigation: A Strategy Session" in 2 YALE REVIEW OF LAW AND SOCIAL ACTION (1971)

43. HOBSON V. HANSEN, May 25, 1971 at 7. In the area west of the Park the elementary school population was 74 percent black and 98 percent in the area east of the Park.

44. Ibid. at 30. On the various meanings of "equality," see John Coons, William Clune, and Stephen Sugarman, PRIVATE WEALTH AND PUBLIC EDUCATION (Cambridge, Mass.: Harvard University Press, 1971).

45. HOBSON V. HANSEN at 23.

46. Irna Moore, "Many Schools Violating Order to Equalize Spending on School Faculty," THE WASHINGTON POST, February 24, 1972. The school system had apparently succeeded, however, in "leveling down" the twelve elementary schools west of Rock Creek Park, for as a group whose twelve elementary schools now showed per pupil expenditures one percent lower than the rest of the city as a whole and only three precent higher than those in Anacostia. The schools out of compliance seemed to show no geographic pattern.

47. IDEM.

48. Interview with Julius W. Hobson, Director, Washington Institute for Quality Education, Washington, D.C., February 29, 1972.

49. President Nixon's message to Congress outlining a legislative proposal for a moratorium on busing is excerpted in THE NEW YORK TIMES, March 17, 1972.

50. See Pious, op. cit., pp. 56-57.

51. Quoted in WASHINGTON POST, March 2, 1971.

52. See James Q. Wilson, "The Mayors vs. the Cities," the PUBLIC INTEREST, Summer 1969, esp. pp. 28-37, and Wallace S. Sayre, "The Mayor" in Lyle Fitch, AGENDA FOR A CITY (New York, Sage Publications, 1970), pp. 563-601.

## Chapter 7

1. A comprehensive, if now somewhat dated, description of Detroit's politics can be found in David Greenstone, A REPORT ON THE POLITICS OF DETROIT (Cambridge: Joint Center for Urban Studies, 1961). Detroit's participation in the New Frontier programs is chronicled by Alan Rosenbaum, "The Model Cities and Anti-Poverty Efforts in Detroit and Chicago." Paper delivered at the American Political Science Association Meeting, Los Angeles, 1970.

2. Dependence on the automobile industry led to periodic severe unemployment, however. The recession of 1958 created an unemployment rate of 10% city-wide and as high as 41% in black neighborhoods. During most of the Sixties jobs were more plentiful.

3. During the Fifties Detroit's mayors were conservative and elected over labor's opposition. Determined to be on the winning side, some labor leaders backed Cavanaugh's conservative opponent in 1961. After the election, Cavanaugh enjoyed considerable labor support, though the black wards that he carried with 80% of the vote were his major constituency. Cavanaugh's political decline is detailed in William Serrin, "How One Big City Defeated Its Mayor" NEW YORK TIMES MAGAZINE, October 27, 1968, pp. 39ff. For a more skeptical view of the influence of blacks in Detroit politics, see: A.W. Singham, "The Political Socialization of Marginal Groups," Paper presented at the American Political Science Association Meeting 1966. Also James Q. Wilson, NEGRO POLITICS (Glencoe, Illinois: The Free Press, 1960) Chapter 2.

4. The inequalities and problems of the Detroit public schools when Norman Drachler took over are documented in Patricia Cayo Sexton, EDUCATION AND INCOME (New York: Viking Press, 1961), and National Commission on Professional Rights and Responsibilities, DETROIT, MICHIGAN: A STUDY OF BARRIERS TO EQUAL EDUCATIONAL OPPORTUNITY IN A LARGE CITY (Washington: NEA, 1967).

5. The history of the system's personnel and student integration policies is detailed in BRADLEY V. MILLIKIN 338 F. Supp. 582 (1971).

6. Some of this history is discussed in Carl O. Smith and S.B. Sarasohn "Hate Propaganda in Detroit," PUBLIC OPINION QUARTERLY, vol. 10, (1946-47) 24.

7. For a description and analysis of the Detroit riots, see THE REPORT OF THE NATIONAL ADVISORY COMMISSION ON CIVIL DISORDERS (Bantam PB 1968), pp. 84-108. This quote is on p. 85. The human tragedies of the 1967 riot are reported by John Hersey, THE ALGIERS MOTEL INCIDENT (New York: Alfred A. Knopf Inc. 1968).

8. An early history of urban renewal in Detroit can be found in Robert J. Mowitz and Deil S. Wright, PROFILE OF A METROPOLIS (Detroit: Wayne State University Press, 1962).

9. For a more favorable assessment of Detroit's economic conditions, see the report by the "Mayor's Committee on Community Renewal" as reported in the DETROIT NEWS, November 25, 1970.

10. City and school demographic trends are discussed in BRADLEY V. MILLIKIN at 585-589.

11. A history of the governance of the Detroit schools can be found in DETROIT: A MANUAL FOR CITIZENS (Detroit: Board of Education, 1958).

12. George Romney, CITIZENS ADVISORY COMMITTEE ON SCHOOL NEEDS (Detroit: Board of Education, 1958) p. v.

13. See the reports of the Citizens Advisory Commission on Equal Educa-

tional Opportunity (1962), National Commission on Professional Rights and Responsibilities of the National Educational Association (1967), and the High School Study Commission (1968).

14. These data come from studies discussed in DETROIT, MICHIGAN: A STUDY OF BARRIERS TO EQUAL EDUCATIONAL OPPORTUNITY IN A LARGE CITY, p. 46 ff., and REPORT OF THE NATIONAL ADVISORY COMMISSION ON CIVIL DISORDER, p. 435 ff.

15. The legislature was responding to the new political strength of the suburbs. In 1940 the population of the city of Detroit was 70% of the metropolitan area; by 1970 it had fallen to 36%.

16. As quoted by William R. Grant "Community Control vs. School Integration-the case of Detroit," PUBLIC INTEREST (Summer 1971), p. 66. Although I disagree with some of his conclusions, I am indebted to Mr. Grant for his accurate and well-written description of the history of the decentralization bills.

17. DETROIT NEWS, March 3, 1969. The bill was co-sponsored by Rep. George Montgomery, a retired white school teacher, who argued that its passage would reduce work stoppages.

18. Jesse F. Goodwin. "A Community Centered School Proposal" (Revised Version), (mimeo), April 1969.

19. Speech by Amos Wilder to the Detroit School Board, April 8, 1968.

20. See, for example, the conflict over the naming of a principal by the Concerned Parents of Butzel as reported by Harry Salsinger, "School Decentralization: Panacea or More Trouble?" DETROIT NEWS, February 19, 1970.

21. For our interpretations of labor union politics in Detroit and school decentralization in this section and elsewhere, we are indebted to the research of Marvin R. Pilo, THE ROLE OF LABOR UNIONS IN THE POLITICS OF URBAN SCHOOL DECENTRALIZATION (unpublished Ph.D. dissertation), Teachers College, Columbia University, 1973.

22. As quoted in the DETROIT FREE PRESS, October 13, 1968.

23. DETROIT FREE PRESS, March 4, 1970. Shortly thereafter, Dr. Robinson, a distinguished leader in the black community became fatally ill. The Presidency was assumed by A.L. Zwerdling.

24. Quotes on redistricting are from Grant, op. cit., pp. 70-71.

25. The minutes of the Detroit Board provide an almost verbatim record of its meetings and are an excellent historical source. Readers interested in the stormy five hour April 7 meeting should refer to the minutes, pp. 497-555. Among other things they make clear the opposition of the separatists to the Board's plans. John Webster who purported to represent Rev. Albert B. Cleage Jr., the Black Teachers Caucus, the Inner City Parents Council and the Ad Hoc Committee for Community Central testified:

I have been instructed to inform you that the black community rejects any plan that does not transfer meaningful power or self-determination to the black community. So-called integration is not only destructive of the best interests of black people, in fact it is a form of genocide from our point of view, but it also suggests an acceptance of the white man's declaration of white superiority and black inferiority. The so-called integration is therefore both undesirable and absolutely unwanted by the black community.

Minutes at p. 523.

26. Revision of school attendance lines is a constant issue in large school systems and it is always controversial. At the April 7 hearing, Superintendent Drachler remarked

I have traveled probably to school meetings as much as anyone in the city. I can tell by the parking lot what the issue is. If the parking lot is packed then the issue is changing of boundaries. If it is empty the issue is curriculum.

Minutes at 511.

27. As quoted in BRADLEY V. MILLIKIN, 433 F.2d 897 (1970) at 899.

28. The school administrators (OSAS) led by Martin Kalish were already opposed to decentralization, but they feared a hostile public reaction if they lobbied very visibly against it.

29. Quoted in the DETROIT FREE PRESS, March 4, 1970.

30. Hearing quotes come from DETROIT NEWS, May 6, 1970.

31. As quoted in DETROIT FREE PRESS, May 9, 1970.

32. As quoted in N.E. DETROITER, April 16, 1960.

33. One can think of more felicitous and objective ways of wording that question, but subsequent polls seem to show that wording changes do not affect the basic trend of public opinion on this subject.

34. REDFORD RECORD, April 8, 1970.

35. Much of the information about the operation of the OSD comes from interviews with its dedicated and cooperative staff.

36. "Guidelines for Regional and Central Boards of Education of the School District of the City of Detroit" (Detroit: School Board, 1970).

37. Much of the information on CCBE here and following comes from telephone interviews with Aubrey Short and other members.

38. For a discussion of labor's role in Detroit and Michigan politics see Greenstone, op. cit., Pilo, op. cit., and John Fenton, MIDWEST POLITICS (New York: Holt, Rinehart and Winston, 1966) Chapter 2.

39. The pre-recall board of four lawyers, one minister, one doctor, and one businessman was the embodiment of the blue-ribbon reform thrust in American politics. These seven board members had earned *nine* graduate degrees among them.

40. When the Office of School Decentralization closed as planned, Larry Doss also left the school system to become executive director of New Detroit.

41. BRADLEY V. MILLIKIN, 433 F.2d 897 (1970).

42. An evaluation of the magnet schools can be found in the DETROIT NEWS November 3, 1971.

43. BRADLEY V. MILLIKIN, 338 F. Supp 582 (1971) at 592.

44. Jerry M. Flint, "Busing is Michigan's Biggest Political Issue," NEW YORK TIMES, October 18, 1971.

45. EAST SIDE SHOPPER, April 7, 1971.

46. If true, this means that CCBE is now twice as large as the more school-establishment-oriented PTA. The figures are probably inflated by the common practice of including the members of constituent organization in CCBE's total, but nevertheless its growth is very impressive.

47. Those skeptical of such honors should recall the arrangement between Elihu Yale and the University that bears his name.

48. In Region 2, the racially mixed, part CCBE and part UAW endorsed, board did institute an evaluation system for tenured teachers which included questions about adherence to administrative directives and teacher relationship with pupils and community. It is not clear what sanctions are available to the board, however.

49. Perhaps as a consequence the OSAS has been more outspoken in its skepticism about decentralization than the DFT. See the comments by President Martin Kalish in "Decentralization: First Impressions (A Symposium)" QUEST (Spring, 1971) p. 19.

50. Grant, op. cit., p. 78.

51. Joel D. Aberbach and Jack L. Walker, "Citizens Desires, Policy Outcomes, and Community Control." Institute of Public Policy Studies Discussion Paper No. 29, 1971.

52. PRIORITIES FOR THE SEVENTIES: THE DETROIT ELEMENTARY SCHOOLS (Detroit: Board of Education, 1971) p. 23. This study was system initiated.

53. See also: Charles H. Moore and Ray E. Johnston, "School Decentralization, Community Control, and the Politics of Public Education [in Detroit] URBAN AFFAIRS QUARTERLY (June, 1971) p. 441.

54. In the short run at least, decentralization did not increase citizen support for school taxes. In a May 16, 1972 referendum, voters not only vetoed an additional millage levy but lowered the existing rate. Several of the regional boards campaigned for the millage to no avail, leaving the public schools in more critical financial shape than before. Newspapers speculated that the defeat was principally caused by the anti-school emotions triggered by George Wallace's primary activities (the referenda was on primary day) though they also suggested that some voters were angry at decentralization.

55. Of course it may be that attitudes on decentralization in 1971 had shifted substantially from pre-decentralization attitudes. Some change would be expected, but there is no evidence about direction. If some blacks were disillusioned about decentralization in 1971; some whites must have been more optimistic. In general the evidence suggests that decentralization did not command majority support at any time.

56. Support for decentralization among whites seems to bear no relationship

to educational level, but among blacks it rises in an undeviating trend with education. Aberbach and Walker, p. 9.

## Chapter 8

1. Fred Powledge, "Flight from City Hall," HARPERS (November 1969), p. 72.

2. James Reston, NEW YORK TIMES, January 26, 1969, p. 19.

3. The most recent history of New York school politics can be found in Diane Ravitch, THE GREAT SCHOOL WARS OF NEW YORK CITY: 1805-1969 (New York: Basic Books, 1973).

4. Two accounts with differing perspectives of this period can be found in Nathan Glazer and Daniel Patrick Moynihan, BEYOND THE MELTING POT (Cambridge: M.I.T. Press 1963), pp. 234-237, and Leo Pfeffer, CHURCH STATE AND FREEDOM (Boston: The Beacon Press, 1953), pp. 442-445.

5. Glazer and Moynihan, op. cit., p. 235.

6. Ibid.

7. Ibid., p. 236.

8. ABINGTON SCHOOL DISTRICT V. SCHEMPP, 374 U.S. 203 (1963).

9. This historical process is discussed in HISTORICAL REVIEW OF STUDIES AND PROPOSALS RELATIVE TO DECENTRALIZATION OF ADMINISTRATION IN THE NEW YORK CITY PUBLIC SCHOOL SYSTEM (Albany: University of the State of New York, Bureau of School and Cultural Research, June 1967).

10. As quoted by Louis Yavner in "Review of Decentralization Plan," Citizens Union, mimeo, 1969, p. 22.

11. Ibid., pp. 3-4.

12. For a muckraking view of the system in the 1930s and 1940s, see David Alison, SEARCHLIGHT: AN EXPOSÉ OF NEW YORK CITY SCHOOLS (New York: Teachers Center Press, 1951).

13. Theodore Lowi analyzes appointment politics and the board of education in his AT THE PLEASURE OF THE MAYOR (New York: Free Press of Glencoe, 1964) pp. 29-34.

14. The two most comprehensive descriptions of the governance of the system in this period and later are Marilyn Gittell, PARTICIPANTS AND PARTICIPATION: A STUDY OF SCHOOL POLICY IN NEW YORK CITY (New York: Center for Urban Education, 1967), and David Rogers, 110 LIVINGSTON STREET (New York: Random House, 1968). The account that follows here draws heavily on both these works.

15. This process is described in Wallace Sayre and Herbert Kaufman, GOVERNING NEW YORK CITY: POLITICS IN THE METROPOLIS (New York: W.W. Norton and Company, Inc., 1965), pp. 235-237.

16. Ibid., pp. 281-2.

17. A history of this episode has been written by Leon Bock, THE CONTROL OF ALLEGED SUBVERSIVE ACTIVITIES IN THE PUBLIC SCHOOL SYSTEM OF NEW YORK CITY 1949-1956 (unpublished Ed.D. dissertation-Teachers College, Columbia University), 1971.

18. A parent's perspective of this problem may be found in Ellen Lurie, HOW TO CHANGE THE SCHOOLS (New York: Random House, 1970), particularly pp. 252-255.

19. Marilyn Gittell and T. Edward Hollander, SIX URBAN SCHOOL DISTRICTS: A COMPARATIVE STUDY OF INSTITUTIONAL RESPONSE (New York: Praeger, 1968), pp. 219-229.

20. As reported by Martin Mayer, "What's Wrong with Our Big-City Schools?" Saturday Evening Post (September 9, 1967), p. 22.

21. Rogers gives a lengthy description of the educational interest groups in Chapters 4-6 of 110 LIVINGSTON STREET. The PEA is the subject of Sol Cohen's PROGRESSIVES AND URBAN SCHOOL REFORM, THE PUBLIC EDUCATION ASSOCIATION OF NEW YORK CITY (New York: Teachers College Press, 1964).

22. NEW YORK TIMES, August 20, 1961, p. 1.

23. Mayer, p. 68. Teachers were often just as frustrated. The difficulties the system presented for sensitive teachers is portrayed in Bel Kaufman's UP THE DOWN STAIRCASE (New York: Avon Books, 1964), and Herbert Kohl's THIRTY-SIX CHILDREN. (New York: New American Library, 1967).

24. Early teacher organizations are described in William Wattenberg, ON THE EDUCATIONAL FRONT (New York: Columbia University Press, 1963).

25. A general history of the UFT can be found in Stephen Cole, THE UNIONIZATION OF TEACHERS: A CASE STUDY OF THE UFT (New York: Praeger, 1969). For a hostile view of the UFT see Robert Braun, TEACHERS AND POWER (New York: Simon and Schuster, 1972).

26. For a discussion of the role of communists in teacher organizations see Robert W. Iversen, THE COMMUNISTS AND THE SCHOOLS (New York: Harcourt, Brace, 1959).

27. As Cole demonstrates, other factors than loss of earnings contributed to the rise of teacher militancy, but the relative decline of earning power after World War II was a very important element, p. 23.

28. A symposium on evaluations of the MES program can be found in THE URBAN REVIEW, Vol. 2, No. 6 (May 1968), pp. 13-34.

29. Inclusion of a group under the category of a minority is largely a matter of convention. Currently blacks, Puerto Ricans and sometimes others from the Caribbean area are considered "the" minority groups in New York. Ethnics which have traditionally had minority "status" Jews, Orientals, Italians etc., are usually no longer included even though none of them are a majority in New York. Indeed the so-called majority group, white Anglo-Saxon Protestants, in

statistical terms is a very small minority in the city. This chapter will employ the term minority group to designate the minorities au currant—citizens of African and hispanic descent.

30. Mayer, p. 66.

31. Gittell, PARTICIPANTS AND PARTICIPATION, p. 69.

32. A discussion of this attitude may be found in Pete Hamill, "Notes of a New York Nationalist," NEW YORK, June 5, 1972.

33. The major modern reports are: George Strayer and Louis Yavner, ADMINISTRATIVE MANAGEMENT IN NEW YORK CITIES (New York: Mayors Committee on Management Survey, October 1951, two volumes). Charles F. Pruesses, BOARD OF EDUCATION ORGANIZATION AND MANAGEMENT OF SCHOOL PLANNING AND CONSTRUCTION (New York Office of City Administrators, 1959). Walter Crewson et al., "Report on the New York City Schools" (Albany: State Education Department, 1962). Mark Schinnerer, "Recommendations Pertaining to the Organization of the City School District of New York" (Albany: State Education Department, 1962). An overview of these reports can be found in Appendix A of the Bundy Report.

34. The work of the Bundy panel, which was convened to make proposals for decentralization, is discussed in the next section. The quote is from McGeorge Bundy et al., RECONNECTION FOR LEARNING: A COMMUNITY SCHOOL SYSTEM FOR NEW YORK CITY (New York: Praeger, 1969), p. 3.

35. The Fleischman Commission, "New York City: A Special Case," Vol. 3, September 1972, Appendix 12A.

36. By 1971 New York ranked last among twelve major cities on that measure. NEW YORK TIMES August 8, 1971, p. 26. Part of this is caused by the enormous overcrowding of schools, particularly high schools. In the worst schools, attendance is not much better than 50 percent and school authorities have become so habituated to this condition that it would be impossible to function if all the students came at once.

37. Since the proportion of poor, minority group children in the system has been increasing, the city wide scores relative to national norms have fallen. But there is no reliable data that would show whether the relative level of failure for minority group children was increasing or decreasing during the sixties. The Fleischman report seems to show the minority group schools in New York were closer to national norms in 1971 than in 1958, but the staff believes that changes in tests and other factors render that improvement insignificant. Whatever marginal gains the system might have made, what is certain is that the expectations for educational achievement for minority children increased dramatically among their parents and public at large.

38. These reports are discussed in HISTORICAL REVIEW OF STUDIES, op. cit.

39. Covellos' philosophy and administrative experiences are chronicled in his autobiography, THE HEART IS THE TEACHER (New York: McGraw-Hill Book Company, Inc. 1958).

40. A history of the project can be found in John Polley, Joseph Loretan, and Clara Blitzer, COMMUNITY ACTION FOR EDUCATION (New York: Teachers College, 1953), p. 1.

41. A discussion of anti-school acts in New York as a form of protest against the system can be found in Nancy Bordier "An Eastonian Systems Analysis of Education Politics" (Unpublished Ph.D. dissertation, Teachers College, Columbia University, 1971), pp. 150-153.

42. Rogers, p. 93 and p. 28. The white neighborhood school forces are described in his Chapter 3.

43. Neighborhood feelings of frustration and impatience in dealings with 110 Livingston Street were partly a typical response to that bureaucracy and partly misunderstanding. The fear that the school was being abandoned to segregation was very real. In 1964, a New York State report called "Desegregating the Public Schools of New York City" documented that integration was actually declining.

Once distrust reaches a certain level even well intended gestures are resented. The Board intended to name the school after Arthur Schomburg, a Puerto Rican who created the great library on Negro History in the district. The parents, however, thought the Board was just trying to name another school after a German Jew. Much of the subsequent bitterness at I.S. 201 might have been avoided if serious negotiations over the architecture, naming, and appointments for the school had taken place. Even in the Board's "model schools" such consideration of local feelings was uncommon. A complete history of the origins of I.S. 201 and the transition in the parents' thinking can be found in Carolyn Eisenberg, "The Parents Movement at I.S. 201: From Integration to Black Power, 1958-1966" (unpublished Ph.D. dissertation, Columbia University, 1971).

44. As quoted by Fantini, Gittell and Magat, p. 4. An early statement of the philosophy that was later embodied in I.S. 201 can be found in Preston Wilcox, "The Controversy over I.S. 201," THE URBAN REVIEW, July 1960, pp. 12-17.

45. This plan was proposed by Gittell in PARTICIPANTS AND PARTICIPATION, pp. 61-67.

46. Decentralization: Statement of Policy, New York Board of Education, April 19, 1967.

47. The economic and social characteristics of these districts are described in the Niemeyer Report, "An Evaluative Study of the Process of School Decentralization in New York City" (July 30, 1968).

48. In addition to the literature previously cited, readers will find additional pieces in "Bibliography on School Decentralization and Community Control" in COMMUNITY ISSUES, vol. 2. no. 3 (June 1970), p. 32. See pp. 21-26 specifically for literature on the demonstration districts.

49. The tension between teachers and community spokesman began to manifest itself during this period, and several UFT people withdrew their support. Niemeyer, pp. 35-46.

50. An evaluation of union tactics in 1967 strikes can be found in Cole, pp. 184-196.

51. Descriptions of the outcome and conduct of the election can be found in the Niemeyer Report, pp. 37-39, and Marilyn Gittell et al., DEMONSTRATION FOR SOCIAL CHANGE: AN EXPERIMENT IN LOCAL CONTROL (New York: Institute for Community Studies, 1971), Chapter 1.

52. Gittell et al., DEMONSTRATIONS FOR SOCIAL CHANGE, Chapter 3, contains a comprehensive analysis of the personnel problem from the project's viewpoint.

53. Ibid., Chapter 4.

54. In his weekly column, Albert Shanker quotes an Ocean Hill teacher who wrote him ". . . we did not define education quantitatively, by scores on tests designed to favor white suburban children. We did define it as black children singing the Black National Anthem . . . None of this could have been mandated by racist bureaucrats: neither could it be measured by their instruments." NEW YORK TIMES March 12, 1972.

55. The best collection of documents is found in Marilyn Gittell and Maurice Berube CONFRONTATION AT OCEAN HILL-BROWNSVILLE (New York: Praeger, 1969). A history of the strike can be found in Naomi Levine and Richard Cohen, OCEAN HILL-BROWNSVILLE—A CASE HISTORY OF SCHOOLS IN CRISIS (New York: Popular Library, 1969), and Martin Mayer, THE TEACHERS STRIKE, NEW YORK, 1968 (New York: Harper and Row, 1969).

56. Mayer, THE TEACHERS STRIKE, p. 15.

57. The problem of evaluation criteria is discussed in Gittell et al., DEMONSTRATION FOR SOCIAL CHANGE, pp. 1-5. Unfortunately the pro-community control institute settled for evaluation techniques and standards that are so subjective that its findings are not completely convincing to a less committed observer.

58. Ibid., p. 112.

59. Diane Ravitch, "Community Control Revisited," COMMENTARY, February 1972. Hentoff's reply is in THE VILLAGE VOICE, March 2, 1972.

60. Gittell et al., DEMONSTRATION FOR SOCIAL CHANGE, p. 87.

61. Ibid., p. 89. Wars create heros and villains on both sides. See Midge Decter, "Is it Still O.K. to Hate Albert Shanker?," NEW YORK, October 25, 1971.

62. The Ford Foundation Annual Report, 1968, p. 26. The issue of the Foundation's role in precipitating the school decentralization movement was discussed by McGeorge Bundy and Walter Degnan of the CSA in U.S. Congress, House, Committee on Ways and Means, HEARINGS ON TAX REFORM, 91st Congress, 1st Session 1969, pp. 370-457. See also Richard Armstrong, "McGeorge Bundy Confronts the Teachers" NEW YORK TIMES MAGAZINE, April 20, 1969, p. 25 ff. The Foundation's own internal evaluation of its role was written by Betsy Levin and is titled "And Then There Were the Children," May, 1969.

63. Gittell et al., DEMONSTRATION FOR SOCIAL CHANGE, p. 86. The

close philosophical and political views of the Foundation and the academic institution it chose to fund are represented in the COMMUNITY CONTROL AND URBAN PROBLEMS, authored by Professor Gittell and Mario Fantini, then program officer for education at Ford and Richard Magat, Ford public relations officer.

64. The research on this controversy was done by Karen Lawrence at Teachers College in 1969.

65. Most of the information in this section comes from Robert T. Simmelkjaer, "Anti-Poverty Interest Group Articulation and Mobilization for Community Control in New York City" (unpublished Ed.D. dissertation, Teachers College, Columbia University, 1972). Mr. Simmelkjear interviewed almost all the major community and anti-poverty leaders, and his dissertation is an exceedingly rich source of information on the development of ideologies and tactics in these districts.

66. For a critique and history of the anti-poverty programs, see Daniel P. Moynihan, MAXIMUM FEASIBLE MISUNDERSTANDING: COMMUNITY ACTION IN THE WAR ON POVERTY (New York: Free Press, 1969).

67. As quoted by Simmelkjaer, p. 74.

68. Humberto Cintron, "We Support the I.S. 201 Governing Board—Join Us" (November 1968), Mimeo.

69. Adele Spier, "Two Bridges Model School District: A Profile," COMMUNITY ISSUES, vol. 1, no. 3 (February 1969).

70. "Report on Three Demonstration Districts" (New York: New York City Commission on Human Rights, 1968), p. 16.

71. It should be remembered that many of the anti-poverty educational programs (job training, para-professionals, etc.) created no confrontation, so the account should not be regarded as a balanced picture of the agencies' overall programs.

72. Gittell et al., DEMONSTRATION FOR SOCIAL CHANGE, p. 128.

73. Education was ranked as fifth most important problem by the parents. Neimeyer, p. 55. More parents than not thought teachers were interested in children and thought the parent-teacher relationship was positive, p. 60. An overwhelming 82% said it made no difference whether their children's teacher was white or black. p. 61.

74. (Champaign-Urbana: University of Illinois Press, 1964).

75. February 22, 1967.

76. In addition to the authors' Laws of New York State, 1967, Chapter 484, Section 2 interviews, on this subject I am indebted to David A. Bresnick's comprehensive "Legislating New York City School Decentralization" (unpublished Ph.D. dissertation, Columbia University, 1972). See also Richard Scher, "Decentralization and the New State Legislature," THE URBAN REVIEW, September 1969, vol. 4, no. 1, pp. 13-19. Fantini, Gittell, and Magat, op. cit., contains a useful section on the Bundy panel on which all three authors played a decisive staff role.

77. Its methodology is discussed in the report's preface. The only exceptions to the no research rule were a feasibility study on district boundaries and some legal analysis. For a critique of the Bundy methodology, see David J. Rachman, "Bundy Revisited; A Look at the Quality of Government Reports," MARKETING REVIEW, May 1969, pp. 9-15.

78. Board of Education, "Statement of the Board of Education and the Superintendent of Schools on the Recommendations of the Mayor's Panel on Decentralization," November 9, 1972.

79. Though not an official UFT statement, Sandra Feldman's DECENTRALIZATION AND CITY SCHOOLS (New York: League for Industrial Democracy, 1968), provides the most comprehensive view of the UFT's leadership philosophy.

80. Bundy Report, p. 11 and p. 28.

81. At that time, the union was still willing to give communities control over the Superintendent's office. Feldman, p. 14.

82. First submitted as a letter from the Mayor to the Governor, State Legislature, and Regents, January 2, 1968. Later called A-6415, S-4512.

83. For a point-by-point comparison of each of the plans, see the NEW YORK TIMES, March 30, 1968.

84. Board of Education, Plan for the Development of a Community School District System for the City of New York, adopted January 29, 1969, pp. 32-33.

85. See Robert Simmelkjaer, pp. 371-375.

86. Bill No. S.5690 and A.7175, amended on May 1, 1969. The best synopsis of the law is in Office of Education Affairs, "A Summary of the 1969 School Decentralization Law for New York City," 1969.

87. Mr. Marchi, the State Senator from Staten Island also had a provision put in the law requiring that Staten Island be a separate district.

88. THE URBAN REVIEW, November 1968, p. 23. Mr. Shanker was arguing for one side of a perennial theory in American political philosophy. For an earlier view of the tyranny of local majorities see James Madison, THE FEDERALIST PAPERS. The proposed New York districts, however, were to have an average population of 250,000 and they were in no way geographically isolated or provincial in the traditional sense of that word.

89. "Plan for Development of a Community School District System for the City of New York" (New York: Board of Education, January 29, 1969).

90. Ibid., p. 4.

91. The Board did resist pressure for a black district in Queens and a hispanic district in the Bronx, but it did not affirmatively try to desegregate either.

92. The U.S. Office of Civil Rights investigated the drawing of the Manhattan boundary lines to see if segregation was fostered. The Office concluded that New York was "the most difficult and baffling place to integrate and did not sustain the charge of discrimination." NEW YORK TIMES, April 17, 1971.

93. Leonard Buder, "I.S. 201 and Ocean Hill Districts Seek to Keep Status," NEW YORK TIMES, November 19, 1969.

94. In the ten largest cities, the average percentage of the public school students that are minority is about 60 percent, while the overall minority population of these cities averages only about 30 percent.

95. This position is taken by the Bundy Report, p. 20, and by the United Parents Association.

96. KRAMER V. UNION FREE SCHOOL DISTRICT NO. 15,395 U.S. 621 (1969). In an earlier case, the Court ruled that one-man-one-vote did not apply to county school boards in Michigan, which were composed of delegates of local school boards. The Court ruled that those boards held essentially administrative powers, SAILORS V. BOARD OF EDUCATION OF THE COUNTY OF KENT 387 U.S. 105 (1967). This issue is discussed in E. Edmund Reutter, Jr. and Robert R. Hamilton, THE LAW OF PUBLIC EDUCATION (Minola, New York: The Foundation Press; 1970), pp. 619-20.

97. AVERY V. MIDLAND COUNTY, TEXAS, 390 U.S. 474 (1968). In accord: MEYER V. CAMPBELL, 152 N.W. 2d 617 (Iowa 1967).

98. HADLEY V. JUNIOR COLLEGE DISTRICT 397 U.S. 50 at 59 (1970).

99. The law permitted non-citizens who were public school parents to vote, but in his report on the election for the Institute for Community Studies, Boulton Demas complains that the legislative requirements of 90 days residency and a minimum age of 21 still discriminated against minority groups. "The School Elections: A Critique of the 1969 New York City School Decentralization" (New York: Institute for Community Studies, 1971), pp. 9-12. Probably the greatest legislatively-created handicap for lower class voters was scheduling the school board election at a special time. The theory was that non-parents would not bother to vote when nothing else was on the ballot. As it turned out class was apparently a more important variable than parentage and lower class voters generally vote less in special elections.

100. Wallace Sayre and Herbert Kaufman, pp. 617-620.

101. These efforts are described in Maurice Berube, "The School Elections: Analysis and Interpretation," COMMUNITY, vol. 2, no. 3 (April 1970), p. 1.

102. Demas, pp. 10-11.

103. Berube, pp. 3-4.

104. The election in Manhattan was delayed by litigation over districting and finally held in April.

105. This problem is described in Demas, pp. 19-20.

106. Ibid., p. 5.

107. Berube, p. 1.

108. Even this two to one ratio probably underestimates the differences in the turnout among minority groups and whites. The districts are based on public school enrollment which is disproportionately minority group. Consequently minority group districts are smaller in overall population than middle class white districts with more childless adults and whose families are smaller or send their children to parochial schools. Furthermore voter registration is almost always

lower in the minority group districts. For example, the number of eligible voters in Manhattan's District 2 (the east side) was 276,092, while in Harlem's District 4 only 27,166. Both districts had a 9% turnout, but that represented almost 10 times as many actual voters in District 2 as in 4. In short, while no precise figures on the number of white compared to minority group voters can be determined, available evidence suggested that whites voted in greatly disproportionate numbers.

109. E.C. Lee, THE POLITICS OF NON PARTISANSHIP (Berkeley: The University of California Press, 1960).

110. After spending two hours trying to pick and then rank nine of the thirty-five candidates in his Manhattan district, this professor of political science gave up and settled for six names.

111. Unlike Detroit, where several unions including the UAW had long histories of school board electoral participation and were active in the decentralized board elections, in New York only the school employee unions were actively involved.

112. Berube, p. 3. See also Fred Ferretti, "Winners and Losers," NEW YORK, May 25, 1970, p. 8.

113. Interview with Albert Shanker, President of the UFT, July 18, 1972.

114. Ferretti, p. 8.

115. Other religious groups participated very little.

116. Interview by Michael Gershowitz in the Long Island Press, June 8, 1970.

117. As quoted by Berube, pp. 5-6.

118. Interview with Selma Kovitz, UPA, August 1972.

119. The complex and tedious work of matching candidates to slates was done by Trudi Prince. Computer programming by Rod Kerr. Since it was impossible to interview all 279 winners, the slate calculations are based on examination of the files at the Institute, PEA, the UFT and other organizations plus some interviews. We believe that the slate calculations, though not perfect, are more than adequate to support the generalization made in this section.

120. The information on candidates and policy attitudes came from a pre-election survey by PEA and the League of Women Voters. 67 percent of the candidates recorded their policy positions. The non-respondents were somewhat more likely to be minority candidates from poorer districts and incumbents. If there is a bias in the sample of respondents, it appears from their backgrounds that they are slightly more conservative than the average elected board member.

121. The Institute regarded the outcome on this question as a good indicator of the overall negative results of this election, but the question as worded "excellent educational experience and ability" vs. "excellent on sensitivity to the conditions and needs of the community" presents a real Hobson's choice. The question received the highest number of no responses in the survey and it is unlikely that its phrasing created a clear cut choice for even community control

advocates. Hispanic and blue collar candidates chose experience and ability and the preference for sensitivity among blacks was very slight.

122. The Institute's apocalyptic judgment and faulty analysis affected others as well. Bernard Bard, education writer for the NEW YORK POST cried "the concept of school decentralization as an instrument of educational reform had suffered a possibly irrevocable setback," March 19, 1970, p. 2. Boulton Demas concluded "analysis of the results in the five boroughs reveals that the local school boards with very few exceptions, are dominated by white conservatives who have little or no commitment to public education; let alone community control (p. 29). The UPA was willing to give up on elections altogether.

It is already clear that the case against elections can be made on the basis of unrepresentative boards, injection of political and pressure tactics, excessive cost and the failure of this section of the law to fulfill the prime purpose of decentralization—to bring parents closer to their schools and give them a voice in the determination of their community schools. The lesson is a bitter one. Election of Community School Boards has proven a failure.

As quoted by Berube, p. 2.

123. The best account of the selection process is found in J. Lelyveld, "Chancellor Harvey Scribner: the Most Powerful Man in the School System on Paper," NEW YORK TIMES MAGAZINE, March 21, 1971.

124. CHANCE V. BOARD OF EXAMINERS (70 Cir. 4141) (1971).

125. Research on these changes was done by Norman Wellan, a student at Teachers College.

126. See Gittell et al., SCHOOL DECENTRALIZATION AND SCHOOL POLICY IN NEW YORK CITY, op. cit., pp. 143-183.

127. Most of this section comes from interviews and Chapter 12 of the Fleischman Commission's Report of New York City Schools.

128. On several issues of implementing decentralization the Board has bypassed the 110 Livingston Street staff and turned to management consulting firms. In addition to the report on allocations among districts, McKinsey and Company also provided a study on decentralizing the school lunch program. Cresap, McCormick and Paget, Inc. did five studies designed to help the CSB in their functions. Peat, Marwick and Mitchell was commissioned to recommend accounting procedures for the CSBs.

129. Community Board #30, Board of Education, NEW YORK LAW JOURNAL, February 1, 1972.

130. "Interim Report of the Special Senate Committee to Investigate the New York City Board of Education," March 5, 1971.

131. COMMUNITY BOARD #3 V. BOARD OF EDUCATION, NEW YORK LAW JOURNAL, October, 1971 and Stay Order of the Commissioner, November, 28, 1971.

In general the courts have restricted the power of the district boards in dismissing teachers, see COMMUNITY BOARD #27 V. BOARD OF EDUCA-TION, GREENWALD V. COMMUNITY BOARD #27, and COMMUNITY BOARD #24 V. THE CITY OF NEW YORK. In these cases the courts overturned board action for lack of due process, however, the CSB's basic right to decide tenure was upheld in BRAMWELL V. COMMUNITY BOARD #3.

132. Information on the operation of CSBs is based on research by Marian Abe, Teresa Babb and Judith Borrell, students at Teachers College, as well as interviews and the research of the Institute for Community Studies in Gittell, SCHOOL DECENTRALIZATION AND SCHOOL POLICY, op. cit.

133. For a study of the way CSB allocated their time see Gittell, p. 60.

134. PTA OF P.S. 222 VS. COMMUNITY BOARD #19, NEW YORK LAW JOURNAL, March 13, 1971.

135. Interview with Sophie Price, President of NYCBA, August, 1972.

136. Information on the impact of judicial review on decentralization comes from Michael Karasik, a student at Teachers College.

137. Interview with Albert Shanker, June, 1972. See also his column in the TIMES, "School Decentralization: Have Its Claims Proved Valid?," November 28, 1971.

138. NEW YORK TIMES, May 8, 1972.

139. NEW YORK TIMES, May 9, 1972.

140. NEW YORK TIMES, August 4, 1972.

141. Bundy report, p. 1.

142. NEW YORK TIMES, February 20, 1972.

143. Marilyn Gittell et al., SCHOOL DECENTRALIZATION AND SCHOOL POLICY IN NEW YORK CITY. These statements are on pp. 81 and 82.

144. Ibid., p. 84.

145. For an argument that tracking is an unconstitutional denial of equal educational opportunity see HOBSON V. HANSEN, 269 F. Supp. 401 (1967).

146. There are some exceptions, for example District 3.

147. NEW YORK TIMES, May 21, 1972. The two following quotations are also from the same source. Increased pension benefits also contributed to the interest in early retirement.

148. Marilyn Gittell et al., SCHOOL DECENTRALIZATION AND SCHOOL POLICY IN NEW YORK CITY, p. 128. Also NEW YORK TIMES, June 17, 1972 and July 9, 1972.

149. Public attention has focused on the appointment of Luis Fuentes, in District 1 (includes Two Bridges) as Superintendent. To some, Mr. Fuentes is a champion of bi-cultural education, to others he is an ethnic chauvinist at best, a racist, at worst. Since he would not have been appointed under the central system, both his advocates and detractors have viewed his career as a test of the validity of decentralization. For comments see NEW YORK TIMES, August 7, 1972 and Albert Shanker, "The Outrageous Appointment of Luis Fuentes,"

July 30, 1972. Also see Fox Butterfield, "Bronx School Changes Stir Hopes, Fears," NEW YORK TIMES, February 1, 1971.

150. Albert Shanker has accused the CSBs of making "a huge patronage pie out of the school system," but no comprehensive evidence has been provided. NEW YORK TIMES, May 15, 1972.

151. See Gerald Yaroslow, "Accountability Procedures in the New York Decentralized Districts," Unpublished MA thesis, Teachers College, 1973.

152. Board of Education, "Parents Associations and the Schools" mimeo, April 21, 1971, pp. 3-4.

153. NEW YORK TIMES January 20, 1971. For the UPA view of the parental role in evaluation see "Facts for Parents–Professional Rating of Teachers and Supervisors and Tenure" mimeo, February, 1971.

154. Don Haider, "The Political Economy of Decentralization," AMERICAN BEHAVIORAL SCIENTIST (September-October, 1971), pp. 108-129.

155. Bundy Report, p. 43.

156. This information comes from Bureau of Audit, "Audit of Community School Board Cash Fund–Imprest Fund No. 61," Letter to Harvey B. Scribner, Chancellor, February 4, 1972 and Elizabeth B. Clark, "Confidential Report on Community School Boards Cash Expenditures," Memorandum to the Board of Education, August 3, 1971.

157. D.H. Wollett, "The Evolution of a Collective Bargaining Relationship in Public Education: New York City's Changing Seven-Year History," 67 MICHIGAN LAW REVIEW 891 (1969).

158. The statements both came from the preface of the 1969-72 contract booklet.

159. Education Law, Article 52-A, Section 2590-g.

160. See the Committee on Municipal Affairs and The Committee on Labor and Social Security of the Association of the Bar of the City of New York. "The New York City School Decentralization, Law and Its Effect on Collective Bargaining," mimeo, May 1972, for discussion of alternative means of representing the community boards.

161. For analysis of this attitude in another context see Fred Barbaro, "The Newark Teachers Strike," THE URBAN REVIEW, January 1972.

162. UPA Newsletter, June 1972.

163. See issue of PEA Educational Information Service, Spring and Summer 1972 issues. PEA also generated a memorandum challenging the legality of the UFT demands. Jeanne R. Silver and Michael A. Rebell, New York Lawyers Committee for Civil Rights Under Law, June 27, 1972. See also the NEW YORK TIMES editorial, "Total Control by the UFT?," July 3, 1972.

164. The Union response to the impact of decentralization on collective bargaining can be found in Albert Shanker, "New Difficulties in Negotiating a Contract," in NEW YORK TIMES, August 13, 1972.

165. The union's public view of the contract can be found in the NEW

YORK TEACHER, September 17, 1972, p. 3. The perspective of the decentralization advocate is in a Public Education Association information packet released October 15, 1972.

166. NEW YORK TIMES Editorial, September 9, 1972.

167. Leonard Buder, "Teachers Pact: Victory for All," NEW YORK TIMES, September 9, 1972.

168. Ibid.

169. This suggestion is made specifically by Richard Reeves, "Solidarity Forever—The Unions Must be Curbed," NEW YORK (May 29, 1972), pp. 35-37. For a more general view of municipal collective bargaining see Sam Zagoria, PUBLIC WORKERS AND PUBLIC UNIONS (Englewood Cliffs, New Jersey: Prentice-Hall, 1972), and R. Harry H. Wellington and Ralph K. Winter, THE UNIONS AND THE CITIES (Washington: Brookings Institution, 1972).

170. OLIVER V. BOARD OF EDUCATION, 306 F. Supp. 1286 (1969).

171. Jinny M. Goldstein, GOVERNING NEW YORK CITY SCHOOLS: OUTLINE OF ALTERNATIVES FOR A CENTRAL BOARD OF EDUCATION (New York: Public Education Association, 1971).

172. Marilyn Gittell et al., SCHOOL DECENTRALIZATION AND SCHOOL POLICY, op. cit.

173. Fleischman, Vol. 3, Chapter 12, p. 411.

**Chapter 9**

1. Frank J. Munger and Roscoe Martin, DECISIONS IN SYRACUSE (Syracuse: Syracuse University Press).

2. E.E. Schattschneider, the SEMI-SOVEREIGN PEOPLE (New York: Holt, Rinehart and Winston, 1960), Chapter 5.

3. Grant McConnell, PRIVATE POWER AND AMERICAN DEMOCRACY (New York: Alfred A. Knopf, 1966).

4. Michael Walzer, OBLIGATIONS: ESSAYS ON DISOBEDIENCE, WAR, AND CITIZENSHIP (Cambridge, Mass.: Harvard University Press, 1970).

5. For a review of these plans, see Annemarie H. Walsh, "What Price Decentralization in New York," CITY ALMANAC, New School for Social Research, vol. 7, no. 1, June 1972.

6. George LaNoue, EDUCATION VOUCHERS: CONCEPTS AND CONTROVERSIES (New York: Columbia Teachers College Press, 1972).

7. Mario Fantini, the REFORM OF THE PUBLIC SCHOOLS (Washington, D.C., National Education Association, 1970).

# Index

# Index

## About the Authors

**George R. La Noue** is a Yale Ph.D. in political science. During the period of his collaboration on *The Politics of School Decentralization*, he was director of the graduate program in politics and education at Teachers College, Columbia University. He has held the Woodrow Wilson, Danforth and Public Administration Fellowships and in the latter capacity served as Assistant to the Executive Director of the U.S. Equal Employment Opportunity Commission. He is currently Professor of Political Science, University of Maryland, Baltimore County.

**Bruce L.R. Smith** received the Ph.D. in government from Harvard University. He has served as a consultant to numerous government agencies and non-profit institutions in the educational and other fields. He is the author of the *RAND Corporation: Case Study of a Non-Profit Advisory Corporation*, (1966) and co-editor of *The Dilemma of Accountability in Modern Government* (1971). He is Professor of Political Science at Columbia University.